The Nature of Special Education

PEOPLE, PLACES AND CHANGE

A Reader Edited by
TONY BOOTH AND JUNE STATHAM
at the Open University

ROUTLEDGE
London and New York
in association with
THE OPEN UNIVERSITY PRESS

First published in 1982 by
Croom Helm
Reprinted 1983, 1985 and 1986
Reprinted 1988 by Routledge
11 New Fetter Lane, London EC4P 4EE

Published in the USA by
Routledge
in association with Routledge, Chapman & Hall, Inc.
29 West 35th Street, New York NY 10001

© 1988 TONY BOOTH

Printed in Great Britain by Biddles Ltd, Guildford and Kings Lynn

British Library Cataloguing in Publication Data

The Nature of special education
   1. Exceptional children — Education
   I. Booth, Tony II. Statham, June
   371.9   LC3965
   ISBN 0-415-010551

Library of Congress Cataloging-in-Publication Data
ISBN 0-415-010551

CONTENTS

Acknowledgements

General Introduction

Part One: Special Biographies

Individuals

Part Two: Perspectives on Handicap

Part Three: Procedures, Places and Change

ACKNOWLEDGEMENTS

The preparation of this book has involved the collaborative effort of a large number of people. In a few cases we have included material in the form in which it was originally published or sent to us; in other cases the final version is the result of drafting and redrafting by more than one person. Ronny Flynn was involved in both the collection of material and the writing for several of the studies. Will Swann and Patricia Potts made substantial contributions, Dennis Briggs and Richard Tomlinson gathered official documents, and Chris Pym did the background work on developments in Oxfordshire. Above all we would wish to acknowledge the help of the adults and young people with whose stories and education we are concerned in this book.

FOR HANNAH, KATIE AND RAINBOW

GENERAL INTRODUCTION

When we tried to think of a term to describe the pieces in this book we could not find one that was entirely satisfactory. They all describe single instances, of a child's education or the job of a professional, of a remedial department in a comprehensive school or a timetabling system. They are examples or cases, but for a while we resisted calling them case-studies. To some 'purists' a case-study implies a detailed and comprehensive account of a single case in which all aspects and angles are described. We have not attempted to provide such a full picture, nor have we chased after an ideal of pure description. In many of the accounts we have combined description with an analysis which attempts to make sense of the facts. Most of our cases explicitly depict the view of one or two people, and often this view is our own. In fact, we have deliberately avoided producing an overall balance of views. We would hope that the cases in total reflect both the needs and wishes of children and their families, and the possibilities for greater involvement of children with special needs in their communities and in ordinary schools.

We thought of calling these accounts case-impressions to reflect their brevity and limited perspective but gave up trying to control the language of our colleagues who persisted in calling them 'case-studies', and no doubt that is the phrase which will be used.

We have concealed the real names of the people and places that are described except in one or two cases where we felt there was good reason for leaving them in. Even with anonymity, people who know a particular school or person will be able to recognise the 'true' identity, and we had some lengthy discussions with the people concerned, negotiating what could be published and what had to be omitted. Sometimes this was a straightforward matter of 'getting the facts straight' but at other times it was an attempt to retain the essence of the truth whilst avoiding conflicts between professionals or between professionals and their employers. We have tried to avoid the

11

'blandness' which such considerations often force on the writers of case-studies, but inevitably the critical nature of some of the contributions has been reduced. This conflict is avoided in some accounts where people write about the places in which they themselves work, but this bypasses rather than overcomes the problem. We or others writing about the same institution from the perspective of an outsider might have portrayed a different picture.

It is particularly difficult to document bad practice, and we have made little effort to do so in this book. Maureen Oswin's study of a ward in a subnormality hospital comes closest to this. We have tried to produce good 'teaching material' which examines some of the things that are happening in special education and offers clues about what is wrong and what can be done.

Although we have called the book *The Nature of Special Education*, the content is in fact wider than that. The definition of handicap and special educational needs which we have adopted is a very broad one. Growing up in care or living in poverty may also be handicaps, and can increase the likelihood that a child will experience educational difficulties too. Our conception reflects the character of the Open University course 'Special Needs in Education' for which this book is a resource. We have included details of this course in an appendix and recommend it and the course books as a comprehensive description of special education.

The material in this book is divided into three main sections; Special Biographies, Perspectives on Handicap, and Procedures, Places and Change. We have tried to make a sensible allocation of case-studies to each of these categories, but there is inevitably some degree of overlap. Every 'special biography' is set in a particular place, viewed from a particular perspective and subject to a process of change.

1. Special Biographies

The case studies in this section are arranged in three parts; individuals, families and professionals, although here too the distinction is not so clear cut in practice. For all of the people involved, handicap creates a 'special career'.

The first part contains descriptions of children and adults whose special needs have been seen as arising from blindness, partial hearing, 'maladjustment', learning difficulties, epilepsy and physical, mental and multiple handicap. The case-studies reflect the perspectives of the people who provided the information on which they are based; parents, teachers, professionals, or adults looking back over their own experiences. The second part of 'Special Biographies' concentrates on families and their relationships with professional helpers. In these studies parents describe the effect of a handicapped child on their lives, the extent to which they have been helped or hindered by professionals, and how some parents have managed to exert a large influence over their child's education. We have provided the final group of case-studies in this section to balance the impression that a 'special biography' is created only for the receivers of services; handicapped people and their families. Special education also concerns, among others, teachers, speech therapists, psychiatrists, residential care-staff, educational psychologists, advisers and administrators. We have included here only a small selection of material describing the career of a teacher in special education, the job of a community worker attached to an ESN(M) school, the work of two teachers in the USA affected by changes in special education law, and a historical account of the life of Dame Evelyn Fox, a voluntary 'professional' who greatly influenced the course of special education in the beginning of this century.

2. Perspectives on Handicap

In this second section we have collected together views on issues and aspects of special education; the views of educational psychologists about their job and the prevention of handicap, the views of children about their school and the teaching they receive, the views of a teacher about the role his special school should play, and the views of adults about the effect on their lives of being physically handicapped or of having grown up 'in care'.

3. Procedures, Places and Change

The third section of the book is the most mixed. It includes all the case-studies which emphasise aspects of the setting as well as, and sometimes to a greater extent than, the people in them. This is least true for the first two accounts, which look at a child in a residential school for 'maladjusted' boys and at the curriculum provided for a partially sighted girl who is taught in both an ordinary and a special school. Later case-studies concentrate on the overall curriculum and organisation of various special and ordinary schools and colleges; such as the individual timetabling system operated for children with special needs in a large comprehensive school, the lavish provision in a primary school in the USA where handicapped and hearing impaired children are taught alongside their 'normal' peers, the curricula offered to special school leavers in two FE colleges with contrasting philosophies. Many of the case-studies look at the possibilities for increasing the participation of children in ordinary schools and in the community. They focus on schools at various points along the continuum of provision for children with special needs. 'Westhall School' describes a special school for children with learning difficulties which acts as a resource for neighbourhood schools and for pre-school children in the community. 'Blueprint for Integration' lays down the steps one teacher would take to increase the participation of handicapped children in a primary school which already houses 'special' units. 'Four Handicapped Teenagers in Transition' describes another teacher's attempt to find out how much or how little support young mentally handicapped people might need in order to live independently in the community. The final case-study, which takes the widest view of any account in the book, looks at special educational developments towards a policy of integration in the county of Oxfordshire.

PART ONE:

SPECIAL BIOGRAPHIES

INDIVIDUALS

1 SPECIAL EDUCATION IN A GARDEN HUT: THE STORY OF HELEN KELLER

June Statham

Source: Helen Keller, *The Story of My Life*, with her letters, 1887–1901 and a supplementary account of her education, including passages from the reports and letters of her teacher Anne M. Sullivan, edited by J.A. Macy (Doubleday, Page and Co., London, New York, 1903).

Special education is often thought to be synonymous with separate education, but it is what is taught, not where the teaching takes place, that makes a child's education 'special'. One of the crucial steps in Helen Keller's education came when her teacher, Miss Sullivan, took her to live in the family's summerhouse at the end of the garden. Miss Sullivan kept a diary recording Helen's progress and her own teaching methods, extracts from which are included in the following account.

In March 1887, Miss Sullivan arrived at the Keller's home in Alabama to begin her task of educating a six-and-a-half year old girl left blind and deaf (and consequently dumb) by a fever at the age of nineteen months. Both she and her pupil, Helen Keller, were to create one of the most famous stories in the history of special education. The methods Miss Sullivan used to teach Helen were based largely on her own experiences and on her gift for communicating with the deaf-blind. Very early in her life Miss Sullivan herself had become almost totally blind, although her sight was later partially restored, and she had spent the years between fourteen and twenty (when she left to become Helen's tutor) at the Perkins Institution for the Blind.

Until Miss Sullivan's arrival, Helen's only means of communication was through pantomime or a rudimentary sign language taught to her by her mother, and her frustration resulted in frequent outbursts of temper, as her teacher soon discovered:

She helped me unpack my trunk when it came, and was delighted

17

when she found the doll the little girls sent her. I thought it a good opportunity to teach her her first word. I spelled 'd-o-l-l' slowly in her hand and pointed to the doll and nodded my head, which seems to be her sign for possession. Whenever anybody gives her anything, she points to it, then to herself, and nods her head. She looked puzzled and felt my hand, and I repeated the letters. She imitated them very well and pointed to the doll. Then I took the doll, meaning to give it back to her when she had made the letters; but she thought I meant to take it from her, and in an instant she was in a temper, and tried to seize the doll. I shook my head and tried to form the letters with her fingers; but she got more and more angry. I forced her into a chair and held her there until I was nearly exhausted. Then it occurred to me that it was useless to continue the struggle – I must do something to turn the current of her thoughts. I let her go, but refused to give up the doll. I went downstairs and got some cake (she is very fond of sweets). I showed Helen the cake and spelled 'c-a-k-e' in her hand, holding the cake toward her. Of course she wanted it and tried to take it; but I spelled the word again and patted her hand. She made the letters rapidly, and I gave her the cake, which she ate in a great hurry, thinking, I suppose, that I might take it from her. Then I showed her the doll and spelled the word again, holding the doll towards her as I held the cake. She made the letters 'd-o-l' and I made the other 'l' and gave her the doll. She ran downstairs with it and could not be induced to return to my room all day.

Yesterday I gave her a sewing-card to do. I made the first row of vertical lines and let her feel it and notice that there were several rows of little holes. She began to work delightedly and finished the card in a few minutes, and did it very neatly indeed. I thought I would try another word; so I spelled 'c-a-r-d'. She made the 'c-a', then stopped and thought, and making the sign for eating and pointing downward she pushed me toward the door, meaning that I must go downstairs for some cake.

Helen's temper hindered her learning, and the battles between her and her teacher grew worse. Miss Sullivan decided that she could do little with her pupil in the midst of the family, who allowed her to do as she pleased. 'I saw clearly that it was useless to try to teach her language or anything else until she learned to obey me.' She persuaded Helen's parents to allow them to live alone for a fortnight in a summer house at the end of the garden. There Helen learnt what Miss Sullivan considered the first step in her education, obedience to her teacher.

> The wild little creature of two weeks ago has been transformed into
> a gentle child. She is sitting by me as I write, her face serene and
> happy, crocheting a long red chain of Scotch wool. She learned the
> stitch this week, and is very proud of the achievement. When she
> succeeded in making a chain that would reach across the room, she
> patted herself on the arm and put the first work of her hands lovingly
> against her cheek. She lets me kiss her now, and when she is in a
> particularly gentle mood, she will sit in my lap for a minute or two;
> but she does not return my caresses. The great step — the step that
> counts — has been taken. The little savage has learned her first lesson
> in obedience, and finds the yoke easy.

Helen and Miss Sullivan returned to the main house, but spent a good
deal of their time outdoors. Helen's mornings were taken up with
'watching' people at work, with digging in the dirt, stringing beads,
sewing and crocheting or doing gymnastics. Between twleve and one
Miss Sullivan taught her new words, although throughout the day she
spelt into Helen's hands everything they did, and in the afternoons she
and Helen would make the rounds of the outhouses and animals, or
visit friends and relatives. Little of Helen's learning took place during
set lessons, but occurred instead as her teacher constantly 'talked' to
her about what they did during the day. Most of the time Helen didn't
understand what the spelling meant, but Miss Sullivan persevered and
the second major breakthrough in Helen's learning came a month after
her arrival.

> Something very important has happened. Helen has taken the second
> great step in her education. She has learned that *everything has a*
> *name, and that the manual alphabet is the key to everything she*
> *wants to know*. This morning, while she was washing, she wanted to
> know the name for 'water'. When she wants to know the name of
> anything, she points to it and pats my hand. I spelled 'w-a-t-e-r' and
> thought no more about it until after breakfast. Then it occurred to
> me that with the help of this new word I might succeed in straightening
> out the 'mug-milk' difficulty. We went out to the pump-house, and
> I made Helen hold her mug under the spout while I pumped. As the
> cold water gushed forth, filling the mug, I spelled 'w-a-t-e-r' in Helen's
> free hand. The word coming so close upon the sensation of cold
> water rushing over her hand seemed to startle her. She dropped the

mug and stood as one transfixed. A new light came into her face. She spelled 'water' several times. Then she dropped on the ground and asked for its name and pointed to the pump and trellis, and suddenly turning round she asked for my name. I spelled 'Teacher'. Just then the nurse brought Helen's little sister into the pump-house, and Helen spelled 'baby' and pointed to the nurse. All the way back to the house she was highly excited, and learned the name of every object she touched, so that in a few hours she had added thirty new words to her vocabulary. Here are some of them: *Door, open, shut, give, go, come* and a great many more.

Almost overnight, Helen's tantrums ceased and her learning began in earnest.

I see an improvement in Helen from day to day, almost from hour to hour. Everything must have a name now. Wherever we go, she asks eagerly for the names of things she has not learned at home. She is anxious for her friends to spell, and eager to teach the letters to every one she meets. She drops the signs and pantomime she used before, as soon as she has words to supply their place, and the acquirement of a new word affords her the liveliest pleasure. And we notice that her face grows more expressive each day.

I have decided not to try to have regular lessons for the present. I am going to treat Helen exactly like a two-year-old child. It occurred to me the other day that it is absurd to require a child to come to a certain place at a certain time and recite certain lessons, when she has not yet acquired a working vocabulary. I sent Helen away and sat down to think. I asked myself, 'How does a normal child learn language?' The answer was simple, 'By imitation'. The child comes into the world with the ability to learn, and he learns of himself, provided he is supplied with sufficient outward stimulus. He sees people do things, and he tries to do them. He hears others speak, and he tries to speak. But long before he utters his first word, he understands what is said to him. These observations have given me a clue to the method to be followed in teaching Helen language. I shall talk into her hand as we talk into the baby's ears. I shall assume that she has the normal child's capacity of assimilation and imitation. I shall use complete sentences in talking to her, and fill out the meaning with gestures and her descriptive signs when necessity requires it; but I shall not try to keep her mind fixed on any one thing. I shall do all I can to interest and stimulate it, and wait for results.

Helen rapidly acquired new words; nouns, adjectives and verbs, and Miss Sullivan discarded her kindergarten materials which she no longer found useful.

I used my little stock of beads, cards and straws at first because I didn't know what else to do; but the need for them is past, for the present at any rate.

I am beginning to suspect all elaborate and special systems of education. They seem to me to be built up on the supposition that every child is a kind of idiot who must be taught to think. Whereas, if the child is left to himself, he will think more and better, if less showily. Let him go and come freely, let him touch real things and combine his impressions for himself, instead of sitting indoors at a little round table, while a sweet-voiced teacher suggests that he build a stone wall with his wooden blocks, or make a rainbow out of strips of coloured paper, or plant straw trees in bead flower-pots. Such teaching fills the mind with artificial associations that must be got rid of, before the child can develop independent ideas out of actual experiences.

Miss Sullivan was equally scathing about the type of education which took place in typical schools for the deaf, like the one she and Helen visited where the teacher constructed an 'exercise' out of Helen's presence, writing sentences about her on the board for the children to copy and thereby learn some grammatical rules.

It all seemed so mechanical and difficult. Nothing, I think, crushes the child's impulse to talk naturally more effectively than these blackboard exercises. The schoolroom is not the place to teach any young child language, least of all the deaf child.

By contrast, Miss Sullivan's method was to take Helen into the garden or out for long walks, describing all she could see and answering Helen's constant questions.

She came tearing upstairs a few minutes ago in a state of great excitement. I couldn't make out at first what it was all about. She kept spelling 'dog-baby' and pointing to her five fingers one after another, and sucking them. My first thought was, one of the dogs had hurt Mildred; but Helen's beaming face set my fears at rest. Nothing would do but I must go somewhere with her to see something. She led the way to the pump-house, and there in the corner was one of the setters with five dear little pups! I taught her the word 'puppy' and drew her hand over them all, while they sucked, and spelled 'puppies'. She was much interested in the feeding process, and spelled 'mother-dog' and 'baby' several times. Helen noticed that the puppies' eyes were closed, and she said 'Eyes-shut. Sleep-no', meaning, 'The eyes are shut, but the puppies are not asleep'. She screamed with glee when the little things squealed and squirmed in their efforts to get back to their mother, and spelled 'Baby — eat large'. I suppose her idea was 'Baby eats much'. She pointed to each puppy, one after another, and to her five fingers, and I taught her the word *five*. Then she held up one finger and said 'baby'. I knew she was thinking of Mildred, and I spelled 'One baby and five puppies'. After she had played with them a little while, the thought occurred to her that the puppies must have special names, like people, and she asked for the name of each pup. She noticed that one of the puppies was much smaller than the others, and she spelled 'small', making the sign at the same time, and I said 'very small'. She evidently understood that *very* was the name of the new thing that had come into her head; for all the way back to the house she used the word *very* correctly. One stone was 'small', another was 'very small'. When she touched her little sister, she said: 'Baby-small. Puppy-*very* small'. Soon after, she began to vary her steps from large to small, and little mincing steps were 'very small'. She is going through the house now, applying the new words to all kinds of objects.

Another time, Miss Sullivan let her hold an egg in her hand and feel the chick peck its way out.

Her astonishment, when she felt the tiny creature inside, cannot be put in a letter. The hen was very gentle, and made no objection to our investigations. Besides the chickens, we have several other additions to the family — two calves, a colt, and a penful of funny little pigs. You would be amused to see me hold a squealing pig in my arms, while Helen feels it all over, and asks countless questions — questions not easy to answer either. After seeing the chicken come out of the egg, she asked: 'Did baby pig grow in egg? Where are many shells?'

Miss Sullivan taught Helen to read by placing cards with the word printed in raised letters on the object, and showing her that each alphabet letter corresponded to a letter she was used to signing on her fingers. She taught her to write the same words and sentences using a pencil and grooved paper, and then to use braille so that Helen could read herself what she had written. Her progress in arithmetic was equally rapid, so that she could easily add and subtract up to a hundred and recite the multiplication tables up to five before eight months had passed.

The difference between Helen's first Christmas after Miss Sullivan's arrival and those that preceded it clearly illustrates the effect of Helen's education on both herself and her family. From being a frustrated, angry, non-communicative child, she had become a full participant in the family's Christmas, hanging up her stocking, excitedly opening her presents, writing her thank-you letters on a braille slate. For Helen, her special education was the beginning of a rewarding and famous life.

EMMA: A CHILD IN A RESIDENTIAL UNIT FOR MULTIPLY-HANDICAPPED CHILDREN

June Statham

Beech Tree House is a unit providing short-term education for multi-handicapped children with deviant behaviour. It is situated in the grounds of a Spastic Society school for ESN(S) children with cerebral palsy. Children are normally referred to Beech Tree from the Spastic Society's assessment centre in London, but some parents hear about the unit through the publicity that is attendant on its research project status, and set the wheels in motion themselves to enable their child to go there. Emma Canny was one such child and her school experience is depicted here as seen through the eyes of the unit psychologist. Her mother attended a lecture given by the head of Beech Tree House, in which he mentioned the type of children the unit catered for, and she campaigned for her local education authority to make arrangements for Emma to be sent there.

Emma was eight when she arrived at Beech Tree House, a very small child with red hair and freckles, described as hiding a 'very manipulative nature' beneath her appealing appearance and mannerisms. She was clumsy but not obviously physically handicapped, and her difficulties had been rather vaguely diagnosed as due to a 'developmental disorder' involving dwarfism, mental retardation, speech problems, hyperactivity and controlled epilepsy. At eight, Emma was unable to communicate apart from screaming, grunting, and using a few signs from the Paget-Gorman sign language which her mother and one of her teachers had learnt. She lived at home with her older sister, her electrician father and her mother, who was the village postmistress. During the day Emma attended a nearby school for ESN(S) children, whose teachers had begun to find it difficult to cope with Emma's disruptive behaviour, which they put down to her frustration at being unable to communicate. However, it was Emma's family who bore the brunt of her most difficult behaviour, which occurred at night. Within minutes of being put to bed, Emma would start to protest, scream and jump out of bed. She refused to sleep alone, and compelled the family to play a kind of 'musical beds' with her, often changing beds every twenty minutes throughout the night. If they refused, Emma would threaten to vomit, urinate or defecate all over the carpet, and carry out her threats if her parents didn't do as she wished. She had the family completely under her thumb, and after several years of this night-time behaviour, relieved only by Emma staying for three weeks in every three months in a sub-normality hospital, her parents were mentally and physically exhausted and their marriage was beginning to suffer.

They felt they could no longer cope with Emma at home, and that it would be best to place her in residential care, both so that she could receive a more structured learning environment in which she might learn to communicate, and so that they could have some space in which to reorganise their lives and think about Emma's future without the constant pressure of her presence. It was at this time that Mrs Canny heard about Beech Tree House, and put pressure on her local authority to obtain a place for Emma there. The authority eventually agreed, more because Beech Tree could teach Emma the Paget-Gorman sign language than because it had been set up precisely to help children like Emma. She arrived when she was nine.

The staff soon realised that Emma was more intelligent than had been supposed, and was probably functioning in the high ESN(S) or low ESN(M) range. She soon learnt to wash and dress herself with supervision and to use a knife and fork and began to speak a few words in a very hoarse, deep voice. She proved to be a sociable child, enjoying pop music and television, liking adult company and 'mothering' the other children in the unit. She could still be very wilful and obstinate, but the staff and her parents decided that if her night-time problems could be overcome, a sensible goal to aim for with Emma would be for her to go back home and attend the reception class in an ordinary infant school in her local community, supported by a welfare assistant. Her home village offered her the best chance of leading a 'normal' life. Emma was something of a local celebrity there, well known and well liked. The school was run by a husband and wife team, and small enough for Emma to be included with little difficulty, given adequate support. Her mother's postmistress job offered Emma the possibility of being able to help out in the shop, perhaps for example by going out the back to weigh up potatoes for customers using colour-coded weights.

Children at Beech Tree House are prepared for one of two possible futures. Those who will 'graduate' to another residential setting are trained to sleep in dormitories, those who are likely to return home are given single rooms. Emma had a single room, but the main problem was to get her to sleep at all. Her night-time tantrums were long-established and gained her the adult attention she craved, even if the attention was in the form of angrily putting her back to bed while her mess was cleared up. If Emma were to successfully return home it was essential that her behaviour at night be changed, so the staff began a behaviour modification programme (described in detail later in this book) designed to reduce Emma's disruptive night-time behaviour by not going in to clear up her mess, and by rewarding her with tokens if she had a clean room in the morning.

The programme began to have positive results, but the school felt it was of little use if the effects did not generalise to the home situation where the problem first arose. Beech Tree House has a policy of maintaining extensive contact with parents, via joint outings and holidays, visits to the pub, teas for parents and siblings, and parents helping out on weekend rotas. Before a child is accepted at the unit, the parents must agree that a member of staff can live in the child's home for several days 'when the time is right', which may be up to a year later. None of the parents have yet refused this condition of entry, although some have initially been reluctant. Co-operation with Emma's parents had always been good, and they agreed to try out the behaviour modification programme developed by the school while Emma was at home on visits. Her bedroom was waterproofed, the windows reinforced and the bed screwed down so that her tantrums could be ignored without fear of her harming herself. Ignoring Emma's screaming and banging proved more difficult for her parents than for staff at the school, who were less emotionally involved, but they managed to stay out of her room until she succeeded with a superhuman effort in wrenching her bolted-down bed from the floor, at which point they felt they had to go in. Even then the spirit of co-operation did not fail, for in the midst of the uproar Emma's mother remembered to fetch her camera and record the incident for the school's records.

Her parents persisted with the programme, and gradually Emma's night-time behaviour improved at home as well as at Beech Tree House. At the same time her daytime learning was also improving. She and two other children at the unit formed an 'academic' group who were given simple number and language work. Emma learnt to add up to five, to count (erratically) up to ten, and to record her sums for herself. She began to read, using the same reading scheme as that used in an infant's school some twenty miles away where a close friend of Beech

Tree's head taught a reception class. Informal arrangements were made when Emma was nearly eleven, for her to spend some time in this ordinary classroom, as a prelude to returning home and attending the village school. Transport proved a problem, with one member of staff having to take Emma and stay with her in order to bring her back again, but there were no problems as far as the teacher was concerned. Emma joined in music and movement and maths games, watched television with the other children, and worked with them on writing and reading games associated with the reading scheme familiar to her from Beech Tree. The teacher reported that 'At no time has Emma disturbed the class or taken more of my attention than any of the other "normal" children . . . in my opinion Emma would be able to cope in an infant class with the help of a classroom assistant.'

Unfortunately for plans for Emma's future, government expenditure cuts meant that such help was no longer available, at least in Emma's county. A further blow to the plan to integrate her into the local village school was the building of a large housing estate nearby, which swelled the number of children attending the school and the size of the classes, and meant it was no longer such a suitable place for Emma. The head of Beech Tree remarked sadly that 'The whole integration project with Emma has fallen flat on its face, not because Emma can't achieve it but because of other circumstances.'

Plans for her future now are uncertain. Emma should have left Beech Tree House over a term ago, having outstayed the two-year limit, but the local education authority has been unable to find a suitable school for her. It is still too soon for her to be returned home, unless her parents are given far more support than the authority is currently able to provide. The possibility of a place at a four-day-a-week hostel in the grounds of an ESN(S) school, with Emma attending a nearby ESN(M) school for lessons, foundered when it was realised that all the self-help skills like cooking, serving food and making her own bed which Emma had acquired at Beech Tree would be irrelevant at this hostel, where everything was done for the children 'as if they were at a nice boarding house', as the matron put it. Part of the problem is that Emma's needs don't fit neatly into any of the usual categories for which special provision is made. Her needs remain, but there is little sign that in the near future they will be adequately met.

3 WILLIAM: A CHILD WITH DOWN'S SYNDROME

Tony Booth and June Statham

William was the Sullivan's second child, delivered at home in their small village. He now has five brothers and sisters and has always taken a full part in family life. He spent several of the early years of his school career in special schools but recently his parents managed to find a place for him with a group of 'handicapped' children in a unit in an ordinary school.

William's parents were told as soon as their son was born that he was a 'mongol'. 'You'll never regret it', said the midwife. 'You've got Nature's own. They bring a new quality and compassion to your life.' The specialist who first saw William was more brusque, turning the baby over and commenting on the parts that were 'not quite up to standard' or 'a bit loose', until the parents felt that their child was being treated like a joint of meat. Years later, sharing their experiences with a group of parents of children with Down's Syndrome, the Sullivans realised that they were not alone in this feeling.

We all loathed the way we were told about our child's handicap, and it was mainly because doctors seemed so insensitive. The parents of one girl were told that she'd be little better than a vegetable. The doctor said to another mother in the group, 'Never mind dear, she'll be dead in six weeks.' Another of the parents asked the doctor how intelligent her son would be, and he said, 'roughly the same intelligence as most animals'. All these remarks by doctors are within the last five years. They're so unbelievably hard-hearted and unsympathetic.

William's parents objected most to the doctors' pessimism:

They believe that the worst thing you can infect parents with is hope, they all think that. They all think that hope is a terrible thing to give anybody, because it might not be realised. It's as if when you think your child might have a spot of talent because he's tap dancing at age four, somebody says 'no he's hopeless, probably got two left feet, might well have a heart attack, children of seven have heart attacks you know . . .' We all have hopes about children, and by the time they're not realised you're onto the next hope.

The Sullivans took William home from the hospital, and searched for someone who could offer them a more positive approach. They found Rex Brinkworth, the adviser to the Down's Children's Association.

He was a goldmine as far as we were concerned. He gave us practical advice, like 'don't give sugar to them because they can't cope with it, give them glucose instead', and he sent us foolscap sheets called 'schedules' with instructions for things to do with Down's Syndrome children. How to stimulate them by pumping their legs, waggling their hands, passing toys so they have to grasp them with their hands. It kept *us* busy and stopped us fretting and worrying. It put value on us as parents.

William's early childhood was a trouble free one. He was an 'angelic little baby', according to his mother, and rarely ill. He never saw a doctor except to have stitches in a cut, and in their small village the family had little contact with home teachers, social workers or health visitors. Mrs Sullivan ran a playgroup in the village hall which included several handicapped children, and William joined when he began to walk at around two and a half. His family grew larger with the addition of a younger brother and sister.

When William was five, the area medical officer came round to tell his parents he ought to go to school, and she took them to visit a school for severely subnormal children. William went too, and was left in the nursery class while his parents looked around. None of them were very impressed, and his mother felt he would learn very little there.

I was shocked by the children there, poor little souls, and I got more and more appalled wondering what he was going to learn there. So I asked the head what he taught them and he described lots of things William had already learnt, like handling scissors, glueing, keeping himself clean. I said 'What about reading and writing?' and he said, 'Oh, we don't bother to teach them to bark at print.'

They decided to keep William at home and educate him themselves, but agreed to having him assessed by the authorities.

They sent a young girl around, very nice but straight out of university and she didn't have a clue. She unpacked her box of bricks on the floor and asked William to do this and that with them. He, being very tidy-minded, packed them all away again neatly in the box, and she wrote down 'has no concept of play'! Then she asked me to go out of the room while she took William around asking him to name things. When they came out she said 'He's got no vocabulary has he?' and I said 'of course, he knows an enormous number of words', and he named them all for me. It wasn't that he didn't like her, he just clammed up.

As a result of the assessment, William was sent to a local educational centre for children with learning difficulties. He was their first pupil with Down's Syndrome and did very well. His parents were quite happy for him to be there, because although it was a special school it was small, well equipped and took children with a variety of handicaps. William stayed there for three years, by which time a fifth child had been born and a sixth was on the way, and his parents had decided to move to a nearby town. The problem of William's education arose again. He was once more assessed, given an IQ of 70 and recommended for placement in an ESN(M) school. However the local policy was to place all Down's Syndrome children in ESN(S) schools, regardless of their ability. The parents visited another ESN(S) school, and were again horrified. They disliked what they saw as the *laissez-faire* 'uncontained' atmosphere of the school and the way children 'slouched around, picked their noses and banged their heads against the wall'; they disliked the locked half-doors 'like a stable'.

William ran out to the car and couldn't be enticed back inside. They decided he wouldn't be happy there, and began a battle with the local education authority to keep him at home. The authority sent the parents forms to fill in to place their son at the ESN(S) school, with a warning that 'steps could be taken under the law' if they failed to comply; the parents resisted and were eventually told of another ESN(S) school some distance away, which they reluctantly went to see. This time they were far more favourably impressed, both by the headmaster and by the teacher William would have, a forceful woman who took great pains to teach her pupils to read and write. They agreed to send William there, only to be told by the local authority that the school was outside their catchment area. The headmaster agreed to make a place available for William, however, and he began at his new school soon after.

He seemed happy enough there, but Mrs Sullivan was still keen on having him educated in greater contact with ordinary children. She felt that the special school was a separate world where strange noises and gestures were taken for granted, the pace was artificially slow and the children only related to each other as 'patients'. When William was ten and had been at this special school for a year, his parents managed to find a place for him in a small unit for 'handicapped' children within a private school. The way this unit was set up, and William's progress there, is described later in this book in 'Parent Participation: Setting up a Special Unit in a Private School'.

4 CHRISTOPHER: A PHYSICALLY HANDICAPPED CHILD IN AN ORDINARY SCHOOL

June Statham

Dogsdale is a large middle school in the West Midlands countryside, catering for around 600 nine to thirteen year olds, and housed in the well-worn buildings of an old secondary modern school. It has also inherited from the secondary modern various large playing fields, and on one of these a new day school for physically handicapped children has recently been built. The choice of site may have been determined by the availability of land rather than by any intention of providing the physically handicapped children with access to an ordinary school, but the schools' proximity has increased the opportunities for integration.

Since the opening three years ago of Elmtree, a day school for physically handicapped children, there has been a fair amount of contact between this special school and Dogsdale, the ordinary middle school next door. The staff are on good terms, the pupils put on plays for each other at Christmas, and some children from Elmtree attend particular lessons at Dogsdale where it is felt that they would benefit from more specialised teaching than the special school can offer.

Ten children have also transferred to Dogsdale full time; pupils whom the head of Elmtree feels will be able to cope emotionally, academically and physically with ordinary school life. There are three children from the special school in the present second year. One walks with a stick, one suffers from hydrocephalus, and the third, Christopher, was born with spina bifida. Christopher is the most physically handicapped of the three. He can walk unaided but with a very unbalanced gait, and is incontinent, needing to use a special bag to collect his urine. Unlike the other two boys who transferred to Dogsdale's register, Christopher stays registered with Elmtree despite taking all his lessons in the ordinary school and spending 99 per cent of his school time there. The headmaster at Dogsdale Middle School prefers it that way, knowing that there is an official as well as a personal link to ensure that

Elmtree will continue to take care of all the medical aspects of Christopher's handicap; treating blisters on his feet, arranging fittings for his surgical boots, providing regular medical check-ups, changing his pads when he has a bowel 'accident' (a procedure which Christopher is capable of carrying out himself, but the teachers at Dogsdale admit it is easier to send him across the playing field to Elmtree where there is a nurse and a changing room than to get him to do it himself without proper facilities). The head at Elmtree would like Christopher to be transferred to Dogsdale's register, but agrees with the head there that this would be a purely administrative change, since the medical back-up would continue to be provided, and since Christopher obviously feels himself to be part of the ordinary school. His contact with the school for the physically handicapped is for medical reasons only, causing the head there to remark good naturedly that 'All we keep are the problems!'

The incentive for Christopher to move across to Dogsdale came initially from his mother. The family live locally, so Christopher's older brother already attended Dogsdale and his younger sister would soon go too. The head of Elmtree felt that Christopher satisfied his three criteria for transfer. Physically he could manage to get around and negotiate steps and was able to cope with the day-to-day management problems associated with the use of his penile appliance; emotionally he was a friendly, sociable child prepared to have a go at joining in with all he could; and academically he was one of the more able children at Elmtree. The heads of the two schools discussed his case at length and it was agreed that Christopher should start at Dogsdale along with the first-year intake of nine and ten year olds, a year younger than himself.

The detailed information on Christopher's handicap discussed by the headmasters failed to filter down to the teachers, or if it did they soon forgot it. They felt it was unimportant, since they had been instructed that these children could be considered as normal pupils, and were quite vague about the medical nature of any of the children's handicaps, knowing only that one had a stiff neck or another some sort of by-pass tubes. They said 'No one ever tells us what's the matter, because educationally we don't need to know'.

Certainly Christopher's handicap seemed to make little difference to his participation in ordinary school life. His form teacher treated him the same as her other pupils, asking him to move desks or take messages, and his school day differed in only a few respects from that of his classmates. When the other children did games or PE, Christopher would do extra work with the head of year, and he practiced hand-writing (which he finds difficult) instead of doing rural science. At lunchtimes the other children would queue for their dinner while Christopher had his brought to him by the canteen staff to save him unbalancing a tray with his lopsided walk. The dinner lady felt he could probably take it back empty himself, but that they'd got into the habit of doing it for him. Apart from these few differences, Christopher was keen to join in everything; excelling at French and drama, throwing himself around in movement classes, joining in the rough-and-tumble of the playground. Some early problems with bowel control resulted in Christopher acquiring the nickname of 'Stinky', but his friendly nature and willingness to join in with whatever was going on soon earned him the acceptance of the other children, and caused his teacher to remark that he was far less of a problem than the more mildly handicapped boy with a stick whom she felt 'played-up' his disability.

Most of the teaching at Dogsdale takes place in mixed-ability classes, but maths and English are setted. Christopher was placed in the top set for English and the bottom for maths. His end-of-term report stated that he had 'settled in extremely well and impressed both staff and children alike with the maturity and rapidity of his adjustment'. On the section of the report where parents could add their comments, Christopher's father and mother wrote that they were 'very pleased with Christopher's progress and hope that he will continue to catch up with lost education. We would like to thank the teachers for their co-operation and consideration'.

The head felt that Christopher fitted in perfectly and that there were 'no problems whatsoever'. The teachers agreed that Christopher benefited from being in the ordinary school and was doing well, but they were more aware than the head of the subtle demands placed on them by the presence of a physically handicapped child in their class.

It's little things. Christopher has to empty his urine bag every hour and a half, and he wouldn't want to do it with all the other children peering in. It was suggested he could go just before break, but that disrupts the lesson, so we arranged for him to use the youth club toilets next door instead.

The special school used to finish half an hour earlier than we did, so the children who came here part-time for some lessons would have to leave early to catch their taxi. They'd need their homework setting, and I'd have to stop the lesson to start thinking about homework before I was ready.

I remember the child with a stiff neck dropping a book he was handing to me to mark. I waited for him to pick it up but he just stared at me, and then said he wasn't supposed to bend down. I later found out he could, although his mother still thought it wasn't safe.

I sometimes wonder whether I ought to go over to Christopher's desk to mark his book, instead of getting him to bring it out to me like everyone else.

For several teachers, the extra attention and preparation needed to make sure that the handicapped child's needs were met was highlighted during the second year's annual outing to York. At first the three physically handicapped children were not invited. The staff felt that they had enough to cope with, staying in an hotel with over 150 children for a full week. However, Christopher's form teacher felt it was important that he be included, and she persuaded the school to extend the invitation to the physically handicapped children too. The parents of the other two children declined, but Christopher's parents were keen for him to go. Plans went ahead, then Christopher's form teacher was taken ill and the responsibility for him fell on the co-ordinator of the trip, who was less familiar with his problems and felt that his inclusion in the trip entailed a lot of extra work. She had to write letters and make phone calls, ask the hotel to give Christopher a ground floor room with a toilet, make sure there was extra help for pushing his wheelchair and someone available to look after it on the coach and train, acquire from Christopher's parents and the special school equipment and information which had been largely irrelevant in the classroom.

He doesn't need a wheelchair around school, but in York we go on long walks, so I had to arrange with Elmtree to borrow a wheelchair for him. They sent one over, and then they sent up a bicycle pump for the tyres which is when I began to feel out of my depth. I worried about what would happen if the chair had a puncture, or if Christopher's shoes wore out or his bag burst. The other children were told to bring a spare pair of trousers, but I didn't know if that would be enough for Christopher. His mother was very good, she offered spare rubber pants and pads and bedsheets. She was very confident and calm, although she got a bit apprehensive on the day we left because he'd not been away on his own with a group of normal kids before.

None of the predicted disasters occured, but Christopher's presence did involve the teachers in extra worry and organisation. His chair had to be left unguarded at the bottom of buildings while the school party went up to look around. Coach trips had to be organised around the proximity of public toilets, to cater for Christopher's need to empty his urine bag every hour and a half. The local Association for the Crippled Child which had offered to provide helpers to push Christopher's chair, tended to supply well-intentioned but elderly volunteers whom the teachers felt would be better off in the chair themselves than attempting to push a large twelve-year-old up steep streets and hills. Fortunately an extra student-helper had joined the trip at the last minute and could devote most of his time to Christopher, and with this additional support most teachers felt that Christopher's presence on the trip had presented few problems and that physically handicapped children should be included in future outings.

Christopher's successful integration into the ordinary school seems to be due to three main factors. The most important one is the physical proximity of the two schools, enabling children and teachers to move easily from one to the other, and the medical back-up and transport resources to be readily available. The head at Elmtree felt that Christopher's presence in the ordinary school 'wouldn't have worked if we were a half, or even a quarter of a mile apart. The teachers there need to feel they can just send a child across the field if there's a problem!'. The second factor is the good relationship and degree of co-operation between staff and heads at the two schools, and the third is Christopher's own ability to cope in the ordinary school. The head there stresses that he can only accept handicapped children who are able to cope with the school on its own terms.

Mentally handicapped children, or those in a wheelchair who would be unable to manage the stairs in the building, could not be included, and he envisages problems for Christopher when the time comes for him to transfer to the high school several miles away, where he would have to negotiate three floors and no longer be able to rely on the special school for transport home. It is possible that Christopher will then have to return to Elmtree, although both heads agree that this would be undesirable and that they will do all they can to ensure that Christopher can continue to receive his education in an ordinary school.

5 HELP WHEN IT'S NEEDED: A PROGRESS STUDENT IN A COMPREHENSIVE SCHOOL

Ronny Flynn

Matthew Birkett is almost fifteen and a member of a third-year mixed-ability class in a large comprehensive school. He has been there for a year, having moved from a secondary modern school twelve miles away. His need for extra help with reading and writing had not been adequately met by previous schools, but at the comprehensive Matthew receives two and a half hours of remedial help a week and feels that the school tries hard to 'help people like me who aren't very good at English and spelling'.

Matthew has had a chequered educational past. Between the ages of five and eight he had frequent and prolonged bouts of tonsilitis. His parents feel he missed the best part of three years of schooling and during this period they noticed that Rosemary, his younger sister, was beginning to overtake Matthew in her reading ability. They voiced their concern to the head teacher at a Parents Evening but Matthew was not given any extra help. They felt that communication between the head teacher and class teachers was so poor that information about Matthew just didn't get passed on; their worries were not taken seriously enough and the impression they received was that they should just 'wait and see'. When Matthew was not given books to take home from school his parents bought them themselves. They feel angry about the wasted opportunities of those years; they regard it as part of a school's job to help students like Matthew catch up on schooling they miss.

Matthew remembers the events somewhat differently. He says that he was able to read as well as anyone at infant school but around the age of 9 or 10 he realised that others were working faster than him and he was getting behind. When he was 12, Matthew's family moved and he spent his next year at a middle school (for children aged 8-12). At this school the class teacher took a liking to him, called his parents to the school and arranged to provide him with extra lessons in reading and spelling. The Birketts noticed a marked improvement in Matthew's work and were very pleased. His school reports were encouraging and teachers remarked in particular on the effort he put into his work.

Secondary education is still selective where the Birketts lived, so Matthew took the twelve plus examination. He failed to gain a place at a grammar school and was allocated to a secondary modern school. He 'cried his eyes out' when he found out but had no choice. The whole family was disappointed as they had been under the impression that he was doing really well.

At the secondary school his fortunes took a downward turn. He was 'shoved to one side and ignored'. He is a quiet, shy child and his parents thought he was just left out of the system. He was placed in the bottom of three streams and was very unhappy. He found it difficult to cope with the amount of work he was expected to copy from the blackboard in a thirty-five minute lesson.

Luckily for Matthew, the family moved nine months later and Matthew changed to his present comprehensive school. Before moving house, the Birketts visited the school and spent a few hours talking to staff and looking around. It was modern, friendly and they liked it immediately.

On entry to the school, Matthew took a routine screening test for reading, and as his reading age was below ten years, he was referred to the Progress department. The Progress department staff do not think of their work as 'remedial' or their students as 'remedial kids'. They have made a deliberate effort to avoid the disadvantages of traditional labels; as one teacher remarked, 'No one understands the term "progress" anyway but I think that contributes to the lack of stigma.' Stephanie, who takes Matthew for literacy work, spoke to him after he had been tested and found him keen to attend remedial sessions.

At the end of Matthew's first term, Stephanie reported:

Matthew has special difficulties in sequencing letters, writing words the correct way round, and in presenting letters – he 'mirrors' them. His hand–eye coordination needs improvement. He is an intelligent, sensitive student, producing work of a high standard in respect of content both in Integrated Studies and in remedial work but he still needs help with his tendency to reverse.

A teacher from the local remedial advisory team carried out some diagnostic tests with Matthew and reported difficulties in letter discrimination, as well as poor 'motor control' and jerky 'ocular pursuit'.

Matthew has two remedial sessions divided equally between reading lessons and writing and spelling lessons. Reading lessons give him the chance to choose and read books with which he can cope, and to develop and practise his reading skills using a variety of materials and activities in a small teaching group in an environment with minimum distractions. Writing and spelling lessons involve handwriting practice, especially with letter shapes he confuses such as b and p, and a variety of worksheet activities using anagrams and sentences with omitted words. Suggestions for help from the remedial advisory team included word games, writing exercises, memory games and techniques for learning spelling.

His form tutor and his Integrated Studies tutor speak highly of him, remarking on his motivation and persistence.

In Integrated Studies lessons, apart from his weakness in writing, grammar and spelling, the actual concepts and ideas he puts into his work are quite good. But it's just the technical details of how he presents it that are problematic. His main difficulty is not to do with verbal expression, just putting it on paper.

Matthew enjoys his present school. His parents feel he has gained tremendously in confidence, has become more assertive and much more at ease with people. They attribute this to the school's informal atmosphere, and Matthew himself thinks that 'it's a relaxed and friendly place'. He is not aware of any burden or restriction attached to being 'a remedial student'. He has made noticeable progress over the year in all areas of the curriculum, and has obviously benefited from working with the Progress staff.

He became aware of the improvement he needed to make in his writing and started to make it himself. I think he knows now what to do, and he does check his work carefully. He is becoming more aware of when he puts letters the wrong way round in a word but that awareness will have to continue and grow before his exams in the 5th year ... I don't think Matthew has 'arrived' at all — he's still going to need support, and there will be support for him.

6 PARENTS' CHOICE: A BLIND GIRL EDUCATED IN AN ORDINARY SCHOOL

June Statham

At fifteen, Helen Williams is a lively, ordinary teenager. Her room at home is full of early schoolbooks, workcards, a cassette recorder, and a phone extension on which she can call up her many friends. Helen is taking seven 'O' levels at a comprehensive school across the town, and plans to go on to take 'A' levels and perhaps a modern languages degree at university. The major differences between her and her fellow pupils are first that Helen is totally blind, and has been since birth, and secondly that her education in the school is supported by a resources teacher employed by the LEA.

Helen's early years were spent at home, with part-time attendance at a nursery school when she was three. She and her two slightly older brothers come from a warm, close family, and her parents were reluctant to follow the local authority's standard policy of sending any blind child away to a residential school at the age of five. The nearest such school was some thirty miles away, and the Williams felt that it made neither financial nor social sense for the authorities to break up the family and send a child away for expensive residential education, rather than for them to provide the necessary support for the child to be educated in an ordinary school and live at home.

In the next ten years the Williams were to become involved in numerous negotiations with the local education authority over Helen's schooling, but at this stage they felt they were 'innocents at the game' and unhappily agreed to send Helen to the boarding school. The year that followed was a depressing one for everyone; for the family who only saw Helen at weekends and holidays, and for Helen herself, who found the change from a close family life to a communal living situation very unsettling. She took refuge in daydreaming, and spent the weekdays looking forward to the weekends when she could go home. Her teachers assessed her as a child of only average ability.

After Helen had been at the boarding school for a year, the Williams decided to bring her home. They had seen what the special school had to offer and felt there was little apart from the braille which differed from the teaching she could receive in an ordinary primary school. During the intervening year they had managed to find a local blind woman capable of teaching Helen braille, and they knew that with her help and their own backgrounds in teaching they could educate Helen at home themselves, as a last resort, if no local school would take her. So they took Helen away from the residential school, and began a long series of meetings with the local authorities to talk about her future. They felt the authorities were being unhelpful, but this time they were more experienced. 'By now we were beginning to get used to what it was like, to realise that it was a game and that they were trying to con Helen out of what we wanted for her.' Her parents had already approached several infant schools to see whether they could take Helen, and when it became obvious that the family could not be persuaded to send her back to the boarding school, the director revealed that the headmistress of the primary school nearest to Helen's home had agreed to accept her into the school.

The Williams were overjoyed. It was arranged that Helen should attend in the mornings only, with an infant helper to assist her, and then should come home for lunch (this being considered too dangerous for her) and spend the afternoons working with the braille teacher that her parents had found. Because the teacher was unqualified these lessons were held at Helen's home and paid for by the family, but they were closely linked to her schoolwork, with all her school readers being translated into braille so she could work on them at home. Her parents also worked closely with the teachers at the school, taking Helen to and from school, preparing braille workcards for her to match those of the sighted children, and going in to assist and advise if there were any problems. But they found that 'there didn't seem to be any problems, because Helen enjoyed it so much'. There were few activities going on in the ordinary infant school in which Helen was unable to take part. She went into morning assembly and sang with everyone else, joined in PE lessons, took out her braille workcards when the other children took out their ordinary ones, listened to stories, learnt tables and counting, joined in making collages and plasticine models and soft toys. Writing was more difficult, but she could tell her helper what she wanted to say and the helper would write it down for her, spelling mistakes and all.

When the time came for Helen to transfer from the infants to the juniors, several of the staff in the junior school were doubtful about taking her. Her parents feared that the battles would begin again, but Helen's progress had so impressed the director of education that he supported her case, and Helen went up into the class of one of the first-year teachers sympathetic to taking her. After this first year, she spent her remaining three years in the junior school with another sympathetic teacher who took the top class. It meant that Helen was always taught with children older than herself, and had to get used to a new set of classmates each year, but for a sociable child like Helen this merely extended her already wide circle of friends. Children she met outside school could be unthinkingly cruel, like those she met in the swimming pool with her father who asked him 'can she talk?', but at school she made friends easily and began to stay to school lunch in order to spend more time with her friends. During her stay at the junior school the school secretary taught her to type.

Things went well until the time for transfer to a secondary school approached and Mr and Mrs Williams had again to look for a school prepared to accept Helen as a pupil. As part of their explorations they visited another special school which impressed them more than the one Helen had originally attended. Helen spent a trial week there, but although she liked it she felt it wasn't like home. 'You'd put your bags down on a chair and the next minute they'd have disappeared into a locker or something. It was the most human of those places I've been to, but it still wasn't home.'

Her parents began enquiries at the local comprehensive schools. The obvious choice, the school where Helen's two brothers went and where all her friends would be going, was reluctant to take her. The head said that the school was too large and open-plan, that most of their resource material was visual and that they would be unable to cope with a blind pupil. The Williams argued, but the head refused to be budged. End-of-term came and went, and Helen's friends all moved on while she stayed behind at the primary school. Her parents tried other secondary schools, generally receiving the same response, and they had begun to think desperately of seeking publicity in the daily papers to win support for their case when an offer came, via the local authority, of a place in a large comprehensive on the other side of the town.

This new school was the furthest away, with a layout less suitable for a blind person than the schools which had already refused her, but from the beginning the teachers there went out of their way to make Helen's schooling successful. Her resource teacher, specially appointed by the LEA, managed to learn braille to prepare worksheets for Helen's lessons. Her domestic science teacher made a model of an egg so that Helen could feel how the yolk was attached to the albumen while the other pupils looked at the real thing, and the craft department made all kinds of additional aids for her. The school provided her with a talking calculator, and a local factory organised a sponsored filing-cabinet push to Wales to raise money for buying Helen's Optacon, a machine which scans ordinary print and translates the letters into electrical impulses for a blind person to 'read'. The Optacon cost £2,000, but was essential if Helen were to do sixth-form or university work, where it would be impractical for all the written material to be translated into braille. The Optacon was presented at a celebration banquet by a famous singer, accompanied by a huge floppy elephant and much champagne and cheering.

The school had originally agreed to take Helen for a two-year trial period, but her obvious success meant there was little question of her not continuing there. Her most recent report contains a string of 'A's for both effort and attainment, and she has numerous friends among the other pupils, among the teachers and in the community. She has failed to fulfil the predictions of either the teachers at her early residential school, who felt she was 'not too bright', or of the eminent man (still giving the same advice) who told her parents when she was five that Helen would be 'crucified' if she went to an ordinary school. Success probably involves Helen in more effort than many of her friends, and certainly requires a lot of dedication. Her work often has to be prepared in two forms, typed on a braille typewriter for herself so that she can read and correct it, and then typed again on a normal typewriter for the teacher to mark. Reading a page of print using the Optacon demands a considerable amount of concentration and time. Even getting home from school involves Helen in two bus journeys, although she has typically turned this into an opportunity for meeting new people. 'I have to ask if anyone is waiting for the 499 bus and could they stop it for me, and that gets me into conversation with people. We often have an interesting chat, and if we meet again I can usually recognise them by their voice.'

The Williams family feel that their battles over Helen's schooling have been more than worthwhile, although there were times when they were depressed by the opposition they encountered. As a family they have obviously been in a better position than most to take on such a fight, both parents being articulate, tenacious and teachers, and Helen herself being a positive and determined character. But they feel that the back-up service they gave to the primary school could — and should — be provided by the authorities and are anxious that the resources that have been built up around Helen in her secondary school, both in terms of practical aids and in terms of teachers' experience, should be used to help another blind child through the ordinary schools — a route which they feel is infinitely preferable to special schooling.

7 ANOTHER CHANCE: A CHILD FROM A DAY SCHOOL FOR MALADJUSTED CHILDREN

June Statham

In theory a 'special' education should allow a child to move freely between different kinds of educational provision as their needs change, but in practice once placed in a special school the child's chances of moving back into mainstream education are not very high. When Max was transferred to a day school for maladjusted children at the age of seven it was recommended that he stay there 'until he reaches senior age at least'. In fact Max has received another chance and has begun attending an ordinary comprehensive school part-time, but the twists and turns of fate in the form of changes in staff and school organisation, as well as his own personal development, mean that his successful reintegration is by no means certain.

At thirteen, Max Thompson attends two schools. For most of the week he goes to Crabhill, a local comprehensive, but for the rest of the time he is a pupil at Garton, a day school for maladjusted children nearby. His time at Crabhill has gradually been extended and it is hoped that soon Max will be transferred from the roll of the maladjusted school so he can attend the ordinary school full time.

His story is one of deprivation, bad luck, and administrative inconsistencies. Born in 1967 and abandoned by his mother when he was nine months old, Max was brought up by his West Indian uncle and his uncle's common-law wife, a Midlands woman who was unable to have children of her own. Max's real father (also West Indian) lives next door, but Max was unaware of his true parentage until he was about ten, when the Thompsons married and legally adopted him. Mr Thompson worked in a laundry until he was made redundant; Mrs Thompson, his stepmother, works part-time in a clothing factory. They live in the ground-floor flat of a house which they are buying on a mortgage and sublet the top half to relatives. The house is generally very untidy and dirty, and one of the main reasons for Max being referred to Garton by the educational psychologist when he was seven was that he appeared 'physically neglected and very dirty'. The psychologist also commented that he exhibited violent and aggressive behaviour in his opportunity class at the primary school, and concluded that he was 'emotionally maladjusted because of his social situation, with his difficult behaviour making him hard to contain in an ordinary school'. On the section of the form headed 'probable length of stay' was written 'until he reaches senior age at least'.

The school Max was sent to was a day school for fifty maladjusted children aged between seven and sixteen, which moved the year after he arrived to purpose-built premises sited at the edge of the Borough between the isolation hospital and a cemetery. The head was liked by his staff, but there was little regularity in either curriculum or routine. Break and lunch-times were frequently changed; both children and teachers were constantly re-grouped. Max was fairly bright but found himself in difficulties socially. He was always poorly dressed and came in for a lot of bullying from the other children, who called him 'Fleabag' and 'half-caste'. He invariably reacted aggressively, and invariably came off worst in the ensuing fight, unless the boys were much smaller and he could vent his frustration on them through the kind of behaviour he was learning from other children. No matter what group he was in, Max seemed to end up at the bottom of the pecking order, losing out on any privileges or treats that were going, and acquiring a very poor view of himself. Various attempts were made by social workers to establish links with Max's family. One who visited when he was eight wrote to the headmaster that there was little she could do.

My work with this family has been very difficult, mainly due to their limited vocabulary and lack of understanding for the need of social work involvement. They either do not have, or at least do not admit to having, any problems with Max at home and it would appear that they are able to exercise adequate care and control over him. You will appreciate that for social work involvement to be effective, it is important that the family concerned acknowledge that they have problems with which a social worker can be of help. With this family I have experienced denial of any problems and my efforts to bring them out have proved fruitless.

I therefore feel at this stage that there is nothing this department can do to assist this family and I have decided to close the case. I do hope my report will be of some use to you.

A year later a different social worker also found Max's family lacking in understanding of his problems, putting them down to 'boyish pranks' or 'a bad temper like his father', but this worker felt that Max had a good relationship with his parents who combined firm handling with warmth and affection. Mr Thompson had a tendency to beat Max, but the social worker felt that his wife prevented him from going too far, and noted that Max seemed fond of both parents. Teachers were less optimistic, noticing scars on Max's body when he stripped for swimming, hearing of him scavenging dustbins for food, and being told by Mr Thompson that Max came to school so filthy because washing was against their religion.

The school was also having its problems. The first head had left soon after the move to new premises, and his replacement failed to win the respect of either staff or pupils. There was an undercurrent of violence, both between children and between staff and children. If all the pupils stayed in the classroom for a lesson, that was considered a good lesson regardless of what was learnt. A curriculum of creative writing and environmental studies might have looked good on paper, but stood little chance of success when few of the children could even be persuaded to sit down with a pencil. The school's reputation began to decline, and so did staff morale and the number of referrals, until the only children referred there by the educational psychologists were those who couldn't be sent anywhere else; mainly large, aggressive, West Indian boys.

It was in this atmosphere that it was decided to try to get Max back into an ordinary school. He was now twelve, and had been at Garton since he was seven. His parents wanted him to have a chance in an ordinary school, and it was felt that if he was ever going to get back it was now or never. The head contacted Max's psychologist suggesting a review, and made various arrangements with Springfields, a secondary school some miles away, which he failed to discuss with his staff. Relationships at the school deteriorated to the point where the head was forced to leave at the end of the summer term and be replaced by an acting head, so at the start of the new school year no one was quite sure where Max was supposed to be. The head of the lower school at Springfields with whom arrangements had been made was also a different person come September, and the school's headmaster claimed to know nothing about any new boy arriving at his school, despite the fact that Max's parents had received a letter inviting them to bring him for an interview. Letters flew back and forth, and eventually Max started at the new school two weeks into the autumn term. He was placed in the second year despite the psychologist's recommendation that he should be put back a year to ensure that he could manage the work. He could in fact cope with second-year work, but the decision to put him there resulted from lack of communication and ignorance rather than from any consideration of his abilities.

The same lack of communication characterised the rest of Max's experiences at Springfields. Like the special school he had just left, it was also in a state of disorganisation. Once an upper-class grammar school, the staff had found it difficult to adjust to the change to comprehensive schooling and to the increased number of black pupils who now made up half the school's population. Staff turnover was high, and communication bad. Garton made fairly frequent phone calls to the new school to check on Max's progress, but admit they did not follow up his placement as thoroughly as they ought to have done. Part of the reason was that they, the secondary school's social worker and Max's parents all received the impression that he was doing very well there; obtaining good marks, happy to be in an ordinary school and causing no problems. Mr and Mrs Thompson were extremely pleased and bought him three complete sets of uniform. His reports emphasised his good academic progress and only noted as an afterthought that his behaviour left much to be desired. It came as no small shock to most of the people concerned to discover that Springfields was considering sending Max back to the special school, mainly because of out-of-school incidents including smoking and fighting. Garton's acting head stressed the importance of telling Max's parents what was going on, so they were called to a meeting and told how close their son was to being suspended: Mr Thompson's reaction was that were Max suspended he would beat him then wash his hands of the boy and let the government take him away. The school agreed to give Max another chance, but still wanted him out and finally suspended him several months later. His mother kept the news from his father to avoid a beating, and Max turned up as usual at Springfields on the first day of term. It was left to the special school to contact his parents and explain that he was to come back to them, but with immediate arrangements made for him to go part-time to another secondary school, Crabhill, which had the advantage of being closer and more prepared to make a success of Max's placement, having successfully taken another boy from Garton some time previously. This school agreed to take Max for PE, woodwork and music. He remained on Garton's roll and went back there for most of his lessons and every lunchtime. The two schools maintained frequent contact, with Max reporting to a particular teacher at Crabhill each time he arrived before joining lessons. After a while maths and English were added to his timetable, so he now attends Crabhill for nearly 80 per cent of the week. Max seems to enjoy it there, and going to the ordinary school has raised both his own and his parent's opinions about himself, besides giving him the opportunity to take some exams and maybe to realise his current ambition of becoming a train driver. It is not a complete success story by any means; the date for him attending Crabhill full time has recently been postponed because of an incident where Max hit a girl who refused to get out of his way. But with the commitment of the teachers at Crabhill and the support of the special school, it seems likely that he will eventually be transferred full time to the ordinary school, and his improved self-image and chances of success will be maintained.

8 ROUTES TO A RESIDENTIAL SCHOOL FOR THE DEAF

June Statham

The following accounts of how two very young girls were identified as suffering from severe hearing loss were compiled from material in the case-files of an educational centre for pre-school hearing-impaired children. They record the 'official' perspective of the professionals involved in the lives of these two girls, and the administrative procedures that resulted in them both being placed in a residential school for the deaf at the age of five.

1. Cathy

Cathy had been born with a cleft palate, was slow in her overall development and had frequent and severe coughs and colds. She was already attending a child development clinic when she was referred by the doctor there to the education service for hearing-impaired children. She was then one-and-a-half years old. Mr Carter, a teacher of hearing-impaired children, tested Cathy two months later but found it difficult to obtain accurate responses to sound from her and suggested that he see her again the following month. This time he used a distraction test of hearing and concluded that Cathy had 'normal bilateral auditory acuity'. Her hearing received little or no attention during the next year and a half, although she frequently attended the child development clinic. She was also treated at the local hospital for croup and bronchitis. When she was three the clinic, concerned at the slow progress she was making, called a case conference. Mr Muir, the educational audiologist and head of service for hearing-impaired children, was asked to test Cathy's hearing again. He had difficulty, too, in getting her to respond appropriately but thought that Cathy '*probably* has fairly normal hearing.' The week after he had tested her, Cathy developed otitis media, an ear infection, and seemed very deaf. The doctor at the clinic

50

decided to refer her to the ear, nose and throat consultant at the hospital and suggested that a teacher of hearing-impaired children visit her home to find out whether she had any hearing difficulties there.

The ENT consultant could find no physical cause for Cathy's apparent deafness, and felt that she probably could hear. Cathy's mother disagreed, and was convinced that her daughter's hearing had deteriorated since she was two and a half. A year previously, Cathy could say a few words, run to answer the telephone and distinguish the sound of her father's car coming home; now she seemed capable of none of these. The ENT consultant cautiously wrote that 'Considerable time will have to be spent with the child to assess the presence of hearing.'

In the absence of any definite decision on Cathy's hearing loss, Mr Muir nevertheless decided that she would benefit from attending the special unit for hearing-impaired pre-school children at a local nursery, where she could be more closely observed and tested. He made arrangements for her to attend the unit part-time and contacted the area education officer to provide the necessary transport arrangements.

At the unit Cathy received auditory training designed to condition her to respond to sound, but testing her hearing still proved difficult. Mr Muir tried to test her twice in the next two months, was unable to obtain reliable responses but was optimistic that he would 'obtain reasonably reliable thresholds sometime in the next three to four months, when Cathy has settled into the nursery'. The teacher of the deaf who had been seeing Cathy at home felt she would benefit from using hearing aids, and these were duly provided. The medical officer also arranged an appointment for her at the university's neuropsychological unit, for an 'evoked response' test of hearing. When the results from this test finally came back they added little information that was new; the university reported that 'The responses were variable and difficult to detect, and we would like to repeat the investigation in order to obtain a more accurate estimation of threshold levels.'

Before the second test took place, Cathy had another hearing test at the unit, having now been attending the nursery for some five months. The tester wrote in despair 'not a good deal of joy today. Can't understand how I managed to get my previous result. Could this child be retarded? Her features are distinctly mongoloid!'

The results from the second evoked response test came back, this time indicating a 'considerable hearing loss', and the clinic called another case conference on Cathy, now four years and two months old. Reports were received from the doctor, who felt Cathy was suffering from progressive deafness but 'is not in my opinion an ESN(M) child; her lack of speech is due to deafness and her intelligence *potential* may well be normal'; from the physiotherapist, who reported that Cathy 'remained very slow physically but was making a little progress'; from the speech therapist, who said she had found it 'difficult to test Cathy even with her hearing aids on because she didn't seem to hear or comprehend instructions'; from the playroom staff, who noted that 'Cathy seemed a clean, well-dressed child but rarely wore her glasses or hearing aids and was not encouraged to do so by her mother'; from the educational psychologist, who unlike the doctor felt that Cathy's limited abilities were 'not solely caused by her deafness as she scored a year below her chronological age level on non-verbal and performance tests'; and from a teacher of the deaf, who had little to add apart from suggesting 'she be supplied with more powerful hearing aids'. The conference concluded that Cathy's primary handicap was deafness, that it was difficult to fully assess her intelligence potential, and that there was a conflict of opinion over whether she had in fact progressed in the last year.

In the months that followed the conference, it became increasingly evident to Cathy's teacher at the unit that far from progressing, the child was in fact getting worse. When she first came to the unit, Cathy was lively and attentive, vocalised and babbled readily and had begun to count spontaneously. Now she did none of these; rarely vocalising unless actively encouraged, often sitting mouthing silently to herself and frequently sinking into lethargy. She appeared physically uncared for, showed no signs of becoming toilet trained and was often tired and pale at school. Her teacher was not sure whether this was the result of poor sleeping habits and routines at home, or whether there was some other cause, but she noted that it had become worse of late. She wrote expressing her concern to the doctor at the child development clinic and sent a copy of her letter to Mr Muir, the head of service, who also wrote to the doctor expressing his concern and suggesting that a placement in a residential school for the deaf might provide the 'caring environment' that Cathy apparently lacked, since her needs did not seem to be adequately catered for at home and since 'Her mother is not too good at keeping appointments or having the child ready for school when the taxi arrives.' He decided to initiate the formal special education placement procedure.

Mr Muir felt that Cathy's parents had not accepted the fact of her deafness and were looking for a 'quick cure', and that their request for her to be referred to the hearing specialists at another university for an assessment was holding up Cathy's appropriate placement in a residential school for the following September, when she would be just five. The ENT consultant agreed, and wrote to the doctor at the clinic

> that the parents' attempts to have their child reassessed were simply a matter of procrastination in grasping the nature of the child's disability, and since time is of the essence I would be against any further assessment when such a complete one has been carried out here. It is, as so often, a very sad case, where the greatest tragedy is the parents' inability to come to terms with the problem.

Mr Muir wrote to the educational psychologist who had been asked to complete Form SE3 on Cathy, describing her history and suggesting that 'The general feeling in this case is, unusually for such a young child, that residential placement would be an advantage.'

He also arranged an informal visit for her parents to a residential school for the deaf, which incurred the displeasure of the area education officer on the grounds that this 'anticipated the SE procedure'. Mr Muir wrote back explaining that it had been an informal visit 'designed to expedite matters as consideration of her placement has gone on for at least seven months'.

The educational psychologist duly tested Cathy, and agreed with Mr Muir and the staff at the nursery unit that she would benefit from a residential placement. She talked to Cathy's parents, and although they were very reluctant to have their daughter admitted to a residential school for the deaf, she managed to persuade them that early admission would be to their daughter's advantage. The parents had managed to obtain a further opinion on their child and the assessment confirmed that Cathy was profoundly deaf. The teacher at the unit for hearing-impaired children reported that Cathy's mother now seemed to want to help her daughter to learn, but was 'unreceptive to advice on this score' and continued to put Cathy to bed when she herself went at 11 p. m. and to allow her not to wear her glasses or hearing aids. The SE procedures were finally completed in December and Cathy transferred to the residential school for the deaf at the start of the following year.

2. Susie

Susie Dixon's deafness was identified at a very early age, partly because her family was under the regular supervision of the social services department due to 'poor standards of cleanliness and tidiness within the house'. The health visitor recommended that Susie should have a hearing test, and at seven months old she was seen by the educational audiologist, who reported that 'I was not able to obtain any response at all to any of our sound stimuli even when the intensities were raised to 100-110 decibels, which is unusual even in such a young baby.'

The audiologist thought that Susie was profoundly deaf, but that more definite results could not be obtained until Susie was old enough to sit unaided and turn towards a sound source. She arranged for her mother to bring her to the assessment unit every Friday for auditory training. After three months she tested Susie again, recommended that she be fitted with two hearing aids, and referred her to the ear, nose and throat consultant for an examination. The ENT consultant could find no physical abnormality nor any family history of deafness or any record of Susie having been seriously ill since she was born, and he concluded that Susie's severe hearing loss must be 'sensorineural' and that it was unlikely that the cause would ever be found. He arranged for her to be issued with the hearing aids and to continue the auditory training sessions, with a review of progress in a year's time. After six months the audiologist tested Susie's hearing again and found a 'slight but encouraging' improvement in her hearing thresholds, and recommended that she be issued with two more powerful hearing aids.

Nothing more occurs in Susie's file for over a year, and then in March 1977 appears the record of a case conference on the Dixon family called by the NSPCC special unit 'to enable the various agencies involved to share impressions of the family' and 'to discuss if care proceedings are necessary in the interests of the children'. The children were Susie, now two and a quarter; her sister of nearly four, and her five-year-old brother. The conference was called because of 'concern being expressed by all agencies regarding general standards of physical care and very poor home conditions', and was attended by representatives from the police and social services (including their legal and properties departments and Family Aid), and by Susie's audiologist, her brother's infant teacher and the family's health visitor. The conference was told that Mr Dixon had a drink problem and that Mrs Dixon was 'very overweight and seems to do no housework'. They were shown newspaper cuttings describing the 'appalling dirty conditions' of the house, and told that the family had to be moved out one Christmas for three weeks while the engineers' department took out and burnt several lorry loads of rubbish which had accumulated there. However it was pointed out by more than one of the agencies involved that the children seemed not to suffer either emotionally or physically from their environment; they were rarely ill, were warmly cared for and appeared clean and well clothed. The conference concluded that it was 'a very unusual case with serious conditions not appearing to harm the development of the children', and that there could be no immediate case for care proceedings.

However the following note appears in Susie's file six months later, written by one of the special education staff in the neighbouring authority Bedbridge,

> Rutford's Service for Hearing-Impaired Children rang to let us know that a little girl by the name of Susie Dixon has been placed in care at St Hilda's Convent in our area. They are going to send us the papers on this child.

The papers arrived, although not before the head of the convent had rung up requesting information on their new child 'who seems to be almost totally deaf'. Bedbridge education department made arrangements for a teacher of the deaf to visit Susie in the convent on a regular basis, even though she was not yet of school age. They maintained close contact with Susie's home authority, who suggested that she be placed in Bedbridge's special nursery unit for hearing-impaired children as soon as she became old enough. Informal discussions took place with the head teacher at the convent school and with the staff at the nursery over the next few months, and Susie visited the special unit several times accompanied by one of the staff from the convent.

When she reached the age of three and a half, the head of service for hearing-impaired children in Bedbridge wrote to the primary and special schools adviser in his area, giving details of Susie's background and recommending that she attend the nursery unit part time, beginning from the end of the following month. He asked the adviser to inform Rutford of this move (since they would be paying the bill) and to obtain their approval. He also wrote to his area education officer asking for a taxi to be provided to take Susie and a Sister from her convent to and from the unit, again subject to Rutford's approval and ability to pay. He felt that transport arrangements were especially important in Susie's case, as 'She has had a somewhat unsettled life and we anticipate very considerable difficulty getting her to settle into the nursery unless it is possible for someone from the convent to accompany her into the unit on a daily basis and of course to collect her on return.'

Susie began at the unit mornings only, and attended full time after a couple of months. She was given regular hearing tests, and after she had been with them for a year the unit sent a progress report to the head of service, concluding that they were 'pleased with the way she is progressing, and feel a place should be sought for future education in a good oral environment together with a stable domestic life'. The head of service sent the report on to the Rutford education authority with the following covering letter:

This child, as you know, is in the care of your social services department, and at present attends the Whitefield nursery unit. I understand that our central area education office has written to you to ensure that you are aware of the child's present placement and, of course, to arrange the financial aspect of the matter.

As we discussed by telephone recently, we feel that Susie is likely to require placement in a residential school for the deaf, possibly Crawford School but this is something which you will wish to follow up yourself no doubt, perhaps by visiting the unit and asking one of your own educational psychologists to carry out the necessary assessment. You will note that she will be five in November of this year.

In the event, one of Bedbridge's educational psychologists undertook to provide a psychological assessment on Susie, on the suggestion of Rutford education department. He found that her co-ordination and performance were appropriate for her age, but that her linguistic development was severely retarded because of her deafness. He recommended that Susie remain at the convent 'where she has found stability and made good social progress', and that she should attend a residential school for the deaf during the week, where 'The special methods of instruction available will hopefully help to bring Susie's linguistic skills more into line with her non-verbal abilities.' Susie's teacher reported that she had made good progress at the unit; that she had 'acquired more maturity and self-confidence' and was 'very friendly and co-operative and good with her hands'. The teacher also noted the co-operative attitude of Susie's parents and of her guardians at the convent towards special residential schooling. She, the doctor and the educational psychologist filled in SE forms, and Susie started at a residential school for the deaf soon after her fifth birthday.

9 'HYPERACTIVE' CHILDREN

Tony Booth, Patricia Potts and June Statham

In recent years a number of terms have been used to define new handi-caps, each said to be the expression of a characteristic 'syndrome'. 'Autistic', 'dyslexic' and 'hyperactive' have all gained currency in the last fifteen years and have been backed by parents' organisations pressing for their increased recognition and far greater provision. The newest of these, 'hyperactivity', has reached epidemic proportions in the USA, and tranquilising drugs are prescribed there for its treatment on a vast scale. The existence of each of these handicaps is hotly disputed, however, none more so than 'hyperactivity', which is seen by many to be a myth propagated in the interests of the medicalisation and personal-isation of deviance. According to this view, problems which are the result of social factors are treated as cases of individual pathology, like whooping cough or brain damage. Excerpts from three stories are presented below which illustrate three different routes to acquiring the 'hyperactive' label. The information for these accounts was provided by the clinical psychologist at the child psychiatric clinic to which the children came.

Geoffrey's father is a design draughtsman, his mother a part-time stocker of shelves in a supermarket for three evenings a week. The family live in a corner house near to relatives and Geoffrey shares a bedroom with his brother John who is three years older. Two miscarriages preceded Geoffrey's birth, but when he finally arrived he was described as a good, quiet baby. When he was three months old the family went on holiday, and according to them Geoffrey seemed to change overnight, becoming very demanding and active. His mother found it difficult to give him all the attention he sought and became very anxious and lacking in confi-dence. She felt dominated by her own mother who lived nearby and who constantly criticised the way she was bringing up her children. Geoffrey became more and more difficult to control, especially when with his mother. He seemed fearless and she was afraid he would hurt

57

himself. She became reluctant to let him out to play, and found it difficult to invite other children in with Geoffrey because of the arguments and fights he provoked. He began to attend a local nursery school, and the teachers soon complained to his parents that he was too boisterous.

When he was four and a half they took Geoffrey to their GP, who referred him to a paediatrician for examination. The paediatrician diagnosed Geoffrey as 'hyperactive', prescribed drugs to calm him down and referred him to the child psychiatric clinic attached to a large hospital. The psychiatrists there continued to prescribe the drugs, which were never officially stopped – it was Geoffrey's parents who eventually felt he could manage without them.

The whole family attended the first interview at the clinic; Geoffrey, his brother and their parents on one side; the child psychiatrist, psychologist and social worker on the other. Geoffrey misbehaved, quarrelling and fighting with his brother, being noisy and bossy and unable to concentrate for any length of time. The psychiatrist who saw him concluded:

He presents as a boy with hyperactive behaviour combined with intense controlling and oppositional behaviour in the family. There is definite evidence of a developmental problem with clumsiness and uneven concentration and attention, and he is self-driven by uncontained primitive impulses and anxieties.

The staff at the clinic made a variety of recommendations on the basis of this interview, including a 'behavioural programme to contain Geoffrey's impulsiveness'. They also recommended 'further examination of Geoffrey's intellectual development', and arranged for him to attend the clinic's day-care centre with his mother. His mother was to receive therapy too, to 'take up her anxieties in relation to her children arising from her own early family experiences'.

Geoffrey began at the clinic's day centre for pre-school children and their families, attending one day a week with his mother, in line with the centre's normal policy. As he was nearly five the question of his future schooling soon arose. Geoffrey's nursery school had hinted that he might be difficult to cater for in an ordinary school, but there was no special school to suit his needs. Schools for maladjusted children began at age seven, and Geoffrey was not educationally subnormal. The clinical psychologist who tested him after he had been attending the day centre for some six weeks concluded that he was:

a boy of good average intelligence who, from an intellectual point of view, would cope well in a normal school. From a behavioural point of view it is important that he should be taught in a fairly structured setting where he can be given a good amount of attention. Enquiries will have to be made locally to see which of the possible primary schools would most suit him.

The primary schools were less certain that Geoffrey would suit them. He was due to start school after Easter, but the headmaster at the school that was chosen was unwilling to take him on without the promise of a welfare assistant to cope with Geoffrey's extra demands. It was a worrying and difficult time for his parents, especially as he had now left the nursery school and was at home all day with his mother until the school finally obtained the welfare assistant and accepted Geoffrey a term late.

Once in the school, Geoffrey seemed to settle in well. His parents continued his medication during the week, but took him off the tablets at weekends and holidays. The clinic maintained contact with the headmaster and class teacher at Geoffrey's school, and he and his mother continued to attend the day centre one day a week for psychotherapy. After a year and a half the clinic considered that Geoffrey's mother had made 'considerable progress, not only in terms of her handling of Geoffrey but in her own development with regard to self-confidence and insight', and that Geoffrey was 'making satisfactory adjustments to primary school, and we would hope that he will continue to do so'. The school no longer felt the need to assign a welfare assistant to 'keep an eye on him'. After a further two years Geoffrey and his mother stopped their regular psychotherapy sessions, although the clinic still keeps in touch with them through occasional 'review' sessions. His mother has recently taken Geoffrey off all medication and finds he seems to manage well enough without it. Now eight, Geoffrey seems likely to follow a normal career through the ordinary schools.

Brian, like Geoffrey, was diagnosed as 'hyperactive' at an early age, but his educational career took a very different path. He was born into impoverished family circumstances, with a father who was often in prison, and at birth had been jaundiced and then suffered frequent bouts of colic. When he started school he was said to be 'very aggressive' and 'antisocial' and he constantly ran around disrupting his classmates. In fact he was suspended from the school at the age of five and this precipitated his referral to the psychiatric clinic. The child psychologist described him as exhibiting the 'characteristic hyperactive syndrome' and remarked on 'the inconsistent handling of Brian by his parents who swung unpredictably from punitiveness to over-indulgence'. However she thought the parents were 'unwilling to cooperate in efforts to improve their child's management'. Brian's school agreed to take him back on trial while he and his parents received 'treatment', but he showed no sign of improvement. Eventually, when he was seven, he was referred to a residential school for maladjusted children.

Matthew in contrast to both Brian and Geoffrey was initially labelled 'hyperactive' by his parents; a diagnosis that was strongly resisted by the clinic to which they brought him on their own initiative when he was eight. Mrs Chalmers said she knew he was hyperactive when she was pregnant. They had read about hyperactivity, and had joined the recently-formed 'Society of Parents for Hyperactive Children'. They were convinced that Matthew displayed what they saw as all the 'symptoms'; he couldn't sit still, he was 'very bright', he couldn't get on with other children. He was naughty at home, and they felt he was misunderstood at school.

His teachers said he was disruptive, aggressive and unable to concentrate. His parents thought that he was picked on by other children. Mrs Chalmers produced a typed list of all the incidents in the previous week where Matthew had been 'victimised' by other children, to prove her point. She wanted special schooling for him, any type of special schooling, even in an ESN school despite her conviction that he was super-intelligent. Any kind of special attention seemed better than none. Both parents brought Matthew along to the clinic, seeking an IQ test to 'prove' his high intelligence. They continually interrupted each other to provide extra information about their son, who was an only child and seemed to be the centre of the family's attention. Mrs Chalmers said that she was unable to cope with Matthew and that the situation was affecting her relationship with her husband. She was an only child herself, and said she hated the noise and confusion of young children. Mr Chalmers was very critical of Matthew's school and teachers and of the family's neighbours.

During the interview at the clinic Matthew was very quiet and subdued. His mother said his birth was normal, although he later cried a lot and threw tantrums, and she described how he learnt to walk, talk and read at a very early age. Both parents seemed keen to have Matthew's intelligence tested. However when the results suggested that his performance was average rather than exceptional, they became very sceptical of the validity and value of IQ tests. Nor could they accept it when the staff at the clinic told them they could find no evidence of Matthew being 'hyperactive', but would like his parents to bring him to further sessions to work on the problems they seemed to be having with his behaviour. Matthew's parents took him away and refused to come back to the clinic.

10 'I NEVER FELT I HAD TO TRY': RECOLLECTIONS OF A WOMAN WHO HAD CHILDHOOD RHEUMATOID ARTHRITIS

Tony Booth and June Statham

The following case-study contains fragments from a series of tape recordings made by Ann, a woman in her late thirties who had had childhood rheumatoid arthritis. She was restricted to a wheelchair and had little use of her hands, but this did not prevent her from developing close friendships and taking a keen interest in painting and the theatre as well as politics. In this excerpt she describes the onset of her illness and her educational experiences.

Ann was born in Cambridgeshire, where her mother was evacuated in 1941. Her parents had come to London from Liverpool in search of work, and Ann's early years were spent travelling with them from job to job. When she was four her parents separated and her mother became a housekeeper on a large Cambridgeshire farm where Ann spent the next four years. She looks back on that time with nostalgia; four golden years of farm life and playing with the village children, although she got little attention from her overworked mother and resorted to lying and taking money for presents in a bid to buy affection. They left the farm when Ann was eight, much to her sorrow, and her mother moved from one housekeeping job to another. It was during this time, when she was nine years old, that the first symptoms of Ann's disease appeared.

I had an acute pain in my hip which I tried desperately to disguise. I don't know why, probably through fear. I think a lot of children do that sort of thing. I was very frightened. It came on very suddenly. Somebody saw me limping, I just couldn't bear weight on the affected hip. The doctor was brought in and I was given half an aspirin, which was considered rather dangerous for a child in those days, and I was put to bed. The first diagnosis was TB of course. I was taken into hospital and saw many different people. All I can remember of what went on in my head was really being very frightened, besides the pain. I was terrified I was going to have an operation. I had a very stiff neck but I kept trying to disguise it, I was terrified they'd cut my neck open.

Having ruled out TB, the doctors eventually diagnosed rheumatoid arthritis, known as Stills disease in a child, and after four months of treatment Ann came home, still in a lot of pain. For a while the disease seemed to abate, and a doctor called in to deal with Ann's bad chest told her mother she had been lucky, the Stills disease had 'burnt itself out'. However, it was decided that Ann was too delicate to attend an ordinary school, and so when she was ten arrangements were made to send her to a residential special school for the physically handicapped in Kent. She missed her mother, and didn't learn very much there.

The teaching was poor. They had an SRN as matron and two unqualified nurses — looking back they knew nothing about my complaint. I was expected to keep up physically with the other children and walk about when we went on trips, and that's just the time I should have been immobilised to enable the bones and joints to develop. They didn't know as much as they do today, unfortunately. The teachers were old cups of tea who taught us things like flower-making in the afternoon. It was a very religious school, with long sermons and hymns. I was quite a devout child, but I found a lot of it boring. No-one was expected to do GCE. You didn't have to try hard. When I was first there I was put in a corner for those who could just get on with their own work — they had no idea of exams. It was very sheltered. I never felt I had to try. Perhaps I should have.

To make things worse, Ann's condition deteriorated during her three years at the school. When she arrived she was able to walk with little pain, but a surgeon there decided to manipulate her feet in plaster to cure their flatness, and when the plaster came off the Stills disease flared up again. The soreness spread to many of her other joints and walking became difficult, even with assistance. She was often in considerable pain.

The other girls didn't understand my position, it was upsetting. Although they were handicapped they weren't in any pain. Many of them were toughies from London who had had polio and missed a lot of education recovering in hospital, but most of them weren't too badly affected. There were some spastics but nobody with my degree of difficulties. I'd probably have received better treatment and education had I gone to an ordinary school. The other children were a bit insensitive and would say 'come on slowcoach'. I'd be hardly able to hold the cloth to clean the tables after a meal, and they'd say 'put some go into it, you can do better than that'. My arm was killing me and I'd have done anything to have a good cry but I had to grin and pretend it was alright. That caused a lot of stress, trying to pretend. If you did cry, they didn't understand and called you crybaby, and no matter how much you protested, saying 'I'm hurt, I'm in pain', even the staff didn't seem to understand, saying I was pulling the wool over their eyes.

After three years at the school, Ann was seen by a sympathetic specialist who decided she couldn't cope there and sent her to Bath for the spa treatment, which she describes as 'putting your knees in mud and things like that'. At about the same time her mother married again, a teacher nearly twenty years her senior with a grown-up son and daughter. Ann's own teenage years were painful ones spent travelling backwards and forwards to Bath for treatment. At sixteen she was hospitalised for a year, lying on her back in bed to allow the joints to 'cool down' prior to surgery. The surgery was a failure because Ann was unable to take a general anaesthetic, and there was little the surgeons could do with bones under local anaesthetic. She was released and sent home.

The pain eased up a bit and I came to life more. I had great plans for art, and realised I had to be able to travel more easily. My legs were stretched out horizontally because my knees were so stiff, so I asked to see a surgeon about a knee operation. Up to that time I'd been under school orders, and this was the first decision I had made on my own. They took me in eventually and I had high hopes of having knees which would bend a little so that I could sit for travelling and going to the theatre. In those days their one thought was to get you on your feet. As all my joints were affected, my arms couldn't help me with crutches or anything once I was on my feet, but it didn't matter what you could do so long as you were upright. They went away and decided behind my back. Next thing I knew I was being prepared and bandaged up to the waist for two hip operations. I didn't think they'd do all that for my knees and asked to see the surgeon, who said 'we decided to operate on your hips instead' — *we* decided! So that was what I had done.

The operation did get Ann on her feet, but only if she was held up by a person on either side, and it caused her a lot of pain. A later attempt at the knee operation also proved unsuccessful. While she was in hospital, arrangements were made for her to go to a training college for handicapped people in Exeter, to learn typing. It was another decision made for her by other people, and Ann's first reaction was one of fear.

I was terrified of going. I'd been sheltered in hospital and school and home, and although I was eighteen I'd never considered working, being so handicapped at nine. In fact I had a marvellous time. I was the most severely handicapped there and they made a tremendous fuss of me. It was easy because I wasn't doing shorthand like everyone else, just typing so I could do copy typing at home. I stayed for five months, and that helped me a lot. Before I'd gone there I couldn't understand that anyone would want to be friendly with me, and there they were. I really didn't expect much of people towards myself, and some even seemed to like me. It did no end for my morale. I was really boosted there — more for that than for learning the typing.

She earned a little money typing for a year, then had an operation on her elbow which meant she could no longer get her hands into a typing position, but which gave her enough freedom of movement to take up painting instead. Her physical health deteriorated in her early twenties, with attacks of pneumonia, asthma and bronchitis keeping her in bed for much of the next six or eight years. Further complications arose in her thirties — bad migraines, a heart murmur, continued insomnia — which meant frequent contact with doctors and a long list of drugs; heart and stomach tablets, diuretics, painkillers, Valium, sleeping pills, steroids. Now in her late thirties and restricted by the rheumatoid arthritis to a wheelchair, with her legs outstretched and with little movement in her hands, Ann feels that these other complaints greatly increase the burden of her handicap: 'I was much more energetic when I was only handicapped, before I had all these bits and pieces.'

A lot of Ann's time now is spent sitting, thinking, reading, writing letters and keeping up with current affairs. She has plenty of interests, but finds many of them difficult to pursue. Art galleries and poetry societies tend to be housed in buildings whose steps make them inaccessible to someone in a wheelchair. Because her knees won't bend, Ann's motorised wheelchair takes up a lot of space and the local art theatre won't allow her to 'clutter up the aisle' because of fire restrictions. Her deformed hands make it difficult to use the phone or write for long periods or put records on a turntable — until she acquired a cheap cassette recorder, listening to records depended on her mother having a free afternoon to play them for her. The painting which provided Ann with a little money and a lot of enjoyment over a ten year period had to be given up when her asthma got so bad that the oils and turps gave her wheezing attacks. She is dependent on the social worker for organising special trips abroad for handicapped people, dependent on her mother for much of her day-to-day living, dependent on the state for her disability income. She is regularly visited by the social worker and the occupational therapist. Much of the time she is still in a good deal of pain, and people still fail to understand.

> They trot out the most stupid stuff about pain being ennobling and good for you and society. I doubt it. I only ever felt that it was an evil. It warped my emotions. You can be quite cruel if you're in pain, like an animal. You lash out at those nearest, at the ones you love.

She tries not to think about the future.

> It's frightening looking ahead, so I don't. I block it off. You learn to live an hour at a time. I suppose having been ill such a lot there's a half thought that maybe I won't be here, so I won't have to face it.

11 LIVING WITH EPILEPSY

Marjorie Blumer

Source: Edited version of Marjorie Blumer, 'Living with Epilepsy', *Epilepsy* (British Epilepsy Association, Workingham, England, 1978).

Majorie Blumer, who wrote the following article, was born in Liverpool and has lived in London since 1965. She is now 32, and had her first epileptic attack at the age of twelve. Dismissed from teacher training college because of her epilepsy, she trained as a secretary and for a time taught typewriting at the secretarial college. Since then she has worked as a secretary for the Duke of Edinburgh's Award Scheme, for St Mary's Hospital Medical School and for a firm of foreign exchange brokers in the City of London. She is now with a large insurance company based in London and Worthing and has recently obtained a driving licence. Marjorie belongs to the British Epilepsy Association, and believes that talking openly about epilepsy will help to overcome the ignorance and prejudice shown by many people to this 'unseen' but very common condition.

I had my first fit at the age of 12. I was on board ship at the time with the Girl Guides. Since it was my first trip abroad, and there was a force 8 gale raging in the North Sea, no one thought that it was anything more than a childish convulsion. No one told me about it either. I had this incredible dream of lying in a cabin wearing a friend's blazer. No one said: 'That's not a dream, that happened to you yesterday.' Why there was all this secrecy I never knew.

I returned home from my trip abroad, and proceeded to 'Relate All' to my parents. 'You haven't told me everything' said my mother, 'You didn't tell me you were ill while you were away.' No one was more astonished than I. Despite my protests I was led off to see the doctor, who gave me tablets to take, told me never to forget them, and said no more.

A year later I went off to camp with the Guides again. I remember being sent off to the farmhouse to collect eggs and bread, with another girl to help carry. 'Thank goodness Sarah had the eggs,' was the comment of the day, since I had a fit just outside the farmhouse door. My mother was sent for and suggestions were made that perhaps it was being away from home that 'upset' me. To her everlasting credit my mother asked me what I felt about the whole matter, and I was allowed to stay at the camp. It was bad enough being the 'different' girl who had the fit: I didn't want to be the 'different girl who went home' too.

I had my third fit a few months after that, and went to see a specialist at a London hospital. 'Epilepsy', he confirmed after tests had been done. It was almost a relief to know that I had a recognisable condition, and was not just having 'funny turns' every so often. 'Pills' continued the specialist, 'these must be taken twice a day.' He explained to me that epilepsy might be with me for the rest of my life but that it would probably go away when I left school/became 21/got married/had children. Meanwhile I was to keep taking the pills.

Pills — how I hate them. In the same way that a motorist's life is governed by traffic lights, so the life of a person with epilepsy is governed by pills. I now have to take them three times a day: I don't mind taking them, it's just that it is incredibly difficult to remember whether or not you have already had the dosage for today or not. This will seem strange to anyone who has never had to take tablets over a long period of time, but you do not know whether the pills you remember taking are those you took five minutes ago, five days ago, or five weeks ago. I have now devised a System which, for me, is more-or-less foolproof, in that I stand the pill bottles up in the morning when I have had my morning tablets, and lie them down at night when I have had my evening dose. The mid-day pills are more difficult, and involve the top and bottom drawers of my office desk (weekdays) and the use of a small pill-box (weekends) to enable me to remember. Thank goodness I don't have to take them four times a day, as I don't know what I should do!

[. . .]

I was very lucky with epilepsy when I was at school: most of my fits have occurred in the evenings, and I never actually had a fit at the school. The staff knew about my epilepsy, but I was always allowed to do everything that my friends did, and so did not feel 'different'. I was, therefore, very unprepared for the shock that came later. I had always wanted to teach domestic science, and was accepted for teacher training college subject to passing a medical (which everyone had to take). I have always been honest about epilepsy, and ended up having not one medical but four because the Ministry of Education (as they then were) were worried about someone with epilepsy teaching domestic science. Frankly I quite agree with them − if I had had a fit whilst teaching, and knocked a pan of hot fat over a child as I fell over ... the consequences aren't worth thinking about. However, instead of saying 'You cannot teach' I was allowed to go to college and was told that it would be 'all right' even if I was ill. Ha ha. I had a fit when I had been there for eight weeks, and was kept in a different hostel for ten days (just like a leper colony). I was eventually allowed to return to my own hall of residence, but two days before the start of the January term my mother received a letter informing her that her daughter could not return to the college to continue her training. I do not know if this was the decision of the Principal of the College or the Ministry of Education, but I feel very strongly that I should never have been allowed to start training there for a career that I was not allowed to continue. It was not as if I had hidden any facts from anyone: I had been very fair with everyone, but they had not been fair with me.

I subsequently trained as a secretary, and have always been extremely honest with prospective employers at interviews. I would not like to be accepted for a job without an employer knowing the full facts about my epilepsy, since I would then dread having a fit and maybe being asked to leave. However, I do leave the subject of epilepsy to the very end of an interview − by which time I feel that the interviewer has usually made his mind up as to whether or not I would be of any use to the firm. Only once have I met with a really unsympathetic response ('the door is over there'), and on most occasions an interviewer has heard me out. I take the attitude that if a firm don't want to employ me and my epilepsy, then I'm sure I don't want to work for them. (Job-hunting can become very depressing unless you feel this way.) I cannot understand why employers don't like employing people with epilepsy, since I tend to turn up at the office in all weathers, and with all sorts of minor ailments that would make most of my colleagues pick up the phone and plead that they were ill.

I cannot describe my fits since I don't remember them. Some people have a warning before an attack, but my only warning is that I go very vague, which is no help at all, since if you are vague then you do not realise it! However, I belong to Medic-Alert and wear one of their 'doggy-tags' round my neck at all times: this I have done since being carted off to hospital on two occasions. The worst bit about having a fit is when you come round: I take ages to regain full consciousness, and it would be marvellous to have someone saying 'You have had a fit, therefore you are lying on the kitchen floor at Mrs Spinks's house'. Most people when pressed will admit that I have had a fit (I usually have to ask the question) but they fail to tell me where I am. Since I am in such a confused state I need all the information I can get at this stage, together with loads of reassurance ('I am here, I am not going away, you are going to be all right').

The most depressing part about having epilepsy is that one cannot do all the things one would like to do: I suppose it is the same with anything in that you always want what you cannot have. On various occasions I have felt that I might like to emigrate; fly an aeroplane; go parachute jumping; take a mad trip along the Trans-Siberian railroad; stay out late every night for a week and generally have a hectic social life, but a line has to be drawn somewhere. I am sure that I would not have done even half of these things if I had not had epilepsy, but I would like to have had the choice.

FAMILIES

12 PROFESSIONAL 'HELP': THE TAYLOR FAMILY

Patricia Potts

The Taylors live on a modern, low-rise estate in Inner London, character-
ised by high-banked ramps and walkways. Both parents are deaf, but
have brought up a family of four children: Christopher (now 17),
Karen (16), Susan (14) and Billy (12). Between them, the members of
this family have had an unusual amount of contact with various pro-
fessional services, not all of them perceived as helpful.

Besides being stone deaf, Mr Taylor is also mute, diabetic and partially
sighted. He is a large man who makes extravagant gestures when using
sign language, and can appear quite frightening to the uninitiated. He
does not have a job, although he did work for a short while some years
ago. He is a Londoner and went to a school for the deaf. Mrs Taylor
does have some hearing and speech. She can chat to her sister on the
telephone so is perhaps not as deaf as she sometimes makes out, but
communication is undoubtedly very difficult for her. She is a Scot and
probably met her husband at their local club for the deaf, of which
they were active members until recently when Mr Taylor, an officer of
the club, was excluded by the club's organiser after a disagreement.

Mr Taylor's physical condition is deteriorating and he has to make
frequent visits to hospital. Mr Taylor, unlike his wife, does not seem to
get depressed by all this and remains cheerfully unconcerned, rather
like another adolescent in the family. It is Mrs Taylor who bears the
burden of the family's social, financial, health and educational worries.
Not surprisingly she often seems at the point of breakdown, quickly
becoming tearful, angry and aggressive when in contact with officialdom,
which occurs frequently. The children are noisy and uncontrolled
around the flats; they have to take responsibility for their parents, who
cannot provide them with an understanding of everyday social experiences. Mrs Taylor wants to move away from complaining neighbours
and intrusive officials, and sees a new house with a garden as the solution

to all their problems. Their huge rent arrears make the housing officer unsympathetic.

With the parents' background of difficulties they were marked out for professional intervention even before the children were born, and each child has acquired a personal history of 'problems' as she or he progressed through the schools. Christopher has been extremely over-weight since he was about six, should wear glasses but doesn't and is noticeably accident-prone. After having his appendix out in 1976, the hospital dietician and physiotherapist between them arranged a slimming programme, but this only had a temporary effect. Christopher has long had to act as interpreter for his parents and this gave him an excuse to stay away from school, a small and declining single-sex comprehensive. As a large fat boy he came in for a good deal of bullying and ridicule which he found very difficult to take. When he did attend school, usually as a result of the threat of court action from the education welfare officer, the teachers said he was of average ability and easy to get along with, despite occasional misdemeanours such as setting off the fire alarm and causing the entire school to be evacuated.

The second eldest, Karen, went to a large, modern, single-sex com-prehensive, where she would often flare up with little provocation, eventually being suspended for attacking a teacher. She always found the work hard, especially after remedial help stopped in the fourth year just when the exam courses began, and was often in trouble at school.

Susan is the only one of the children to suffer some hearing loss. This was not suggested until she was about seven and not properly investigated until she was eleven. The doctor was of the opinion that it was the result of a perinatal difficulty rather than the family's genetic history, but the Taylors could not accept that Susan had any hearing loss and she refused to wear aids. At primary school, Susan was occasionally moody and difficult in class and aggressive in the play-ground, but was more solitary than troublesome. For her, it was the transfer to secondary school that was disturbing, with all the changes of teacher and classroom. She was described as bewildered, too immature to cope with the organisation of a large comprehensive; she became difficult in class and her conversation disjointed. Susan's attendance fell away sharply at the beginning of the second year, and by the end of it she was allocated a home tutor.

The youngest child, Billy, was described by his primary school teacher as violent, a bully, hostile, self-critical, disruptive, restless, rude, unco-operative; he fought and he ran away and the teacher was afraid that he might hurt another child or himself. All four Taylor children went to the same local primary school, some of whose teachers, therefore, knew the family for more than a decade. They were often critical of the children's parents and unsympathetic to their home background. One wrote of Susan:

> Having seen the attitude of her mother towards Susan, I am surprised that Susan is not worse than she is . . . As I taught her elder sister I'm sure that has something to do with her less than aggressive attitude towards me, but in the wrong hands she could be disruptive. Although the children are very close, and will defend each other to the hilt, a lot of love and attention is needed, which I fear is lacking at home.

Another commented on Christopher's school report:

> Parents' general attitude to school: 'Parents have never attended any parents' evenings'.
> Attitude to children's educational progress: 'Do not seem very concerned'.
> Attitude to children's behaviour in school or elsewhere: 'As above'.

All of the children's attendance at the primary school had been erratic, but Billy seems to have had more problems at this stage than the others. He was put in a remedial group where he could relax and work only if he had the teacher's full attention. He has recently been in trouble with the police for breaking into a nearby theatre. Mr Taylor couldn't see that this was any sort of offence because Billy didn't stand to gain anything.

Reading these descriptions, it is not surprising that the Taylor family is well known to various 'professionals': doctors, psychologists, psychiatrists, social workers, educational welfare officers (EWOs), teachers (including a home tutor and a peripatetic teacher of the deaf), the housing officer and the police juvenile bureau.

Christopher was originally referred to a child guidance clinic in 1974, when he was coming up for secondary transfer, but did not attend until 1976 when his truancy was followed up. The other three children were referred to the clinic by their schools, mainly for aggressive behaviour, and their contact spanned three years. In March 1976, there was an initial case conference, with teachers, clinic staff (psychiatrist and psychiatric social worker), EWO, the social services worker and the educational psychologist. The first family session was in June, after which it was arranged that Christopher would see the psychiatrist and Karen the psychiatric social worker, who would also continue to see the parents. Christopher and Karen each kept two appointments. In May 1977, Karen and her mother came to the clinic after a violent incident at school and in June the whole family, except for Karen, came to discuss Susan and Billy. In August, the Taylors cancelled their appointment and did not attend again. However, three more case conferences were held to discuss the family, in March 1978, September 1978 and March 1979. The September conference led to the following 'decisions':

1. Psychiatrist to write to the consultant paediatrician at the district hospital re Susan's hearing loss and appropriate school placing in view of this.
2. EWO to contact the educational psychologist re assessment, and to follow up the possibility of a remedial class in school in the meantime.
3. Psychiatrist to contact the senior medical officer, local AHA community health services, with particular reference to the Birchland Audiology Unit.
4. Special social worker for the deaf to check that the peripatetic teacher of the deaf will be seeing Susan in school.
5. The importance of encouraging Susan to wear her hearing aid was stressed.
6. EWO to write to the school re Karen.
7. Psychiatrist will initiate getting Special Education forms done for Billy.
8. EWO to look into possible ways of helping Christopher, and in particular the link courses between school and further education college.
9. Conference to reconvene . . .

Special education was never recommended for Christopher, whose problems were seen as obesity and truancy, but placement at a day school for maladjusted children was considered for all of the younger three children. In the event, Karen went part-time for several months to an off-site support unit designed for children who were involved in fighting at school, after which she successfully returned to regular schooling with improved attendance and behaviour. The primary school's difficulty in coping with Billy's disruptive behaviour made him an obvious candidate for placement in either a day school for maladjusted children or in a tutorial class from ordinary school, but he failed to turn up for all the appointments made for psychological testing so the SE forms could not be filled in, and he remained where he was. The authorities considered various possibilities for Susan: a school for the partially-hearing, a school for delicate children or a school for the maladjusted. She could not cope with comprehensive school and she would not wear her hearing aid, so was considered to have both social and physical problems. In July 1979 she was recommended for day maladjusted school on the grounds of 'neurotic and conduct disorders', ranked 2 (scale 1–3) in severity. It was felt that 'If she wears a hearing aid properly and all the time she would be better placed in maladjusted school where there are smaller classes etc.' The SE forms were duly filled in, but Susan was turned down by the special school, not for the commonly-used reason that the family would be unco-operative (her parents didn't like the idea of any special school, but were more willing to accept the maladjusted recommendation than the physically handicapped one), but because the head teacher in question cited the case of a partially-hearing child in another day maladjusted school who never became socially integrated.

Susan is now about to attend the partially-hearing unit of an ordinary school in the autumn. Billy's secondary school, a large, modern, co-educational comprehensive, has not referred him back to the clinic. Karen is working and Christopher has had a job at a bookbinders since Christmas. The family is still in the same accommodation. Mrs Taylor's feelings about professionals and their involvement with her family are clearly illustrated by the letters she wrote to the psychiatrist at the child guidance clinic.

August, 1976

Dear Doctor,
Will you tell me We want know. If I can get other
house. Please help me. Iwant go away now. I has fed
up. The children from outside hit Karen, 7 boy 6 girl
She never done nothing. My husband want get out this
flat Because the police say to me keep your children
in. That is very cheeky of him
I was a lot of crying everyday.
Can I go back C. Street or L. Road.
Please help me anywhere houses with garden,
(Deaf)
Mrs Dianne Taylor

Spring, 1977

Dear Doctor,
Just a few lines to let you know.
Did you ask about house for me. I want get out here.
I fed up. We are not happy now.
Will you please stop talking about Christopher and
Karen.
That Mr Taylor is fed up because of you. I thought
you were help me. Now me and husband say to me, I
don't want any social worker come my house. They
don't help me.
So Please do not bother my Karen and Christopher. I
do not want them away. Why you ask people come my
house.
I told her get out my door. Mr Taylor will fight
again he is not worry about himself Diabetics.
That was 4 time people come for Karen and Christopher,
Susan and Billy. I do not want any help me. I will
never speak to you social worker any more my houses.
We go out everyday not children with me.
They go out park or swimming.
So sorry I don't want any help here.
                    Mrs Taylor
I try fight myself look for other houses.

Summer, 1977

Dear Doctor or Miss Brown,
Sorry that I am not coming see you Because I am
getting fed up. The people are try be funny. I has 3
worker now. Because I fed up.
I want get out this flat.
I want move to L. Road or H.
My children are not happy here.
They make me ill and worry about.
I has buy shoes, cloth and pay my bill. No one will
help me. I be wait for long time. That why I fed up.
Why you want them for.
I has no good friend here I want out other place. I
saw lovely house at beside market name

P. Street near beside L. Road or C. Street.
I want get out here That place make me ill and worry
too much.
I sorry I not see you. Sorry.
If you see S.H. tell her I see her Tuesday morning.
                        Mrs Dianne Taylor

13 'THERE'LL NEVER BE A TIME WHEN I'M YOUNG AND FREE'

Mervyn Fox

Source: Edited version of Mervyn Fox, 'There'll Never Be a Time When I'm Young and Free' in Mervyn Fox (ed.), *They Get This Training but They Don't Really Know How you Feel* (National Fund for Research into Crippling Diseases, Hersham, 1974).

The birth of a handicapped child has a major impact on the lives of the parents, and creates a whole new set of needs; for information, advice,. support and practical help. Mrs Whyatt, who was eighteen when her second child Sally was born with Down's Syndrome, describes here how she first learnt that her daughter was handicapped, and the effect that Sally has had and will continue to have on her life.

I'd already had one child, quite normal, when I was seventeen, and he was five months old when I fell for Sally. She was born at home, with the cord round her neck, and was a deep purple colour; she had oxygen at home. Right from the beginning I knew there was something wrong, she had really ugly features, she wouldn't feed properly. She always snuffled and had sticky eyes. When she was three weeks old, we thought she should be properly examined. I didn't stop to think to ask our doctor, although he was present at the delivery, and I took her into the Casualty at the children's hospital. My mother had asked the midwife if Sally was mentally handicapped, and the midwife said 'it's more than we dare say, we can't commit ourselves'; the GP said nothing at all, and I think that's why we didn't go to him later on. At the hospital they asked me why I wanted her examined, and I said I thought there was something wrong; they asked me what, and I said obviously I didn't know or I wouldn't be asking them; I just wanted her to be thoroughly examined. They did this, and asked me to come back in a fortnight. I saw a specialist who said 'What do you think is wrong with your child?'; I said I had no idea, and she said I must have or I wouldn't have brought her here. I said I had no idea at all. The specialist said I must have some idea, and I said 'No, I don't'. I got quite annoyed, she was just pressing me to say what I thought, and all I could say was that I thought there was something wrong, with all the vomiting, and the eyes. Eventually I said my mother thinks she's mentally handicapped and the specialist said 'your mother's right, she's a mongol'. She said she'll never be independent or marry, never hold down a job, and will always be a responsibility to me. Maybe I'd think about having her put in a home – but this was never further from my mind.

In an ideal world I'd like to have been told in the first two days, because in that eight weeks so many horrors went through my mind that weren't necessary. Nobody had mentioned the possibility of mongolism until that woman came out with it. Some people may be able to hide things from themselves for years, but I couldn't, and I needed to know. I don't mind the two weeks' wait before I saw the specialist, I know there's plenty of people waiting on her time, but somebody could have called.

I never saw a health visitor. They usually pop around after the baby is born to see what you're feeding them on. I've never felt that health visitors are much help really. I always feel that they're only able to talk things over with you, and I'm not a person that talking helps, I like something practical done.

Mrs Whyatt feels she was told very little when she did see the specialist.

I was just given a rough outline of what mongolism meant, and this was it. I wasn't asked to take my husband, but I took him along as I wasn't sure what I'd be like if the news was bad. I wasn't asked ever to come back. Then I took her home and told the family. My mother-in-law was more than upset, she urged me to think seriously about having her put away, to think what it was going to mean to my life. But I thought, Sally didn't ask to come, she didn't ask to have a handicap, she's my responsibility. I was given the impression that she could have gone into a home straight away, but I realise now this wouldn't have been possible anyway.

After being told when Sally was eight weeks old that her daughter had Down's Syndrome, Mrs Whyatt had little further contact with professionals for the next year and a half.

I was left completely alone, the situation wasn't discussed with me, I just carried on as though Sally were normal, and when she was five months old I fell pregnant for my third child. They were all pure accidents. Nobody said a word until after the third, when I went to the family doctor about the Pill, and he said he'd meant to speak to me about it some time. I was young and silly and my husband was irresponsible, although he was six years older. I managed and coped alright, but I never had anyone knocking on the door to say 'Are you managing OK?' I met lots of people but nobody ever mentioned this. Looking back, I don't know how I did cope. I used to have two children on high chairs and one in my lap with me in the middle . . . It was worse than triplets, worse because one of them wasn't developing. I did go to a clinic, but not regular because after coping with my first child I didn't like being told my child needed four ounces of milk if I knew that my child was hungry after four ounces and really needed five, so I never really bothered, unless I went along to get them weighed occasionally.

I know the clinic is supposed to see to hearing, and dental, and sight, and give IQ tests to see that people aren't mentally handicapped or brain damaged. But all the advice I was given was about milk and feeding, and I didn't need it. I was twenty with three children, and I didn't even see the health visitor regularly. Eventually we moved to East London and my records were sent over to the nearest clinic, and the health visitor came round, and she told me about the centre which had just been opened for the mentally handicapped.

Although she was only eighteen months old, Sally was taken into the centre on an experimental basis, after attending a selection meeting with three other 'competitors' for this much wanted place. Before starting at the centre, Sally was very unfriendly to all at home apart from her mother, but through the centre she became more outgoing and lovable.

When I got to the Centre I didn't know if mongols could even talk, so the head grabbed one out of the classroom and she spoke quite normally. I didn't know whether I was going to have a child or a vegetable, until then; I took it she wouldn't be able to walk at all.

She feels it would have been a help to have met somebody like herself now, with a Down's Syndrome daughter, when Sally was a baby.

Even now, I still wish that I had someone near with a mongol of say fifteen, to help me know how they manage with puberty. And now I'm active on the school committee and so on, and there's still nobody I can discuss intimate problems like that with. No-one should pressure mothers into what they do with their children, but there should be people able to talk to mothers early on.

Mrs Whyatt reverts to the question of institutional care for mongols, and the present fact that only by leaving their child behind them in hospital can a couple who feel unable to change their lives to accommodate one of these children be spared the imposition of an unshared burden. If a mongol is born at home, she explains, the parents have little hope of ever being rid of it. She feels that for some couples, and for some mongols, an institution is the proper solution, but the only way to secure admission seems to be to abandon the child.

People aren't interested enough. I was left entirely alone when she was young. Neither the doctor nor a health visitor came knocking at the door. I should have been told right from the beginning what to expect, all the symptoms. Until she was at school I never knew that mongols tend to vomit, it always worried me. I was scared there was something wrong internally. A booklet would have been good enough.

Actually, at the hospital, I was told, very quickly, that mongols can die at any time, and this worried me for quite a time, every time I went into her room I thought 'What shall I do if she's dead'. She used to make a funny noise when she breathed, and when it got better and I couldn't hear her in her own room, I thought she was dead, and I waited outside the door to hear her make the noise. I was petrified, I waited a long time. I don't know the point of telling me that, perhaps they knew about her heart defect. She suffers all through the winter with coughs and catarrh, but you can't keep calling the doctor with something that's normal for mongols, so I look after that myself.

The future is something she thinks about often.

When I'm fifty she'll be thirty. I'm young. There's no possibility of my ever having a break from her, probably I will outlive her, so with us there's no problem for her; but for us, this is the problem that does worry me: I started the family young, and had she been normal they'd all have been off my hands by the time I'm forty, but with her, this is never going to be, there'll never be a time when I'm young and free. We couldn't go anywhere without Sally. The biggest need of all is for a home where the child can go to give the parents a break . . . this might sound silly to someone who hasn't got a handicapped child.

Mrs Whyatt has considered the possibility of self-help; parents of the handicapped exchanging their children to give the parents, in turn, the chance of a week's holiday, but she feels that the responsibility of having two handicapped children under the same roof is too great for an ordinary person, and favours institutions for this purpose. She stresses that by not abandoning their children at birth parents of the handicapped have saved the local authority a considerable expenditure, and deserve some recompense.

People don't think about all this, purely because they haven't had to deal with it themselves. If it's alright for the school to take children away for a week's holiday without them coming to any harm, why can't the Authority do this too — I don't mean a place with high grey walls. There should be more schools. There should be more of these little residential homes where they can go for a break. But overall I've been very lucky. I'm really very lucky indeed.

14 'THEY GET THIS TRAINING BUT THEY DON'T REALLY KNOW HOW YOU FEEL'

Mervyn Fox

Source: Edited version of Mervyn Fox, 'They Get This Training but They Don't Really Know How You Feel' in Mervyn Fox (ed.), *They Get This Training but They Don't Really Know How You Feel* (National Fund for Research into Crippling Diseases, Hersham, 1974).

Mrs Barker lives in a small, externally uninviting terrace house with her husband and her two sons, Mike and Kevin. The younger son's handicap has brought Mrs Barker into contact with many different professionals and left her mainly disillusioned with their help and advice.

I've always carried a chip on my shoulder since they first found out what was wrong with Kevin, his hypothyroidism. When he was six weeks old I detected that something wasn't quite right, and I took him back to the maternity ward where I had him; they told me he had hydrocephalus. The doctor just turned round to me and said 'We suspect hydrocephalus.' Well I didn't know what hydrocephalus was. I thought he was just going to die in my arms . . . and I'd already lost one baby six months old, with congenital heart. I thought, My God, what is hydrocephalus' you know, and I went home to my husband expecting him to die in the night. I went down to my own doctor the next morning and he told me what to expect. I was given an appointment at the Hydrocephalus clinic, seeing terrible sights, for six months, and during that time they had him in, and investigated him, kept measuring his head which wasn't getting that much bigger, and at the end they gave him a lumbar puncture and said he didn't have any extra water and they couldn't see any signs of hydrocephalus. They said they didn't know what was wrong and they transferred me to the Endocrine clinic, but while I was going up there I never saw the same doctor, which is another point I'd like to make. These different doctors, they all used to comment on the dryness of his skin, and his distended umbilical cord and all that, and I just — I was green, then, I didn't know what they were talking about — he went to the Endocrine clinic and he used to say 'Come back next month, it's just something you've got to live with, got to accept.' But what I had to live with I just didn't know, it wasn't explained to me at all. I kept going back every month, month after month, I was sitting for hours and hours with little drops of milk in the bottle, Kevin was eleven months old but looked a little thing of five months, like a little ball of yellow fat, until one particular day I went up there and said I just couldn't carry on, I had another little boy of three who didn't know he had a mother and my husband who didn't know he had a wife. I was just screwing myself in corners, I didn't want to go out, I didn't want to wash myself, or anything: I just felt as though I had to keep grinning and trying to feed him. When I had my other boy, Mike, perfectly normal, I couldn't get rid of the welfare lady . . . they kept coming round, week after week, but when I had my Kevin I never saw a soul, on my life; and that was a time when I sorely needed somebody: I really thought I was going out of my mind. When you've lost one baby, it makes you feel a thousand times worse. I was sitting for hours just trying to feed him, and on this day when I went up there and said I couldn't carry on, you'll have to do something, either I'm going to leave home or I'll do something to myself, I told him, and I'll take the baby with me; so he said 'We'll have you and the baby in our annexe, and we'll learn you how to feed him.' I thought you're not going to learn me in a fortnight what I've not learned in a year; I said, he's my third baby, not my first. But I agreed to go in; I had to make arrangements with the almoner, she arranged that I would go up there, and when I got there I saw the admission doctor.

He didn't even touch him! He just looked at him, and he was just a doctor, not a 'mister somebody-or-other'. He said to the nurse, 'Are there any more notes on this baby, because I feel there should be.' 'If your baby has got what I think he has, we've got a lot to be thankful for, because we'll be able to do something for him,' he said to me, 'I think he's hypothyroid.' I thought to myself, 'My God, something else.' They never explain anything to you, that's what I don't like about doctors, they never take the time to explain. I don't know whether they think that you just ought to know all these long medical words. Anyway, the matron of the annexe found she couldn't feed the baby at all, and she came to me and said 'We've got nothing to learn you about feeding babies', and from that day nobody came near me at the annexe at feed times, I was just left entirely by myself. For a few days they did these tests and it was proven that he was hypothyroid. But why, oh why wasn't it found out when I first took him up there when he was six weeks old . . . I shall never know. They should have gone through these tests before. I saw another specialist after he was put on thyroid tablets and he told me that owing to the fact that he didn't have the thyroid from birth he had got a bit of brain damage which could have been prevented if it had been found out earlier. And that is what has made me so bitter, I don't think they take enough time and trouble; I don't know if they haven't got the time, I know they're busy, but when you're given an appointment then they should take the time and trouble, and look at everything, not palm you off with 'Come back next month, come back next month.' Because that's what I was told for nearly a year.

I got a medical book out of the library, to find out what hypothyroid meant, it stood out a mile. It all came back to me, what the doctors had said when I was attending the hydrocephalus clinic: about the dryness of his skin, and the yellowness of him, all the fluid under his skin; when I looked back, I could only think how on earth it could have been missed . . . I went to the clinic to have him weighed, but that was as far as it went, nobody used to bother to come around to see me. I can't say I've got any help from anybody, once that doctor knew what was wrong. He carried on under Mr G. [she mentioned a well-known paediatric endocrinologist], whom he'd been seeing since he was six months old. Of course, when he didn't find it out, and the admissions officer did, I lost all confidence in him; I had none whatsoever at all, even up to today. I've got no more confidence in that hospital . . . but I still go for Kevin's sake. There's no-one up there I can really talk to. The almoners come and go . . .

She described her early struggles in two rooms above a shop, with her children growing up. Kevin walked when he was three, and then became hyperactive and noisy, so that she had suffered from being closed in with him and he had suffered for want of grass to run on, until when he was eight they had moved to their present lodgings. Neither the almoners nor the doctors had been able to help, although she knew both had tried. Only when her landlord had summonsed her and an eviction was pending had the council been able to offer her adequate accommodation, after seventeen years on the housing list. She said

that only twice since Kevin's discharge from hospital had she seen a
health visitor and she seemed to have had little contact with the local
authority services and stated her impression that they didn't know
about Kevin at all.

She soon stopped going to the clinics:

> I got past it. I thought, if they're not going to worry, then why
> should I? It just used to annoy me to think that nobody came
> round. As I'd never had much to do with the clinic — when I went
> down there with my first baby, everything seemed to be so secre-
> tive. They don't tell you anything, and I hate to be treated as though
> I'm ignorant. This is the whole crux of the matter. When I used to
> go to the childrens' hospital nine times out of ten Mr G. would have
> students sitting with him, and I well remember one particular time
> when I took Kevin up there . . . I noticed one side of his face seemed
> to be different to the other, and I happened to mention this . . . you
> do, you try to tell them every little thing that's worrying you; when
> I told this to Mr G., one of these young fellows started laughing, he
> sort of looked around at the others, grinning, as though I'd said
> something stupid. I felt about as big as that! I just gave him a terrible
> look . . . if looks could've killed he'd have dropped dead, and I just
> shut up.
>   I'd have liked somebody to be visiting me, knowing how I felt,
> but I wouldn't have liked someone in authority. What gets me is the
> almoners: they've not had any children . . . I know they get this
> training, but they don't really know how you feel. They don't know
> how real demented you are, indoors. You get this terrible feeling
> that you are absolutely . . . all . . . on . . . your . . . own. It's you,
> you are the one that's important, you don't think of anybody else,
> you're the only person in the world with this worry. You go up to
> hospital on the day you see all these other terrible cases, and — it's
> a pity to say it — it makes you feel better just for one day, to see
> those others worse off than your own, you think of those parents
> . . . but then when you get back indoors you're all . . . on . . . your
> . . . own. This terrible depression comes over you. If I could have
> seen someone I would have liked someone who had the same, or
> nearly the same problem, the same kind of worry. A parent. Some-
> one you could have really poured your heart out to and known that
> they could have fully understood.
>   My own family doctor? No, they haven't any time for him.

They've got so many on their books it's a waste of time.

We're in contact with quite a few parents now, as my husband is on the committee at the physically handicapped school. He went to a normal school for three years, and it's only since he was eight that we've really met any other parents. I don't know if he saw the school doctor when he was at the normal school, I know I didn't. I can remember seeing Doctor R. [she named the most senior of the authority's child health medical team] because she used to come down every six months and give him tests to see whether he could carry on at that first school, and then I got a letter to see her about going to another school. Naturally I felt straight away that she was going to send him to a mentally handicapped school and I felt – although I knew in my heart that Kevin couldn't carry on – he used to come home full of bruises, he used to fall down ever so easily and he couldn't stand up for himself against any other children – I felt he wasn't bad enough for that! I felt if he went to one of those schools it would drag him down, undo everything that had been done; he could read before he went to school – I mean, only surface reading, it wasn't sinking in, but he got each word out. So then she asked me how I felt about him going to a physically handicapped school, and of course when I went to see the headmistress I felt so relieved. Now they've opened the new building and it's been wonderful.

She was the first person I met in whom I had any confidence definitely. She's a marvellous woman. I could go to her . . . It must be a gift that she has, because she's a spinster, she has had no children of her own, but she has got this marvellous way with her, she must have been born into this job. You can ask her, and tell her anything whatsoever. I know her so much better than anyone else . . . I really feel such a . . . a love for her, that's it, she is a real love. I could go down there any time and she would only be too pleased . . . she's never too busy to see anybody. She's tremendous!

When I talk to Mr G. he doesn't even look at me, he's looking down and going through the notes, he never looks at my face, not once while I'm talking . . . a few months back, I visited the childrens' hospital, and he asked me what school Kevin was attending. He'd been at the PH School for seven years and now he asked me what school Kevin goes to!

This is really what gets you! I told him the name of the school, not for the first time, and he told me to go and see the almoner, for what reason I didn't know, and I spent an hour sitting outside the

almoner's office, waiting for her to come back from somewhere
. . . it was a young chit of a girl, about twenty, a foreigner; I suppose
they're trained at their job but it just gets me! She was telling me
that Mr G. thought that it was in Kevin's interest to go to a mentally
backward school . . . and all this is boiling up inside me, and I was
thinking to myself, I come up here once in three to six months, he's
had just one report from the school (the headmistress says she won't
send them to hospitals unless they ask for them, and they'd never
asked) on Kevin since he'd started there, and now he's suddenly
thought of this! I was furious! I'd like to know why he couldn't tell
me himself instead of asking the almoner to tell me! This is what I
mean by being secretive . . . They're never out with anything. Apart
from being furious, which I told the almoner in so many words I said
I'd keep him at home rather than let him go to a mentally backward
school now, I went straight off to the headmistress and she was so
furious too; she looked at the psychologist's report, which Mr G.
had never seen, and she just said she couldn't understand it.

Mrs Barker is not sure what an almoner or social worker does, or what
sort of training they are likely to have had.

I should imagine they're trained in Welfare and how to interview
people, but I don't really know, because they come and go so much.
People that see them very often must just get used to one, and then
she goes, and then they have to get used to another one all over
again. As far as I'm concerned, they seem to be miles apart from me
. . . you feel as though they're forced. The last one, for example, she
was sitting there looking all attentive, and agreeing with every word I
said. She knew her job very well because when I first got in there I
didn't mean to say anything, I just wanted to be awkward, but I
came out of there telling her everything . . . I was annoyed with
myself, but I still felt she was too young, and, perhaps because she
was foreign, I felt separate, I felt she wasn't one of my own.

She resents the attitutude of many professionals who have given her
'advice'.

When you're sort of lower class and you get a person speaking really
posh you feel . . . I don't know how to put it . . . there's a wall.
People can talk nice, and it comes natural, you know that it isn't
put on; but then you get another person, really talking lah-di-dah
and you feel they're putting on an act. They speak as though they
know more than me . . . about my child. Or they know better than

me . . . about my own child. They won't accept what I have to say.
That's what people in authority are like . . . Once I even went so far
. . . you know, I still have this feeling Mr G. doesn't take any notice
of me, there's this barrier there, and it's as though I'm just ignorant,
not worth talking to, this is the impression he gives me, not worth
talking to because I wouldn't understand what he said. So once,
when I was reading up about this hypothyroidism, and Kevin wasn't
walking at the time, and I read about the brain damage, that it could
damage the cerebellum and that could affect his walking, his balance
. . . so I didn't know how to pronounce it, but I asked one of the
nurses before I went in, and she told me it was 'cerebellum', so when
I went in there − I knew I wouldn't really know what I was talking
about, but I did so want to sound interesting so that perhaps he'd
say something back to me, you know, and so I said to him 'Do you
think there could have been any damage to the cerebellum?', and he
just gave me one look and then he got all the X-rays out, Kevin's
head all along the wall, and he's walking up and down and I was saying to myself, 'Oh good, I've said something bright', and he said 'Oh
no, Mrs B. I don't think so, I feel sure he'll walk in time.' Do you
know, for a few visits after that he seemed to take me seriously, and
he was more interested, but as time wore on we sort of slipped back
to the beginning again.

[. . .]

When I go to see anybody, any of these people I've mentioned,
I'm up in arms . . . I feel all this resentment inside, resentment to the
medical profession. I try to console myself that if I hadn't pushed it
when Kevin was eleven months old he wouldn't be as good as he is
today . . . but then I sometimes feel that I should have pushed it
earlier. I would have liked to have had more children, but I was too
afraid . . . I would have loved to have had some more . . . I asked Mr
G. and all he would say was that if the woman next door had five
children perfectly normal and healthy and you both became pregnant, you would stand more chance of having a perfectly normal
healthy baby than she would. But as to seeing another doctor, perhaps with more experience, I never got anywhere. He said it's
nothing out of the ordinary for a woman to have one abnormal
child, but to have two is just bad luck.

If I was to have a baby now, I would like all hospitals, to really
test these babies, all babies, for any abnormalities, before the mothers
take them home.

15 THE WILSON FAMILY

June Statham, adapted from Tom Wakefield

Source: Edited version of case study entitled 'Babs Wilson' in Tom Wakefield, *Some Mothers I Know: Living with Handicapped Children* (Routledge and Kegan Paul, London, 1978).

Kenny and Babs Wilson live at number 13 Fortescue Avenue, a street of Victorian terraced houses amid the high-rise flats and demolition areas of London's East End. There still exists in their area a kind of family community; Kenny's sister lives at number 27, his mother at number 9, his aunt at number 3. Kenny and his brother are London taxi drivers, and Babs worked in the cutting section of a clothing factory before her children were born. They had two daughters, followed by a son, Andrew. The following description of Andrew and his family is adapted from a much longer account written by Tom Wakefield, the head of the special school that Andrew attended.

Babs had a difficult labour with Andrew, but she took him home from the hospital with a clean bill of health. The celebration was short-lived. Babs noticed that Andrew seemed a bit 'floppy'. She had been informed that there was a slight toxaemia during the pregnancy, but had been reassured this had not affected Andrew in any adverse way. Nevertheless, at two months, during a periodic medical examination, it was mildly suggested that Andrew was not progressing as well as could be expected physically. At two years Andrew was referred to the Hospital for Sick Children at Great Ormond Street and there was subjected to many tests of a varying nature in order to come to some kind of conclusion as to the nature of his physical debilities and what might conceivably be the cause of them. This proved a very testing time for Babs, as Kenny probably externalised his concern and anxieties more than she did. Apart from these pressures, she already had two young daughters to care for, and organising the priorities of attention towards the individual children gave her some problems, as clearly a handicapped child would

90

demand more time and special thought by definition. Fortunately the two daughters, Jackie and Carol, realised this and never seemed to resent the fact, although much later, after she was married, Jackie did discuss with her mother the feelings of guilt and resentment at the extra attention Andy had received, feelings which she had hidden at the time.

Babs and Kenny found the physical diagnosis easy to accept because it was apparent. They were informed that Andrew was suffering from a dorso-lumbar scoliosis and that this would result in a curvature with regard to his stature. At this early age the degree of curvature did not seem too apparent. Even so the clarity of the condition gave them cause for deep sadness. Perhaps more worrying for them was the addendum on the report. This read quite simply 'In addition to scoliosis he appears mentally retarded.'

Both parents questioned the addendum and the hospital went through an exhaustive series of tests to see if the physical defects had in any way contributed towards the retardation. The conclusion remains still a very 'open verdict' and from a medical viewpoint it was termed as unexplained, but apparent.

Brain damage was not suggested – an EEG test showed moderate diffuse abnormality, but this in itself might not cause any retardation whatsoever. It is the question marks that caused the stress and the difficulties of accepting what still remains a somewhat mysterious condition. Babs knew that on an educational level there would be difficulties with Andrew and it is in this area where she and Kenny combined together to defeat medical, and to some extent, educational prognosis.

Before Andrew was due to commence schooling, they spent a great deal of time with him on social training, initiative undertaking and speech. All of the family must have provided him with intense pre-school training to equip him with the amount of independence he had acquired by the age of five. Nevertheless, it was felt by medical and educational authorities that Andrew should attend a special school. Kenny fought this decision and the local authority accepted his views and agreed to Andrew being admitted to an ordinary infant school if a sympathetic head teacher could be found.

The Wilsons found one, and Andrew spent the next three years in her school. His social skills improved, and at eight he was able to wash and dress himself, help around the house, take messages within the immediate environment and be sent on errands to shops near to his street. Had his family lived in a high-rise flat or on a big estate Andy would have found it much harder to cope, but the area around Fortescue Avenue is more like a village, with small streets, nearby shops and people who know each other and him. His mother feels that he 'couldn't achieve the sense of community he needs on the newer estates' and is worried what will happen when the plans for their 'village' to be demolished are finally passed by the council.

At eight, Andrew could also build and draw, and help his father with his taxi. However the headmistress at the infant school felt that in his three years there they had helped Andrew all they could in the more obvious social areas, and that he would now benefit educationally from attending a special school. His parents were still reluctant and refused placement at one special school, so the headmistress, who took a great interest in all of her pupils and was sympathetic to Andrew's parents' worries, contacted an ESN(M) school which she had heard other parents recommend, and arranged for the Wilsons to visit the headmaster there.

They were impressed by the look of the building even before they went inside. 'It looked more like a small hotel than a school, with big gates and the high wall around the playground built of bricks with holes in them so there was nothing "shut off" about the appearance, like there is in some buildings.' Once inside their favourable impression was reinforced; there were bright pictures on the wall, and in the doorway a list of everybody who worked in the building; teachers, speech therapists, the welfare woman, cooks and cleaners. A pupil at the school saw them looking and told them where Mr Wakefield's office was and they were told by the secretary that they were expected and could go straight in. Babs recollects that 'My first impression was that it was a friendly place, there was no anxious waiting outside like it is when you visit a hospital.'

Mr Wakefield had Andrew's papers on his desk, fulsome and varied reports from teachers, headteachers, psychologists, doctors, health visitors and consultants. The combined weight of opinion was that Andrew should be given a trial period in the ESN(M) school, but would probably prove to be ESN(S). The head explained the situation and offered Andrew placement at his school 'on trial'. Kenny reacted angrily, listing Andrew's capabilities as proof that he was unsuited to ESN(S) schooling, but both parents were reassured by the head's admission that he too disagreed with the Ministry's category of educationally subnormal. They explained that they weren't denying that their son needed to go to a special school, but that they 'didn't see any kiddies as subnormal'. Andrew was admitted to Mr Wakefield's school the same morning, still officially 'on trial'.

He settled in well and was soon definitely accepted as a pupil, much to his parents' relief. Babs began working as a bus attendant to show her appreciation of the school, and found that having a job for the first time since her children were born gave her a sense of independence and of being valued. 'It's probably done as much for me as it has for Andy.' Having a handicapped son caused other changes in the Wilsons' priorities and interests. Both became much more interested in education generally, with Kenny reading the education section of the Guardian and Babs eventually becoming a school governor, and Babs felt it had affected the way she and Kenny related to each other.

I suppose Kenny and me would never have talked over so many things if we hadn't had Andy. In this sense I suppose Andy has brought us closer because Kenny has always wanted to be the one in charge. We talk things over much more and it's not always a case of me just listening now.

Things went well for eighteen months after Andrew started at the ESN(M) school. His physical deformity appeared static, and did not prevent him taking part in the other children's play and games. Then his parents and teacher noticed that he had begun to drag his left foot, and an appointment was made with Andy's specialist at Great Ormond Street. The news was not good. Andy would have to wear a specially fitted brace all the time for quite a long time, in order to correct his posture. The brace arrived three weeks later and Andrew appeared at school encased in it like a giant plastic clam. It extended from his chin to just beyond the base of his spine. Babs and Kenny were worried that the other children would tease their son, but after the first novelty had worn off the other pupils paid little attention to the device. Andrew bore the contraption stoically, but it clearly made physical demands on him. He was much less active and by the end of some days at school was obviously very tired. Emotionally it was causing some disturbance, as he had sporadic bouts of bed-wetting throughout this period. The brace was worn practically all the time, and both parents were diligent in seeing that all the hospital's instructions were carried out.

In the months that followed Babs was confronted with more visits to the hospital for adjustments to the brace than would have seemed necessary. In spite of the continued adjustment the brace began to cut even more deeply into the child's back and the consultant eventually called Babs and Kenny for an interview with him. They went with a deep sense of foreboding, taking with them Mr Wakefield, the head of Andrew's special school who was by now a close friend. The consultant told them that the brace would have no long-term effects in correcting Andrew's posture, and that the curvature was increasing. The only alternative was major surgery, with no guarantee that it would be 100 per cent successful.

Both parents were deeply upset. They hated hospitals and feared the idea of an operation, but when they realised that if Andy didn't have the surgery he would eventually be bent right over, they gave their permission. Arrangements were made for Andrew to be admitted to a hospital which fortunately was near to his school so he could be visited each day by the head or one of the teachers, to maintain contact and help make the experience less traumatic for Andrew. It seemed a good choice, but when they took him in on the appointed day Babs and Kenny were shocked by the physical conditions of the ward. The beds were unmade, the linen dirty, the dead flowers giving off an unpleasant smell. The hospital was badly understaffed, as an official later explained in a letter of apology, but Babs and Kenny's confidence was completely undermined and they refused to allow Andrew to stay. They went back to Andy's school and the head helped them to make other arrangements for him to be seen by a specialist at a different hospital.

This new specialist established a good rapport with Kenny. He explained in detail the delicate type of operation he was to perform, and indicated that Andrew would be hospitalised for five months. The hospital arranged for Mr Wakefield to attend with Babs and Kenny on their second visit so that the staff could discuss Andrew's educational needs with him. There was a school attached to the hospital, which also possessed plenty of playrooms, well-designed wards and large grounds. Kenny and Babs were impressed, and the detailed information they were given about Andrew's operation helped to ease their fears on that score. Andrew was to have a 'halo' screwed into his head, back and hips, then later it was to come off and a Harrington Rod would be clipped onto his back. The operation was difficult, and not without hitches. Some time after the surgery one of the clips dislodged and the process had to be repeated, although in the event this proved a blessing as the curvature was decreased even more and the operation proved totally successful. Andrew bore the discomfort well, although he hated the halo and his mother felt that 'He won't be quite so interested in "Dr Who" after this is all over!' Mr Wakefield arranged for one of the teachers from his school to visit Andrew once a week during his five months stay in hospital, and he also met and talked to the headmistress and some of the teachers who would be working with Andy after his operation. Five months later Andrew was back at school, with a straight back and no more worries about scoliosis. Her experiences with Andrew have changed Babs' feelings about special schooling.

I know more about it now and that helps, and all schools vary anyway. I suppose if the world were perfect there would be no children with handicaps, and if all schools were perfect then they could be designed, equipped and staffed to cope with all kiddies. But I know the world's not perfect, and certainly I don't see how all schools can be. Andy couldn't have got through all of this without special schooling. Yet in a way, it's special people that count for more. Just look at my Andy now — he has got a future.

16 CARING FOR A MENTALLY HANDICAPPED CHILD: THE DAILY ROUTINE

David Wilkin

Source: David Wilkin, *Caring for the Mentally Handicapped Child* (Croom Helm, 1979), pp. 106-10.

The notion of 'community care' for handicapped people often means in practice that the burden of care falls on families, and in particular upon mothers. The effect this has on the lives of the people who do the caring is illustrated by the following description of the day-to-day experiences of three families with a child categorised as ESN(S). The descriptions are taken from David Wilkin's book Caring for the Mentally Handicapped Child, *and are based on research he conducted in the early 1970s for the Department of Health and Social Security, on the provision of services for families of mentally handicapped children.*

Sheila

Sheila was a profoundly handicapped twelve-year-old girl with a level of social and intellectual functioning which was below that achieved by the average one-year-old child. She lived with her parents and her elder brother and sister (16 and 18 respectively) in a well maintained owner-occupier terraced house with a small garden situated in a quiet street. The house was modernised and Sheila had her own bedroom. It was, however, rather small and, as is true of many older houses, the stairs were steep and difficult to manage with a non-ambulant child. Sheila was unable to walk at all, although she could shuffle and crawl, she required somebody to feed her, could only manage a liquid diet and wore nappies day and night, since she was doubly incontinent. Thus she was totally dependent for physical care on the other members of the family. In addition to this, she appeared not to respond to any

96

form of communication, had a tendency to bang her head repeatedly on the sides of her cot or on the floor and frequently slept very badly at night. Not surprisingly the family's domestic routine tended to revolve around Sheila and her requirements.

She usually woke in the morning at about 8.00 a.m. and was carried downstairs by her father before he left for work at about 8.15 a.m. Although her mother could just about manage to carry her up and down stairs this was becoming increasingly difficult. Between 8.15 a.m. and 9.10 a.m. her mother was more or less fully occupied in feeding, washing and dressing Sheila before the ambulance arrived to take her to the special school. She often refused to eat any breakfast at first but could usually be persuaded to eat something. Washing and dressing Sheila was not easy at the best of times, but was made particularly difficult when she was unco-operative. Being co-operative meant a passive acceptance of her mother's attempts to wash and dress her, but when she became difficult in a morning she tried to scratch or bite anybody who attempted to dress her. One way or another Sheila had to be ready by the time the ambulance called, and her mother was then able to get on with general housework. The fact that she wore nappies and required a complete change of clothing twice a day meant that her mother had to wash clothes at least three times a week. She was, however, more fortunate than some mothers who faced similar problems in that she had an automatic washing machine. At about mid-morning she usually had to postpone the remainder of the housework in order to visit her elderly father who lived in the same neighbourhood. After checking that he was all right and doing some cleaning and shopping for him, she was able to do her own shopping and return home in time to prepare lunch for her husband. Any remaining housework and the preparation of the evening meal had to be completed by about 4.00 p.m. when the ambulance brought Sheila home from school. Although Sheila would usually play with her toys until the family gathered for tea at about 6.00 p.m., she could not be left in a room alone for more than about one minute. She usually wanted something to eat at the same time as the rest of the family, but this required one person to feed her whilst saving their own meal. For the rest of the evening she would play as before under close supervision and was usually ready for bed between 9 and 10 p.m., although she often did not go to sleep until midnight. She was carried upstairs to bed by her father who, because she slept poorly, went to bed at about the same time so that he could be in the room with her until she went to sleep. During the night he would get out of bed every two to three hours to see that Sheila was not banging her head and had not become uncovered. Weekends were similar except that Sheila had to be occupied throughout the day, but since the whole family was usually at home, the tasks of playing with her, feeding her, dressing her, changing her, etc. could be shared. School holidays, however, were much more difficult since, although the routine was essentially the same as at weekends, the burden of care fell very heavily on her mother. The older children were not around and her father was working. For about four weeks of the summer holiday (her father arranged two weeks holiday to coincide with the school holidays) her mother had to look after Sheila all day in addition to performing all the usual household tasks and helping her invalid father.

Paul

Paul was an extremely active fourteen-year-old whose mental and social capacities were similar to those of the average four-year-old child. He was fully ambulant, fully continent and capable of performing most self-care tasks with only minimal supervision. However, these abilities were combined with an over-active temperament, very little sense of danger, a desire to wander and an ability to overcome most obstacles that might be placed in his way to prevent his wandering. His older brothers and sisters had all left home, leaving only Paul and his elderly parents in a small rented terraced house. His father was an invalid and had been unable to work for a number of years and his mother had suffered periods of ill health during the previous two years.

There was no regular time at which the day could be said to begin, since this was largely dependent on what time Paul decided to get up, which varied between 5.00 a.m. and 9.00 a.m. One parent had to get up with him in the morning, usually his mother, since he could not be left alone for fear that he would injure himself or manage to get out of the house (he once went to school at 6.00 a.m. dressed only in jumper and socks before his parents realised he had left). From the time he got up to the time he was ready for school somebody had to be with him in order to keep him out of mischief. Dressing, feeding and washing him had to be accomplished during this time and, although he was quite capable of performing these tasks for himself, he often refused, which resulted in a long verbal battle since he was becoming too big for force to be effective. The school bus called at a collection point not far from Paul's home, but his mother had to wait anything from five minutes to half an hour for the bus to arrive. She found it a great relief every day when Paul eventually went to school. However, she found that the time he was away — between 9.30 a.m. in the morning and 3.30 p.m. in the afternoon — only provided just sufficient time for her to get through the usual domestic chores. Paul's over-active behaviour meant that he was extremely hard on clothes and created a great deal of extra housework. The housework and the preparation of the evening meal had to be finished by the time Paul returned at 3.30 p.m. If the weather was reasonable his mother would take him to the local park in order to try and work off some of his seemingly limitless energy, otherwise he would have to be occupied at home which meant more or less constant supervision. The evenings provided some respite as Paul was prepared to sit and watch television, although he could not be persuaded to go to bed until 11 or 12 o'clock.

When he did eventually go to bed he insisted on sleeping with his mother and, even so, there was no guarantee that he would stay asleep. It was not uncommon for his mother to wake and find that Paul was downstairs playing records at 2.00 a.m. One consequence of Paul's behaviour at night was that his parents had not had a satisfactory sexual relationship for a number of years. Without the relief provided by Paul's attendance at school, weekends and school holidays could be torture. His mother felt that she was incapable of physically keeping pace with Paul's needs, her invalid husband's needs and the housework. Nevertheless, she managed to get by with the assistance of substantial periods of short-term care for Paul during the school holidays.

Graham

Graham presented a sharp contrast to the two children already described. He was nine years old and lived with his family in a modernised three-bedroomed council house. Like Paul he was fully ambulant and capable of basic physical self-care with only minimal supervision but, unlike Paul, he presented no behaviour problems. His mental and social capacities were similar to those of a normal five- to five-and-a-half-year-old. He had two older brothers and one twin brother and seemed to fit into the normal pattern of family life as the youngest child in the family. The family's daily routine appeared to be adapted to Graham's needs but to no greater extent than one might expect in a family with a young child. He rose in the morning at the same time as the older children and was quite capable of getting himself ready for school with minimal supervision. The school bus called for him at a local collection point at about 8.45 a.m., and his mother was able to work between 9.00 a.m. and 1.00 p.m. in a local supermarket. She was able to complete her housework after returning from work and before Graham came home from school. The amount of housework was not excessive since the children, including Graham, helped to keep things tidy. The family usually had tea between 5 and 6.00 p.m., after which Graham would play with his brothers and their friends either indoors or outdoors. He went to bed at about 9.00 p.m., the same time as his twin brother. Weekends and holidays were similar except that Graham played out more. Holidays presented a bit of a problem but his mother had been able to continue working because Graham's 16-year-old brother was able to keep an eye on him during the school holidays.

17 HELP YOURSELVES: SUPPORT SERVICES FOR PARENTS OF A SEVERELY HANDICAPPED BOY

David Thomas

The burden of caring for a severely handicapped child can be eased by the provision of adequate services. This brief account indicates the amount of help one family has been offered, and the additional services that the parents would like to have received.

After Richard and Christine Bowman married they managed a public house and lived above it. Their first child, Tom, was a healthy baby but at the age of two and a half his speech began to deteriorate. At first his GP thought that inflamed adenoids and tonsils were the cause of the problem but then Tom developed defective hearing. He underwent several operations on his ears but these made no difference to his condition and soon it became clear that his hearing and speech problems were only part of a general physical and mental deterioration. It was not until he was five that the doctors arrived at a final diagnosis. Tom was suffering from a rare degenerative disease of the central nervous system and would be unlikely to survive into his teens.

The Bowmans reacted to the final 'knowledge' of their son's handicap by deciding to give up the pub and apply for a council house, where they might give Tom proper care. Mr Bowman took a job as a supervisor in a local factory and Mrs Bowman became a housewife. They were allocated a damp prefabricated dwelling and told that they would be rehoused within a year. After five years they were still in the same home but with the addition of a second son and they applied to their MP for his assistance. The housing department responded to the MP's letter almost immediately. The Bowmans obtained a three-bedroomed house which they are now in the process of buying from the corporation. They have converted one of the downstairs living rooms into a bedroom for Tom. Ideally they would have liked a bathroom on the ground floor so that Tom could use it easily but they are relieved to have a decent home for him and his brother.

Tom is now eleven and a half years old. He has no speech and cannot move without help. He is incontinent and unable to wash, feed or dress himself. During the day he attends the special care class of a school for the severely subnormal but after school, at weekends and during holidays he is the sole responsibility of his family. He sleeps poorly at night and his parents often have to come downstairs to settle him down. Tom's bedding and clothes constantly need washing, but the drying facilities in their new house are inadequate. It is difficult to get all the housework done, especially when Tom is at home all day. Christine and Richard cannot afford a car but find it very awkward to take Tom with them on public transport, so whenever he needs to travel anywhere they are forced to hire a taxi. A car would also have helped them to take advantage of the shopping facilities in the town instead of having to buy everything from the local shops at greater expense and with less choice.

The Bowmans feel that one of the most difficult problems they have to deal with is the effect Tom has on his younger brother. Joe is four now, too young to fully understand the situation. He has temper tantrums and often refuses to do things for himself, but they find it difficult to discipline him. They don't want him to feel pushed out, but they often can't give him attention when he wants it, because Tom needs changing or feeding. Joe has said that he wants an older brother who can walk and run like other boys.

Richard and Christine do manage to go out together once a week, when a baby-sitter comes. They arranged a caravan holiday three years ago but Christine returned from this experience worn out. Looking after Tom in an unfamiliar environment left her no time at all to relax. This year short-term care is being provided for Tom, but the dates were confirmed too late to enable them to book a holiday for themselves and Joe. Relatives and neighbours are all very sorry for them but never offer to help. Christine feels that they are probably afraid of the responsibility.

The family receive a Constant Attendance Allowance to help cover the cost of Tom's clothes, bedding and napkins which rapidly wear out because of constant washing. Travel is expensive because of having to use taxis, but they have spent the allowance mainly in obtaining a colour TV, which Tom loves to watch.

The social services department have not been very helpful. Whenever Richard or Christine asked for something, the department's response was so slow that they finally had to appeal to their MP to obtain results. They had to do this to obtain a telephone, transport from their new house to school and a particular type of table for Tom to use. Christine found the occasional visits from social workers in the past of little use. 'They didn't seem to know anything.' Each worker who visited spent all of his time just trying to find out about Tom's unusual illness and so could not give any practical advice or provide her with the opportunity to talk to someone who understood her particular situation. She said Richard was helpful and supportive but she could never discuss Tom with him as they 'couldn't face it', and the opportunity to talk things over with a sympathetic person would have been very welcome.

Apart from transport to school, the family receive no other services, and never have done. They say they would be interested in a laundry service, incontinence aids, literature, holiday programmes and particularly classes for parents, as Christine feels a great deal of time and energy could be saved by being in touch with other parents and finding out how they deal with similar problems. Their major need, however, is for advice about available equipment and aids to cope with Tom's severe handicap. Richard had to build him a bed with movable sides, like a cot, to prevent him from falling out, since beds offered by both the corporation and hospital proved unsuitable. Christine mentioned some other equipment which would considerably improve their situation – a covered wheelchair to protect Tom from the weather, with a place provided in which to carry shopping, and a reclining chair similar to those used in hospital.

Tom has been away from home for short-term care five times in the past, and was once recommended for permanent care by the hospital paediatrician after a period of particular stress, but no place was available. The Bowmans contacted their MP and got Tom placed in hospital for six weeks, in a ward for active children. On his return home Christine found him 'rather knocked about' and will no longer consider permanent care, especially as they now know that Tom has not much longer to live. They still feel that two periods of short-term care a year would help them, but Christine is ambivalent about how long these periods should be. She feels a fortnight would be too short to give her a real break, but is not sure that she would want Tom to be away for as long as four weeks at a time, because she misses having to do things for him, even after only one night.

18 DOUBLY HANDICAPPED: DISABLED AND POOR

Peter Townsend

Source: Peter Townsend, *Poverty in the United Kingdom: a Survey of Household Resources and Standards of Living* (Penguin, Harmondsworth, 1979).

In his book Poverty in the United Kingdom, *Peter Townsend describes many families who in the 1970s were living below the national subsistence level. Lack of money is a handicap in itself, but for those who are poor* and *handicapped life is doubly hard. The Nelson family were interviewed several times in 1968/9 as part of a research project concerned with the impact of poverty on individual families, and again in 1972.*

In 1968 Mr and Mrs Nelson, 35 and 32, lived with their three sons of 13, 9 and 6 in a four-roomed council flat in a poor district of Oldham, overlooked by a rubber factory belching smoke all day long and near a canal. They believe the flat is a danger to their health. 'One bedroom is so damp it stripped itself.' The living room has a fire but they can only afford a one-bar electric fire to heat the bedrooms which are terribly damp. The fire is taken from one room to the next. At Christmas the bedroom window was smashed by a brick. Because the family cannot afford new glass, the room gets too cold and the boys sleep in one bedroom. The family had been moved out of a house which was also very damp and had been demolished in a clearance scheme two years before. They have no garden or yard, and though there is a playground attached to the flats, Mrs Nelson thinks the slides and swings are dangerous and too near to an adjoining busy main road. The flat is poorly furnished with linoleum and no carpets, no washing machine or refrigerator and just battered settees and chairs.

Mr Nelson is an epileptic. His fits began eleven years ago. He also has blood clots which keep touching the brain, and bad hearing. He can go out for a walk, but if he goes far he must have somebody with him. He tends to be in bed a week in every four, from the after-effects of fits and the blood clots on his brain. His nerves are bad, and, for example, he is afraid of holding scissors to cut his nails, in case he has a fit. His wife says that the doctor told her that not much could be done for him. He had not worked for six and a half years, when he had been a driver earning a wage well above average (then £25–£30 p.w.), for a decorating firm. He had, in fact, served a six years apprenticeship in painting and decorating. Five years ago he had been sent to a government retraining centre, where he entered an engineering section. After three days he had an epileptic fit and the doctor said that the work, and travelling six miles each way, was too risky. Now he goes once a month to his doctor for prescriptions and a sickness certificate, and once in every four months to hospital for a check-up.

Mrs Nelson had given up her work as an office cleaner twelve months earlier to look after him. Formerly she had been a spinner in a cotton mill. She suffers badly from bronchitis and rheumatism and has pain in her chest, following a spell in hospital with fluid on the lungs two years earlier. Her health varies seasonally, and from week to week, and she feels tired all the time. She goes to the doctor three times a month for a prescription for tablets.

Their second son Jonathan, aged 9, is very thin and delicate and has intermittent deafness. He is very susceptible to colds and has had several spells in bed this year. He has been to hospital to see a specialist three times about his hearing. For much of the year he has had nasal catarrh and wakes up in the middle of the night shouting, 'I can't breathe. I can't breathe.'

The eldest son is in reasonably good health but has a so-called 'lazy eye', of which he is self-conscious. He goes to a special school. He is not mentally backward but was slow to begin to read and was considered to need such schooling. He is collected daily by school bus. The youngest child is also in fairly good health and, like the second son, goes to a neighbouring primary school. They wear plimsolls to go to school because they cannot afford shoes.

The family have little social life, partly, they say, because they moved into the district less than two years ago. Mrs Nelson sees a number of her relatives once or more a week, including a sister, her step-mother and father and her husband's mother, but there is little exchange of help. They can depend on a neighbour for emergency help, but Mrs Nelson's family seem to be keeping their distance, perhaps out of fear from the husband's epilepsy. Or perhaps the Nelsons themselves feel the need of protection from barbed gossip and want to hide in privacy. 'We keep ourselves to ourselves', as Mrs Nelson said. They have not had a summer holiday, but twice in the year Mrs Nelson has saved up and taken the children by train, just for the day, to her sister in Yorkshire. 'It gives them a good day out. Good air. It is the only holiday they are likely to get.' They have not had a meal or snack with any relative or friend in the last fortnight and have not been out any evening. Similarly they have not entertained anyone in the home. None of the children has had a birthday party and none of their friends has come in to play. They are Church of England but have not been to church in the last year.

At the time of interview (March 1968) they had £10.25 a week in sickness benefit, and £1.05 supplementary benefit, as well as 90p family allowances. Their rent of £2.60 was paid directly by the Supplementary Benefits Commission because they had got into arrears and had agreed for the council to be paid direct. Their total income appeared to be marginally below the state poverty line, and if they had been judged to be entitled (because of the poor health of three of the family) to an additional allowance, would have been more than a pound below. In the week following the interview, family allowances were to be increased by 70p, but sickness benefit and supplementary benefit reduced by the same amount. 'It is scandalous, and the government say they are trying to alleviate poverty.' They had received two single grants from the commission in the last year of £4.50 for shoes and £1.62½ for glasses. The grant for shoes was supposed to cover the cost of boys' shoes. An application for clothing was refused. Once, when Mr Nelson had recovered from a particularly bad fit and had spent a fortnight in bed, he asked for a visitor to judge an application for a grant for shoes. No visit was paid for six weeks. He said he was not embarrassed to receive supplementary benefit. 'It is a case of necessity. We cannot live without it.' They have no savings or other assets. 'There's nothing we own which would fetch a decent price.'

Wednesday is benefit day, and Mr and Mrs Nelson do not have a cooked meal on Tuesdays (and sometimes Mondays) because they have no money left. They rarely have fresh meat, but their children have free meals at school (and also free milk). The family has a pint of milk a day, which is watered to eke it out. If Christmas so falls that the household gets two weeks' benefit, they spend it on 'giving the children a good time and starve the second week'. They have also depended a bit on a Baptist Mission which caters for the poor and needy. When Mr Nelson is well, he organises games for poor children at the Mission on a Sunday afternoon for three hours. He is not paid for this, but at

Christmas receives a big food parcel and a toy for each of the children. They cannot afford a hundred-weight of coal at once and only buy it in 28-pound bags as and when they can afford them. The children receive 2½p pocket money apiece. Mr Nelson hands over his benefits to his wife, and when he is well, receives back £2, with which he buys cigarettes and has an occasional drink in the pub. They feel worse off than family or friends and feel they have never been worse off in their lives. When asked to describe poverty, Mr Nelson said, 'The circumstances we are experiencing now. Poverty is when you are living from hand to mouth and you have no security.' They had not voted at the last election and laid responsibility for poverty with the government. What could be done about it? 'Increase benefits above the subsistence level', was Mr Nelson's reply.

After this interview, the family allowed the research team to take up the question of rate of benefit on their behalf. The allowance was agreed by the Supplementary Benefits Commission to be wrong and the weekly payment was increased by 35p. An exceptional needs grant of nearly £30 was also paid for clothes and bedding.

In 1972, the family was visited again. Mr Nelson was very frail. He now had sixteen or seventeen epileptic fits each day during severe episodes of epilepsy which seem to come every eight weeks or so. He was assessed for an attendance allowance but was turned down. He had been visited in the course of a disabled register survey. Mrs Nelson said, 'I asked them about a holiday for him.' As for supplementary benefit: 'After you were here last time they put everything right, but we haven't heard anything since, only when we ask them to come.' After having an exceptional needs grant in 1968, they had not received another until a grant for £12.20 was paid this year. Mrs Nelson pointed out that when her husband had fits he pulled and tore the bedding. The officer told her, 'You've had enough grants from us.' 'We need new beds. They are all falling to pieces. They were all second-hand when we got them. I've asked the WVS if they can find us any . . . The only visits we get are from the Mental Health, but the visitor has left and I don't know if we shall get another. She was nice. She tried to fix my husband up with a holiday. But it was going to cost £17 for him to go to an epileptic home for two weeks. I couldn't afford that.'

Their eldest son, Arthur, is now 17 and he took a job as a labourer with a cardboard-box firm a year ago. 'He just loves it. He's never late.' For a forty-hour week he gets a gross wage of £8.80 a week, and takes home £7.94. They were delighted because in Christmas week he got a bonus of 50p. The family's rent has increased by 45 per cent from

£2.60 to £3.76. Invalidity benefit is now £15.70. To this a family allowance of 90p and supplementary benefit of £1.35 is added. Even allowing for Arthur's share of the rent, his parents' total income seems to be about 30p below the basic scales of the Supplementary Benefits Commission (including 50p long-term addition). No additional allowance is made for Mr Nelson's special needs. There has therefore been an improvement in their situation only to the extent that the eldest son now earns a small wage. About supplementary benefit and sickness benefit, Mrs Nelson commented, 'You get fed up always having to ask for everything. I hate going down. If I have to go down because the book hasn't come they say I've just got to wait until it does come.' Subsequently the income from the commission was investigated. Not only was the allowance confirmed to be an underpayment, the extra amount agreed to be necessary in 1968 for Mr Nelson's diet was no longer being paid. The underpayment was put right and the dietary allowance restored. A further exceptional needs grant was paid.

The evidence of deprivation is as strong, and in some respects stronger, than in 1968. They go to bed early to save fuel. Mrs Nelson buys second-hand clothing at jumble sales. For breakfast, she cooks porridge for the children but she and her husband have nothing. They are used to days without any cooked meal '. . . especially Mondays and Tuesdays. We give it to the kids. We get the money on Wednesday and it doesn't last long.' They have little fresh meat. 'We have a few chops if cheap enough, perhaps once a fortnight. Arthur's that good. I like to give him a nice lamb chop as a treat sometimes.' She has no shoes for rainy weather, 'Just these boots, which are three times too big.' At Christmas, 'I got a lovely piece of lean bacon and boiled it and roasted it. It cost £1 but it was worth it. Anyway, it was a long holiday, wasn't it? My husband's sister bought a Christmas present and Arthur bought sweets for the kids and we got some second-hand toys from the welfare.' The two younger children get pocket money 'now that Arthur is working. He gives them 5p each a week.' She said that they did not go out in the evenings. 'Mr Nelson walks down to his mother's most evenings if he's feeling well enough. Sometimes she gives him money for half a pint. It does him good.' When the coal strike was on, Mrs Nelson was seriously ill at home with pneumonia. At the same time, Mr Nelson was having severe fits through the night. 'That was the worst time I have ever had.'

The problem of doing right by her children obsessed her. Her second son Jonathan is at a secondary modern school which insists on uniforms:

The school moans at the lad because he goes in jeans, but a blue shirt alone costs £2; and the trousers are £3.15. Then there is a grey pullover and a blazer. I can't possibly afford it. There's PE equipment and swimming. I haven't any decent towels and the school complains. The headmaster keeps complaining. That's when I went to the council about a grant, and they turned me down. I bought some shoes last week for both of them, £3.25 a pair. I got the money from the TV rebate. Jonathan can't read very well and the school don't do special reading. He doesn't bother to try now and has only had one special lesson since January although the Child Guidance people said he had to have them. He still gets stomach pains. They fade and come back. The games teacher made him do games even though I sent a letter.

When asked how she described poverty, she answered, 'Not being able to buy anything for the kids . . . I'm hoping things will be better for my kiddies in time to come. I never thought life would be like this.'

There is not much change in the furnishings. One dresser which had been rather chipped and discoloured had been repainted. The living room has been papered with some wallpaper given to them by Mr Nelson's sister. A single cup and saucer stands proudly on the dresser, a memento of a relative's holiday. The interviewer was allowed to look at it, though Mrs Nelson kept a firm hold on it with one hand stretched underneath for fear it fell. 'Everything in here, except the TV, which we rent, has been given to us.' The TV is on a meter and every three months is emptied by the company. The difference between the rent and the money in the box is refunded. 'In another couple of years the TV will be mine. Then they can't take it away. I can't wait for that day.'

She has a slipped disc and has been having prolonged investigations in hospital for ulcers and gall-bladder trouble. She had just learned that very morning, however, that she is pregnant and the baby is due in eight weeks. This news has stunned her. She was bewildered by the fact that although she has had a number of X-rays as well as examinations at the hospital in the past months, no one had said anything about a baby. She had been handed a diet sheet. 'As if I can afford steak.' She had nothing for the baby and had gone that afternoon to the welfare to ask for an old pram, but was told they had none.

Mrs Nelson was as sharply critical of the government as her husband had been in 1968. The government was responsible for poverty. 'Put governments in a bag and shake them up. It doesn't matter which one you get. Each one is just as bad as the other . . . They promise everything.

They're going to give you this and give you that. The only thing they do give you is the transport to vote for them.'

The interviewer, a skilled and sensitive woman with long experience of fieldwork, herself the mother of three children, described Mrs Nelson as 'quite the bravest person I have ever met. This house is full of respect for everyone else, and affection.' Perhaps an answer to a question about holidays was most telling of all. Had the family had a summer holiday recently? Mrs Nelson immediately said

Oh yes, we saved and saved for weeks. We put the money in that pot up there. Mind you, we had to take it out sometimes, but we managed to put it back. Then the time came, and we really did go together to see *The Sound of Music*. Oh, it was lovely — that opening scene where she was dancing on the mountains and all free. The children each had an ice-cream, and when we left we walked up the High Street and you know that wallpaper shop, well, we saw that picture, there, above our fireplace. We counted up our money. If we walked home we would just have enough for it. So next morning I walked down and bought it, and there it's been ever since. When you're fed up you can look at it and it reminds you of *The Sound of Music*.

Mr Nelson died in 1976. He was 43.

19 JACQUELINE CUNNINGHAM, A DAUGHTER

Tony Booth

Mrs Cunningham's experience of her daughter's handicap has involved two major crises. Twenty years ago when Jacqueline was seven she was informed that her daughter was ineducable and would have to be taken out of school and kept at home, a decision which her parents disputed. Recently a new major issue has arisen. Jacqueline now has a chance of a place in an assisted group home. Mrs Cunningham sees this as both an opportunity and a cause for concern about her daughter's independent future and about her own new life without full responsibility for her child.

The Cunninghams realised when their daughter Jacqueline was young that she was 'a bit of a slow developer', but prior to school nobody ever suggested that she was mentally handicapped. Mrs Cunningham remembers:

She started at an ordinary school when she was five, just as a normal child. When she was moved into the second year her teacher said she was at the bottom of the class but wouldn't need special education. Then, I don't know how it came about, but she had this IQ test. We had a terrible time with this man. He was very abrupt. Quite the wrong type. He immediately made you feel nervous. He had a strong Scottish accent which I had difficulty in understanding, let alone her. He showed her pictures of household things saying 'Which one do you *coo*k on' and of course my daughter didn't know which one you '*coo*k on', it was a 'cooker' you see. So she did get a lot wrong. She was all nervous and she could feel the tension in us. He didn't have the right manner at all. I told him he needed to be more gentle and kind and understanding, and he got on his high horse about being a fully qualified psychologist. He might have been, but he certainly didn't have the right manner!

I complained because of his Scottish accent and he said he would agree to do another IQ test, but when we went in he was even more

111

put off by us because we had complained. He sat her in front of his desk and told me to sit in the far corner and not to make a sound, so of course my daughter was even more nervous than she normally is, and when he started firing questions at her she just couldn't answer them, though they were things I knew she knew. Anyway she was given an IQ of 49. At that time if the IQ was below 50 they were deemed ineducable and came under health.

They said she couldn't go to school, but it was their duty to inform us that we could appeal, so we appealed and we had to write to the Minister of Education. We had to get references from her teacher and headmaster. Any rate I didn't keep her away from school at this appeal time, I kept her going. I didn't know whether they would send her home again but they kept her on. This went on for some months. Letters from the education authority used to come by recorded delivery and I was in such a state, I used to hide them away unopened for several days. I imagine women used to do that in the war when telegrams came, they were so afraid to open them and see what they said.

Eventually they sent another man from London to test her. He was a different kettle of fish altogether. He came in and just got to know her and made friends with her. He said he was quite prepared to sit there for 2–3 hours and play with her and gain her confidence. He thought she had done badly in the tests because she could feel the tension in the whole house. When he'd finished he told us that she wasn't ineducable but would qualify for special education when she finished primary school. There wasn't a special school for children under eleven in our area.

We were really pleased, but then we received a letter from the education officer. He wrote: 'I have to congratulate you that you've won your appeal but unfortunately there aren't any places in the school so we cannot readmit your daughter.' Of course she'd never been away, so how could there not be a place for her? They just didn't seem to know we'd kept her at school.

My husband went flying up to the education offices. The education officer told him 'You're not the only ones — this happens to hundreds of parents' as if that made the worry or the problem any easier. Any rate they did agree to let her stay at that junior school.

I don't think it made their life terribly easy having her at that school. Jacqueline did get on all right there and we didn't get called into school about her. But perhaps we were selfish, I don't know.

When she went on to the special school she was very nervous and unsettled and they wondered whether they could keep her. I don't know what she did — disrupt the classes, to a certain extent, I suppose. But after a few weeks she settled down.

Later on we had to leave the area because of my husband's work. We had a few choices of places and we decided to move where there was a special school for her. The new ESN school didn't think much of the education she had received at her previous special school.

I was pleased with the new school but she did get into a spot of bother at one time. She used to go to a Wednesday evening social there but there was some trouble with one of the boys, going outside, you know — I had to go up and put a stop to that. He was quite sensible this boy, he rides a motorbike around town so he has got road sense but he's been in trouble with the police several times.

When the time came for her to leave school I had to go to discuss her future with the headmaster and the careers officer who dealt with ESN children. They said 'What about a supermarket?' I didn't think she could do that but they were sure she could stack shelves. So I began to think 'Gosh, perhaps she's better than I really think she is.' So she got the job in the supermarket where she did everything wrong — putting the wrong prices on everything.

Then they opened a work preparation unit at Westerport and she was one of the first to go. She was there for quite some time and then they found her a job in a bacon factory and she's been there ever since. They process sausages and bacon. She does packing — bacon pieces is her main little job which she feels very important about. But she gets a lot of the cleaning jobs — cleaning the machines. She loves doing these bacon pieces because they're in great demand in the shop. She says to me 'They want some more bacon pieces you know.' She feels very important about that.

Jacqueline is 27 and still lives at home with her mother, who is now widowed, and her two younger brothers of 15 and 22. They live in a village on the outskirts of a small town. Her elder sister has left home and has a family of her own. Her brothers don't have much to do with her. 'Obviously they don't have much in common with her. I mean it drives me up the wall sometimes, you're having the same conversation with her that you were having twenty years ago. You never got on a higher level really.' When she is not at work she spends most of her time in the house with her mother. Her two main interests outside the home are adult literacy classes and activities organised by the local mental handicap society:

She really enjoys the literacy classes, it's all right when she's sitting down concentrating all the time, but as soon as she leaves off, it goes. But she likes going, I think she feels its part of being normal, just like everybody else. A while ago she said to me (it's terribly heartbreaking), 'I wish I was normal' and there's absolutely nothing you can do about it. She's got enough intelligence to know she's different and wish she was normal. That's the heartbreaking thing really, you get more severely handicapped people and they don't know they're different, do they? She realises she's different and that's hurtful to her.

But she enjoys the mental handicapped society. She loves going out with them. She has a friend who went to the same school who wouldn't be seen with them at all. She goes on holiday with them to Skegness every year and thoroughly enjoys it.

Apart from these outings she only goes out with me. She used to go into town on her own but she got knocked down one time and now I would worry too much. I think I've got worse about that. It's easier for her to always be with me than for me to let her go out and worry myself sick. She's terribly vulnerable. Her friends can't come here, they've all got to be taxied around you see – I suppose their parents are the same as me and worry about them. She goes down to the shops in the village, and she goes to work, but otherwise she never goes out on her own. It's the roads, she can't really handle busy traffic. Her work is within walking distance, but she catches a bus, just to get her across this one busy road.

Of course she does take up a lot of my time. I don't like leaving her on her own though I do sometimes leave an hour's gap between my son going out and my returning from evening classes. I tell her to lock the door and not to answer it. She's afraid of the dark too.

She's not as demanding as some who need dressing or feeding but she does need a lot of attention. I always get her packed lunch in the morning – she could do it herself but she's so slow. She does her hair but if she wants a perm I have to do that. I get her breakfast in the mornings but at the weekends I leave her to get her own. She could do it, but she doesn't have any breakfast if I don't get it, it's laziness in her I suppose. She is good with the ironing. It's just a case of having to do all her thinking for her.

Holidays present Mrs Cunningham with a particular problem now she has a three-quarter time job. Jacqueline has four weeks leave each year and Mrs Cunningham takes her own holidays to coincide with her daughter's.

I don't like the thought of her being at home on her own for a solid week. She'd have the television on all the time and she'd not know what to do if anything went wrong. She might do some cooking, she likes that, but I'd be worrying, she'd be setting the house on fire.

One week shortly after my husband died I took Jacqueline for a week to a local 'home' for one of her winter weeks holiday. I'd never do it again. It was terribly institutionalised, four or five beds to a room. They showed me around before she went and told me how clean it was. I said 'you don't want it too clean and tidy'. It was nothing like a normal home. I took her on a Sunday. All the boys were watching football on the television and all the girls were at the end of the room knitting. There's a games room there with records and everything but no-one was using it, it all had to be 'neat and tidy'. She was waiting with her case when I came to pick her up and she came running out to meet me.

Now I take my holidays when she gets her winter holidays. I hardly get away from her and she hardly gets away from me.

She has this boyfriend in the background, that keeps her morale up. He's moved away now, but they ring each other up every Sunday and she talks about 'my boyfriend'. She does say 'I wish we could meet again' or 'I wish I could marry Jeremy'. I remember years ago saying to her, when she was talking about getting married and this and that, and I said 'oh you can't get married, you can't look after yourself let alone looking after a husband', and I often wonder now if I should have said that. They do get married now don't they? A while ago I saw a programme on the television about a mentally handicapped couple in America who got married. There were lots of protests about it. They were just like my daughter as regards being able to go out to work but having had problems with jobs. They had wanted to get married and even though the law in their state forbade it, they were allowed to marry. They were taught birth control and they had enough sense to take that in. They wanted children at first. The girl thought about it and she was confident that she could look after it but she realised that when that child went to school the others would say 'you've got daft parents' and they decided that they wouldn't have children. I found that remarkable that she could figure that out for herself.

They shouldn't have children, oh no, but I don't think marriage should be denied them. I should never have said that to my daughter. Why shouldn't they get married if they could cope? As long as they were in a sheltered environment and didn't have children.

I'm now coming up to another crisis in my life. I'm a widow and I've got to face up to what happens to her if something happens to me. Whilst you're married you can push that to the back of your mind because if anything happens to you there's someone else to look after her. My other children won't want to look after her and that's understandable — why should they?

For some time I've been looking into the possibilities for her. I'm on the accommodation committee of the mental handicap society. There's a residential small group home opening in January and her name is down for it. I know, when I think clearly and stand back from the situation, that it's the thing to do. She's very keen on the idea because she has a friend who is already in such a home and is happy and Jacqueline wishes she could have her name put down for it. It's not a hostel, there'll be four mentally handicapped and four physically handicapped people and some university students. They're hoping for some support from the students in taking the others out. There will be 'living-in' houseparents too and that's the most important thing from my point of view.

If they are able to cope, it might be possible, later on, for them to move out into a house close by. It would be wrong for them to be plunged into an unsupervised house when their parents have died. There was a social services place which was just dreadful. They said it was supervised but the only supervision came from one woman who went in for a few hours a week — when she turned up. If she was ill they were just left. They lived on beans on toast all the time.

I really should jump at this opportunity. I think she'll be quite happy about it. It's going to be me who's up the wall . . . I'll worry that they won't give her the care I've given her — perhaps I've made her too dependent on me.

I haven't thought about myself for so long that I just don't know what I'd do with the freedom. Some people said where would you go for a holiday if you could go anywhere in the world, and I said I've no idea. I've just never thought about it. You just live from one day to the next. But if she goes, it's going to make a hole in my life, to be free and able to think about things . . . I don't think it'll be a bad thing, but it'll mean a terrific adjustment on my part.

20 PARENT PARTICIPATION: SETTING UP A SPECIAL UNIT IN A PRIVATE SCHOOL

Tony Booth and June Statham

When a local authority adopts a particular educational policy for a category of handicapped children, the wishes of parents and the needs of individual children may be ignored. In many areas, all Down's Syndrome children are sent to ESN(S) schools regardless of their level of ability. For the parents of the more able children, this often means sending their child to a school which they feel offers few opportunities for extending their abilities, and for many it means learning undesirable social habits and behaviour. The pressure put on parents to send their child to an ESN(S) school, and the lack of any real alternative, means that parents must be well-organised and very determined if they are to secure the kind of education that they would like for their children.

The parents of William, Kevin, Valerie and Peter met each other through their local branch of the Society for Mentally Handicapped Children, and started a campaign to get their local authority to set up a special unit for their children within an ordinary school. They met with adamant refusal on the part of the authority, and had to go outside the state system to set up the kind of unit they wanted in Priory Bridge, a small private school. Its progress was supported and monitored by Tony Booth, whose observations and interviews with the parents and teachers provide much of the information and quotations used in this study.

The Children

When it opened the unit catered for six children aged 5 to 10; the four Down's Syndrome children plus two others already at the private school but with a history of special schooling and finding it difficult to cope in the normal classes. The parents' descriptions of their children's

117

early education show some basic similarities, particularly among the four Down's children. All of their parents had experienced pressure from the authorities to place their child in an ESN(S) school, all had done so for varying periods and none had been satisfied with the experience. The reasons for their dissatisfaction were also very similar, and Peter's story is typical of the experiences which the families had had with the authorities. Peter, now six, was diagnosed at birth as suffering from Down's Syndrome. He went to a mother-and-toddler group where he mixed with non-handicapped children, and his parents hoped that he could continue in an ordinary school.

> At the back of our minds we always felt that there may be a chance that we could get him into a normal school, even for just a year. He could have handled a small reception class.

They planned to ask for a place in the small school in the village where they used to live, but then the family moved and the new local school had a reception class of forty children, 'so we never even asked'. They started taking Peter to a playgroup in their new area, but felt it was 'too unstructured' for him, and so he began attending three mornings and then five at the nursery attached to the ESN(S) school. They weren't very happy with this decision, and his mother recalls 'getting increasingly depressed as the day approached when he would start being educated there'. The school was anxious to take Peter full time before he reached the age of five, and the parents felt that the head took it personally when they insisted on taking some responsibility for Peter until statutory school starting age.

Both parents felt under a lot of pressure to send Peter to the ESN(S) school, not only from the school itself but also from the home teacher. Peter's mother appreciated her help and support, and liked the way the home teacher also involved Peter's older brother and came at a time that enabled her to pick the other child up from school, but she didn't like her constant suggestions that it was time Peter began attending the ESN(S) school full time.

> She obviously thought it was the right thing and that eventually I would come round to her way of thinking, but I never did. The pressure increased when Peter was three-and-a-half, or four. The decision of where he was going to school upset me tremendously, I found that far more difficult to accept than coming to terms with the fact of having a handicapped child.

Their feelings were reinforced by Peter's experience in the 'baby group' at the special school.

It was a diabolical time; most of the time in the baby class for at least an hour and a half every morning was spent on ablutions; sitting kids on pots; rubbing down; some of them had been on the bus for an hour at least so they were in a bit of a state when they got there. The first hour each morning was spent on toilety things: which Peter was past, he was trained for years past. Up to this point we had never had any trouble with him going to the toilet; but at that time, oh, he messed in his room, and plastered it all over the walls and carpet, three days running it happened and then it went on for two or three weeks . . . at the beginning of him starting at the special school. Of course if you mention it to the headmistress, its nothing whatever to do with the special school, but it was; and I think as well that he'd gone back to a baby stage that he was beyond; he had gone back to just slapping around with his hands in paint and what have you; I know that they do go through all that playing about with paint, but he was beyond that and they were taking him back to a stage he had got past and he was using his mess as paint and going all round the room; so that really was an awful stage — plus the fact that he was picking up all sorts of stupid mannerisms. He recognised them as abnormal behaviour and he used to think it was a bit of fun to say 'Roger' and then act like him; he would have the imitation fantastically well; he's a great mimic; and you've only got to have someone with abnormal hand actions and he can do it. I remember taking him out in his buggy when he was younger and we went to a big store and he was copying a child from school who is always in a buggy, kicking and grabbing hold of people, and I thought this is just about the last straw, I've brought up a sensible child that behaves properly and can sit up and behave nicely and he's turned into this idiot in the buggy doing all these loony actions; I mean, I just couldn't cope with this, I was trying my damnedest to bring him up so we could take him out and be proud of him, and then to have him picking up all the mannerisms of all the other children.

Peter's parents didn't think, as was suggested, that he was 'so much better than anyone else', but they did want to prepare him for as normal a life as possible when he grew older.

We basically asked ourselves what do we want the education system to do for him, and we felt that if he was to have any separate existence, sheltered work or whatever, he's got to become socially accepted as well as to have some skill, and we felt that if we could get him in a more normal environment he was bound to learn from the other children socially acceptable things; normal movements, how to hold himself . . . you can always tell a mentally handicapped person from the way they walk.

The ESN(S) school formed a new group with eight of the more able children, including Peter, because of pressure from a few parents who felt like they did. At first they were quite pleased with this new arrangement, but then Peter's mother began to feel that:

every time I turned around there was another child in the class. The headmistress tried to please too many people, including many parents who felt their child should be in the class, so before we knew it there were fourteen in the class, and there was no benefit to Peter being with fourteen quite handicapped children with one teacher and one assistant.

They also felt that Peter's progress depended a lot on individual teachers, and that although at that time he had one of the best, they were worried about the teacher he would have the following year. Although he seemed happy and settled at the ESN(S) school, they began looking around for private schools which might accept him, despite the disapproval of the home teacher who still kept in touch and who warned them that ' "Private" schools might take him but they are just after the money and are not very good, they wouldn't really benefit him.'

When the campaigning of the education group in which they were involved resulted in the offer to set up a unit at Priory Bridge, Peter's parents 'jumped at the chance', despite a few reservations about moving him from an environment in which he seemed settled, to one which offered more opportunities but also more possibility of his being unable to cope.

The stories told by the parents of the other three Down's Syndrome children had much in common with Peter's. Valerie, also six, had settled well into an ordinary nursery school, but her place there was closed down because of pressure from the head of the special school, who wanted Valerie to attend her school full time. The one day a week that Valerie already spent in the ESN(S) school nursery had convinced her parents that 'The normal nursery was the place for her – the whole environment at the other place just was not good for her development, there was no example she could copy except that of the teacher, nobody could *do* enough to get a game going or understand a game.' The home teacher who had Valerie on her books but had never taught her backed the special school in their attempt to get Valerie to attend full time; and the health visitor, 'although she didn't advocate special education, didn't help us to look for anything else either'. Kevin's parents were warned against trying him in an ordinary school by their home teacher, despite his success in mixing with normal children at a social services day nursery, where his mother felt that 'He came on marvellous, and was just like any other child.' Although assessments placed him in the ESN(M) range, Kevin was placed in the local ESN(S) school where his parents were pleased at his educational progress but dismayed by his social regression. He began to eat with his hands instead of a knife and fork, to pull strange faces and to copy the more handicapped children he saw at school.

William was nine when the unit at Priory Bridge opened, and had a similar history to the other Down's Syndrome children; early integration in a playgroup and within his family, pressure from the authorities to send him to a special school, growing dissatisfaction on his parents' part with the kind of behaviour he was learning there. William's mother was the driving force behind the establishment of the unit at Priory Bridge; it was her article about William for a local paper which prompted the headmistress there to offer to set up a unit in her own school. His parents for a long time avoided joining the Society for Mentally Handicapped Children, 'not because of pride, but from an instinct that that wasn't the sort of thing to be associated with if you wanted to have a positive attitude to your child'. However, the social worker attached to the society heard Mrs Sullivan ask a question at a meeting about handicapped children and encouraged her to join.

Finding a Unit

When William's mother began attending the Mentally Handicapped Society meetings, the interests of the group were not very well defined.

There were all sorts of parents representing several different priorities, and we spent several months sorting out what we all wanted. We drew up a report for ourselves and we split up into various groups pursuing their own interests. The education group was left with school education, Jane was supposed to do the pre-school interest, another girl took up the parent support aspect which actually came to fruition in the Parent Support Group. That was for people with very severely handicapped children who were quite satisfied with special schools, because they felt their children were so handicapped they needed constant attention in a place where they could walk in at any time and sit down and play with them – they were happy that it wasn't primarily an educational establishment.

The education group included the parents of William, Kevin, Peter and Valerie. They decided to focus on the issue of integration, and to press for a special unit to be set up in an ordinary state school, which they felt would 'provide the best of both educational worlds: specialist teaching and the company of ordinary children'. They collected information at the suggestion of the principal educational psychologist in charge of special education, and at the end of 1977 presented proposals to the LEA for a unit of this kind, with details on spare capacity in local primary schools, transportation costs, and a copy of the timetable of one special school indicating the amount of individual tuition and the range of activities undertaken by children in that school. They explained the major cause of their dissatisfaction with ESN(S) schools for their children. They were concerned about the very narrow band of the ability range catered for and the consequent lack of suitable models for behaviour, language and education for the more able children and mentioned the waste of resources and strain on the children in journeys to and from the special school. They pointed out that the local authority had plans to close down primary schools in the area because of falling school rolls and that some of the available space could be used instead for integrated provision.

A reply eventually came, after several repeated requests. The education authority were 'not in favour of integration on the lines described', feeling that such a unit would not be 'practicable and compatible with the provision of efficient instruction in the school'. They preferred a policy of mild fraternisation of special schools with normal ones, and dismissed the parents' worry about the lack of good models of behaviour for their children with the comment that 'It would be wrong to rely, for these children, in more than a minimal way on chance learning as a result of copying other children.' To those who live or worked with the children daily, it was obvious that they had well-developed imitative skills and would copy movements and gesture which would show up in their fantasy play.

To some of the officials in the education authority, the parents' reluctance to have their child in a special school demonstrated a 'common psychopathology' and an inability to accept the child's handicap. One of the officials referred to the problems they had with 'overcooked mongols'. However, in talking to the researcher all the parents made a 'realistic' or conservative assessment of their child's present abilities and future development. There was no evidence to suggest that the parents were looking to an education in an ordinary school in order to gloss over the limitations of their children. They were concerned, however, that their children should have the best chance possible of participating in the life of their community. They did not want the evident handicap of their children to be a reason for putting them at an additional disadvantage. That, they felt, is what happened to their children in the schools for the severely subnormal.

The group met and wrote to the education authority several times more, but were unable to persuade them to reconsider their policy on integration. There was no attempt on the part of the authority to understand the reasons for the parents' request or to discuss it seriously with them. Not all of the relevant officials even seemed sure what their policy was. At one meeting the chairperson of the primary and special education sub-committee, when asked her views on the matter, began confidently enough, but soon faltered and turned to the principal educational psychologist to ask 'What *is* our view on this matter?' The parents seemed better informed than some of the education officials, who had not heard of the Haringay project, a similar scheme in operation on an experimental basis in a London school.

Despite their lukewarm reception from officials concerned with special education in the education department, the group were more kindly received elsewhere. The child psychology unit of the university wrote to the local press who published their letter, and also articles and editorials which prompted subsequent letters of enthusiastic support and also fervent disagreement from teachers and members of the public. One of the group was interviewed by the BBC in an item favouring integration, and the child psychology unit expressed support for a pilot scheme and a willingness to monitor it: 'Finally, and for us most encouraging of all, the headmistress of a local private school approached us with the offer to set up just the unit we wanted in her school.'

The headmistress made her initial approach to Mrs Sullivan, William's mother.

She phoned me up just after having seen my letter in the paper even though she hadn't seen the original article and so didn't know much of what it was about. She just knew that I wrote certain things about ugliness and children that she agreed with. She's obviously impulsive; she just phoned up and said that she thought it was great.

Mrs Sullivan's first thought was to put the headmistress in touch with Valerie's parents, who were particularly keen for her to go on from the private nursery school to further integrated education, but she then decided to try for something more ambitious. 'I asked if she would consider having a unit of mixed ages rather than the odd child, and the existing scheme came from there.'

The Unit Provision

The scheme was planned, discussed and established during the 1978 summer holidays. The headmistress rang Mrs Sullivan in July; in August a part-time teacher was found for the unit and the parents came in to decorate the basement room allocated to their children, and in September the new unit opened. The speed of the whole enterprise surprised and pleased many of the parents, used to long complicated deliberations with the state education system, but it did mean that there could be little teacher consultation, and the staff had no time to work out their feelings and adjust their teaching styles and techniques before the four Down's Syndrome children arrived at the beginning of the autumn term. The unit began with several other disadvantages. It lacked adequate space or facilities, occupying one small room and a corridor in the basement of the big Victorian house that was the school's main building, with access to a craft room shared by several other classes. The unit's room had a carpeted stone floor and blow heaters, and because Down's Syndrome children, due to circulation problems, do suffer more than most from the cold, the group was often cramped inside during cold spells. There were few resources apart from those created by the teacher or donated by parents, like the tea-set and a few dolls which arrived in the second term. Fees for the Down's Syndrome children were the same as those for other children in the school, which in 1978 was £270 per year. At the same time the per capita allowance for a child in a state ESN(S) school was around £2,000 per year.

The headmistress appointed a part-time teacher, Mrs Price, to teach the unit children in the mornings only. She was helped out one morning a week by a student volunteer, on another morning by an unemployed teacher, and on a third by the researcher from the child psychology unit who was monitoring the unit's progress.

Clearly the provision in the unit was far from ideal. If the unit had become part of a development plan in a local education authority the facilities could have been planned and developed in a totally different fashion. A state primary school could have been selected because of the availability of space, the interest of the staff and its connection to a sympathetic and appropriate secondary school. The teachers could have been prepared through discussion and information meetings and through visits to similar units for the needs of their new pupils. The group would have had their own full-time teacher and a welfare assistant, and a system of staff cover could have been arranged in the event of staff illness. The teaching space would have been sufficiently large for separate activities to coincide comfortably in the same classroom and for children to be away from others when they didn't wish to be in constant almost-touching contact. The group teacher would not have had to take sole responsibility for the supervision of her group at playtime, and other teachers would be involved in setting the examples which foster integration. Integration between the unit children and others would have been built up on an individual basis at the times of day when lessons or activities were compatible.

But the unit was not set up in this way. It was not part of a local authority scheme nor was it an 'experiment' financed and copiously staffed by research money, like the Haringay project. It was simply the result of an expression of choice by a group of parents who wished to have some control over the education of their 'handicapped' children. They were aware that their choice involved a risk but after careful consideration they felt it was worth taking that chance.

The Unit Day

Mrs Price had made a point of visiting the parents of the Down's Syndrome children before the unit opened to establish a personal link and to find out their thoughts and feelings about their child's education. Since all the parents seemed to share the same worry that their children had been copying the less able children in their special schools, she decided to 'model my class as much as practical on a "normal" class, and to form quite high expectations of the children'.

The day usually started with group songs and then children presented their personal 'news'. Individual work on reading and number would follow with some time for free play activities like building and puzzles before break. Break was a social time for chatting, sharing fruit and drinking milk. It also served a teaching function as some of the children had difficulty in chewing and swallowing and in drinking through a straw. The children then joined the rest of the school in the garden, accompanied by their teacher. At first the children huddled around her, chatting with her and sometimes competing for her attention, but she made a point of talking and playing with the other children and setting up joint playground games. Gradually the groups merged until after a few months the unit children were spread over the play area engaged in activities with a whole range of children. After break the children might do some painting and be joined by some children from the reception class, followed by further individual work and finally by group language games until lunch. At lunchtime, after eating their packed lunch with the reception class which they were to join in the afternoon, the unit children also mixed with the rest of the school in the playground. The games which Mrs Price had initiated soon became part of the playground culture and carried on even over the largely unsupervised lunch-break, with the other children insisting that the unit children take part.

The afternoon sessions produced predictable problems particularly for two of the younger children. They lost their home base and point of adult security when their teacher left after lunch. Their teacher was also the person who knew them best and was therefore most adept at responding to their needs and aware of the signs which indicated impending disturbance. Kevin at the best of times was an active physical child who needed more space than the unit classroom could offer and more physical games than were permitted in the sedate garden of the school. It soon became apparent that the school could not adapt to his needs in the afternoons and he went home when Mrs Price left. Peter had a different problem. At first he found a full school day simply exhausting and his parents took him home for a rest. After the first half-term he was gradually reintroduced for full days. Priory Bridge school closes on Wednesday afternoons, so the unit children initially spent four afternoons a week with a middle infant class. The teacher there was unfamiliar with their level of ability and their needs, and felt that much of the work required too much concentration especially for the younger children. As the afternoon sessions with the middle infant class were obviously not working out well, the unit children began to join instead with a smaller reception class, usually with a voluntary helper, where the children were younger and the teacher got to know both Mrs Price and her pupils well. This worked much better for a while. Mrs Grant, the class teacher, planned an afternoon's activities that she felt could be adapted to the level of the unit children. She incorporated poems or songs with which they were familiar, and it was clear that their interest and concentration on activities and stories were better at times than some of her own class.

Then in the second term, during the winter, a flu epidemic hit the school and many pupils and teachers, including Mrs Price, were off sick. Mrs Price's absence precipitated what the parents now look back on as 'The Crisis'. There was no cover arranged for her, so the children stayed in the ordinary class full time, several of them unwell themselves and restless, and with Kevin in particular reacting badly to the change of routine. There was a distinct possibility that the unit would be closed down. The headmistress obviously felt some conflict between her desire to help handicapped children and the need for her school to have a high academic standard in order to attract fee-paying parents. The difficult behaviour of some of the unit children while Mrs Price was away, was observed by some of the parents of the other children, and the headmistress worried that they would 'begin to wonder what they are paying for'.

The sense of unease persisted even after Mrs Price returned, centring around Kevin but with the headmistress casting real doubt on the continuation of the unit. When it became apparent that the unit would close down and most of the children be asked to leave unless an alternative scheme could be produced, William's mother stepped in. She organised voluntary helpers and parents to take the unit children swimming on one afternoon and to the town's Sports Centre for another two afternoons. This eased the situation to some extent but left several parents disappointed at the loss of integration, since the unit children were now only joining the ordinary class for one afternoon a week. The headmistress was still unhappy about keeping Kevin in her school, and the summer holidays were reached a year after the unit had opened, without any firm commitment to continue the unit in the following year. Some parents felt rather disappointed, one felt despairing: 'It's been a strain for us, its not been easy for us as parents. I feel we've tried to help, to meet the school more than halfway, but we're never going to feel at ease there.'

In fact the unit has continued. Kevin left, and went to an ESN(S) school, but not the one he had attended before he began at Priory

Bridge. His parents were disappointed, but had always preferred this second ESN(S) school. Mrs Price also left, but despite the low wages and lack of holiday pay, the headmistress appointed another excellent teacher to replace her. The current employment situation may well have contributed to the ease with which good teachers have been found for the unit. This teacher also stayed for a year, and then was recently replaced by a full-time teacher, who will have the unit children all day, rather than just for the mornings. The parents hope that this will improve the quality of their children's education, and make their integration with the non-handicapped children in the school a positive decision rather than something arising from the lack of available teachers. They are still concerned that integration should take place, and one parent recently donated a Portakabin no longer needed by his company to the school on the condition that it be used 'for the purposes of integration'.

Parents' Evaluation of the Unit

Having fought so hard to get some kind of alternative educational provision for their children, how do the parents of children in the unit feel about their child's education there?

Mrs Sullivan feels that the pace is much better for William than at the special school, where everything was very slow. His reading has improved, and so has his language. They have noticed his use of idiosyncratic speech like 'it's great' which enables him to sound more like other boys. His parents think that this is because what he hears at home is reinforced by his school experience now. 'He doesn't have two worlds which he can easily get confused. At special schools they have this frightful shorthand where they get what they want by making a few suggestive noises that the others know by habit means something.' William's parents have also noted a decrease in another of the habits they felt he had picked up at the special school, the over-enthusiastic greeting of strangers:

> One of the things about special school is the tremendous amount of instantaneous cuddling, it becomes simply a way of greeting people that's not always appropriate, and used to irritate the other children. It's fine when he knows people and they're friends, but not throwing his arms around some complete stranger. He doesn't do that so much any more. On the other hand, William seems more able to form real

relationships since attending the unit. He has started going round to see neighbours and adult friends to talk about school, as if testing out his own ability at being able to mix normally, and he has also begun to relate better to other children.

I never remember any genuine relationships at all with the children at the special school. He never spoke much of them or asked if they could come to play. They were more like 'patients' to him as in a hospital. The 'real' children were in his home environment. Now he refers to many other children at school and he greets them warmly, but naturally, when we are out and about and meet any of them, and they do likewise to him. This is perhaps the area of the greatest difference since he's been going to the unit.

William's parents see him as having two sets of behaviour, 'one that is the sort of tolerated behaviour of the special school; loud noises, silly laughs, belches and other rude noises, which he doesn't do much when he's out of school, at home or at the theatre or someone's house'. The longer William has been out of the special school, the more they feel he is dropping the first kind of behaviour in favour of a 'school-boyish sense of humour' and becoming 'much more ordinary'. They are very enthusiastic about the unit and the progess William has made there. He runs errands that don't involve crossing major roads, cleans and tidies up, gets his own lunch and goes swimming or to the library with his brother. William always has been well-integrated at home if not at school. They are a large and boisterous family, and William takes part in everything. His five siblings accept his handicap as a medical fact deserving little attention, and they respect the things he is good at, like swimming. They also enjoy the 'perks' of free teas and outings arranged for handicapped children and their siblings, but are dubious about these treats continuing, especially as their brother no longer attends the special school. As one of them remarked, 'What will happen when they find out that William's not really handicapped?' William's parents feel that attending the Priory Bridge unit rather than a special school has helped William both socially and academically.

Valerie's parents were initially very pleased with their daughter's progress in the unit. She was happy there, liked the teachers and the other children and seemed to be benefiting from the routine. Her mother thought that Valerie was more willing to learn because of the presence of older and more able children in the class. 'I think she's seen the other children reading aloud from a book and it's given her that bit of incentive to try the same.' However, the parents were very disappointed when the afternoon sessions broke down and the unit children ended up spending very little time in class with non-handicapped children, although there was still a good deal of playground contact. They felt that the unit was 'very much a self-contained little group', and although this provided both parents and children with a sense of solidarity they wouldn't get in a larger special school, Valerie's parents worried that she was getting less contact with 'normal' children than she had done in her previous nursery school. For a short time they began to wonder if they should have taken up the offer of a place for her in a small class in a village school. They had liked the teacher and the mixed ability age groups within the class, but had turned it down partly because of the long journey and partly because they were not sure that Valerie would have been able to manage without a helper. If it hadn't worked, they would have had no alternative but to send Valerie back to an ESN(S) school, and they were quite clear that the unit at Priory Bridge, for all its lack of space and resources, was infinitely preferable to that.

> There's no comparison. At the special school they never get a normal model, and they don't have a work programme like Priory Bridge. The general standard there is so low, behaviour and everything. The very thought of her going to that special school is revolting.

Recent developments such as the employment of a full-time teacher and the possible use of a Portakabin, have made them more enthusiastic again about the possibilities offered by the unit.

The parents of Helen and Eileen are bound to view the unit in a different light from the parents of the Down's Syndrome children, who were largely responsible for it being set up. Helen and Eileen were both in ordinary classes at Priory Bridge before the unit opened, and their transfer there several months after the Down's Syndrome children arrived came initially as something of a shock to their parents. Helen had started at Priory Bridge at Easter and towards the end of the year was moved to Mrs Price's class. Her mother knew she had changed classes, 'but I didn't know it was a unit until it was almost Christmas'. She admitted being surprised and at first slightly disappointed, because she felt Helen had 'come up in the world' by being in a normal class, but after a year she was very pleased and felt that Helen had benefited enormously from the individual attention and made 'tremendous progress', especially in reading and in developing her imagination. For the first time she could feel competent and relied upon, rather than always being the slowest and least capable.

The parents of Eileen, like those of Helen, were slightly shocked to find she had been moved from a normal class at Priory Bridge into the unit. They had sent her to the private school in the first place because she didn't seem to be learning well in her village primary school and they hoped the smaller classes would help her to get on. Their first reaction to her transfer was that she would lose out on academic work, and they sent several notes to her teacher asking for her to be encouraged to work hard. A typical note suggested that 'Eileen would take greater pride in a page of well-executed and meaningful writing than in a pretty picture.' However Eileen seemed to progress well, particularly in her reading, and her parents now feel that her presence in the unit 'works very well'.

Kevin's father summed up many of the benefits the parents saw in integrated education when he described how he felt about the unit shortly after it opened, and before his own child was excluded.

> I'd have to give it a whole year before trying to assess it properly, but at present I think it's marvellous for him. Not just for him, I think it's marvellous for the normal children he's associating with, it brings them a bit nearer to what a handicapped child is. I think with the severely handicapped, when any child has come into contact with the likes of Kevin, when they come up against the severely handicapped they're about half way there, because they've experienced it. It's like with all the children in the unit, they're not so severe that the other children are afraid of them. And when they do come up against the severely handicapped there will not be the fear there.

Of course Kevin's parents were disappointed when he was rejected by the school. They were told right at the end of the school year that he wouldn't be able to return and they felt hurt about what they saw as inconsiderate treatment. They were embarrassed at having to go back to the school authorities to ask for a place at a special school. But fortunately the head of Kevin's new school treated them with kindness and respect and they have now recovered from the initial blow of 'failure'.

Peter's parents are very happy with his progress at the unit. He no longer talks with his tongue out, a habit that was tolerated at the ESN(S) school, and he has become much more enthusiastic about going to school. He has formed real friendships with the other children in the unit, unlike when he was at the special school; 'He plays better with William than his brother does with his friends.' But apart from these social improvements, his parents also remarked on his increased self-awareness and conversation, and his reading and writing. The strong group feeling among the children is something that several of the parents remarked upon. The older or more able children will look after the younger ones in the group, blowing their noses, praising them for good work and encouraging them to learn. Each child is seen as making a particular contribution to the group – Valerie will always join in and try things, William is the comedian who is very perceptive to other's ideas, Kevin was very good at retaining information needed for games.

Peter's parents can't imagine what they'd do if the unit at Priory Bridge collapsed. 'We just couldn't bear the thought of it.' Their determination to avoid segregated education for their child was strengthened by a visit to the seaside where they saw a group of mentally handicapped children on an outing.

They came to the beach holding hands, all plodding along with their heads down. They looked as though they'd come straight from an institution. Peter was half a mile away by the sea, having a great time. They didn't do anything, they just sat and stared into space. They didn't communicate at all, whereas Peter has always got something to add to the conversation. Half of them had Down's Syndrome. Why is there such a contrast between Peter and these others?

Postscript

As we have made clear the unit at Priory Bridge cannot serve as a blueprint for other people to copy, it has too many obvious disadvantages for that. What is quite remarkable is the relative success with which the unit has been established despite the meagre means at its disposal. The children have learnt well and have blossomed socially, and this seems to be the result of many factors. The first is one of scale. It is commonly thought that special schools provide a small secure environment for handicapped children. But watching the children in the unit over a year developing a sense of group identity and solidarity has prompted a rather different view. Children and adults within special schools may become overwhelmed with the large numbers of children with severe problems which surround them. A unit base for handicapped children, even within a much larger school, may be much more humanly manageable. In the particular case of the unit children they would certainly be in the higher ability range within the schools for the severely subnormal. It must be to their advantage to be with children who are more developed socially and linguistically than they are. It was quite clear that they did watch and learn from others. The idea that such children 'cannot learn by imitation' is mistaken, potentially damaging and easily disproved by observation.

But the unit at Priory Bridge does confirm that it is possible to successfully educate Down's Syndrome children within an ordinary school; a rather unsurprising conclusion already amply documented both in this country and abroad. It demonstrates even more forcibly the degree to which parents are made to struggle in order to exert some choice over the special education of their children.

We have deliberately avoided making this report an 'academic' document. It is a story; an episode in the lives of some children and their families. We hope that it will be used by parents wishing to know of the experience of others and by professionals who wish to evaluate the effects of their decisions on the lives of their clients. We would like to see it as a spur to other parents, who want to exert their influences over the educational options open to them, to develop their own schemes in their own areas.

PROFESSIONALS

21 DAME EVELYN FOX (1874–1955)

Patricia Potts

This description by Patricia Potts of the career of Dame Evelyn Fox illustrates how much influence voluntary initiatives could have on local and central government committees, how they allocated resources, co-ordinated services and made significant changes in the legal status of the mentally deficient. It also illustrates how the training of relevant professionals was organised, officially recognised and rewarded; and how piecemeal was the way in which a system of special education developed, with the impetus frequently coming from voluntary associations.

Evelyn Fox's family came from county Longford in Ireland, but she was born and educated in Switzerland. Her enlightened mother allowed Evelyn to travel alone and become more independent than was common for young, upper-middle-class women. She read history at Somerville College, Oxford (1895–8) and then spent a year at the recently-founded London School of Economics. Between 1899 and 1906, Evelyn Fox worked as a publisher's research assistant, a routine job to which she felt no particular commitment, and it was then that she became attracted to the cause of the mentally handicapped. The Royal Commission on the Care and Control of the Feeble-Minded sat from 1904 to 1908 and Evelyn Fox saw that its report could initiate far-reaching changes in legislation and provisions. She had the confidence, private resources and energy to make a success of her sudden, but serious, decision to devote herself to the welfare of the mentally deficient.

Evelyn Fox started clubs for children from special schools, joined the National Association for the Promotion of the Welfare of the Feeble-Minded and, although always a voluntary worker, undertook a social work training at the Women's University Settlement in Southwark. This was followed by experience with the Charity

134

Organisation Society. When the Royal Commission reported, a 'Joint Committee in Support of the Mental Deficiency Bill' was set up, composed of representatives of relevant voluntary organisations, and Evelyn Fox was an active member. The Act was passed in 1913 and came into operation in April 1914; mental deficiency was defined as 'a condition of arrested or incomplete development of the mind existing before the age of 18, whether arising from inherent causes or induced by disease or injury'. Four categories of defectives were described: idiots, imbeciles, feeble-minded and moral imbeciles.

Local authorities were not forced to take the initiative with regard to the ascertainment, certification and placement of defectives; they had 'duties' and 'powers' but few statutory obligations. Their mental deficiency committees often financed voluntary mental welfare associations as this spared them appointing their own officers. To make sure that local authorities were zealous in their efforts to implement the Act and that the voluntary bodies worked efficiently, the 'Central Association for the Care of the Mentally Defective' was formed in October 1914, with Evelyn Fox as Honorary Secretary. The chairman, Sir Leslie Scott, KC, said: 'At that time Miss Fox was already showing the qualities which were later to make her the architect of the mentally deficient services.'

The voluntary societies that belonged to the Central Association (from 1923 the Central Association for Mental Welfare), had four main activities: the identification of children as mentally deficient; the undertaking of case-work with their families (both of these done on behalf of the local authorities); the setting-up of occupation centres for children and young people; and the education and training of teachers and other professionals who worked with the handicapped. These developments were largely the result of Evelyn Fox's versatile crusading. Occupation centres had first been advocated in 1914 but there was no official financial support from the Board of Control until 1923, when a trained organiser was also appointed. The first training course for special school teachers was set up by the Birmingham Education Committee in 1915 and Evelyn Fox was responsible for the employment of peripatetic educational psychologists, and speech and occupational therapists.

The shortage of funds, staff and equipment during the First World War meant that many local authorities did nothing to implement the Mental Deficiency Act. In 1918 Evelyn Fox published an article in the 'Eugenics Review' that was partly a critical discussion of the 1913 Act and its achievements and partly an exhortation to the authorities to take immediate action in a cause of 'national importance'. The main problem was the imprecision of the categorisation of mental defectives, which made medical officers reluctant to certify individuals, especially when information about their early history was lacking. How could you certify a 'moral' imbecile and demonstrate that 'some permanent mental defect, coupled with strong, vicious or criminal propensities, on which punishment has had little or no deterrent effect' had been present 'from birth or from an early age'? The whole process was dependent upon subjective interpretations, some officers using a yardstick of literacy and some of instability. Regional variations in standards meant that some 'persons obviously defective in their mental attainments and conduct are not considered certifiable, and they must be left now as before the passing of the Act, to voluntary organisation to assist.'

Evelyn Fox argued that mental deficiency was not sufficiently understood, that those in authority were too ignorant to make competent assessments and that the situation could not be improved by extra medical examinations but only as a result of large-scale, longitudinal epidemiological studies. 'It is only with the actual experience of the troubles, miseries and dangers which beset the ordinary feeble-minded boy or girl, when competing in the outside world, that a just estimate can be formed of what is involved in the term feeble-minded.' She thought that special schools benefited feeble-minded children because of the additional discipline and the tailored curriculum but that special school leavers would be likely to need permanent institutional care because segregation would protect. Segregation would also be cheaper in the long run because 'To allow defectives, who are a danger to others and are unable to protect themselves, at large, is to spend money on them directly or indirectly, through the police, the courts of law, the prisons, the workhouse, charitable sources; it is economy to spend it in protecting them in institutions.'

Evelyn Fox concluded her article with a description of the work of the voluntary associations, which she saw as a social-work role played with official support. She argued that the voluntary associations' help with notification, assessment and the provision of accommodation should decrease and local authorities take their responsibilities seriously. She finished her article by discussing 'one of the gravest dangers to which the state is exposed: the continual increase of the number of illegitimate children of defective women'. The War should not hold up the work because of 'the importance to the nation of caring efficiently and kindly for the mentally defective'.

Between 1914 and 1924 Evelyn Fox was a co-opted member of the LCC Mental Deficiency and Mental Health Committees which brought her into contact with professional civil servants, local government officers and politicians. Between 1924 and 1929 she sat on the Wood Committee appointed by George Newman, chief medical officer to the Board of Education, to discover the numbers of feeble-minded children and to examine their educational provision. The main recommendation was the abolition of certification so that children who were not feeble-minded, but nevertheless severely retarded, could be provided with special education without the stigma attached to certification; they were to be regarded as 'social failures'.

If the majority of children for whom these schools for retarded children are intended are, *ex hypothesi*, to lead the lives of ordinary citizens, with no shadow of a 'certificate' and all that it implies to handicap their careers, the schools must be brought into closer relation with the Public Elementary School System and presented to parents not as something both distinct and humiliating, but as a helpful variation of the ordinary school.

In 1926 Evelyn Fox was elected honorary secretary of the new Child Guidance Council which included Cyril Burt as chairman of the executive committee and Dr William Moodie as director of the first clinic. She resigned in 1932 to concentrate on her work for the mentally deficient, a decision thankfully accepted by the council, with whom she had often had disagreements.

Evelyn Fox was determined to develop the role of the specialist social worker in the field of mental welfare and at a conference held shortly after the Mental Treatment Act became law in July 1930, she made a speech advocating training for all social workers. A training course for psychiatric social workers had been established at the LSE in 1929, financed like the first child guidance clinic by the Harkness 'Commonwealth Fund' of America, but there was no recognised training for mental health social workers, as distinct from the PSWs who were based in child guidance clinics. The Central Association for Mental Welfare arranged short courses for mental health workers in the thirties and, after the war, the National Association for Mental Health ran diploma courses for local authority mental health officers and for teachers of the mentally handicapped in occupation centres, recognised by local education authorities.

At the biennial conference of the CAMW in 1934, Evelyn Fox made a speech about the way in which mental deficiency had been ignored in favour of mental illness: 'The subnormal, unstable group of cases were left to be dealt with by the non-expert, despite the fact that their social adjustment invited the cooperation of the best that psychiatric, psychological and social services could provide.' This time, she was concerned that the government was not implementing the recommendations of the Wood Committee and the CAMW therefore undertook to mobilise public opinion. Evelyn Fox's speech has been described as 'a watershed in the history of the CAMW'. Between the Wars, Evelyn Fox enlisted the support of several influential Cambridge women. Ida Darwin founded a mental hospital (the term 'asylum' was abolished in 1930) and later became a lay commissioner of the Board of Control. Dame Ellen Pinsent, a colleague on the Wood Committee and the first woman commissioner of the Board of Control after its reorganisation in 1930, had, as a member of the National Association for the Feeble-Minded, been involved with the placing of children in appropriate special schools in Birmingham since the 1890s and as a result of this had given evidence to the Royal Commission on the Care and Control of the Feeble-Minded (1904-8). In 1901 the Board of Control had appointed Ellen Pinsent to chair the new After-Care Committee through which she advocated boarding schools and sheltered residential workshops for the feeble-minded. She had a considerable influence on the development of Evelyn Fox's own views and their acceptance by civil servants. Ida Darwin's daughter, Ruth Rees Thomas, was also a commissioner of the Board of Control and a generous benefactor to the NAMH for which she worked as an educational psychologist. Ellen Pinsent's daughter, Hester Adrian, became the second Vice-President of the NAMH and was active in mental health affairs in Cambridge, particularly with the Fulbourne Hospital.

Between 1936 and 1939, Evelyn Fox was a member of a Committee, chaired by the President of the Child Guidance Council, Lord Feversham, that undertook a survey of voluntary mental health services. Like Evelyn Fox, Lord Feversham thought that social work should be taken seriously and he was a trained probation officer, believing that a secure childhood would prevent many problems. But unlike Evelyn Fox, he was not regarded as wonderfully bright. The publication of his Report in 1939 was unfortunately timed and resulted in it not being as widely read as it might have been. The Committee recommended that the Mental After-Care Association, the CAMW, the National Council for Mental Health and the Child Guidance Council should amalgamate to form a single, co-ordinated, national mental health organisation. In 1942 the Provisional National Council for Mental Health was set up and in 1946 the NAMH was established with Evelyn Fox as a vice-president. In 1937 she was awarded the CBE and in 1947 the DBE.

Dame Evelyn Fox retired to her cottage in Sussex, suffering from increasing deafness and rheumatism. She had always been a great country woman, although inclined to talk shop with her visitors, and she would bring flowers for the office on Monday mornings. Those who worked with her described her as energetic, devoted, enthusiastic, inspiring, sympathetic and affectionate, with an Irish sense of humour. She was formidable in argument but enjoyed 'low-brow' cinema for relaxation. One colleague says that Evelyn Fox reminded her of an Oxford don, who was also witty and charming; a 'fascinator'.

As a committed pioneer, Evelyn Fox was tenacious, intolerant and dictatorial, impatient of 'official caution' and very demanding of those who worked with her. At the NAMH, Evelyn Fox's henchwomen were Aphra Hargrove, Marjorie Welfare and Jean Mackenzie, full of character, clever and cliquey. Only Jean Mackenzie was a paid administrator; she was Evelyn Fox's secretary and greatest friend. Evelyn Fox was both intellectual and warm, an expert fund-raiser and organiser; she could not bear to see children hanging about on the streets doing nothing. But by the 1950s her style was out-of-date and the supply of educated, self-sacrificial women with private incomes was drying up. Evelyn Fox's comrades were very badly paid but she regarded money as unimportant. With the establishment of the welfare state in the late 1940s, the role of the NAMH had to change, from being a provider of services to an informed pressure group and government critic.

Evelyn Fox loved to tour the country to canvass support and stir up public opinion, arguing for a recognition of individual educational needs and for a separation of 'defective' from concepts of 'mad' and 'immoral'. However, there are contradictions in her attitudes: she was in favour of segregated education and living for the mentally deficient because it was more efficient, cheaper and protective, but she was also anxious for their socialisation and involvement with local communities. She was affectionate towards mentally handicapped children but also fearful of them for what they represented as a social group within the nation, an incongruity not uncommon at the time. As an educated, independent and confident woman, Evelyn Fox found in mental welfare her life's work, and in the co-ordinated voluntary association her ideal channel. She had more freedom to publicise her views than if she had been a career social worker, teacher or civil servant and she enjoyed considerable power.

22 JENNY: A CAREER IN SPECIAL EDUCATION

Jenny Woodward

Jenny is a teacher in the special needs department of a large city comprehensive school. She did an initial training course primarily in special education, unlike most teachers entering special education who have no additional qualifications beyond their teaching certificate, but who may take a diploma in special education after they have been teaching for a while. Jenny's first job was in a day school for maladjusted children, where she worked for three years. She describes here the twists and turns in her career.

It's difficult to remember now why I got involved in special education. At school I knew I wanted to go to a teacher training college, but there wasn't a particular subject that I wanted to teach. I'd worked in play centres after school and in the holidays to earn a bit of money, and I had a boyfriend whose sister was very severely subnormal . . . I think that was one reason I became interested in subnormality. I took two 'A' levels, geography and religious knowledge. I wasn't a brainbox at school, I found exams very difficult. That's partly why now I'm a teacher I keep saying schools shouldn't be concentrating on academic learning all the time. There are so many other important things. I find the whole exam system appalling, perhaps because of my own experience of finding things quite hard at school.

I applied to a teacher training college that had just started offering a three year course in special education. There were only a couple of colleges where you could take courses like that. By then I was absolutely sure that that was what I wanted to do, and I worked hard. There was a certain amount on the history of special education and we looked at different sorts of handicap, but the course concentrated mainly on ways of overcoming learning difficulties. I did my first teaching practice with a reception class in a primary school and my second long one I spent in an ESN school. During the last year we had to do something associated more with mainstream education so I went into a primary school again, but all through the course I knew that I wanted to get into special education — I was never so interested in physical handicap, I wanted to work with children who found learning difficult but whose bodies were intact.

On the course we went on visits to different kinds of schools. I remember going to a boys' approved school for a weekend. And we looked at practical ways of helping children when they've got difficulties with reading, like word wheels and techniques for dealing with reversals. I remember one set of work we were assessed on which involved preparing ideas and materials for a reading lesson. We had to read around a bit, and make up our own apparatus with cards and boxes. So much of the course was practical, it wasn't just a load of old theory.

The first job I had was working in a day school for maladjusted children and I found that the course I had done did provide me with ideas. I was very lucky because I had a gradual introduction to the school. Our course finished early so I started six weeks before the end of the summer term on a supply basis. The teacher I was replacing was still there, so I had a chance to see how she worked with the group, to do some team teaching with her and to just get to know the children. Some days I would only teach a couple of lessons and see what else went on in the school for the rest of the day.

After the summer holidays I started full swing into it. It was hard work, but there was a lot of support from the head and the staff as a whole. After a year and a half, two years maybe, I was still enjoying it but I felt I ought to move on. It began to feel a bit claustrophobic working in such a small school and I felt I needed some mainstream experience, to work with a larger number of staff in an ordinary school. The head kept telling me I ought to do that too, for the sake of my career. But I didn't look too hard for other jobs. Then towards the end of my third year at the school, things started to go wrong. I started to realise that many of the children we took shouldn't be there, that they hadn't been offered the kind of help in their mainstream school that could have kept them there. I began to see that there were many times where children probably would never have got referred out of particular schools for special education if there had been less pressures on teachers within the mainstream, if the teachers had had smaller classes and chances for retraining. There were certain things that really bothered me about what was being offered — or rather not offered — to the children in my school, and I started speaking out against the things I didn't approve of. The new head who had just come into the school seemed to make far too many changes too quickly; changes in curriculum and break times, changes in classes and groups of children.

From that time I started finding it difficult working there. When things are happy and secure and there's plenty of support you can put all your energy into problems that occur. You can cope if a kid blows out, or if there's a difficult home visit. There are plenty of stresses and strains in the job anyway, and if your private life or social life are stressful too, or if you're not happy and secure in the job, then you don't feel able to cope. You begin to feel maladjusted yourself, like a nervous wreck. The head seemed to be worrying about so many trivial little things while we were coping with one crisis after another. All the time I was speaking out about the things I disagreed with. At one stage it got to the point where I could hardly face going in in the mornings. That's when I knew I had to get out, or I wasn't going to be any good to anybody.

I decided I wanted to work in a comprehensive, with a wider variety of children. I didn't want to be a subject teacher; I wanted to develop some expertise in ways of helping children to cope with their lessons in the mainstream, by giving them extra support in reading and writing and spelling. I applied for a job supervising a remedial department in a secondary school, but the post required experience of teaching in the mainstream which I didn't have. So I started instead at my present job, working in the special needs department of a large London comprehensive.

It took me a while to get used to the big building and the timetables after being at such a small school. The school had mixed ability teaching for all subjects except English, maths and French, and during my first year I taught some of the low English groups on a withdrawal basis. In my second year I got involved as a deputy head of house too and took on some pastoral duties. It made me look more closely at what caused children to be seen as problems, what made them be disruptive and end up getting referred by the psychologist to an opportunity class or ESN class or a 'maladjusted' group. I felt we should be looking more at what was offered in the way of curriculum to children in the mainstream — all children, not just the academic ones who can pass exams and work hard. I started spending a lot of time discussing ideas like this with the co-ordinator of the special needs department, and we both went on courses and conferences where we met other people and heard their point of view. I'd been in the school long enough by then not to worry about what I was going to teach in next week's lessons, so I had more time to think about the implications of what I was doing. I

felt our department was becoming a dumping ground for children that
other teachers couldn't cope with. Children with learning problems
were supposed to come to us for extra help with reading and writing in
small groups instead of going to French lessons. Instead it seemed like
a lot of the children who were being sent to us were in 'B' groups for
English and came because they were disruptive in French lessons, not
because they needed our specialist help. Yet there were many first
years who really did need extra work with basic reading and writing to
help them to survive in the school, and we couldn't fit them in. The
school had a tutorial unit for children with behaviour problems, our
role was to support children with learning difficulties so they could
cope in their other lessons. We couldn't do that if we were also seen as
a dumping ground for kids who were kicked out of their classes for
misbehaving.

Often they were misbehaving because they couldn't cope in certain
lessons. There are many teachers in comprehensive schools who are
not really committed to mixed ability teaching, who prefer to take the
'O' and 'A' level groups and leave the new teachers with the first and
second years. There are many who see mixed ability teaching as
teaching to the top or to the middle of the band. It's unrealistic to
expect teachers to work with the whole ability range anyway when
they get inadequate preparation time, less and less resources and little
support from their departments.

I'd like us to get more involved in the school as a whole, and try to
support those teachers so that they *can* work out programmes to teach
children of all ability levels. I would prefer it if our department didn't
get any money, but instead all the subject departments contributed
money to the special needs department, and we provided them with the
resources to teach the less able children themselves. That has started on
a small scale already. We discovered some history worksheets at the
last Remedial Books Exhibition which were particularly good for
children who find reading and writing difficult, and the history budget
contributed towards these. We've also tried to get the library to order
interesting books for children who don't read very well, and we've
given remedial catalogues and inspection copies of useful books to
various mainstream teachers. But we have to be very careful and
diplomatic. If we stood up and said directly some of the things we
believe, about the curriculum not meeting children's needs, there would
be a lot of bad feeling within the school.

During this last year I've had the chance to get a different kind of
experience in my job. Instead of just withdrawing children for small

English groups, I was asked to set up withdrawal groups for the thirty or so most needy first years, the ones who were coming into secondary school with reading ages of six and a half to seven and were going to need a lot of extra support no matter how well the subject teachers organised their lessons. So instead of teaching seventy children once or twice a week, I could concentrate on working with those twenty-eight first years.

They are allocated to various tutor groups and take most of their lessons with the other first years in their group, but for six or seven lessons a week I withdraw them in nines or tens to teach in a small group. Often I teach them the same subjects that their tutor group are taking with the subject teacher. I run it more or less like a primary class; there is an interest table and we talk a lot. The children have the security of spending much of their time in the same classroom with one teacher. I don't agree with the idea of having a special class but I think the transition from a small primary school to a very large comprehensive is especially difficult for children who have problems with reading and writing, and if we can give them the security of spending some time in their first year in a small group with a supportive teacher, then that can prevent problems developing later. It's been interesting and I think successful, and I'd like to do it again with next year's intake, if I'm still here.

I've been thinking lately about what I should do next. I've had experience now of two different schools, and of being deputy head of house in one of them. I feel that I now need a year without any practical teaching, to read and study. I'd like to develop more theoretical knowledge and become aware of what's been written in the six years since I left college. There's no time to read a lot of books and have interesting philosophical discussions when you're teaching all day. You spend all your time either doing school work or making sure you have a good social life as well, because the job isn't your whole life. I'm starting to build up ideas of my own now. I'd like to go and talk to other people who are working in special education within the mainstream, to see what they are doing and what materials they are using, to see what is successful and what doesn't work. There's not enough pooling of ideas and knowledge. Everyone is working in isolation in their own school. So I've applied to be seconded for an advanced diploma course in the teaching of ESN(M) kids next year, and hope that will give me a chance to look around a bit. After that I might try to get a position of responsibility, so that I'd be in a position to try and change a few things. I don't think I could ever go back into a special school now. At one point last year I thought that after two years away I'd like to go back to my first school. But I feel that we shouldn't have so many special schools, so that would be going against all my beliefs. I might consider working within a special school if I had a particular responsibility to liaise with ordinary schools and see how children could be supported within the mainstream rather than kept at the special school. I don't know what jobs are around at the moment. I don't just want to be a teacher who takes children out for extra reading and writing help. I'd like to be in a position where I could change things in the mainstream, and help to make the whole curriculum more relevant to children's needs.

23 BARRY MARKS: A CALIFORNIAN PROGRAM SPECIALIST

Tony Booth

Barry Marks works as a program specialist in a relatively small school district in California serving a largely rural school population of 30,000 students. The creation of 500 new posts in California with the title 'program specialist' was an indirect result of the passing of Public Law 94-142 by the Federal Government of the USA which directed each State to provide an education for all *handicapped children in the* least restrictive educational environment *compatible with their educational* needs. *Following the passing of the Federal Law each State formulated its own law which specified the manner in which the law would be implemented in the State's school system. California, the largest and richest State, surpassed the Federal Law in terms of the spirit and cost of implemention of its own legislation. The job of program specialist was one of the posts created by the State in its attempt to go beyond PL 94-142.*

When Barry left high school he studied for a degree taking courses mainly in the area of international relations. He had had no intention of becoming a teacher but:

> after a year of law school I started into teacher training mainly because of the Vietnam War. There were deferments for teachers and after a year of training I gained my certificate, received a deferment and taught in a Los Angeles continuation high school, a form of alternative secondary education peculiar to the United States which is less competitive and more flexible than the standard schools. I taught normal students — whatever normal is — at least they weren't labelled handicapped. Most of them came there after they had been in trouble with the law or school authorities. They were trouble makers and dropouts. I taught there for three years and then moved to Santa Cruz to a program for students who had been found guilty

of a criminal offence and sent to a juvenile hall, or residential detention centre. The aim of the program was to get them out of the juvenile hall and into the community. I did that for a year and then I started teaching the severely mentally retarded.

Without specialist training Barry soon developed a considerable interest and aptitude for his new work. He became increasingly fascinated with the problems of the Down's Syndrome students who were often unwilling or unable to display what he felt to be their true competence. He considered that their biological inheritance had given them thought processes which were out of step with those of biologically normal students. His interest was further elaborated when he became involved in an art project which examined the 'creative potential' and style of Down's Syndrome students. He was astounded by the beauty of their art work and by the long periods of time for which they painted without needing or seeking supervision in stark contrast to their approach to other periods of the school day. They were able to use an unending inner source of ideas which were not more basic but were of a different quality from those of 'normal' students. Barry considered that, through their paintings, they yielded 'a glimpse of what it was like to be a person who was biologically different'.

Barry has taken an academic as well as a practical interest in Down's Syndrome. He scans the literature and has written and spoken on the subject. He became well known within special educational circles in his school district and it is not surprising that, when the post of 'program specialist' was advertised, it was suggested that he should apply. In selecting applicants the authorities sought people who had expertise in a particular area of handicap and classroom experience. Barry was duly appointed to the post along with three others in his school district.

He saw the task of defining the scope of his job as 'like asking me to describe the Pacific Ocean':

The idea was to have someone who would be an implementer and instigator of new ideas. Special education had become fairly stagnant around the country. New ideas have been very slow to creep into the system. I'm not sure whose idea it was but when the State plan was drawn up this was part of it — that there would be a position that was neither an administrator nor a classroom teacher but was somewhere in between.

Program specialists have the responsibility to come up with better ideas about how the system can function solely in terms of what is better for the students and not in order to make life easier for the staff or principal [administrative head of a group of schools].

It's quite peculiar to have such a vague position actually prescribed by State law and being such a vague position it's been open to tremendous criticism. The only thing that saved it was that the law required it. The words in the law which define the position like 'co-ordinate' and 'facilitate' can be interpreted in any way. It suits those people who like a wide latitude to determine their own work but others who like a clear job description have found it disconcerting. I spend some weeks working entirely at my desk fulfilling bureaucratic demands.

Others may involve meetings with professional administrators and teachers and at other times I may spend a four day stretch devising an appropriate educational plan for an individual child.

In the same way that each State had to satisfy the requirements of Federal law by producing a State plan, each school district within California devised its own implementation policy. In Barry's school district there were three other program specialists and this permitted some degree of specialisation. In other parts of the State a program specialist might work for a 'huge mammoth urban district'. (In Sacramento with a total population of 600,000 there were 18 program specialists.)

The system in my part of the State is grafted onto past developments in special education and also depends on the political history of the area. The number of new posts is based on how many Individuals With Exceptional Needs or IWENS — they don't even sound human any more — are discovered in the district. It's gotten to be a joke because each district actually determines its own number of IWENS; individual children who have been identified and for whom the paperwork has been completed.

The plans of some school districts did not appear to conform to the spirit of State law and an attempt was made to bring them back into line.

Some of the districts decided to make their program specialists administrators with responsibility for evaluating teachers and overseeing programs. The State had to remind those areas that that wasn't the purpose of the job and threatened to cut the monies for these kinds of position unless they changed the nature of the posts. These areas have been slow to respond and so far the State hasn't made them but things are moving rapidly at the moment.

Barry had to interpret the nature of his job as the demands of his school district responded to constant revisions of State law. The post which he occupied and the other new post created by State legislation, a resource specialist assigned to each school with the job of co-ordinating the educational plans for IWENS within the school, seemed to be two of the very few fixed points of the legislation.

Whilst many of his duties were left up to him there were some clear directions to his role. He was meant to foster plans for mainstreaming of children traditionally excluded from schools because of their handicap and was closely involved in the process of developing Individual Educational Programs or IEPs; a process which involved a considerable increase in paperwork and lay at the heart of the discomfort and changed working life of several professional groups.

It's part of our job to explain the paperwork to others and many of them find it a mystery or resent doing it or resist doing it. I've spent many hours trying to communicate to parents that it's not just paper − there's a meaning behind all this − and that meaning is that these children who really need the services should be receiving them.

Whenever it is suggested that a child has a special need all those who are actively involved in the education of the child, including the parents and even the child when it seems appropriate, meet to develop jointly a future educational plan. For every child who is identified as having 'exceptional needs' a further meeting has to take place once a year. The plan which is developed is not just a list of general guidelines but specifies the form of additional support the child will receive. It then becomes incumbent on the school district to deliver the services. The IEP is a legally binding document and failure to fulfil the obligation it specifies can result in litigation:

In theory the paperwork is a good idea but meetings can vary greatly. With some parents or teachers it can become very volatile and they can become very angry. It depends on the chemistry of the people involved. Sometimes it can be just an exercise in filling out the forms; just a formality to rubber stamp a child into a particular program. But I have seen children whose needs have never really been carefully thought through before being given proper consideration for the first time during this process. At such times parents, teachers and other specialists have been surprised that they knew so little about what was going on. So it can be a really thoughtful, creative process particularly from the parents' point of view. It is very different from sitting down with a teacher and hearing 'she's got on fine this year' or 'she hasn't progressed much' – general statements which don't mean a thing.

Each meeting has a chairperson and a case manager. The chairperson is usually an administrator or program specialist and the case manager is generally a school nurse or school psychologist, who unlike an educational psychologist in the UK is generally attached to one particular school. The chairperson's role is largely clerical. It involves notifying participants about meetings, obtaining permission from parents to conduct assessments, providing test materials for teachers, keeping the file up to date, ensuring that reports are handed in on time and that agreed deadlines are met. The meetings have introduced a new set of power relations for the participants. In some school districts school psychologists have responded to the threat of a new professional in an elevated position in the hierarchy by gaining an agreement from the educational administrators that program specialists would receive one quarter per cent less than them in salary.

The roles in the meetings are unique to our area. In our small rural district the level of administration has been mediocre at best. When the new requirements were introduced for drastically increased paper work the administration had to recruit psychologists and school nurses to keep track of students and ensure that IEPs were 'in compliance' with the law. People were taken out of traditional roles and became care takers of the system. At the same time as psychologists and nurses were removed from the classroom under the weight of administrative pressures program specialists who often had considerable classroom experiences and already had contacts with the teachers, were moving into the classroom, forming coalitions with teachers and changing things that had been the same for many years.

School nurses had had a role in normal education which was limited to checking eyesight and hearing and problems of general health. Their role in special education had always been much broader but even so the special meetings required a considerable increase in their professional competence. They are responsible for the health area and have to interpret, for the meeting, everything that's in the medical folder and ensure that the physical tests are up to date and reliable. It used to be the task of administrators, when they had the time, to check that assessments were brought up to date but now it's being done at these meetings right out in front of the parents. This has created an entirely new world where inefficiencies just cannot be hidden. The whole procedure has placed tremendous pressure on school principals who had very little interest in special education or were even antagonistic to it and school nurses who rarely dealt with handicapped students and schools psychologists who only used psychological tests to determine whether a student was severely retarded or not. Suddenly they were thrust into these meetings to interpret data with which they were totally unfamiliar.

In practice the person who has most influence in a special meeting may depend more on the force of their personality and strength of their arguments than on their formal position within the hierarchy. It is quite possible for parents, with a clear and firm commitment to the provision of particular services for their children, to have these written in the educational plan.

Once a child has been recorded as an IWEN and an IEP has been produced the school district can claim $2,400 from State funds which goes into a central pool for the development of special educational services for the area. The school authorities have to keep a careful watch over the services that are recommended, particularly where the support of professional staff is involved. Speech therapists, for example, have been in short supply and whilst in theory the additional State money can be used to employ new staff you cannot conjure up trained professionals at will. The whole process takes time and planning. Special meetings can take a farcical turn when some participants urge the provision of services which others know cannot be delivered. PL 94–142 was framed with the naïve intention that services could be based on a pure concept of need. However there is no way in which the constraints of both the existing system and of limited financial resources can be avoided in practice.

In common with most developed nations the USA has experienced a declining birth rate and falling school rolls. Many of the additional teachers required to co-ordinate the IEPs within each school were simply recruited from the overabundance of staff in the ordinary school system. They may have had responsibility for withdrawal groups of children with learning problems but in their new posts they could devote no more than fifty per cent of their time to teaching.

In theory there is no limit to the number of children recorded as having exceptional need. But in practice the State authorities have issued informal guidelines that they cannot fund any school district which 'records' more than ten per cent of the school population. In fact most areas could not reach that number simply because they do not have the administrative and professional staff either to conduct the necessary meeting or to fulfil the requirements of the educational plans.

As far as the other formal requirement of the post was concerned, that of fostering mainstreaming, Barry had seen limited changes.

> They are including many of the physically handicapped students that they did not have previously who are close to the normal range or even above the normal range intellectually. They have been readily accepted because the law is rather clearcut that they must be. In the past schools claimed that their architecture was unsuitable but a whole series of laws including 94–142 have meant that children with severe physical handicaps have been mainstreamed even if they have needed an individual teaching aide to accompany them around the school. The severely mentally handicapped have presented a much more difficult problem. Some who were excluded from education are now going to school but very few have made it into the regular programs.

The position for children with 'learning handicaps' has been complicated. Children with mild learning problems have been the fastest-growing category in special education, a category which gained further impetus with the implementation of the law. Although some of these children who were previously 'following' the normal curriculum are now in special classes, this is balanced by those who are included in special provision under the new law but who had fallen so far behind in the past that they had just dropped out of school. The 'new regime' may have further repercussions for the education of these children in the future. Almost every school district in California has one or more 'continuation high school' which were established as an alternative form of education by the public school system. Many children who could not cope with the rigid age grading system of regular schools drifted towards the continuation high schools. Although they were not intended to be special schools for handicapped students, they have inevitably attracted a large number of children now regarded as having exceptional needs.

Sometimes they water down the regular curriculum so that students who couldn't handle the material of the regular high school can tolerate it. They provide a less structured and less intense setting. Students who didn't like the requirements of a large high school may do better in a continuation high school where the groups are smaller and there's more of a relationship with one's teacher.

Barry found it difficult to work out what was happening to particular groups of children because of the moves to abolish categorisation of children with exceptional needs. Children who had previously been called emotionally disturbed were now absorbed into the learning handicapped category.

At the present time only four categories are in use; severely handicapped, physically handicapped, communicatively handicapped and learning handicapped. But as far as I know the new revision of the law does away with these four categories so there's just handicapped students generally or special needs students since they are trying to do away with the term handicap altogether.

In the face of all the changes it was clearly difficult to maintain a sense of direction. Barry assessed the current state of special education in his school district in this way:

I've been thinking about all the trouble which has followed the introduction of the law and wondering whether all the turmoil has been worth it. I think so because even though there's been many problems it's the first time in the ten years of my involvement with retarded or handicapped students that new ideas have come in. It's created tremendous chaos and confusion which has allowed an opportunity for these new ideas to emerge. The old system has been thrown over and no-one knows quite what to do. But if a person is able to live within a system that is going through all this confusion and is able to provide some direction then it's possible for some very positive changes to take place.

24 JULIE LORRAINE: A TEACHER OF MENTALLY HANDICAPPED STUDENTS IN CALIFORNIA

Tony Booth

Like Barry Marks, Julie Lorraine works in special education in California and her job, too, has been affected by recent legislation. The following description of Julie's career and the school she most recently worked in highlights a number of features common to much of American special education; for example, the amount of money available for new buildings (like J T Cobb School described later in this book), and the ready acceptance of new philosophies in special education.

Julie has just left her job at a school for handicapped children operated by a small county in California. It was built as a ten acre farm, 10 miles from the nearest urban centre, to provide an alternative education for mentally handicapped students aged 14–21 years and to prepare them for eventual work in the farm industry. Nearly 50 per cent of the students come from residential 'foster homes'. These 'homes' were developed as private businesses (licensed by the State) to fill a gap created by the general absence of social and residential services for these individuals. Such homes might contain anywhere from two to eighteen handicapped residents. The level of emotional and material support varied greatly from home to home; but staff were often untrained and inexperienced.

The allowable maximum age for handicapped students to remain in special education schools has gradually risen to 22 years. However, provisions for vocational, educational and residential place merits have traditionally been quite limited beyond that age. This absence in support services sometimes resulted in mentally handicapped young adults being placed in large residential state hospitals. Those young adults with higher social and vocational capabilities were and are heavily penalised by a system which withdraws social benefits once a certain parental income level is reached.

The school was conceived and built prior to recent changes in law

154

and philosophy relating to handicapped children in the USA. It was set up at great expense by the Californian authorities at a time when special education was taken to imply separate facilities for handicapped pupils. However it had become caught in the crossfire of changing educational philosophies. The barn, built at a cost of $100,000 to house the farm animals, was standing empty. There were a few rotten apples on the trees in the orchard, left to decay for want of pruning and spraying. Some of the students travelled two hours each way from their urban homes. Whereas previously a municipal bus had called each day to take some of them on trips away from their farm, the service had been cut leaving the staff and students isolated for the entire school day. The identity crisis of the school and school staff was further fuelled by the reduced possibilities for employment. There were limited prospects of the mentally handicapped students finding jobs in agriculture.

Julie studied psychology at university but had no clear idea of her future career until she worked on a summer education scheme for learning-disabled children. She found the work interesting and in the absence of a teaching qualification took a post as an 'instructional aide' working under the direction of a class teacher with mentally retarded children. She continued with this work for five years and depending on the inclinations of the teacher involved, experienced varying degrees of autonomy to develop her own teaching approach. In fact she eventually obtained a teaching qualification by a combination of evening study and a year's supervised teaching practice. When she applied for and gained the post as a teacher at 'The Farm School' she conceived of the work as rational and challenging and felt it would offer a real contribution to the quality of life for the mentally handicapped. She found the experience a disillusioning one. We include below her description of the organisation and curriculum of the school and the difficulties faced by the staff:

During the years from January 1978–June 1980, the Farm School had either 5 or 6 classes of students. Each class consisted of 1 teacher, 1 instructional aide and a maximum of 12 students. There were, in a few instances, extra aides hired to help with students who were visually or orthopedically impaired, in addition to being mentally retarded.

There was a wide range of student abilities at the Farm School. Some children functioned barely above the Development Center level [profoundly handicapped or special care in the UK]. Other students had come from higher functioning classes attached to the local schools — i.e. Educable Mentally Retarded [now Learning Handicapped in California, USA and ESN(M) in the UK]. They were now attending the Farm School perhaps because of inappropriate social behaviour or protective parental wishes. The problem stemmed from the inability of the local school district to offer the proper educational setting and there was nowhere else for these students to go. In between were those students who had been labelled when young as Trainable Mentally Retarded [now Severely Handicapped in California and ESN(S) in the UK] and had attended separate schools for the entire length of their educational experience.

A scheme of 'rotation' was developed each year and usually scrapped in disgust at the year's conclusion. Generally students had a homeroom that they would go to at the beginning and end of the day. During the rest of the day the students 'rotated' to various classes offered by the different teaching teams. These classes could be:

1. Vocational — i.e. crops maintenance, grounds and custodial maintenance, pre-vocational workshop skills.
2. Cognitive — maths, reading — either 'survival-practical' type or more academic.
3. Self-care — home skills and basic skills for daily living.
4. Physical education — sports, yoga, running.
5. Creative arts — painting, weaving, music.

The staff attempted to group students in these classes according to:

1. Goals listed on the IEP (Individual Educational Program).
2. Similar functioning level.

Rotation occurred on 3–4 days a week with the other days being self-contained. Rotation was devised ostensibly so as not to duplicate teaching students certain skills. Covertly, other reasons existed. No teacher wanted to work exclusively with the lower functioning students. In addition we also were covering up for the incompetence of certain staff members by not exposing some students to them for the entire day or week. So the incompetence was spread out in lesser doses.

The Principal of the Farm School, like other principals in our county, was the administrative head of up to six other special

schools. The job involved multiple administrative duties and meetings, and the six school sites were separated by great distances and
served children with a variety of special educational needs. There
were three changes of Principal in the two and a half years I was
there. The result for our school was the almost complete absence
of the leadership and support of a principal. None of the three
really had any idea of the teaching which took place in the classrooms. They did, however, provide much verbiage on how 'wonderfully' we were handling things. As long as we didn't cause too much
trouble things were fine.

Additionally, the principals were usually involved in one of the
various current projects or methodologies that were in vogue. These
new ideas have great claims attached to them and much excitement
is generated about these 'miracle cures'. There was, of course, a
'back-to-basics' movement, which might have been successful if staff
could ever agree on what the 'basics' were. Were they reading and
writing as parents pressured for?

One year, Sensori-Motor Integration became the latest method to
provide a groundwork for further learning. Workshops were given,
equipment ordered and a specialist was hired as a consultant. Many
teachers devoted a good deal of classroom time to sensori-motor
exercises. Suddenly, we didn't hear any more about sensori-motor
integration because of a new project.

This year's emphasis is on a form of acupressure, which by pressing points on the body promotes relaxation and readiness for learning. It is being tried on an experimental basis on students with a
variety of handicaps. Our area administrator appeared on a local
news station describing the project's benefits and showed up at
staff meetings extolling the programme.

It's not that there is pressure for every teacher to try this method.
But this new 'cure' gets all the energy, attention and publicity. The
regular classroom teachers doing their job get little reinforcement
or attention.

All of this happened, I feel, in the absence of a sound and viable
curriculum. We needed leaders who had the authority to ensure that
the agreed-upon aims were being carried out. We needed resources to
support these aims.

I think the net result of all this was an incredible confusion on
the part of the staff and lost educational opportunities for the students. There was never a logical progression of acquired skills that
continued for a few years. Progress was haphazard since we always

seemed to be starting over again. I think that if students learned much of anything it was due to their own maturation and self-sufficiency in gleaning what they could.

The direction of the school was not helped by the three changes of principal within two and a half years. This turnover was an exaggeration of the turmoil in administration which was a consequence of local political changes and the election of a new county superintendent of schools. The head teacher of the school, who received only a 5 per cent addition to his salary for his post, had to take on additional responsibilities but did not receive sufficient administrative support to successfully carry out these duties.

The staff was divided about the future of the school. Some, who had past experience of weathering the storms of change, regarded the implementation of PL 94-142 [see introduction to case study 23] as a bewildering procession of fads that would eventually blow over. They pointed to the two complete changes in documentation of children with exceptional needs in two years and regarded the special meetings as a game played by administrators and professionals that had little relevance to teachers or students. They argued for the regeneration of the farming community.

The remainder of the staff believed that the school would disappear. They felt that the students should be returned to their communities in the urban centres and become more a part of the normal school system. Julie was one of this group. She felt that she needed some time away from the classroom so that she could reconsider her aims as a teacher. As she put it: 'I'm burnt out, I've been around the classroom too long.'

25 A COMMUNITY WORKER IN A SPECIAL SCHOOL

Tony Booth and June Statham

Janet is a community worker attached to an ESN(M) school for pupils aged 3–16 years. Her job is funded through the National Elfrida Rathbone Society, the only national voluntary organisation devoted to helping young people categorised as ESN(M). She is one of very few community workers attached to special schools.

Janet sees her job as 'increasing and strengthening the links between the children and their community and between the school and the parents of the children'. The community in which she operates is defined officially as 'the school and the area from which the children come'. At times this definition may lead to a conflict of interests. The school's catchment area is large, and Janet's attempts to involve the children and their families in the school may actually be at the expense of greater involvement in facilities in their own areas.

Before beginning this job Janet had taught for several years in an ESN(S) school, and most recently had worked in an experimental special education unit attached to an American university. The parents of children with special needs in the States had far greater power and involvement in their children's education and she felt that much could be done to foster co-operation here:

> In many schools the attitude is that children would improve if only the parents were more capable, while parents often feel that teachers are the ones with the training and that they have very little to contribute themselves. There's an atmosphere of distrust on both sides and teachers can be defensive. It's my job to try as hard as I can to be a middle person, not to take sides, but to represent the parents to the school and vice versa.

At the beginning, Janet took over several tasks involving contact with parents which had previously been carried out by teachers, such as

159

collecting money for the weekly lottery, organising the Summer Fayre and writing the School's monthly newsletter. She saw this as a way of establishing relationships with parents and teachers, rather than as an end in itself.

> Normally I don't like to take on something that's already been done, because otherwise at the end of a year I'll merely have taken the load off other teachers' shoulders. But on the other hand I obviously can't work unless I have reasonable relationships with the school and the teachers, so if I can show I'm willing to help them by taking over the things that are a real burden to them and that fit into my job description, then I'm going to get a lot more co-operation when I need their help.

She is aware of the overlap in her job with the work of the teachers and also with other groups such as social workers and education welfare officers, and is keen to pass on to them the work she sees as falling in their domain. She is particularly careful to encourage contact between teachers and parents and feels that she would be failing badly if that were to decrease as a result of her presence. Teachers do visit parents at home but she has the advantage of being able to see them at any time during the day.

> Also I think it can be easier for them to relate to me as a person than to a teacher in the school. I don't feel I have sole visitation rights — teachers can visit parents without telling me, and do. But often they're relieved if they can send me, partly because of time, sometimes because some of the parents can be quite hesitant about communicating their worries to the school staff. I always say, to both parents and teachers, that I can't make things happen but I'll do my best to explain what you've said to me to them, and I'll see what can be done.

Being a go-between does have its problems. She has found herself being used when parents and teachers don't see eye-to-eye. Janet recalls one father who rang her up with a list of grievances about his daughter.

> They were the sort of things which other parents would probably have accepted, but he felt strongly about them. He said that his child had been hit and someone had stolen her coat and the teacher hadn't tried to find out who was ganging up on her. I told him I'd see what

I could do. The teacher said he was overreacting; one of the children had taken the coat as a joke and given it back later, the child who had hit her had been punished and all kids have gangs at that age; she's got a gang just like the girl who was supposed to be ganging up on her.

Janet wrote to the father explaining the 'misunderstanding'. She thinks that just knowing he'd been listened to was a great help. 'Often the parent needs attention as much as the child.' She hopes that taking on a task such as this which she does not really see as part of her job may have long term benefits for her relationships with parents and staff.

Although Janet does visit and deal with parents on an individual basis, she aims to work with parents as groups, and to try to get them to support each other. Most parents don't know parents of other children at the school, partly because of its wide catchment area and partly because of its location in an expanding new town. Nearly half of those who answered a questionnaire Janet sent out soon after starting the job said they would like to meet other parents.

So as well as backing up on normal school events like Thanksgiving Service and Parents' Evenings by sending notes home to parents and picking up those who want lifts and that sort of thing, I've also set up monthly evening meetings for parents who'd like to meet each other, in their own homes. Six to ten people come, and the meetings seem to work well. I hope to start up afternoon ones soon on the various estates, so that parents can bring younger pre-school children.

She has also organised group sessions for various money-making activities, such as relabelling plastic coal bags to raise money to build a garage for the school's minibus.

For me the fund raising is maybe less important than it is for the school. For me what's important is that it gets people involved in the school. Some parents don't want to come and just talk, perhaps because they don't think they've got problems or perhaps because they're afraid, but they're willing to help the school and participate in more practical ways. It's a matter of finding as many different ways for parents to participate in the school as possible, hoping that that will lead to them being more involved in the education of their children.

Janet has made some progress in getting the community more involved in the school. 'The idea is to get people in the community in general to know what special schools are, in particular what ESN(M) kids are and what they're capable of, because it's people in the community who are going to give them jobs.' She has sent the school's newsletter to various interested local people, written an article on the school and her job for the local paper, involved local businesses in the school through donating products or money and receiving in return publicity or thank you letters from the children, and recruited as many volunteers as possible from the outside community to help in the school. She had hoped that the newspaper article would result in more volunteers than it did; a better source has been the local Volunteer Bureau which has so far produced eight helpers. Some of Janet's time is spent introducing them to the school, supporting them once they are there, and making sure that both they and the teachers are happy with the situation. Last summer she also set up a playscheme at the school which ran for two weeks and which she hopes to repeat on a larger scale this year. The scheme involved children from outside the school as well as within, and was run largely by volunteers from the community – a parent, a teacher from an ordinary school, three students from a local FE college and a home-school link assistant.

Her attempts to increase the children's participation in the community have centred around the older children at the school, trying to get them work and community experience. She has helped the careers teacher to find work in a playgroup for four senior school girls, and has made sure that the Volunteer Bureau is aware of the school as a possible source of volunteers. Janet's job description also includes helping pupils who have left the school to become more involved in their community.

A school-leaver might come to me and say they couldn't get a job and didn't know where to go, and I'd direct them to the Careers Office or the Careers Teacher. I see myself as a referral point, I'm not there to get them a job but I'm perhaps there to tell them what there is and introduce them to someone who can help them.

She hopes that the youth club she plans to set up will also help these older pupils. Initially Janet was keener to take the children into their local youth club, but the head teacher of her school persuaded her of the importance of developing school facilities, and she agreed to start one at the school instead. 'The kids here do often have trouble mixing socially, so perhaps it might be better initially to have their own school youth club, provided we could get outsiders in too.' She hopes that the children will feel easier about joining community facilities once they have come to the school club.

Janet is responsible in her job to a management committee which meets once or twice each term and consists of the school's headmistress, the school medical officer, one representative from the Development Corporation and one from the voluntary organisation, the divisional education officer, one of the teachers at the school, and the chairman of the School Governors. She would like to get a social worker and a parent on to her management committee too. She admits that working for so many different bodies has its problems. 'I'm answerable to the voluntary organisation through the headmistress and the management committee, so I have to keep all their demands in mind as well as make judgements of my own. It's quite complicated — I think everyone's got the kids' interests at heart, but they vary in the way they put this into practice.'

Although she would like to be seen as a 'halfway house' between parents and the school, Janet sometimes finds that she identifies more closely with the school than with the parents. She introduces herself as the 'community worker from Hazelwood School' and some parents do see her as aligned with other school staff. A further difficulty can arise in the occasional case when she sees it necessary to make a confidential report for the school which is unavailable to parents. 'I'd be no good at my job if I didn't have a good relationship with the school and teachers. But it does make a difference to your allegiance, if you write reports which parents don't see.'

The future of Janet's job is uncertain.

It's guaranteed for a year, probable for two, possible for three and unlikely for any more, because of money. I think the voluntary organisation would like the County Council to take it over then, but that's unlikely the way things are at the moment. I try to keep in mind that I won't be there for ever, so when I set something up I've also got to think about getting it to the point where its running itself.

She is uncertain too, about the future of jobs like hers if properly resourced schemes of integration could be fostered:

I do see some advantages for my work of having the children in a special school. In some cases, the fact that their child attends a special school makes parents face up to their child's problems, though some of them had literally to force professionals to recognise their children's difficulties. That is an advantage, but it's a side issue. It couldn't actually be a reason for placing a child in a special school. The more I work there the more I see that whatever its advantages, I am trying to unravel the problems created by having a special school in the first place. If the children were in their own schools they wouldn't need me as much. They might need someone to build up their confidence so that they could take advantage of youth clubs for example, but they would know more children in their own areas and would be aware of the facilities that were available. You would still need to cultivate relationships with parents, but it might be easier.

PART TWO:

PERSPECTIVES ON HANDICAP

26 OFF DUTY: EDUCATIONAL PSYCHOLOGISTS DISCUSS THEIR JOB

Patricia Potts and June Statham

Despite the fact that the educational psychologist is often seen as one of the key personnel in the special education system, there seems to be little agreement as to what the job involves. Teachers may have one idea, parents another, and the educational psychologists themselves are by no means unanimous either about what they do or about what they should be doing. Neither do they share a common background of training or experience. The group of educational psychologists who took part in the following discussion have come to their jobs via very different routes, and they differ in their attitudes towards the value of IQ testing, the nature of any alternatives, and the relevance of their training to their job.

Jack: I invariably use a standardised intelligence test to start with, in any assessment that I do. I do that because of my personality, to provide a structure that is very clear cut so that it doesn't seem threatening to the child and gives me time to become more flexible.

Tim: I gave up IQ tests for a number of reasons: meeting people and doing the same thing with them every time would be excruciatingly boring. Secondly, I think giving an IQ test is a very misleading project because they're not able to do the job one gives the illusion they can do.

Roy: I totally disagree but I don't quite know why. I feel that I ought not to be using a standardised test, but . . .

Tim: Standardised tests only have meaning when applied to group differences. That's something that psychologists ought to learn in their training, and presumably they do; they're aware of this elementary statistical fact. IQ tests have very little meaning when applied to individuals. Now if you use it in a different way, to structure your relationship with a child, then I'd argue

167

that there are better ways of getting to know a child than using IQ tests. I think that had one never had the illusion in the first place, that you can ascribe meaning to an individual encounter using an IQ test, then you'd never have developed the idea of using it to structure the relationship.

Roy: One needn't quote an IQ to use an IQ test. I tend to forget about the figure, but it's a standardised interview.

Jack: As soon as I flip open the case with the tests in, the machinery goes into gear and I no longer have to think about how I'm putting things out, what the words are and so on; it leaves me free to observe that child. I saw one the other day whom I knew I'd only see once. Afterwards I was able to write 'over-shot the mark on block design', 'disinhibited' and so on. A mass of remarks because he was so engrossed he wasn't worried what I was writing down; I was free to record my observations. I could reassure his father that he wasn't making a song and dance about nothing, for all the things he said he was worried about were down on the test report. In that framework, in a brief time, I'd been able to pick out his main points of concern.

Pam: So much hangs on one interview. You can write a Special Education referral form for a child you didn't know before that hour and the child's whole life may depend on what you say.

Roy: You learn to work with the job. The one-off interview tends to be what you can manage.

Tim: But if your aim is to do something useful for the child, how can you possibly do that based on a thirty minute interview?

Roy: I wouldn't say that was my aim. I don't really know what my aim is.

Tim: Earning your living?

Roy: Yes, although I get my living whether I earn it or not. I saw a child today in a head's study and I gave a standardised IQ test, because I didn't know what else to do. That was there and I can do that and watch the child and write things down. With this child I could see that he was bright, but if he didn't get things right first time he found it very difficult, the thinking process was very difficult for him. I was able to point this out to him and then he was able to do it. I told him his thinking processes needed oil, and in the end I was able to say 'oil' when he was stuck and he could do it. The teachers hadn't noticed that.

Jack: If possible I have a teacher, or someone who regularly works with the child, in to watch my assessment to see precisely what

I'm doing and the reason for any comments I make at the end. They often find it helpful, it gives them the opportunity of looking at the child in detail.

Pam: But what does that imply for educational psychologists as a special breed if teachers are let in on the secret world of assessment and can then make informal assessments themselves?

Jack: But not formal ones. They do see your test materials, but it also provides them with an opportunity to do nothing but watch one child for a whole hour.

Roy: The advantage of using an IQ test is that you can see the strategies they use, how the children cope with problems and frustrations in a situation in which you know what the rules are. If you don't know what the rules are it's very difficult to make sense of what people are doing, and psychologists know the rules of IQ tests.

Tim: But if I meet a child down the road and he's crying, I don't think 'poor boy, he's got a problem' and invite him into my house for an IQ test! I'm used to meeting people so I have all kinds of ways of relating to them and I don't need to erect artificial ground rules.

Jack: But given the structure and framework of an IQ test, I can organise things so that the children go out thinking they're great. They've had a positive experience, they feel they got things right. I'm able to organise that in a structured situation; it's important for children to go out feeling better than when they came in, especially if I'm going to see them again. I need the structure to make sure I can rely on that happening.

Tim: If you started from scratch you'd never have discovered IQ tests. Somebody has given you a way of conducting your life which from the outside seems strange. Why does no one else structure their encounters using IQ tests, at a party, for instance? You already have the IQ test, wonder why you're giving it to the children and then think, oh, it structures the relationship.

Jack: But at parties you still use some kind of structure when you meet new people and often it gives you a very superficial view of them which may turn out to be completely wrong. The danger of judging wrongly is greater when you don't have ground rules like you have in an IQ test.

Tim: If you're saying that assessing people is part of life, then yes, but I don't use an IQ test! I don't know you, but I'm not giving you an IQ test!

Pam: What do you do with a child in an interview if you don't use an IQ test?

Tim: Most of them can talk, so the first thing to explain is why you've come. With little kids you probably wouldn't want to take them out of the classroom anyway, just watch them and their friends round a table. That would be the closest you could get. You have to work out what questions you want to answer. If the child is transferring schools you're trying to answer the question 'How can I produce for this child a curriculum that's compatible with his interests?' and you have to follow that line, which may take you away from seeing the individual child. There's a lot of children who can't do things compatible with their interests.

The group then went on to discuss how they felt about their training, and its relevance to the work they found themselves doing.

Pam: Do you think it is relevant that educational psychologists have to have been teachers?

Roy: Once you stop being a teacher, you stop being a teacher. I think it's a bit of a red herring.

Pam: What does the year of training actually involve?

Tim: It's a year off. I'd been working for three years after leaving university. There were only six of us on this course and it was an easy year when I didn't do much hard work.

Roy: It's like passing your driving test, it's only after you've passed that you start learning to drive.

Tim: I had this 'welfare' motive. I thought I'd like to do something of value to people so I went into educational psychology. On my course the teaching was terrible. You'd go in in the morning and the lecturer would suddenly remember he was supposed to be teaching so he'd pull some old volume off his shelf, blow the dust off it and start reading. That was the standard of tutorials. It was very painful and in such a small group revolution was impossible, it would have been too personal, so we would endure it for about twenty minutes and then make a joke and break up the class. It was very childish, but I suspect my experience is quite common, that the academic content of these courses isn't that high.

Jack: On my course it certainly was; the lectures were well-prepared, we each had to prepare seminars during the course and were given lengthy up-to-date reading lists. We had to write detailed reports on the places we visited, quoting all the relevant references. I think it was a fairly high standard.

Roy: I trained at two places; they were very different. At one I saw a hundred people and there were lectures and exams, it was very heavy going. At the other I saw four or five children and it was all talking and thinking and considering conceptual models to look at children with.

Tim: People tend to think 'What does an educational psychologist need to know?' and then try to cram it all into one year, instead of thinking 'Life's a long time and you can learn things after you leave.'

Roy: It's the same with children: you're not going to solve their problems for them in the time you've got, just open up other vistas for them. I could speculate that the child with the funny thinking process had a background of stabbings and so on and that there were lots of things he wouldn't want to put together and think about. All right, that's a psychoanalytic-type speculation but it's something worth thinking about, even if you don't take it anywhere.

Tim: But it's only worth looking at if you're going to take it somewhere, surely?

Roy: No, I'll have to wait and see how this child progresses. I was trained on the idea of coming in as an educational psychologist for intervention, plonk, and I've moved very much away to not seeing a child unless I've known about him for at least a year. I encourage schools to discuss problem children with me. I tell the teachers I'm not going to intervene in the child's life, I can't run my own life let alone theirs, but if they can persuade me there is something useful I could do then I'll see the child, and try to tell the child what I've learnt during the interview.

Jack: Ninety per cent of the children I see can't talk: I've got special responsibility for deaf children. You can't just chat to them, you've got to make it quite clear that there's some reason for their coming to see you. I do watch them in the classroom and I used to run a playgroup, which I wouldn't have considered doing without my training. Without it I wouldn't have known about these children and I wouldn't have had any guidelines. But I have had a lot of other experience: I did a year working with handicapped children and I taught for about thirteen years before I did the educational psychology training. I also did an extra postgraduate year.

Tim: I am the opposite; I was quite raw when I started as an educational psychologist. I'd done a psychology degree, which was highly experimental, mainly animal psychology, so that wasn't much use to helping troubled children. I'd read a few books on reading and helped a few children with their reading and thought I must be a real expert on helping children with remedial problems. It hadn't occurred to me that there were people who'd had a lot of experience. I set up courses for teachers; when I think back, I'm amazed. I soon discovered that there were people with very specific experience of teaching children with reading problems, so I certainly wasn't an expert compared to them. I'd come out of the course feeling 'I'm an expert now', but it gets increasingly difficult to work out what one's an expert in.

Roy: Meeting a child and talking to him is a nice experience for everybody, but if you're only going to see the child once, for an hour, which is what usually happens, either it's a job you get out of because there's no sense seeing a child for an hour, or . . . how do you explain to a child what you're there for? You've got to set up a contract with a child, find out beforehand what the child thinks you're seeing him for, what the parents, the school and you yourself think you're seeing him for, work all that out and then still be in the very odd and difficult position of having to get close to that child in an hour.

Tim: So you mustn't do it.

Roy: So what do you do instead?

Tim: If the psychologist bit of the job is having deep meaningful relationships with people then you've dumped it by only seeing them for an hour.

Jack: I'm surprised that you should look at being a psychologist like that; I'd have thought that was a much better description of a psychotherapist.

Pam: Is being an educational psychologist impossible, a contradiction in terms?

Tim: You've got to get away from this idea of the role being the person. People who are earning their living by being educational psychologists have got all sorts of different interests in life as well as education and psychology.

Jack: What do you see as the psychological side?

Roy: Well I give IQ tests, so I've got it all sorted out!

Pam: Wouldn't it be better if you knew the children?

Jack: I think we're getting far too child-focused. Educational psychologists have such a range of functions that affect or involve children, but to talk as though that were all we were doing or are responsible for is to miss out the many administrative functions and the work with parents and other professionals. Our work varies according to the child we are dealing with: preschool, handicapped, disturbed. Part of our training and experience is going to help us recognise whether it is the child, his family or somebody else we should be seeing. It's a question of finding the best educational setting for a child and you've got to accept the parents' difficulties. You may have to work for a long time before they can agree to your recommendations. So it's wrong to say that the job concentrates on one child and his relationship with one other person during an hour's interview.

Pam: But a one-year course cannot qualify you to call yourself an expert in all that.

Jack: No, so the selection procedures pick out those who stand a good chance of developing a lot of these skills.

Eva: I trained last year and they seemed to select the people whose backgrounds they liked the look of: people with a lot of different experiences, they tend to take fewer young people now. People with a good psychology degree and a variety of relevant experience, not just the bare minimum of teaching, and they hope you're in a good enough position in your present job to get secondment.

Pam: If it was all relevant experience beforehand, how does this time of training change you?

Eva: It doesn't particularly. My two placements were the best part of the course, and a year's break from teaching. There was a high academic level, not particularly demanding, but with a lot of meat. You had to get through all the etiology of subnormality and autism, but it's not yet been useful to the job.

Jack: But doesn't it help you recognise these conditions when you see them?

Eva: But when am I going to see them? In the ordinary run of things I don't see a handicapped child or a deaf or a partially sighted child. I often see children in groups in ordinary secondary schools, as well as working in the classroom and with groups of teachers. Sometimes I do see two or three children for ten minutes each, for 'low-level counselling,' every time I go. The most interesting things I do are with ordinary secondary schools. I see the individual children to try and keep them in the ordinary school and prevent them being sent out to maladjusted schools, that's why it's an ongoing thing.

Tim: Why wouldn't you want to refer children to the maladjusted schools?

Eva: I have reservations about what goes on in the special schools I know. I feel there's little educational opportunity there, and I also don't feel happy about segregating children according to some often dubious categorisation.

Pam: But do teachers accept this new role of yours? Traditionally, educational psychologists are used by teachers to facilitate rather than prevent referrals.

Eva: At the same time as stopping some children being sent to special schools, I do assess others. Also I'm the psychologist for one of the local special schools, so I'm trying to build up their reputation. I'm trying to do it both ways: help make those schools viable, educational and therapeutic institutions, but at the same time keeping out a lot of children whom the ordinary schools want to throw out.

Pam: How far is it your previous experience or your training which gives you the confidence to make decisions about which children to send and which to keep out?

Eva: Mainly the experience. From working in secondary schools, I have a feel for which children will survive and which won't. On the course we rarely talked about schools, we hardly even mentioned secondary schools. You could easily go through your training without necessarily entering a secondary school.

Jack: I never ever worked in a normal school during the whole of my teaching career. I worked in a private residental school for the deaf, very abnormal, and then as a peripatetic teacher of the deaf, mainly seeing individual, pre-school children. So where did I acquire such diagnostic skills as I seem to have developed to place children appropriately in a school for the maladjusted?

Tim: You're assuming it's a high-level skill, but maybe you just have to ask any kid at school about the ones who'd be appropriately placed at maladjusted school and they'd be able to tell you just as well.

Roy: But our particular standpoint is useful, I think. We're free-ranging, not attached to one school, just like advisory heads and

	some Inspectors. Class teachers don't share our kind of involvement with children.
Pam:	Have you more to offer by being detached like that?
Roy:	I think so . . . It'd be much more challenging to be in one school all the time but I think we're useful in throwing a different light. I try to see the child in a wider context than education.
Jack:	In order to become reasonably proficient in any sphere you have to specialise. A counsellor, psychotherapist or social worker can give support to the family. I'd find that very difficult; I'd think what the hell am I meeting you for this time? But when I meet parents with their deaf children, I have a specific aim and I have specialised in deaf children so I can cope.
Eva:	The logical extension of the Warnock Report would be very few SE forms. You'd close down most maladjusted and ESN(M) schools and have a group of specialists to deal with the 'real' handicaps. SE procedures don't justify your existence.
Tim:	They are the end of a long struggle with the school medical officers; that was a major victory for the educational psychologists.
Eva:	One could close down a lot of special schools, apart from the physically handicapped and ESN(S), and just call all schools 'schools', doing away with marginal handicaps. You wouldn't have any maladjusted kids or ESN(M) kids, and you wouldn't have any SE procedures. These are the only two categories I have anything to do with, and we could well do without them. We could get rid of the SE procedures and it wouldn't be doing anyone out of a job.

27 MINDS OF THEIR OWN: ONE TEACHER'S PHILOSOPHY

Gerry Serpell-Morris

Gerry Serpell-Morris is the deputy head of a school for severely mentally handicapped children. He is responsible for the part of the school that contains some of the most difficult children, many of whom are not only mentally handicapped, but also quite severely disturbed. He has recently returned to teaching from being a senior lecturer in a college of education where he ran courses in teaching the mentally handicapped. Over the past four to five years he has become more and more discontented with received wisdom about the curriculum in this area.

My job is continually throwing up the practical problem of what teaching action I should take with a particular child. I know there are many books that set out to assist teachers in making such decisions. When I was lecturing I felt I should include such practical books in my courses — books advocating careful prescriptive planning, largely based around what is called the behavioural objectives approach. However, now I am personally facing these problems I find little assistance from such material. Rather than planning tightly structured prescriptive programmes I tend to proceed pragmatically within a developing set of principles and the books to which I turn for help are philosophical.

My concern extends beyond how to get over an immediate problem with a particular child. I find myself continually querying my reasons for the action I take. Was it meaningful to the child? Was it purely arbitrary? Was it merely a piece of child-minding? Is what I have done consistent within a set of carefully considered values? I've been struggling with the philosophy of the curriculum because once I have established clear principles on which to proceed I feel that I shall have a basis for a more consistent course of action — a more consistent curriculum.

What considerations can help me to put together a consistent set of principles of procedure? If all the children in this school were going to an adult training centre, we might just look at that ATC and ask: what is it they are going to demand of our children? Then we would come back and gear our curriculum to preparation for the ATC. That would be one way round the problem: education as a means to a preconceived end. Nevertheless I have been struggling for a philosophy that is not based on means to ends, largely because I believe it is a fallacy to presume that we can know for certain what these ends are.

One can also consider what society appears to conceive as the future of these children when they leave school. Curricula for severely handicapped children cannot be based solely on preparation for employment, particularly when the likelihood of their success in the job market is so remote. Furthermore such a curriculum policy tends to promote entry into employment as a major criterion for evaluating the child's education. But if they leave school and there are no jobs for them, are we to declare their education a failure? What matters, educationally, is the development of a viable personality at ease with himself and others.

My principles are founded on a belief that education can only *ameliorate* mental handicap; it cannot solve it. The only way we could move towards a real solution would be by radically restructuring the complex demands of our society and this seems most unlikely. The reason these children are with us is because they have been handicapped by their inability to make sense of the complexity of the normal world from early in life. Our job is to lower the complexity of their environment so as to enable them to perceive and relate as meaningfully as possible. To arrange things so as to capitalise on what they can do — not emphasise their disabilities. It seems to me that badly planned integration could put a lot of mentally handicapped people in situations which would be meaningless and unbearable. Integration by itself will not change the high level of complexity of thought and action required to survive in our society.

When education is perceived as amelioration then it immediately becomes more than a means to a set of ends. It becomes enabling the mentally handicapped person to make the most of his life at *every particular moment*. The present is always as important as the future. I see my job as making the most of every little bit of potential that they show. For example, a child in my class, Clare, comes in: she's tearing at her hair, jerking, she's like a thing possessed, she won't smile at you, she can't concentrate on anything. So what do I do? I put her in a warm bath. I use soap bubbles, pour water down her back, work for her relaxation. My job is to ameliorate this uptight little person's condition and if I succeed – is that education? In my view it *is* her education because it is amelioration of her handicapping condition and in the process an enhancement of her *present* life experience. I don't sit down and think 'My God I've spent two months with her and she's no further forward today than she was when she came to me.' It's inappropriate to think of education as a means to an end with such a child. I must concentrate on making her life stimulating and full by interpreting her needs almost from moment to moment.

I can't hope to eventually hand a child like Clare total responsibility for her own life, which is what normal education sets out to do for children. These children are very rarely going to take complete responsibility for their own lives. They're always going to be in the care of one responsible adult or another. There's always going to be in their lives a restriction on their personal freedom. So we've got to be very sure that the adults who are responsible persons at any time try to give them as much freedom and choice of action as possible.

I think teachers in this work have got to throw aside the traditional role of an instructor with a clear idea of the end in view and the means to achieve it. At the moment I'm sailing against the wind. The inspectorate and the government are very keen on teacher accountability. And teacher accountability leads to curricula based around specific behavioural objectives. I see this as a most dangerous trend. If enough people are sufficiently entranced by it it could reduce the possibility of teachers viewing handicapped people as human beings with a mind and life style of their own and a need to be themselves. It leads to adults making these vulnerable people dance to their tune. They'll say 'You will do this because I say you need to learn it.' In other words, it leads to people defining future needs for those who cannot respond.

This is the crunch issue in curriculum decision-making. If you subscribe to prescriptive planning it's very easy to write a book telling people how to write instructional objectives, but such books will rarely tell you *which* objectives. But as a teacher you can't evade the value issue, because somebody has got to decide what the objective is. You can't get round it by saying 'Let's look at them to see what their needs are.' You can never evade the fact that when you said 'he needs', it was your judgement; you've got to take responsibility for that judgement.

For example, I can take a child in my unit and say 'He needs to be toilet-trained.' Now who does he need to be toilet-trained for? You might say 'It's because it would make the lives of everyone around him easier.' But that's nothing to do with his needs. So you say: 'It will make life nicer for him. If he were toilet-trained he wouldn't have this discomfort, and he wouldn't have to wear nappy pads.' But there's nothing he seems to like better than to mess himself and then play with it, eat it and smear it on the walls. So from his point of view he doesn't need to be toilet-trained at all. Perhaps all he wants is to be left alone. So we must realise that the needs we identify have more to do with what society wants these children to be than with what these children are.

I have no difficulty rationalising the need for toilet-training, but with children in the senior unit at our school it's far more complex. Benedict, for example, has got good expressive language, but it obviously indicates a restricted cognitive function. To all intents and purposes he's gone about as far as he's going to go, yet he's in school for another four years, and I find it extremely difficult to pin down worthwhile and meaningful objectives. A year ago I decided it would be valuable if he could write his name. I devised a carefully structured programme based on simple objectives, with daily practice in a variety of situations. A year later he was making exactly the same mistakes as when he started.

Many teachers would say that the one thing you can be sure of is that wherever children are they will need to communicate. So the core of the curriculum is language and communication. But Benedict communicates, he's communicating beautifully. He'll tell you if he's hurt, if he's sick, if he's depressed, if he's happy. He'll tell you what he did at the weekend, he'll tell you what he's going to do. He's communicating as well as *he* needs. He's not communicating as well as society would demand. So you could say he needs to communicate better. What he really needs is to be normal, and we can't make him normal, it's a question of cognitive ability. What people really want is for the curriculum to make them normal.

We are not dealing with normal people and we can't perform miracles. Our concept of education should not be one of training. There may be a place for the training of skills but we should try to enable a handicapped person to be as free a person as possible, given a dependence on others. They must be free to opt out on occasions. They may need to do nothing or be lazy, as much as to follow a tight prescriptive line aimed at making them normal. They have got minds of their own; they are often bizarre minds. Special education must be about developing those minds, bizarre as they might be.

28 GROWING UP IN CARE

Barbara Kahan

Source: Edited extracts of Barbara Kahan, *Growing up in Care: Ten People Talking* (Blackwell, Oxford, 1979).

In 1970, the Children's Officer of what was then a local authority's children's department organised a series of discussions between ten young adults who had spent the whole or a significant part of their first eighteen years in the care of the authority. She taped the meetings, which were held monthly for about a year, and used them as the basis for a book Growing up in Care, *from which the following material is taken.*

To go to school every day is a statutory requirement for all children, unless they are unable to do so by reason of illness or some other legitimate cause, or are educated at home. This is a continuing reality for each child from five to sixteen, most of their childhood years. Thus five days a week, forty weeks of the year, a child is expected to arrive at school even if families move frequently, parents become ill, desert their children, lose the family home or job, change partners, go to prison, or put the child in care. Such expectations can be both a stabilising influence and a demanding constraint. Children may be unsettled, filled with grief, overwhelmed with anxiety, deprived of normal family support; they may be attending one of a succession of schools in none of which they have been able to put down any roots, or the school may, by good chance, be one of the few long-term, familiar and reassuring elements in a background shattered by events beyond their control. Either way, to give their full concentration to their work or to be able to maximise the opportunities that are offered is likely to be difficult. Children in care are often handicapped simply by the consequences of being in care. When these are associated with school failure, they may become doubly handicapped.

180

The discussions between the group of ten young adults were wide-ranging but one topic to which they constantly returned was their previous educational experience. They had all been to day primary schools and most to what were then known as secondary modern schools. Three had undertaken periods of further education, but many of the participants shared feelings of regret about 'wasting' their educational opportunities, and were able with hindsight to identify some of the difficulties and problems which had made school a largely unsatisfactory experience for them.

They recognised very clearly that their attitude to school had been related to where they were living and whether the adults caring for them were concerned about their educational progress. Barry described how when he was in a children's Home he was fifth from the bottom in a class of over forty, but when he was boarded out his class results got better each term until he was third from the top. He could not explain why this had happened except that his foster mother and an older boy in the family had both taken an interest in his progress and encouraged him in a variety of ways, some direct, others indirect. Two other group members, both men, confirmed that when they were in residential Homes' groups they found it hard to become really interested in school. One of them, Andrew, described himself as 'absolutely useless in everything at school' until to his own surprise he had developed an interest in woodwork and metalwork and had finished top of the class in one and quite high up in the other. But he 'felt retarded' in other subjects because he hadn't been able to be interested. 'I wasn't really committed in my own mind to what I wanted to do with myself.'

Many of the group members felt they would have done better had they been 'pushed', either by teachers at school, or by a particular person in their Home. They used the word 'push' in contexts which suggested they felt children in care needed very strong support and backing, to help them overcome the uncertainty and indecisiveness which resulted from the traumatic experiences they had suffered. 'Pushing' meant caring enough about them to help them to make something of themselves. Margaret, who had been born and adopted in another country, experienced not only the problems of going to school from a children's Home, but also those of having to adapt to a different educational system as well as numerous different schools. She had great regrets about her education.

Education, that is something that I desperately, when I was in care, wanted somebody to help me with. And yet there didn't seem anybody that I could turn to. I came from Canada to England, the method of teaching was so different that it took me until the term before I left school to really get a grasp of what was going on, because of all the different schools I'd been to in this country as well. And that last term if there had been somebody, in fact I think I did say to someone, 'I don't want to leave school, I want to stay on.' And I really wanted somebody desperately then to say 'Come on, work hard at it and perhaps you can!' I can remember that as a real grudge that I felt at the particular time. I didn't want to go out into the wide world, I wanted to stay at school, I wanted to better the educational opportunities that I felt there were. I would like to have been made to sit down at night and do homework. At school I found they made allowances for the fact that I was in care, and that I came from Canada, too many allowances. I felt that if only they had come down with a rod of iron it would probably have helped: 'You sit there until your homework's done,' or 'You sit there until that's done and if you can't work it out ask me how.' I used to long to be like other children that I knew had to take homework home.

Margaret wanted to ask for homework but thought it was no use because she did not think there would be anyone at the children's Home to help her, and she would need help. Ironically two of the house parents on the staff of her Home were qualified teachers. Margaret summed up her feelings by saying, 'I felt I had a lot more to give, and there was no one, well, not no one to give it to, but no direction in which to give it. I didn't know which way to turn.'

The experience of being one of a group from a children's Home attending a local school had a number of adverse consequences, and often made the children in care feel 'different' and discriminated against. 'One of the things that does impress on my mind thinking back, is the fact that in a Home we were regarded, to outsiders, school and in the village and things like this, as "the Home kids" ' said Andrew. 'At school when there was a medical examination or something like this the teacher used to come out and say "Now all the Home children stand over this side and all the other . . ." '

Instead of going forward each with his or her own class group, the children from his Home were extracted from their individual classes and all put together in a line.

This is where I felt very aware of it. I would rather have been mixed up with the others; I'd have felt more secure that way. You felt that

you were detached, you were different, you were something of
a Martian, you weren't the same as them and yet you wanted to be
the same as them. In anything you were sort of segregated. 'Now
the Home people, all the Home people together!' Looking back and
trying to remember my feelings at the time, in my own heart I
objected to this. I thought 'How can we be different to them? We
want to be the same as them.'

Andrew was describing his experience in the children's Homes and
schools he knew. Barry was in a different Home and a different school
but his experience was very similar.

Everyone knew you were in a children's Home and you tended to
be not exactly lined up one side, but that type of thing. I can
always remember that one of the things was that you didn't pay for
school dinners and other kids looked strangely at us you know. You
weren't one of the other kids at school really. You came from
children's Homes. When I was fostered out I carried on at the same
school and I was still taken for one of the Homes children; I never
went over to the other side of the grass. When teachers were dealing
with matters in which money and parental permission were required,
school outings, for example, they would say, 'Oh, you're from the
Homes, so we needn't bother about you, we'll find out.' So you'd
really got nothing to say in it.

Like many of the others, Barry resented being made to feel different
from children in their own homes, even when the differential treatment
was a form of positive discrimination. He recalled one occasion where,
without his prior knowledge, arrangements were made for him to go
on a six week adventure and education course in the mountains. He
enjoyed it a great deal when he got there, but was angry that he had not
been given a choice. It was a rare opportunity, only one place for his
school and village, and he realised in retrospect that the social worker
and the school had been involved in positive discrimination, but no one
likes feeling helpless even when it is for their own good and fourteen
years later Barry remembered the feeling of helplessness as well as the
benefits of the course which were 'marvellous'.

Other group members recalled similar discriminations; being excused
homework, assumed to be unable to answer for decisions about themselves like involvement in school outings, and separated out from other
children when school medical examinations were being carried out.

The adult reasoning which led to these differences was not understood at the time, and even if it had been would probably have been rejected by the children concerned. It was resented as a form of discrimination, something which increased self-consciousness already painfully over-developed by the experience of having to leave home and he brought up in care. But there were other effects with perhaps more serious long-term consequences. Andrew analysed the group pressure as follows:

> The group reaction that was within oneself sort of came in to encourage you not to knuckle down to anything directly responsible and get on with things. I think in certain circumstances you'd have been more independent of the whole group and perhaps less aware of being separate from any other individuals if you'd come from a normal home; if I'd been with a foster parent, a solitary individual rather than say one of twenty, all boarding the same school bus, all fighting for the seats, all diving for the ashtrays at the back of the seats. Even at school I think we gained some sort of comradeship about being a little group rather than being a mixture in a classroom, and say, for my argument's sake, you weren't getting on very well or something like this, in maths, you'd talk it over amongst yourselves, 'Well, we couldn't care less' and it was all sort of bravado, being a whole group as it were. You threw all your emotions into that one group rather than having some sort of independence or some mind of your own. And you took refuge in that. It encouraged you to neglect getting on.

Another member who had experienced the same pressure said, 'I didn't like school and I didn't bother to learn. I'd rather just mess around.' He thought if he had been in a foster home he 'would have settled down and studied more' but

> because I was in the children's Home and the lads from the children's Home went to the same school and the same class, and we messed about at the children's Home as well, then you think school is another children's Home, whereas if I'd been fostered I wouldn't have had them (with me) and I'd have had to start off again. I regret it, you know. That part of my life I feel I made a mess of, terribly.

The sense of regret at wasted educational opportunities was a feeling shared by many members of the group. Andrew, the oldest at 34 and one of those cared for during the very early years of the children's department, felt himself 'to be about three years retarded' when he left school at fifteen years old, and was saddened by his lost chances.

Possibly the organisations at that time didn't really cater for the attention that people are getting today. Possibly the children that are in care today develop and advance much better than we did in our day and probably end up in better positions than we did and are better educationally.

The experiences of Anne, one of the youngest in the group at 20, suggest that the critical factor is still the amount of individual attention and support which the child receives, which often comes from someone taking a particular interest in their progress. In Anne's case, this support was lacking in her foster home and it was not until her emotional needs were recognised by teachers in her secondary school that she began to progress educationally.

I was at this comprehensive school for about a year and a half, and tension had built up inside me so much that I just had to talk to somebody and some perfectly trivial thing at school happened in a domestic science class, I can't remember what it was, and I started crying a bit, weeping, and the teacher was ever so sympathetic. She asked me to tell her all about it and when my tears had dried up a bit I went out and went home. It was the last period of school so I was OK. She must have spoken to the headmaster about it because soon after that a lot of the teachers assessed my work and I got a lot of individual attention from them, not to do with my own private affairs, but it made me feel as though, at last, I belonged to somebody or something or a group of society. I wasn't so cut off any more. I was very grateful to those teachers, especially the headmaster. He arranged that I could take 'O' levels and if it hadn't been for him I don't think I'd have had the courage to go into anything. I think I'd have been a very backward sort of person if it hadn't been for his egging me on to make something of myself, for myself. If my foster parents weren't interested I wasn't to worry. If nobody else was interested it didn't matter. He was interested, and I had to be for my own sake, for earning power and this sort of thing. It really was a pep talk I got and he did quite a lot for me. I took some exams and passed them and it boosted my morale tremendously. I really felt as if I had something then.

29 FOUR PHYSICALLY HANDICAPPED GRADUATES
June Statham

The four studies described below are based on interviews conducted in 1977 by the National Foundation for Educational Research as part of a study of physically handicapped graduates. Although the four people concerned have all attended the same Further Education college for the physically handicapped to take 'A' levels and prepare themselves for university or polytechnic, their earlier experiences of education have been very different. Josh spent all his educational career before university in special schools or colleges, while Ray was a pupil in a normal comprehensive for three years until he found he could no longer cope. Anna attended a residental school for the visually handicapped and entered the special FE college as a mature student, while Anita only became handicapped at sixteen due to a motorcycle accident and therefore received a normal integrated education. The interviews reveal various similarities and some important differences between the four in their attitudes toward special schooling, in their experiences of coping with the academic and social life of a university or polytechnic, and in the reactions they have encountered from able-bodied students.

Anna is seriously handicapped by blindness, partial hearing and arthritis, which not only restricts her movements but frequently causes her intense pain. Although she is able to walk and to climb stairs, the general restriction of movement in her joints is very disabling. She is unable to carry heavy loads or perform fine movements. She has been totally blind since the age of nine but can still visualise things mentally. Her deafness is relieved by the use of a hearing aid, but she has the added disadvantage of her blindness making it impossible to lip read.

Anna had no real social life during her time at her school for the visually handicapped, partly because of its geographical isolation and partly because access to fellow students was limited to term time. 'During the holidays you stayed at home and you were protected.' Her brother and sister were allowed out normally but Anna's parents were over-protective and hindered her efforts at independence. This made her feel very 'different', and she began to avoid situations where her feelings were likely to be hurt or she might be 'treated oddly'.

Her parents felt sure that Anna would be dependent on them for the rest of her life and had adjusted themselves to this, telling her as her brother and sister prepared to leave home that 'we'll always have you'. When she was 21, they gave Anna 'a thumping great birthday party' on the assumption that 'they might as well pay out for that, because they were never going to have to finance my wedding'. Anna did marry soon after starting FE college, but her earlier experiences made her feel that most people assumed handicapped people 'oughtn't to marry anybody', and that she was 'obscene' to express a liking for babies. She recalls encountering frank prejudice from parents of boys she dated, who feared Anna might become permanently involved with their sons.

Anna was always certain that her capabilities were underestimated and that people were aware of how different she was rather than of her similarities with themselves. Her intelligence coupled with what she calls 'pig-headedness' led to her entering a college of further education for physically handicapped students in her late twenties and obtaining 'A' levels there which enabled her to go on to study philosophy at university. She found no difficulty with the academic work, but some of the organisational aspects baffled her. Her blindness made it difficult for Anna to estimate the required length for essays, and the time limits set meant that she had to learn to organise her time carefully. Preparation was more important for her than for other students as she had to rely to a large extent on having material read to her beforehand – braille facilities were available at the university, but she found an external reader more efficient. Although the university was generally accessible, movement from building to building took Anna a good deal of time. She was able to walk but her movement was limited and slow, so that if lectures ran close together she would have to arrange for someone to guide her from one to the other in order to be on time. She also needed help in getting up the steps to the library, although a room was provided inside for her to store books. The lecturers were helpful and agreed to speak more slowly, but Anna did not feel that she could make demands on the university other than those which were more than justified. She felt a great responsibility for others who might follow in her footsteps, and made a particular effort 'not to make a nuisance of myself'. She tried not to stand out in any way, preferring to queue rather than sit and wait to be asked what she wanted, and she tried to wear fashionable clothes which would mask her handicap as much as possible.

Anna found that the other students were initially wary of her, largely through ignorance of her capabilities. She felt that they were nervous of 'doing the wrong thing', and less straightforward in their curiosity about her disability than the young child who asked her why she had one big shoe and one little one, and went away satisfied after she had taken off her shoes to demonstrate that without them she leant sideways. Anna feels that segregated education for the handicapped is partly to blame for the other students' uneasiness.

"I'm all for bunging everybody in together and making them cope right from the start. I think that's the way. It has advantages both ways because the handicapped learn to cope, learn what the *real* world's like rather than just being thrown into it at 16 or 18 or whatever, and they (the able-bodied community) learn that you're not freaks."

Josh is definitely not in favour of 'bunging everybody in together'. Born in Africa, Josh contracted polio in infancy and came to England paralysed from the waist down with no use whatsoever of his legs. All his education has been spent in schools for the physically handicapped, where his intellectual and physical talents have enabled him to feel 'a big fish in a little pond'. He was one of a group at his special school who took 'O' levels in three years, and he participated in a great deal of sport, particularly basketball and table tennis (he now plays international wheelchair basketball).

Success seemed to come easily to Josh, without his really trying. The institutions he attended were very willing to do his fighting for him and he responded by succeeding with apparently very little effort. 'We've arranged for you to have an interview at FE college. I went and they said "oh well, you've been accepted." It was the same at university.'

University was Josh's first experience of a true able-bodied environment. He had always prided himself on being very fit, but he soon realised that he was no longer the fittest in the group, and for the first time had to 'ask for favours', which did not come easily. He felt impatient with people who did not respond immediately to requests for help; 'if they hummed and hawed about it I would say don't bother'. Josh's initial contact with other students was not entirely successful. He felt that if he asked for help they expected him to demean himself in some way, and gave an example of when his car battery was flat and he asked some fellow students to push him. They said they would 'in a couple of minutes', but Josh found their casualness off-putting and left his car in the middle of the road, using his wheelchair to get to his destination instead. On the other hand, he also found it hard to deal with 'those people you say "no" to who still insist on giving you a hand'. Josh found that his physical disability tended to curb racism. 'People tend to see your chair first, and then when they get to know you, your colour.'

When he first began at the university Josh used to play table tennis in the students' union, but he found that other students would often patronise him, 'playing soft' at the start of a game and then 'when you mopped them off the table, they'd claim that they weren't trying'. He also used to go to discos, but found that girls either turned down his invitation to dance or accepted 'because they were too embarrassed to say no'. He started to spend most of his free time away from the university, playing wheelchair basketball. Among the disabled community Josh could excel both physically and socially.

> When you go down to the disabled games, you talk to girls with more self-confidence because you feel they're not going to mind you being in a chair, that's what they're there for. But when you are in the university, they don't expect a bloke in a chair to ask a girl to dance.

Josh's success in the disabled environment, where he has 'always been king pin at something or other', has given him a lot of confidence. He does not think that his difficulties in relating to non-handicapped people are due to his having attended special schools, nor that his schooling has held him back — he admits it took longer for him to get to university, but as he says 'I got there.' According to Josh, 'If I had grown up in an able-bodied school I wouldn't have been the person I am. I'd have felt inadequate.'

Ray's feelings about special schooling are less clear than those of Anna or Josh. He has a fairly rare condition which affects the muscles in his legs and back and keeps him in a wheelchair, although he is fairly independent physically. Much of his education has taken place in special schools, although for three years he attended a large comprehensive where he found his physical difficulties made it hard for him to cope, especially as he received no special help. He wasn't in a wheelchair then, but walking was very difficult. At the end of the school day Ray was taxied home and saw no one. He became very depressed and was transferred to a school for the physically handicapped, later going on to the same special FE college that Anna and Josh attended 'to avoid any outside pressure for a while' and then to a polytechnic to study social administration.

He feels that he got on better once he left the comprehensive: 'I was struggling there and didn't do very well, but once the pressure was taken off academically I improved quite a lot.' However he also feels that his shyness and lack of confidence largely stem from having spent so much of his time in special education. The sheltered environment left him totally unprepared for university, 'I really wasn't used to the size, and that really worried me for a long time, just the sheer pace and size of it all.' He finds it difficult to mix with non-handicapped students, often wanting to break into a group but not knowing how. Being in a chair means that Ray would have to assert himself to bring the group down to his level, and he is normally too diffident to do so.

> I think it's a problem that's particular to disabled people when they get out of institutions, it's not till then that you realise . . . at college I didn't feel at all threatened, here I feel threatened by people. You're on the same level (at special college), not talking up to people all the time. If they are parallel with you you can relax far more. You really have to know people, you've got to know them before you talk to them.

Anita has no such problems relating to the able-bodied community, probably because until she was sixteen she was part of it. A motorcycle accident left Anita with spinal injuries which paralysed her from the waist down, although seeing her sitting on a bed it would be difficult to tell that she is handicapped. 'I look normal, if I wasn't in a chair people wouldn't know.' Anita feels entirely at ease with other students and will often initiate conversations with them. Her background of an integrated education and a full social life before her accident may well have helped, as does having an extrovert personality.

Anita is well aware of the mechanisms used in the able-bodied world to deal with disabled people, and tends to use them in a way which some handicapped students regard as exploitative. 'I started sort of "giving up" and getting people to do things for me. I knew all along that I could cope, but I didn't let them know that I could.' She plays up her femininity to get help from men. 'I'm always saying "Right, I want a man" . . . Well, men can't say "I want a lady to carry me down the stairs". There's a lot of sex in it, carrying and humping me up and down stairs. I do feel very female.' Anita resents the fact that although she has 'seen people look at me twice if I've been sitting on a bed', they back off when they realise she is handicapped. She found this less of a problem at the FE college, where 'we all knew the environment and understood one another'.

At the FE college there were, however, less opportunities for independence. 'Here I have to make my own bed; it was always done for me when I was at FE. Now there's not always somebody to run after you . . . you can't always rely on somebody being there to help you if something goes wrong. Say I got stuck in the bath. To get out of this bath I have to use a seat . . .' Anita relates the story of when she did get stuck in the bath, emphasising the importance of 'the ability to alert others to come to your rescue'.

Anita's eagerness to enlist the help of able-bodied people is the method she has chosen to deal with her handicap. Josh adopts a policy of mixing with other physically handicapped people among whom he can shine, Anna tries to make her handicap as inconspicuous as possible, and Ray is still trying to find a way of coming to terms with his difficulty. All four have succeeded against heavy physical odds in following a university career that should increase their chances of an independent future.

30 THE PREVENTION BUSINESS

Tony Booth and June Statham

Whenever a group of people discuss the future of special education the idea of prevention, of avoiding the need for special provision, is bound to be voiced. But prevention covers a very wide area, from measures to avoid high-risk pregnancies to methods to detect foetal abnormality, from compensatory education to social revolution. Everyone believes in prevention but few agree on what can be prevented, even fewer on what should be prevented and fewer still on the means by which prevention can be achieved. For the following discussion we gathered together people who have a professional interest in advocating and planning schemes to prevent handicap. All of them had a background in psychology but their views are diverse and do not always exhibit a secure grounding in fact. We have edited the discussion into three sections which look at prevention before birth, early childhood intervention, and the influence of social problems on handicap. None of these topics are covered exhaustively but each section gives an insight into the wide variety of opinions that are held by people with some similarity in professional background.

Preventing Handicapped Babies

Richard: Severe mental handicap is the area a lot of people think about in connection with prevention. With amniocentesis and other prenatal measures you could remove 50 per cent of mental handicap.

Simon: What should you say to someone if following amniocentesis you discover that they're going to have a Down's Syndrome child? After all you don't know how Down's Syndrome is going to turn out.

William: But you can make probabilistic statements about it. It's unlikely to go to university and won't raise a family. A lot of people not only want children but want grandchildren too.

Sonia: You could make more powerful statements than that. You could say this child will demand a disproportionate amount of time from you. It wouldn't cut much ice with some people to say he won't be going to university. But you can make enough certain statements to make parents face the practical issues, like the time, emotional draining and social stigma with which parents will have to contend. Like the educational decisions and conflict with authority.

William: You'd be saying these are likely to happen.

Sonia: No, they are certainties. Any parents with a child out of the norm to that extent are going to have to face these problems. I think it's the responsibility of professionals to spell out the consequences of having such a child more bluntly than may actually be the case.

Richard: In our area the Down's Children's Association have produced a letter for new parents of Down's children. It begins: 'This is a joyful occasion you have given birth to a special child.' You can't tie ethical issues to knowing that a child will take up more of your time. People may actually want to have that child.

William: It's not always up to them. There are Roman Catholic doctors who don't do abortions.

Chris: Different philosophies amongst doctors produce very different survival rates in handicapped offspring. We've seen dramatic changes in the survival rates of children with Spina Bifida.

Richard: In our area we get a fair number of marriages between Asian cousins. One or two families have produced three children all of whom are in ESN(S) schools.

Simon: You think marriage between cousins is the cause of severe subnormality?

Richard: One cause, yes. I'm not sure how you could prevent it, but it is preventable.

Simon: I read a book called *Walter* recently. He's a severely handicapped person and he's meant to be the product of an incestuous relationship. My reaction to that was this was literary licence. There isn't any evidence to suggest this should happen. Is there really an increased likelihood of severe subnormality in children born of cousins? Do the children you are talking about have some recognised genetically caused syndrome?

Richard: No, but the medics for these families talk of intermarriage as a possible explanation. Maybe it is a myth, but in our area it seems a hell of a bit of reality.

Chris: What about children born of subnormal parents? There's this trendy view that says that not only have the handicapped the right to intercourse but they also have the right to have children. I think this is quite the wrong direction. Even if there isn't a genetic component to the child's depressed attainment in the future he's going to have the most awful home to live in. The kids I work with — a number of them could breed — to have them bringing up kids would be senseless. They're mentally handicapped, violent, physically handicapped. I don't think they'd actually get round to feeding their children. I believe that every child has a right to have good parents who can bring it up adequately and that it should have a reasonable chance of being physically sound. To allow some of the children that I work with to have children would be to deny these rights to any child they might have. This is an area where prevention is possible. Many handicapped people are actually separated in male and female wards at present so they can't have children anyway, but I'm concerned about what could happen if we remove all constraints. I don't deny that rather than masturbate they should be permitted sexual intercourse, but they shouldn't have the right to have children. It's only affecting a small number of people but it's an area of such obvious need to prevent that I don't see how you can argue.

Anne: There aren't enough mentally handicapped people who've had children to know what kinds of parents they would make.

Richard: You'd have to be talking about people for whom there was a very high degree of certainty aboult what would happen. If you took a typical ESN(M) population of kids you'd find a high incidence of ESN(M)-ness amongst their parents, but the degree of certainty would be far too low for there to be any ethical justification for limiting their right to have children. The case where dull parents produce dull children in deprived circumstances is different from where an abnormality is detected by amniocentesis and the degree of certainty is fairly high.

Simon: But even if you could 'predict' with 100 per cent certainty
           that someone would have a handicapped child they still have
           the legal right to have it. If you were to attempt to prevent
           people from having children under the current law you could
           only do it with people who were powerless to stop you.

Anne: I saw an article in *The Futurist* which suggested that parents
           might have to acquire a Mom and Pop certificate. They'd
           have to take a sterilising drug and the antidote would only be
           provided if they passed their parenting exams. Who is to
           decide who can breed? How could you put these ideas into
           practice anyway?

Chris: It's ironic that people are now bewailing the fact that there
           aren't enough referrals. At one stage they were saying oh
           God wouldn't it be wonderful if you could prevent all handi-
           cap but now that they're not coming through and schools are
           beginning to close and people's jobs are at stake, they're say-
           ing where are these handicapped children?

Richard: A head in an ESN(S) school in our area has said why aren't
           the psychologists getting them in? As if you could go out and
           find them!

Early Intervention

Richard: There's a big confusion when we talk about prevention.
           Prevention is linked very much to medical categories. What
           do you prevent? You prevent something – behaviour prob-
           lems or maladjustment or dyslexia or ESN-ness. But short
           term foster care can be a very preventative strategy. It may
           not prevent mental handicap, but it can prevent the parents
           being driven to such a point that they push their kids into
           permanent care. I think that's a useful way of looking at
           prevention, not that it prevents the child from having the
           problem, but that it prevents other things that may be conse-
           quences of the problem.

Chris: The children who come to my residential unit have mostly
           been badly handled by their parents. I believe we need a
           decent preventative service, training parents who are having
           problems with their child in management techniques, whether
           that child has a physical, mental or behavioural handicap,
           What you'd be doing is preventing initial problems becoming

intolerable. That's the most exciting area of prevention. Even with not particularly bright families you can certainly teach them a lot about how to handle their kid. There's a set up like that in Nashville in the States. They have six professionals at the Centre, and they bill all the parents for hours that they receive in treatment in hours that the parents have to recontribute to the system. If they're a reasonable typist they can contribute 100 therapy hours as a typist. Or if they're good at counselling other parents they can do that. So you have a self perpetuating, self help organisation.

William: Does it work for people who aren't middle class?

Chris: There certainly was a social hierarchy. You wouldn't have a down-and-out taking visitors around the unit. That was an articulate lady. But they're still involved — someone has to clean the place. Parents learn from each other. One will interact with their child in a room while others systematically observe and code the interaction, and others sit behind them watching how to do the coding.

Anne: How do the parents get involved?

Chris: Anyone who comes forward and contributes can join in. Anyone who has a child who's causing a problem, by the parents' definition. They're seeing forty kids a day. The professionals are very much in the background. They may be doing studies but basically it's trained parents who help others. The professionals encourage parents with particular skills to concentrate on particular areas such as counselling or observation and recording but it's the parents who mostly deal with other parents. There's a physiotherapist and two psychologists, and they've got the backing of the Peabody College — but they're more like resource people called upon by the parent group. There are 13 or 14 of these groups scattered around the States. Some have been going for 14 years. It also appears to be highly cost effective. Why aren't we using parents in this fashion instead of rejecting them? My one worry is whether a system like that has much relevance to this country, because of course they don't have a state system like us. They don't have all these lovely facilities that we have, you get up off your backside and join something like that or you get nothing.

Sonia: Wouldn't we have to go in for a lot more education of the public for parents to be that involved? I've just come back from Canada and I felt there was easier community access and more potential for including parents, in a way we haven't even started in this country, apart from the odd Portage scheme.[1] I wonder how many teachers and heads there are who feel under threat at the thought of sharing and therefore weakening their expertise?

Simon: Parents do get together and help each other in groups here, although they organise themselves without the intervention of professionals.

William: But you get some weird orientations . . . I had something to do with the hyperactive children's support group, and their sole therapeutic approach is a dietary intervention, they put out complex diet sheets, and parents get worried when the diet sheets don't work and they think there's nothing else to do. I think if you haven't got some kind of professional . . . not exactly guidance, but oversight − you might get an almost mystical, witch doctor approach.

Simon: Unless the professional happens to be turned on to diet too!

Richard: I've got little belief that there's a miracle cure if only we could get the techniques right; prevention through management and things like that. I read recently about someone who looked at the end results of research on behaviour management with parents in America, and found that even though there are the initial successes that almost all programmes throw up, the parents who can actually sustain the effort and the success in the long run are the parents who often have very good neighbourhood links and friendship ties. That interests me a lot at the moment, we're hoping to get a family centre started soon. It's the parents who will have the power; they will run it and work alongside professional helpers.

William: What would happen if someone who was really big on the laying on of hands gained a lot of influence in your centre? Would you just go along with children getting the 'devils' cast out of them, or would you feel professionally or morally obliged to intervene?

Richard: Each individual would be able to make a choice about whether or not to accept such an idea. The parents might decide themselves to boot the person out. You find that the parents who are drawn on for help by the others are the ones who actually are supportive and useful to the other parents.

It happened like that at a Family Centre I know in Gloucestershire, in a largely Asian community where the parents' particular needs were to learn the language, how to fill in forms, how to get certain benefits, medicals . . . in my area there's no extended family network, lots of parents with young children and lots of consequent problems, no granny round the corner or even anybody they know very well, and I think it's important to bring people together so that they can help each other. I think professional skills, such as they are, have to infiltrate rather than be imposed on people — particularly for that kind of area. The Portage scheme is to some extent different because it's dealing with an obviously physically or mentally handicapped child, and parents can see an identifiable entity that needs help.

Sonia:　I'm very interested in early identification in an educational context. By the time children usually get referred for learning difficulties in ordinary schools — normally much later than five or six — their problem areas have ossified, sometimes absolutely irreversibly, and if you can get into the classroom early you can maybe prevent the problem. There's a dispute at the moment about whether you should pick out children who have a lack or deficit which you are trying to repair, or whether you should be helping all children to reach their potential.

Simon:　Aren't there more than those two alternatives? You may pick on a few children, not because you think they have something wrong with them but because you have a limited amount of money. Then you can either focus on the child or the curriculum or the teacher. Haven't most British screening approaches tended to focus on doing something to the child?

Sonia:　That's too simplistic. Some have had a tremendous focus on the teacher; in-service training for example.

Anne:　They don't screen teachers and pick out the ones that are unlikely to help children develop their learning potential.

Sonia:　It'd be highly political to screen teachers.

Simon:　It's highly political to screen children! There seem to be two aspects of having a model, what you write about and say you're doing, but also what effect you have. Don't teachers, involved in your screening procedures, think that you are looking at deficits in children? It all sounds like smoke-screening to me.

Sonia: It's impossible to think of it except in terms of children posing problems. I get very irritated with people who attack a screening device as being deficit oriented when that's the whole function of educational psychologists, advisers, remedial specialists; to deal with problems that teachers define in the first place.

William: What's wrong with the deficit model anyway – I like it. Why is there a need to defend it?

Richard: I don't see how you can get to this level of sophistication, discussing models, when so bloody little is done about the kids that you know about. Raybould's[2] research is so nice, this huge elaborate system to help teachers identify kids and then after 6 years he finds out there's a 0.98 correlation with teachers' own identification. If you went into a class and asked 'tell me which kids are having problems', in three minutes you'd get the same kids as if you'd spent two months screening them! Why go to such a level of sophistication in screening them when the real question is what do we do about it? In our area we haven't got the means to do anything. We did screen one whole school once, not really being interested in what we found but with the express notion of making a case for extra resources for this school, which we did. I found a 25 per cent rate of maladjustment in that school, it was superb.

William: On what criteria?

Richard: We didn't bother about that! What the hell – what does the screening matter? The fact is that the school had a very high proportion of kids with problems of one kind and another and we wanted resources for them. The school got a special education teacher attached to it permanently.

Anne: It seems like screening isn't a form of prevention at all. If you're saying all you can do is pick out the kids and then you don't have the resources to do anything with them, you could argue it actually increases handicap, because once you've screened and labelled a child they might do *less* well if you don't do anything about it.

Richard: And you need resources to do the screening which could go elsewhere. Our authority has started a screening system for pre-schoolers of two and a half. It's purely about finding the kids who've got the greatest single educational need, to

push in resources for those kids. We use a parent questionnaire; a list of developmental items administered by a health
visitor. The kids get allocated on the basis of those into a
priority nursery group. It's only done on those children of
two and a half plus in the area who are thought to have some
developmental problems; language, mental handicap, or other
specific difficulties. Screening only confirms what people
already know, it doesn't usually show you anything new but
it formalises information and so gives you access to resources.

Simon: Early screening is often associated with a particular structured style of teaching based on the setting of classroom
objectives. That's the approach Ainscow and Tweddle
recommended.[3] But it's not realistic to think we could
prevent classroom failure by a change of method, unless that
change of method was compatible with teaching a group of
30.

William: You're talking really about restructuring the normal school
curriculum. Ainscow's work was mainly in an ESN(M)
school.

Simon: There's a common assumption in the discussion of prevention that it's better to expend resources with children at age
six or better still at age three, than to help people at age 15
or 18. I don't know that the evidence supports that, or
whether even in theory it ought to be true.

Richard: It must be a myth that if you got all the kids early enough
and did all the right things, there would be no more problems. At the very least there's going to be a residue of adolescent problems that you won't pick up at an early age. Prevention could never get rid of all the problems.

Preventing Social Problems

Richard: I think we've been talking very idealistically. The thing that
perturbs me is what to do with families living in the area,
who've got three kids in special education, another three pre-
schoolers, mum's pregnant again, services are pouring in:
social services, health visitors, probation officers — the whole
works. Then a special education mop up job. It's going on
and on, and it's going to continue going on and on. No

matter what you might think about prevention, it isn't going to happen in the foreseeable future. There are going to be the hard core, social deprivation families who for social, political, economic, or whatever reasons are going to continue to produce these difficulties. The kids are going to keep coming through. We've got families with 15 kids, 12 of them in special education. The kids are picked up even at two, you know exactly where they're going, it's a predictable pattern. They're one group that you've seriously got to think about prevention for. The other ones, like what do you do when you know the results of an amniocentesis, are straight ethical questions, but for this group it's much less clear but much more important. And you're not even talking about money, because the money's already going in; a phenomenal amount of money. Residential education, community homes, the services continue to pour in and people continue to pull their hair out — these families become jokes. In our area there are names which have historically been attached to such families. They say, 'It's a such and such family situation.' The labels are conveyed from one family to another. They're the families one lies awake at night about, wondering what can be done.

William: But you have to ask yourself whether those families would consider themselves handicapped. Sure, they're a headache as far as you are concerned because they're failing in school and are socially inadequate, but some of them get jobs, they survive within the framework of society. You're always going to get some people at the low end of the continuum. If you are thinking of preventing handicap, you have to ask yourself to what extent these individuals are 'handicapped' in their own terms. If I were an unemployed drunk and my child wasn't reading I might not see him as failing.

Chris: We haven't faced the problem. We've been talking about families and children who are handicapping the community rather than being handicapped. We're talking about the degree to which these families handicap *us* given the scarce resources available. Isn't that the nettle you won't grasp? I worked in a docks area for a while as a social worker, and I didn't meet many families who realised they were the bottom of the pile. They had tatty photographs of their kids on the wall and, just as some people might talk about their kids going to Eton or Harrow, they would say 'He's in Durham Jail' or 'He's at

Borstal.' The only people who saw them as being at the bottom of the heap were us.

Simon: But there are many extremely poor people.

Chris: The poverty that they are suffering is nothing to do with any injustice. We live in a society where you get back what you put in.

Sonia: What about those who are genuinely unable to because they were handicapped from birth by lack of opportunities or options?

William: What are you suggesting could be done about it? That the people who are very poor should be given more money?

Richard: I don't think one could deny that. Material conditions do affect kids. When you talk about special education it conjures up in people's minds a little twisted kid with funny bones, and wheelchairs and big heads and lesions in the spine, and Down's Syndrome. Not only to most people in the street, but to most people in the business too. But they're a fraction of the kids that we're actually concerned about. About 85 per cent of the kids I'm involved with every day aren't like that, they're kids who don't learn, who have social problems. You almost don't have to ask about home problems when you see a kid with behaviour problems, it goes without saying. If you want to get resources for visually handicapped kids, everyone's interested, we can get a scale 3 teacher even in these times of financial stringency. Could we integrate mental handicap? That'll come soon; physical handicap, fine. But there's this huge group of kids with moderate problems of one kind or another, behavioural or learning, or they simply don't fit. They're a great majority of the kids. They have preventable problems. What can we do for them?

Simon: There are answers. There's no doubt that the big housing blocks were a disaster and exacerbated the problems that families had in bringing up their kids. We could distribute resources in a more rational way. One knows what could make things better.

Richard: But what can you tell psychologists and educational welfare officers and all the social workers and teachers about what they do about those families *tomorrow*? You can't say it's all a social problem and needs social revolution when those people don't hold it within their grasp to do anything about that. The families are there, and their jobs are there. I'm not interested in what it needs a revolution to overcome. 'If only we could change society.' That may be a correct analysis, but what about tomorrow?

Notes

1. A home visiting scheme. See case study 45, p. 358.
2. D.J. Leach and E.C. Raybould, *Learning and Behaviour Difficulties at School* (Open Books, London, 1977).
3. M. Ainscow and D.A. Tweddle, *Preventing Classroom Failure: An Objective Approach* (Wiley, Chichester, 1979).

31 ORDINARY SECONDARY SCHOOL: WHAT ITS STUDENTS SAY

Peter Woods

Sources: Peter Woods, *The Divided School* (Routledge and Kegan Paul, London, 1979); Peter Woods, 'Negotiating the Demands of Schoolwork', *Journal of Curriculum Studies*, *10*, 4 (1978), pp. 309–27.

The logical extension of the concept of 'special needs in education' is that all children should be provided with a stimulating education that meets their particular needs. For many children this is far from being a reality. The following material, collected by Peter Woods during a participant observation study of a secondary modern school, illustrates how irrelevant is much of what is taught in an ordinary secondary school to the needs of many pupils.

The conversations I had with a particular class of fifth form non-examinations pupils about their life at school revealed widespread dissatisfaction with the organisation and teaching of the school. Many regretted not having been allowed to take examinations. Some had lost out by choices in the third year. The 'work' they were doing and had been doing since the beginning of the fourth year was too 'boring', too 'simple'; they were simply repeating work; or did 'useless', 'meaningless' work or 'nothing'; lessons were not 'helping for the future'; they were 'ignored', 'forgotten about', 'practised upon', 'made use of'; some teachers agreed with them, others 'didn't care', 'picked on them', took it out on them.'

The following examples are given to demonstrate how ingrained this boredom is within these pupils.

Example 1

PW: Do you get anything out of school subjects?
George: No, not very helpful I don't find them, just boring.
Len: Some of them interest yer.

204

Harry: Everybody likes an easy time, don't they? Like our English group now, it's mad ain't it? He tells you the answers before you ever do anything. Says 'Oh well, I'll write it up on the blackboard first and then I'll copy it out.' Huh! rubbish!

Len: It's like Mr Brown, you don't learn nothing on that, you just copy off the board.

Harry: Blackboards and blackboards of writing, it's just meaningless. You write it down. Can you tell me what we done last week?

George: Done nothing.

Len: I wasn't here last week.

PW: What use do you make of this writing, do you ever read it again, are you ever tested on it?

Len: No.

Harry: We haven't 'ad an exam in two years, it's pointless.

Example 2

Kim: I can do it, I just don't like it, it's too boring. The maps we are doing now are so simple really.

Christine: I've not learnt anything these past two years. The English we're doing is exactly the same as my sister's doing in the first year, and the maths work, she's doing 'arder work than what I'm doing.

Kim: What I'm doing is fractions, but 'alf of this work is only second form stuff, I just sit around doing nothing either because it's too easy or because I'm not bothered about it.

Christine: See, we're not learning anything, we've done it all before. I wish they'd give us some work, some proper work to do. It's so boring. We have two lessons with Mrs Nelson, that's interesting because she talks to us about life and things like that. Nobody plays about there because it's interesting. In chemistry the boys sit around and throw things about.

Example 3

Sally: I'm repeating work, it's making me sick because I can remember doing it before and it was quite exciting then but now we're painting and washing up and everything else.

Susan:	. . . ever so easy . . . (All talking at once in agreement.)
PW:	Isn't there anything you enjoy doing?
Joanne:	Art, and that's about all — for a laugh.

Example 4

| John: | There's nothing to do here. There's a long dinner hour, not that we mind that but us being fifth years, we can't have a room to ourself where we can talk. If you go in the cloakroom you might be suspected of stealing if something goes wrong, but if we had us own room we could go in there and talk, but we're all outside bored stiff, there's no activity to do, it really does depress you. We 'aint got nothing to do, you're just waiting for the next lesson and when it comes, you're bored stiff. |

Example 5

| PW: | Looking back on school, what do you think you're going to remember about it most? |
| Paul: | Boredom, of all the lessons and that. Same thing day after day. I liked primary school better, there were more things to do and I seemed to get on better there. |

Example 6

| Alan: | When they had speech day everyone started ripping off these bits of foam under their chairs and started throwing them about. Suddenly I noticed a line of teachers at the door taking names, everyone in the hall, you know, spaced out, sort of gestapo, spaced out, standing up for the interrogation . . . 'Did you throw?' . . . 'Were you in?' . . . some people got the cane, but it was so *boring* it weren't true speech days. If you're sat there for a whole afternoon with nothing to do you do get bored, don't you? |

Example 7

| Simon: | It's not a bad school really, you know. I don't mind it you know, but . . . coming every day doing the same old thing one day after the other, same lessons, you know, gets a bit sickening. You can't wait until the end of the week or the end of the day, you know, when you get here. |

PW: Do you find the work difficult?
Simon: No, it's not difficult, it's boring. You just sit there with
            a whole lot of work to do.
PW: What do you do, say in English?
Simon: Wednesdays, teacher reads to you which you nearly fall
            off to sleep, I do anyway. You get so bored with it you
            know.
PW: What else do you do?
Simon: It's hard to think. I remember once I got so bored I did
            fall off to sleep in English. Yeah, so bored with it.

Example 8

From field notes 5 March 1975; art-periods 1 and 2, 4th form. Carol,
Janice and Susan seem lost for anything to do. 'Have you any jobs sir?'
The three of them shimmy idly over.

Teacher: 'How am I going to find jobs for you three for all of
            next term?' (Teacher sets them arranging magazines in
            a file, the three exchange looks of resignation.) Teacher
            tells me they're not interested in art. They came to him
            for negative reasons. He sees some of them three times
            a week, twice for half days. There are four more terms
            to go yet.

A considerable amount of 'mucking about' was mentioned in
association with expressions of boredom, itself often connected with
routine, ritual and regulations. Thus speech days, assemblies and other
forms of ritual which the vast majority of pupils I spoke to described as
'boring', 'useless', 'meaningless', 'a waste of time', taxed their ingenuity
in remaining sane. I witnessed many assemblies. On the surface they
seemed rigid, militaristic, well-drilled affairs. Pupils filed in by form,
were inspected for uniform as they passed through the door, and lined
up in serried ranks. Teachers ordered them, squaring off rough corners,
tidying up lines, filling up spaces. They stood among them at strategic
points while those not on 'duty' mounted the platform. There followed,
usually, a talk, a hymn, prayers, then announcements. The beginning
and end were monopolised by the band. For most of the pupils I spoke
to in the senior school it was twenty minutes of standing boredom. Here
are some typical reactions:

'Assemblies are a waste of time. For religious people they're OK, it's

a good morning's start, but there aren't many religious people in the
school. You're all in there together, it's a great temptation to kick
somebody's legs and make them fall down just for a laugh, just
temptation to trouble.'

'No, we don't listen in assembly, we just muck about. Sing to drown
everyone else and that.'

'Useless, rubbish.'

'The boys keep tickling yer . . . All mucking about . . . boys pulling
your hair and that.'

'Waste of time I reckon, 'cos while you're standing there you might
as well have an extra ten minutes on your lessons. All you do is sing
a song and say a prayer, and that's it, you're out again. You could
do that any time, couldn't you, at home?'

Among the pupils assembly activities that I observed were the
mutilating of hymn-books, whispering messages along the row, general
scuffling, teasing the nearest teacher, communicating by coughs,
making faces at the teachers on the stage. The hymns seemed to be
quite an exciting affair. Among the competitions I witnessed were
trying to be the last one to finish a verse, getting a word in in the
middle of a pause (the most amusing one I heard was a cacophony of
'harks' in the pauses between the lines in 'Hark the Herald Angels Sing'),
trying to drown the senior mistress, inventing new words for the hymn
as you go along, mutilating your hymn-books some more.

'Mucking about' is often a reaction to lessons that seem irrelevant
and incomprehensible, like this fourth year maths lesson with the
bottom set.

4th Year Set 5, Marks Observation: Excerpts from Lesson

Noisy lot. First few arrivals are quite jocular with Len. David asks 'What
are we doing today Sir?'

Len:	Decimal division this afternoon, page 46.
Harry:	Oh these aren't too bad, sir.
Len:	Right now, pay attention everybody, just like you did yesterday. [Len explains how to divide decimals.] Tell me what you do Jane. [General commotion while Jane

tries to explain division of decimals.] Just shut up talking when I'm talking, will you, you have the chance of talking when you're working. Listen to me now! Now pack up this chatting and turning round will you!!

Fiona: What do you do with the decimal point, Sir?

Amanda: Which side goes which, Sir?

Derek: What page are we on, Sir?

Len: The idea of this introduction is to tell you how to do it, so stop asking questions! ... Now, when dividing, you move the decimal point two places to the left.

Amanda: Right, Sir?

Len: No, left!

Amanda: That's what I meant Sir, right, left, Sir.

Len: You said right!

Amanda: I meant you were right, Sir!

Sheena: I said left Sir, I did!

(Later)

Sheena: Oh Sir, do we have to do these?

Len: Yes, you do, it's very important. [He explains some more.]

Sheena: You haven't moved the point.

Len: You don't have to with this one.

Sheena: Oh, it isn't 'alf' ard, Sir! [Len explains some more.]

Sheena: Can I have another piece of paper then?

Len: Well you shouldn't have started yet!

Sheena: I did, I thought we 'ad to!

Len: I've been here explaining, how do you know what to do before I've explained it?

Sheena: That was before I knew!

(Later)

Amanda: Sir is that right?

Len: No, that's not right! Look, you're all working, and half of you don't know what you're doing! Why don't you put your hands up and ask?

Sheena: Init 'ard?

Len: No it's not hard, it's ever so easy, it should've been done in the second year!

Christine: Who invented the decimal point, Sir?

Len [to me]: I thought I'd given them something easy to do so I could get on and mark their books — blimey!

The lesson continued in this vein. The pupils played with the teacher, pretending at the game of learning, contriving fun and jokes out of it where they could and devising their own amusement where not. The teacher's complete immersion in his own paradigm was shown at the end when he confided to me 'that wasn't too bad. They worked quite well in that lesson.' Most of the pupils, however, had played their way through the two periods.

It is not only the students categorised by the school as 'less able' who are mystified by much of what teachers expect them to do. Those taking examinations are also critical of the way examination work seems to consist of attempts to commit to memory slabs of knowledge by various means of varying tedium.

Dave:	The metalwork homework was to copy 10 pages out of a book, and that took three to four hours.
PW:	Was that usual?
Dave:	Every week, for a year.
Ken:	It seemed pointless, because we kept the book anyway.
Des:	The idea was to make us learn it, I think, but he said 'copy it down and learn it', but I just copied it down word-for-word and didn't achieve anything from it anyway.
PW:	Did it have any bearing on the exam?
Des:	Not all that much.
PW:	Did you revise your notes?
Des:	There was too many of them!
Steve:	Time you'd learned your tools an' everything . . . you couldn't learn it all. Not like history.
Dave:	In history, we do the same thing — just copy — but we have tests, you see — so we have to learn it.
Daphne:	I would have been much happier taking fewer exam subjects, because there's so much forcing you to do what you don't want. Then you try to cram more in at the end, and that was too much. Especially physics, I found that very hard, and chemistry.

I found few expressions of 'enjoyment' of work. This answer was typical:

PW:	Was there anything you really enjoyed?

Julie: No. Nothing I really enjoyed.
Elaine: I didn't mind English, but I wouldn't say I enjoyed it.
Julie: It's just something you had to do. You had to do it, you couldn't get out of it.
Kate: I don't think its been really hard work. I mean when people go out to work, I bet they find it a lot harder than at school.

The demands of examinations appear to militate against the personal relationships so highly regarded by pupils. What seems fairly clear is that there is a misfit between demands and resources. Suddenly and dramatically between the easily negotiated calm of pre-exam work and the rather exciting prospect of remunerated, independent, responsible and meaningful employment, comes this period of peculiar pressure, for which it was difficult to find a consistent rationale.

Shirley: I thought the normal homework during the year was quite interesting — maths and English I didn't mind doing them. But at the end when it gets towards exams, it gets you down a bit. They say you've got to learn this, you've got to learn that, or you won't pass your exams, and things like that.
Christine: When you start going over things all over again, that's what I don't like.
Caroline: Well, it was out of proportion. Physics we had hardly any homework, and we didn't learn much. In French we had a couple of hours every time, and we don't have the time to do that in one evening, we've got other subjects.
Beryl: You're supposed to spend an hour for each subject, but physics, you can do that in a quarter of an hour, French would take us three hours.

This work has a mechanistic quality:

Debbie: I don't like geography because it's all on the blackboard all the while, and I can't stand the teacher so . . .
Angela: He doesn't speak to you as . . . well, I dunno . . . 'e kind of treats you as machines really [yeah]. Its 'come in' he'll say, probably talk about something, not very often, its usually straight out of a book or atlases, of off the board.

Also it seems to squeeze out those other (non-work) areas of school life that make it a humane institution. So that, for some, it is the total impact of the exam programme that impinges.

PW: What will be the thing you remember about school most of all?

Heidi: Hard. No end of homework in the evening especially in French.

Shirley: Teachers tend to push you too much in the fourth year, they watch everything you do, and generally keep getting on to you all the while.

Caroline: Yes, and, you know, a bit strict with you, they don't let you have no freedom whatsoever.

Barbara: It starts the first day of the fourth year. We have homework sheets every month. If we miss a lot of homework or two lots of homework we get 'unsatisfactory' and if you get two 'unsatisfactorys' you have to see the year tutor and get told off by him, get put on report and everything. Really gets us down. That's why half of us don't do it really, to rebel against them, I think [laughs].

Not all my conversations with pupils were so dominated by a tone of 'complaint'. Many did express an enjoyment of the work, here and there, although that was more difficult to pin down and was invariably because they got on well with a particular teacher.

Many pupils in the examination forms worked hard but it was a strange activity, at times difficult, tortuous, and much disliked, not at all involving the ingredients of 'fulfilment' — opportunities for choice, decision, acceptance of responsibility, self-determination and growth. It was often the opposite of these, suppressing rather than encouraging them. Non-examination pupils saw school as for kids, almost a separate compartment of life, a glorified creche for adolescence. As a preparation for adult life the school failed most of its students.

32 PLEASING TEACHER

Patience Tuckwell

Source: Patience Tuckwell, 'Pleasing Teacher', *New Society*, 27 April 1979, p. 185.

Primary schools, with their child-centred philosophy and flexible timetabling system would seem to be in a good position to respond to children's individual needs. However Patience Tuckwell suggests here that instead of helping children to learn, primary schools may instead encourage the development of counterproductive strategies to avoid the stigma of failure.

I have seen a lot of jaded looking juniors and seedy, saturated secondary school kids lately, so it was refreshing to spend a day in the company of infants where that aura of world weariness was largely absent. Nevertheless, I was surprised to see in some of the children a teacher-pleasing strategy in its infancy.

These were 6 and 7 year olds, about 35 of them, in a large, colourful classroom, under a kindly and enlightened regime. I was not introduced to them, by choice. I wanted to see if it made any difference, not being a 'Miss'. I simply sat and watched them working and observed the way they behaved. They took no overt notice of me, beyond a few shy and self conscious smiles, until I began to play with the Cuisenaire rods. These are coloured rods of various sizes which children build with, play with and all too often use simply as counters to do conventional sums with. A little boy came and watched me laying orange rods end to end along a desk.

'What are you doing?'

'I'm seeing how many of these orange rods it will take to reach the end of the desk,' I said without so much as looking at him.

'I should think 12,' he commented.

Another kid stood by him and suggested 13, on the safe side. Another said, with characteristic caution,

213

'About 11, or it could be what Simon said too.'
Simon began to lay the rods end to end. About half way along he had already got 10 rods. I stopped him and told him to have another guess. He sighed and said,

'It must be more than I said. I'll say 15.'
The others hedged their bets and said quickly, without thinking,

'14. I say 14.' and 'Make it 16.'
The result was 20. At this a girl said dolefully,

'Oh! I *knew* it would be 20!'
Perhaps she did, too. Haven't we all kept quiet at times like these, afraid to be wrong, offering only safe answers. Safe, because if they are wrong, others will be wrong too. It sometimes seems as if, to many children, being wrong in company is preferable to being right alone.

I began to line up blue rods, which are slightly smaller than orange ones.

'I should say 16,' Simon ventured.

'But it can't be,' Laura said, 'cos, look, orange ones are bigger than blue ones and there are 20 orange ones. It must be more than that.'
At this juncture, a large, untidy boy called Eliot came on the scene.

'Oh! 150,' he said. Then he saw, because he looked for clues, astonishment on the others' faces and changed his mind. 'Well, only 20,' he said. 'I say it's 20.'
He was a typical strategist. He knew all too well, even at his tender age, that answers are what are noted and collected at school. He was very anxious to be in on the fun but unwilling to surrender himself to actually giving the problem his serious attention, in case, as happened all too often, he was wrong. Better to be wildly out, so that you can say to yourself, 'I *knew* that would be wrong,' than to risk an answer that might be right or might be wrong.

'Well, you lay the rods end to end and see,' I said. He began to do this but it took too long and when he had only put 4 rods end to end, he gave up and danced off to interfere with another experiment that was taking place. Laura had taken over from Simon and was now laying yellow rods (half as big as orange ones) along the desk. She got 40 of them. So then I asked her and the other kids who stood around, how many they thought would be needed to go across the width of the desk, given that there were 40 for the length.

'Well, less than 40', she said, after giving the matter some thought.
Other kids, not willing to commit themselves to a brave new estimate of their own said,

'Much less than 40.'

and
'Not as many as we think.'
Eliot, who was both more committed to his complete distrust of real
thought and also less skilled in disguising the fact, said,
'There will be 50, yes, I say 50.'
He started piling up yellow rods, his eyes darting round for clues as to
what was really required of him, now that it seemed he would have to
support his theory in practice. Did you have to pile them up or lay
them along the desk? He didn't really know. I thought that it would
prove too long and arduous a job for him to lay them all end to end.
I gave him a small box and asked him how many yellow rods he thought
would be needed to go the length of it. His eyes darted around again
for clues but nobody helped him. He ran his hands through his hair
and started talking about Bonfire night which was a recent event.
Eventually he began to lay out the rods. He wouldn't risk a bet. When
he had measured several boxes in this way and had seen that heaven
didn't fall if he was wrong, he started laying bets. He muttered to
himself, 'I'll say 6, or 7 . . . or perhaps 8.' It was a long time before he
would commit himself to one bet and risk being wrong.

The others did a lot of experiments and began to guess more
accurately. Other children, as they passed, offered guesses too, and the
scatter of their accuracy was not always related to what we should call
their conventional skills. Sometimes those children who might, in other
circumstances, be described as 'slow' were more reasonable in their
estimates and less easily discouraged if wrong, whereas those whom we
should call 'bright' were sometimes both unwilling to risk a guess until
the rods were almost all in place and also more easily put off by a
wrong guess.

When they had covered the desk in a multi-coloured pattern I
thought it might be a good idea to write down how many of each
colour we had used, i.e. that 40 yellow equalled 20 orange rods and
so on. But they were not enthusiastic about this new direction and,
although they did what I had suggested, in a resigned sort of way, it
took the fun out of their work and some of them drifted away,
disillusioned. Now, I think they were right. After all, writing at that
age is a labour of its own and the facts they were writing did not need
to be remembered in the same way as a shopping list or a list of dates
needs to be. They were learning to make experiments and to estimate
and they needed practice at this. Mere secretarial work was out of
place.

The things one learnt by watching their behaviour during these guessing games were borne out by their behaviour during class lessons, in which the teacher showed a film and asked them questions about it. Those who had not minded being wrong during the guessing games, were the ones who did not mind volunteering information, right or wrong, and were not put off by correction, but would answer other questions. Eliot, in the class lesson, waved his hand wildly with the rest when the teacher asked a question. He judged, rightly, that the chances of his bluff being called in a class of 35, were small. When, by bad luck, he was called upon to answer, he gasped as if he had momentarily forgotten what he had meant to say and when the correct answer was given by someone else, he said, 'Oh! Yes! That's what I was going to say.' He had very little to contribute to any discussion because his attention was always diffuse, split between seeking clues from the faces of the other children and the teacher and playing, chatting, fidgeting, anything rather than concentrating and so being shown up as someone who tried hard to do work but couldn't. The trouble with his way of life and that of many like him, is that they will probably go through school in this same manner, fooling their teachers by their eager eyes and waving hands but really remaining out on a limb and learning little. There were other children, besides Eliot, who practised the art of teacher-pleasing, of never showing their cards on the table and of hedging their bets and covering for failure. Of all the children I observed that day only a small number of them, like Simon, who had been interested enough to ask me what I was doing in the first place, and Laura, were confident and honest enough to make mistakes, to ask questions and to say those forbidden words, 'I don't understand.' These are the children who will always get the most attention in school, the ones who benefit most from school. The others manage to con us into thinking them lazy or naughty or stupid when they are simply fearful. Some, like Eliot, even manage to convince us that they are with us and they go through the motions of being educated without being detected as imposters.

The teacher's real job is one of sabotage. The strategies children employ for muddling through have got to be rumbled so that they have to declare themselves and learn to meet failure without turning tail. Perhaps we should put less emphasis on right answers if Eliot and his like are already at the age of seven, so frightened by the prospect of failure, censure and exposure that they cannot allow themselves to learn. I wonder what we have already done to these children to make them so aware of the way the world looks on failure. After all, these kids were relatively new to school. They still had an eagerness about them that made one think all was not lost.

Too often, of course, we make the rewards of being a good scholar, too much like punishments. We ask who can write and when someone volunteers his skill he is stuck with the boring job of writing up the work for the group. Later on, we require those who are conventionally bright to pass exams and if they fail them we make them try again. I know many children who do not feel that they can 'waste time' on hobbies during the year that they take 'O' level and 'A' level examinations. Even children who have not reached that exalted position on the school ladder, have so much homework to do that out-of-school activities have to be curtailed. It must be tempting to drop out at the earliest possible moment, to coast along until that moment, and when that moment comes, to drop books and learning with a whoop of relief, never to return to them. Like the old soldier, children learn not to volunteer for anything, lest when the sergeant asks who can play the piano, the volunteer be required to move and not play it. Only mugs volunteer.

Do infants already have intimations of what is to come? That the brighter you seem, the more hoops you will be required to jump through? For many, a policy of spurious teacher-pleasing seems to be the wisest course. If this is so, it is disturbing to see such a cynical attitude in such young children, the more so when we consider that these children were in a 'good' school, a pleasant building, with a kindly and imaginative teacher. They were nearly all from 'good' homes, well cared for and of at least average intelligence according to the standard tests. If cynicism is the answer these children, a particularly pleasant and well-endowed set of kids, have found, what answers are others, in poorer and bleaker surroundings going to end up with?

33 CHALKWAY SCHOOL: A REMEDIAL DEPARTMENT IN THE PROCESS OF CHANGE

Tony Booth and Ronny Flynn

Comprehensive schools differ markedly in the way they organise their remedial teaching. Some, like Bridgewater Hall described in 'Towards a School Policy for Remedial Provision', withdraw children for relatively brief periods of special help from ordinary mixed-ability classes. Others teach children they classify as 'remedial' in separate class groups. Chalkway school, at the time of this case study, was contemplating a change in its organisation from a system based on separate classes to one of 'supportive learning'. In what follows we have given an account of the views held by children in the school's first year remedial classes and mixed-ability groups about their position in the school, and then gone on to describe the changes in remedial organisation.

Background

Chalkway comprehensive school was formed from the amalgamation of two secondary modern schools on the same campus, one for boys and one for girls. Prior to amalgamation, boys with remedial problems were called the 'progress group' and received their remedial help in the attic of the girls' school. There was a tradition of separate remedial classes for the very slow learners, and 'near-remedial' classes for the children of slightly higher ability.

In 1980 the school had a nine-form entry and in that year class 9 was the remedial class and class 8 was the near-remedial group. The grouping of these classes at one end of the numbering system was a chance occurrence since the numbers of these classes were changed each year in a deliberate effort to avoid easy classification. There were two full-time members of the remedial department who acted as form teachers to the first and second year remedial groups and also taught English to the third and fourth year groups. A further part-time

218

member of the department taught humanities to the first year group and English to the fifth years. The English teaching of the near-remedial groups was entirely the responsibility of the English department.

Although the other seven tutor groups were mixed ability and taught as such in some subjects, by the end of the first term of the first year the children were divided up into four ability sets in each half year for English, mathematics, science and French. The near-remedial groups joined the setting system for all subjects except French, but the remedial group were only involved in maths sets. The children in the 'mixed-ability' groups remained within their forms for humanities, art and crafts and PE/games; approximately half of their timetable.

However a number of pressures coincided to cause the school to question the continued existence of its near-remedial groups after September 1980. For some time there had been lively discussions amongst the staff. A few thought of the near-remedial groups as an identifiably separate group of emotionally and educationally retarded children. Others thought that their capacities overlapped with those in the rest of the school and pointed out the difficulties for the children of joining the mainstream teaching groups and curriculum if they improved. The situation was complicated by the presence in the school of two ex-heads of the remedial department who were very anxious about the change, and a new one who favoured it. A discussion group was set up which examined the scores of the groups on school tests and found that there was indeed considerable overlap in performance. They also looked at the trends in the intake for the school and noted a rapid improvement in their ability in recent years. The head of the school agreed on the basis of this evidence to explore the possibility of abandoning near-remedial groups entirely. The balance of opinion, but not necessarily of power, within the school was in favour of making changes, but such changes were fraught with difficulties. A new and possibly powerful factor began to emerge in the following year; how would the administration of educational cuts affect the situation?

This study of Chalkway school is divided into two sections. In the first part we have looked at the differences in view of the school between children in first year remedial classes and those in other classes, and depicted the feelings the children have about the remedial groups. All the children in a mixed-ability class and the first year remedial and near-remedial classes completed a questionnaire which examined their knowledge of the school organisation and their participation in school and out-of-school activities. We spoke to six children from each group to find out, in greater detail, their views of school life and their position within it. Using this as a background we have gone on to explore, briefly, the changes the school made after September 1980 and the difficulties they have faced.

Starting a Remedial Career

In examining the consequences of special class provision people have often concentrated on one set of issues; do the children in special classes feel stigmatised by their position and do others look down on them and alter their expectations about them? But placement in a special class may do more than affect the thoughts and attitudes of people. It may be associated with a distinct school career which reinforces the separation of the children involved and may contribute to the production of a marginal group within a school. It is just as important to find out the differences which attending a special class actually make as it is to see how the children and their teachers feel about it.

One of the most striking features of the remedial classes at Chalkway is their physical separation from the rest of the school. Their form bases are in single storey huts in the school grounds. The first year group spend all their English and humanities lessons in their hut which amounts to half their timetable. In subsequent years they may spend less time there depending on who teaches them humanities. There are ten children in each class and as the head of the department commented, 'They stand out as a group in assembly because they are by far the smallest class.' The size of the remedial group has other consequences too; they did not have enough children to compete in the interclass swimming gala. They follow a simplified and modified curriculum without modern languages and this limits their possibilities for transfer and makes any comparison between their progress and that of other children very difficult. This is not true of mathematics where they join the setting system and not all of them are in the bottom set. In fact the mathematics department had been running remedial provision on a different basis from the rest of the school since 1979. They started a withdrawal system to help children who were experiencing difficulties at any level. One child, for example, who had come to the school from the USA, just did not have the same background of studies as the other children and was being helped in the areas he had missed.

The curriculum for the near-remedial group, containing twenty pupils, only differed from the other first year classes in the absence from their timetable of French. The rationale for excluding them from

French clearly had much to do with the idea that children should master their own language before mastering another. Historically it may also be tied to a British view that foreign languages are an exotic and inessential part of the school curriculum.

Children are assigned to the 'mixed-ability' classes at Chalkway school so as to produce a spread of ability in each group and also to leave their friendship groups intact. This does not apply to the remedial groups. Before September 1980 the children were chosen for the near-remedial and remedial groups on the basis of visits by one of the ex-heads of the remedial department, now a member of the pastoral team, to the childrens' primary schools. This system, whilst being administratively simple, raised problems about the comparability between primary schools, their referral policies and the competence of primary school teachers. For a small group of children this approach had the finality of the 11 plus examination. At 11 years of age they were to be offered a distinct secondary curriculum which would make it difficult to recognise and act on subsequent progress. This was high-lighted by the comments of a pupil in one of the first year mixed-ability groups (class 7) about children in classes 8 and 9. He had had problems with reading in the junior school, himself, but had improved whilst still there:

> They can't work as well as we can but we're all the same. It's just that some of them are a bit slower at learning than what others are. I'm not all that fast — when I was in the junior school I got stuck at reading so during the lessons I'd go out and I'd get taught how to read better and that. We had a teacher who wasn't very good then when I was put in a different class I caught up two years . . . I think a lot of them in class 8 and 9 could catch up.

Most of the children in classes 8 and 9 were aware of the reasons for their placement because of their poor attainments in reading and spelling or because they were 'not very clever'. Some children however were unsure whether placement was for ability or for effort and behaviour. One child in class 9 said: 'The other classes are for the clever people — it's not really clever people — it's the people who really work hard and don't mess about — they go into the good classes.'

Another child who had been 'demoted' from class 8 to class 9 clearly thought it was because he 'messed about':

> My brother who's a 3rd year now said when he was a 1st and 2nd

year he messed around all the time. He said now he's a 3rd year it's
the best time to be good all through the year and then you might
just get a proper job because they'll forget about the 1st year. I
might just be naughty in the 1st year and then be good for the
rest of the time.

Whilst the remedial staff are themselves clear that children are not
put into the classes on the basis of their behaviour, some other
members of staff certainly do think of the remedial classes as also being
for 'disruptive' or 'disturbed' pupils and it is quite possible that their
confusion is passed on to the pupils.

One child we spoke to from the remedial class was keen on the
benefits of her group. She had had remedial help at junior school and
thought it sensible for her to be placed in a small group now:

I think if you're in a class with lots of people the teacher can't just
be with you all the time. She has to be with everybody else and it's
hard for you to get what you want if she's with another person
. . . They're very kind to you in class 9. They give you more form
points. We win the trophy nearly all the time. It sort of gives us
more confidence. In one way it's not fair on the other people, in
another way it is.

She was aware though that the favouring of her class might be double-
edged:

It encourages us, but if they are in a better class and get harder
work and if they don't get it right they don't get any form points
. . . there was one comment I overheard — someone said 'You
must cheat, you must put them down yourselves.'

Most of the children who spoke to us from the remedial groups
felt that they would prefer to be in a different group. One child tried
not to bother about it but was made aware of his position by other
children:

I don't know why I'm in this class. Some say its because of the
age, some say its because of the brain. I just don't take any notice
of it. I just think, oh, you're just in the class, you've got to learn . . .
The other children they sort of, like, feel sorry for you. They don't
make fun of you but they don't really like you.

Two children said they had learnt about the nature of their group from others: 'People told me, they said "What class are you in?" I'd say class 9 and they'd say "That's a slow class" . . . I don't say I'm in class 9 now I say I'm in a different class.' 'Kids kept coming along and saying "What class are you in?" You'd say class 9 and they'd say "oh, it's a dopey class."'

But even if other children hadn't pointed it out, the children we talked to from class 9 knew they were different for other reasons: 'The other classes, they look brainy. They don't stay in the same classrooms like us. They change around and we don't. We just stay in our class.' 'Class 8 don't do activities like we do, like going into the gym and practising clown things. They do lessons all day long. I'd rather be doing other classes' work.'

One child picked on the 'chance' occurrence that year of his class being class 9:

> They shouldn't make a name for us like class 9 because its high — we think it's high but it seems low. I'd feel better if they changed it because they wouldn't know if I'm good or bad . . . the trouble is they'd find out when they saw you weren't moving classes.

Their dislike of their position in the remedial group made some of the children determined to work their way out, an aspiration which they could see might be frustrated by their lack of ability and which might also be blocked by the distinct nature of their curriculum: 'I've been trying to work my way "down" [to a lower numbered class]. Next year I'm going to try more than anybody in the school because I really want to get down.'

> I tried to get into a different class but I think I went down a bit on reading. I tried ever so hard. I must have gone off it. I think its the books because I went down in books [graded readers] I don't like the stories very much. Sometimes you miss out half of it when you're away. Today I've missed the finish of the story. I did read it but I didn't understand it.

The children in the remedial classes were well aware of their 'status' in the school and most of them would have liked to be mixed in with the others. We also spoke to children in class 7 about their knowledge of the remedial classes and their views on the current remedial organisation. One child who thought that the first year's classes were sorted out by ability ranging from class 1 to class 9 thought it was right that children should be 'sorted' in this way: 'You have to sort all the classes out into different grades so that the brainy ones can work at a fast pace and the middle ones at their own pace and so on. The slower ones get so far behind if they're mixed up.'

Three of the children we spoke to from class 7 thought that it was unwise to separate the children by ability. One related her ideas to what she saw as the consequences for one of her junior school friends who had gone to a school for the educationally subnormal:

They shouldn't put them all together in classes 8 and 9. Some people learn quicker than others but they shouldn't put them out because they're a bit slow . . . They could feel sad and get naughty and people could call them names . . .

I know a boy from my primary school who was a bit backward. He goes to the special school now — it's for people who can't learn as quickly as others. He was a friend but he's different now. He talks stupid and mucks about a lot — he didn't used to do that. We've broke friends now, I don't talk to him anymore. If he was here we could be friends. He just got silly since he left junior school.

Another child commented on the amount of English the children in the remedial classes were expected to do: 'I don't know what happens to them if they don't like English. They must get bored doing English all the time.'

A third child went into some detail about the way the system might be improved:

They should have a few bright people with them to help them — they could see what other children can do — it wouldn't hold the bright ones back because if you're brainy you won't suddenly become stupid . . . They should be able to mix more, they feel stupid if they're kept away from other people. Some of the boys in class 8 mess around and stop the others working. They ought not all to be in the same class.

The answers to the questionnaire which we gave to the children broaden the picture we have of the separation between children in mixed-ability classes and remedial classes. To give an indication of the children's knowledge of the distribution of power within the school we asked them to name the senior members of staff such as the deputy head and head of English. In the case of the mixed-ability group 90 per cent of them could name more than four senior members of staff correctly and 50 per cent could identify more than nine. Only 50 per cent of the remedial group could name more than four senior staff and none of them could name more than nine. The near-remedial group occupied an intermediate position on both these counts.

We also looked at their knowledge of the examination system and the setting system in the school, as well as their membership of clubs inside and outside school. The results were again clear. By the third term of the first year 70 per cent of the children in the mixed-ability group and the near-remedial group were aware of the different types of examination in which children were involved in the fifth year; only a quarter of the children in the remedial group had such knowledge. All the mixed-ability group were familiar and accurate about the setting system, some of the near-remedial group were confused about it and only a quarter of the remedial class had any idea of what it entailed. More than two-thirds of the mixed-ability group belonged to school clubs but in the other two groups less than half were involved. And the remedial group also took little part in organised activities outside school.

This gradation in knowledge about the school may seem unsurprising. The differences may merely reflect the levels of ability of the groups and the degree to which they actually come into contact with members of staff. Whether such differences are important depends on how they are interpreted and also on the attitude one takes to children in the remedial groups. It is possible that their lack of knowledge and degree of participation in school life mutually reinforce each other and contribute to the creation of a distinct set of aspirations and a feeling of separation from school life.

There are differences then between the 'remedial' and other children's position, knowledge, perceptions and attitudes. From our discussions with the children it was clear that these differences were most keenly felt by the remedial group. We did not look in detail at the way these affect their life higher up the school. Although many of the children were not happy to be in the remedial classes, they were constructive about ways of changing the organisation or teaching. None of the children interviewed appeared to have given up on school. They were still trying hard and still wanted to do well.

The effects of a remedial education on the options of the children involved was brought home to one child in the third year remedial group who had been examining the fourth year option groups. He had decided that he wanted to be a chef when he left school and tried to select his subjects accordingly. He put down French because as he argued, 'All the menus are in French.' He was dissuaded from pursuing his choice because of 'limited numbers' but both he and his parents found it difficult to accept the explanation.

A glimpse of a further possible consequence is provided by the head of the remedial department. In the fifth year non-examination 'option' group several children from previous remedial and near-remedial classes are mixed together:

> In upper school you end up a little more mixed; in one non-examination option group you get those who were near-remedials trying to score points off the remedials to make themselves look better; they call the remedial group 'thick' as if they are trying to deny that they are the 'near-thicks'.

A Policy Shift at Chalkway School

It is extremely difficult to capture on paper the processes which surrounded the attempts to create a new approach to remedial education at Chalkway. The implementation of change is rarely a simple matter within a school; if the change emanates from a centre of power then it may become transformed by teachers in face-to-face encounters with children. If it emerges from a group of teachers who may have the appropriate knowledge but little power, then it may be changed to coincide with the perspective of those with the power to implement it. The departmental system of most comprehensive schools gives each department a measure of autonomy over the development of their curriculum and manner of working. In a remedial department, at the best of times, this may be far more difficult to achieve. For the central issues within remedial education impinge on the total structure of a school. Should children be taught in separate classes or on a withdrawal basis? Should remedial work be confined to literacy skills or should it be broadened to include not only numeracy but any area of the curriculum where support is required? Should a remedial or educational support department have responsibility not only for children who are slow or have a specific learning problem but for other children with special needs such as the physically, sensorily and mentally handicapped who might usually be excluded from secondary schools?

In Chalkway school the remedial department, in contrast to the number of children categorised as remedial, was small. It consisted of the head of department together with one-and-a-quarter other members of staff. The school contained two ex-heads of remedial work, both of whom could lay claim to knowledge and experience about remedial provision in the school. In order to promote change through the decision-making system of the school, through the heads of department meetings, the meetings of senior staff and the headmaster's office, the views of the remedial department required powerful support. Whilst we cannot document all the details of the discussions and decisions which took place we will try to indicate some of the major considerations.

The head of the remedial department wanted to move from a system of separate classes to a system of small group and individual support of children, all of whom would be in mixed-ability tutor groups. The discussion group which met to discuss remedial work in the school opted to propose a less complete shift of policy in the first instance. They argued to replace only the near-remedial group; some members of the group wanted it replaced by a system of 'supportive-learning' involving withdrawal from 'mixed-ability' classes for teaching in specific areas. This policy was pressed through school committees by one of the deputy heads of the school, though not without considerable opposition, and at the end of the summer term it seemed that the new scheme would come into operation at the beginning of the following school year. The deputy head recalled the events in this way:

The year tutor who moved up with the 1st years as they became 2nd years tried to unscramble the near-remedial group for the 2nd year but it was difficult because they had missed French and although they're not now a separate form, they still follow a mod-ified timetable. But at least we didn't have a near-remedial, non-French group coming into the first year. Out of nine groups we had eight mixed ability and one small remedial group.

But when the timetable was devised for the following year, things were changed. Although they would still be in a mixed-ability form, certain pupils, 'possible near-remedials', were designated to miss French and receive supportive English and maths instead. The deputy head continues:

So when I came back after the holidays I realised that some children in the new intake were going to have a separate curriculum just like they always had done. The second year near-remedials were no longer a form group but they still missed French. They were still, therefore, a distinct group who were referred to by staff as the ex-near-remedials! Things stayed completely the same further up the school. However there was to be a month's grace for the first years, a diagnostic month, when the particular children receiving remedial help were to be finalised. During this period a group of us came together to see if we could devise an alternative system for supportive learning. The head of French came along too because she thinks that the children should do French for the first year. It was partly through these discussions that I realised that it wasn't only the so called remedial children who can have a learning problem, its something that affects all children. I know that was something the head of the remedial department thought but I came to it myself too. I'd also seen that my own son could have problems or 'hitches' even though he could learn well for most of the time.

In the end we became very ambitious; we screened the whole year and made lists of children with difficulties in spelling, reading, writing and numeracy. Then we went back to the timetable to arrange groups for each area. We looked at the staff that were time-tabled for the groups and by juggling around free periods we managed to avoid taking them out of French except for one period of French studies which the head of French said was inessential. We ended up by re-creating the scheme we had wanted to run in the first place.

Although initially given the go-ahead on a trial basis, this scheme was allowed to continue for the whole of the year. Almost a quarter of the first year intake, apart from the remedial group itself, were receiving additional support. They ranged from one child with a specific spelling difficulty who was in the top set in all subjects to others who needed support in several basic areas. The group receiving support was larger and more varied than the previous conception of a near-remedial group. The scheme appeared to be successful, some children who progressed no longer needed to be withdrawn.

The 'remedial support group' began to devise their system of total withdrawal for the following year beginning in September 1981 and prepared documents giving precise details of their plans. They envisaged having eight mixed-ability groups with an 'impressive resource base in the old remedial huts'. Children would visit the base 'to the extent that they needed support'.

It is difficult to predict the extent to which forces besides the

development of a remedial philosophy might impinge on future
planning. Chalkway school has to make 'savings' of staff both because
of a marginal falling roll and cuts in government expenditure. In
common with other schools, the head has to decide on a set of priorities
in administering the cuts. It was possible that the proposals emanating
from the remedial department could be seen to be double edged.
They had argued that the school should not have two remedial groups
and this could be interpreted as implying that the work of one teacher
could be saved.

The developments at Chalkway have reached a critical stage. As
things stand at Easter 1981 there are definite plans to move the children
in first year and second year remedial classes into the mixed-ability
groups and to avoid the creation of a separate remedial class in the
intake for the following year. A small remedial 'non-French' group will
be withdrawn during English and French lessons. The 'remedial support
group' appear to have achieved most of their immediate objectives,
but as this account should have made clear, the formation of policy
in a school is a continuous process. The remedial support group are
actively promoting their philosophy and attempting to prevent any
possible cuts although they recognise that supportive, withdrawal
schemes can be seen to be costly in terms of staff. Their effort will be
one of several determinants of an evolving school philosophy, structure
and curriculum.

34 AN ESN(S) SCHOOL AND THE LABOUR MARKET

Peter Beresford, Tony Booth, Suzy Croft and
Patience Tuckwell

*The education of all children is fraught with contradictions. Educators
often espouse a liberal, romantic view of education in which the development of the potential of each child is seen as their central aim. But they
also prepares children for the harsh realities of the labour market which
for many may involve a life far removed from the flowering of this
potential. The role of state secondary schools is inextricably connected
with the reproduction of a stratified labour force in terms of inculcat-
ing discipline and differentiating students on the basis of skills expectations, training and qualifications. But, although they may not have the
obvious trappings of examinations, schools for mentally handicapped
students have to construct and come to terms with the economic
position of their students no less than other schools. The following case
study, adapted from material collected by Peter Beresford, Suzy Croft
and Patience Tuckwell, looks at one ESN(S) school and examines
contrasting philosophies involved in attempting to provide an education
suited to the needs of individual students whilst preparing them for a
life after school.*

The school from which the information for this case study was obtained was described by its local assistant education officer for special
education as 'typical of ESN(S) schools in the country'. It has seventy
students of both sexes ranging in age from 3 to 19 years. Most of them
come from the surrounding city. There is a separate secondary unit for
five autistic students and a special care class for the twelve most
severely handicapped children, described by the headmistress as
'severely mentally and physically handicapped, needing nursing as well
as teaching'.

At the time of the study twenty students were in the senior section
of the school and coming up to or above school leaving age; two in the

special care unit, the five in the autistic unit and 13 from the rest of the school. Sixteen of these 20 students were interviewed, three were unable to communicate and one did not wish to take part. Nineteen of the 20 families of the students agreed to take part. Some of these interviews were with one, some with both parents, one with a foster parent and another with the two workers mainly involved at the hostel of a student in care. Further information was obtained from interviews with the assistant education officer for special education, the head teacher and other teachers in the school.

A Child Centred Philosophy?

Although all the pupils at the school were regarded as mentally handicapped, like other ESN(S) schools, it caters for a wide range of ability and handicap. There were students without speech, with brain damage, physical handicaps, Down's Syndrome, and with none of these conditions. One 15 year old girl, an elective mute with petit mal, had been described by a doctor in 1970 as 'in my opinion unsuitable for education'. The teacher described another girl as 'able to read and write fairly well, can copy and keep things together, would stick a job and has a basic understanding of money'. The parents of one boy described as 'borderline ESN(S)' said he couldn't read or write very well, but apart from that was 'no different from other boys', while the parents of another girl summed up her handicap and abilities as 'diabetic, can't read or write, won't make conversation', but 'can do the housework and washing up properly, understands TV and can do puzzles'.

The routes by which the children arrived at the school were equally varied. Some had transferred in 1971 from the junior training centres. Others started school there at age three or five, whilst eight had initially attended ordinary schools but had been moved, according to their families, because they 'didn't fit in' or 'the school couldn't cope'.

Given this diversity an attempt was made to discover the general aims of the school as perceived by staff and parents. Inevitably there were a range of different ideas expressed about the purpose and philosophy of the school. One member of staff stressed the need to help parents to adjust to their child's handicap as well as 'looking to the child's future', another placed emphasis on enabling students to be 'reasonably happy and content', a third emphasised the role the school served in protecting students from society and a fourth felt that the school really didn't have any philosophy. One teacher summed up the school's goals as 'to help these children come to terms with themselves, to learn social skills, to develop their personality and as far as possible to teach them academic skills'. The head teacher suggested that the school was educating its children towards 'being as full a member of society as they will ever be able to be. Hopefully they can cope with it morally and physically and intellectually to the best of their ability.'

Although most of the teachers felt that the school's goals were not carefully worked out and explicit, underlying and unifying their responses were several common themes; to educate children to their full potential, to equip them with the best opportunities for the future and to bring them as near to normality and integrate them as much as possible into the community. It was striking how little mention was made of future employment for the students or of preparation for the adult training centres or for a life without work. In contrasting their philosophy with the aims of ordinary schools this emphasis was made explicit. One teacher said: 'We're concerned with the whole personality of the child whereas in ordinary schools they are more concerned with employment and holding down a job.'

Several of the staff felt that their students hadn't the mental ability to pass exams and this freed them to be more 'child centred' and 'do whatever is best for each child'. This broad, child-centred approach to education was echoed in some measure by the comments of families of students. Twelve of the nineteen families saw the purpose of their child's education at the school in terms of developing their potential and equipping them with the social and academic skills to benefit them in life. Only one specifically mentioned preparation for work. However, four families thought the school only served to occupy their children:

It's to keep them occupied. He hasn't come on too well with the 3R's.

To be honest I can't see if there's any purpose or method. They go there and they're treated like babies. If they don't do anything they never force them.

Most of the families agreed that ESN(S) schools differed from ordinary schools in their purpose; many judging this from their experience with their other children's education. They felt too that the ESN(S) school was more child oriented; concerned more with social training and 'keeping busy' and less geared to formal teaching and getting a job.

Preparation for a Life after School

In contrast to the teachers and families, the assistant education officer was quite explicit about the relationship between what went on in the school and the labour market:

> They do have the demands of employers and the labour market – in the sense that there are children there who would like to be employed who wish to be employed and must be employed – and must go onto the labour market in some form, protected or not. It's different obviously from an examination entry to the market, but it's entry nonetheless.

It is interesting to compare the aspirations of the families and students with regard to employment after school with what the teachers expected them to do. Only five of the nineteen families expected their child to get a job, and another two hoped their daughters would find a 'career' in marriage. In the light of traditional values for women, the proportion hoping for jobs might have been higher if there had been more boys, since they were outnumbered seven to thirteen. The rest of the families expected that their child would continue to attend some kind of institution; they hoped it would be a place where they could develop skills and abilities. Less than a third of the parents were confident that the adult training centre could fulfil this role and the rest were merely resigned to the prospect.

> We've just got to accept it. It's all she will be able to do.

> Sometimes you get the impression the aim of the school is to shunt them into ATCs.

> As I imagine it'll be a big, noisy confusing place, I don't expect her to fit in. Either she'll be a nuisance or she'll do nothing.

> I'd rather he stayed at school if he didn't get a job.

> I don't think it will suit her, but she will go there as there's no other outlet.

> I think the only good thing they do there is keep them occupied so they have friends and somewhere to go.

Not all parents viewed the ATC negatively. The parents of one girl would rather she went there than took on the menial domestic work that was within her capability. They were determined she would not have to 'go out washing up and scrubbing floors. She can do that at home and I'll go out to wash. I'd prefer her to go to the training centre. She'd be happier' said her mother.

Most of the students thought realistically that they would go to the ATC but fewer said that was what they wanted. When independent employment was suggested as an alternative to the ATC most students said they would prefer it if it were possible.

These aspirations need to be set against what actually happens to young people when they leave the ESN(S) school. The reality for most of these students at the end of their child centred education is entry to an adult training centre. Of the students who had left the school between 1977 and 1980 only two had gone on to open employment. The conflict in aims of the school was reflected in the answers the staff gave when questioned about the relationship between the school and the ATC. When asked how far the education students received at school prepared them more for ATCs than for anything else, the headmistress replied:

> It's very difficult to say because I'm afraid we all realise that the majority of them will go to the ATC. I suppose that you might say that our programme is geared to this, but we like to think we are gearing it to being able to cope with open employment — all things being equal, that they could get into open employment.

Most teachers felt that few of their students would be capable of obtaining open employment, including one teacher in the ordinary unit who took some of the more able children. They saw the transition to an ATC as a more or less automatic process, and generally encouraged students to want to go there by telling them that they would be doing a 'real job' with 'real wages'. However only one of five members of staff interviewed thought that an ATC, in its present form at least, was the most suitable provision for the school leavers. The others were more critical:

> It's all that's available. They'd be better if they had more education.

> If they took young people up to the age of 25 to 30 no more . . . Training alongside the work situation should have achieved something

by then; either have got them into work or if not, into a work centre. [sheltered work]

I think we know when the children leave here they haven't reached maximum potential – they couldn't do. But they don't have teaching at the ATC. It's more how viable they are to earn money. They need further education. Once the young people leave here, if they haven't learnt something, then that's it. They won't learn it. The ATC won't teach them.

We're not at all concerned with financial gain, but they are tied by this. We're more concerned with the family and the family problems. They're not at ATCs . . . At ATCs they all go into little rooms . . . They have to fend for themselves.

The word training should be operative and [they should] not just be a dumping ground.

Because the transition to an ATC is seen as more or less inevitable, the goals of the ESN(S) and the training centre 'run together at the top end of the school', as the teacher of the top class observed. In their final year students spend one or more days a week at the ATC in preparation for leaving and going there full time. It is here that the conflict becomes more explicit between the individual/child centred values expressed by the staff, and the role the school actually serves in sending most of its students on to the work-oriented ATCs. From what the staff said, the centres offered a typical range of work; simple and repetitive packing and assembling items like fireworks and cutlery on contract for outside employers, or gardening, producing concrete blocks, rug-making and woodwork, all for very low wages. Several members of staff however seemed rather vague as to exactly what the trainees did at the centres, and although one ATC was nearby there were no regular meetings between school and centres.

While the school is closely linked to the work oriented ATCs, it does not seem to be similarly geared to finding open employment for its students. While rising unemployment is likely to make this an increasingly difficult task, significantly it does not seem to be one which the school is or has been organised to achieve. It does not have a careers officer. The disablement resettlement officer does not seem to be involved at all in advising students. While the local education authority careers officer is involved on a regular basis with the ESN(M) school, he is not with the ESN(S) school.

While more efforts are made to arrange work experience or for a student to go on an OPEX (opportunity and experience) course, the school does not have any close ties with employers. The main provision for decision making and advice for the future of students is the 'Leavers Conference' held in the November of the school year in which the student may be leaving — although in future this is to be augmented by a preliminary discussion in the spring of the year before. This is attended by school staff, doctor, social worker and similar professionals. At present getting a job for a student does seem to depend more on the efforts and contacts of parents than the school. When we asked families before the Leavers Conference, all said they had had no careers advice from the school and only one had had careers advice from elsewhere.

It is not clear why the school does not have a closer relation with the labour market. It may be because this seems to conflict with the broad educational and social goals staff express, although as we have seen, so apparently does referral to ATCs. Staff did not seem opposed in principle to students working on the open labour market, even in its less desirable sectors. The assistant education officer said:

> The sort of jobs that the children would have . . . wouldn't satisfy people in the open market. A lot of our children in a rural county like this do agricultural work where they would not for example be driving a tractor but would do a lot more of the basic manual work — the sort of work other young people aren't prepared to take any more.

However in practice they didn't seem to facilitate this or initiate alternatives, and concentrated on sending students to the ATCs instead.

What stopped the students getting jobs? While there was some recognition of the role of the labour market and the effects of the worsening economic situation and their interaction with students' handicaps, two of the teachers, including the teacher in the ordinary unit, saw their students' handicaps as the primary obstacle to their holding down open employment. Only one of the school staff saw the employment system as primarily to blame for students not getting jobs.

This was an interpretation families shared no less strongly. Fifteen of the 19 thought their child was incapable of holding down open employment; only two thought they could. Thirteen of the 19 interviewed thought their child's capacity to get work in open employment was primarily limited by their handicap(s), four by a mixture of that and the market, and only one that it was the market that primarily restricted the young people's opportunities. Yet the students themselves seemed to have higher expectations. Eleven of the 12 who answered thought they could keep an ordinary job, including all those in the ordinary unit. All 12 thought they could do a job well. This may be related to their different conception of work than to their 'unrealistic' expectations. One girl when asked what she felt the difficulties would be for her in getting a job, clearly saw them lying in the outside world rather than herself: 'People will be horrible.'

One student felt painfully aware of his problems in finding open employment.

I can't be a policeman. Not so long ago when I was seven I was knocked down by a bus. I'm all right in a way, but mum says I can't be like a policeman. I could cope with the job, but boys would call you funny names and say horrible things like spastic. They're so tough because they go to a different school. They would bully you.

The assistant education officer expressed clearly the economic realities facing ESN(S) students.

The market obviously in general is a profit market and you want people who will help you produce efficiently and most of our children tend to become adults who need to be helped rather than just help, so it needs to be a sympathetic situation, a supportive, philanthropic view as opposed to a bustling profit-making enterprise.

It is clear that the school is constrained by the labour market as is the ATC which is supposed to offer an alternative to it. The work-oriented ATC reflects and is subject to the demands and values of the market; the requirements of outside contractors, the need to get work done on time. It also restricts who the ATC will take. The teachers said that ATCs did not welcome some students; the same ones we would also expect the labour market to reject; those clearly needing support, 'with little language, disruptive, not toilet trained, disturbed, who can't fit in'. When we asked them what skills students needed to go to the ATCs, they were similar to those thought necessary for open employment — 'the same to a lesser degree', as one teacher said. With increasing general unemployment more students from ESN(M) schools are losing their place in the labour market and being sent instead to

ATCs, so there are fewer places and increased competition for ESN(S) school students.

The staff at the ESN(S) school are caught in a number of dilemmas. While some have reservations about ATCs and would prefer them to have the 'strong educational bias' recommended by the Warnock Report, they know there are few alternatives. As one said, without them 'It would be terrible, [the students] would just sit at home.' They also know that neither the headmistress nor the assistant education officer share their view that the ATCs should place much more emphasis on education. As the head and the AEO said:

> Most of us expect to work as adults and we should gear these children to thinking of themselves as adults. It gives them a dignity.

> I think you must give them a work situation because they have had hopefully some twelve years in an educationally oriented background and although I agree that it would be very nice to have teachers, [ATCs] should still be oriented towards the work situation.

Further education, which is increasingly being offered as another alternative for ESN(S) school leavers, would have been acceptable to half of the families and many of the students, but it would not necessarily have provided an escape from the constraints of the labour market or of the ATC. Further education may actually only serve to postpone exclusion from the former and entry into the latter.

The Contradictions

If in an ordinary school the espousal of a child-centred philosophy appears to conflict with the idea of preparing children for work, in an ESN(S) school the contradictions are even more glaring. Children designated as mentally handicapped are treated as an identified and homogeneous *group* in being placed in special schools in the first place — a process in which there may be very little attention paid to the wishes of *individual* families.

When the families in this study were asked about the assessments on which a decision for their child to attend the school was based, 12 of the 19 said they didn't know: 'they just took her out of the room'; 'they didn't tell us', and 14 didn't know on what basis the decision was made. Several complained they had not been told. From what families said assessment was not standardised, although the headmistress and assistant education officer say that standard procedures involving the school doctor and a psychologist are now employed. Only one family was able to describe their child's assessment in the following detail: 'She examined her, made her walk up and down stairs, X-rayed her, tested her IQ with puzzles etc.'

In fact, eight of the families thought the decision for their child to go to an ESN(S) school had something to do with their expected (low) employment capacity. Families seemed to have little say in what happened to their children. Seventeen of the 19 interviewed said there had been no discussion about their child's future – 'She said she'd be there until she was 16 and then she'd go to an ATC.' Eighteen said they had been offered no choice but an ESN(S) school and this was justified either on the grounds of their child's handicap or in two cases because there was nowhere else. Eleven parents had negative feelings about the decision, two were resigned, only three pleased. In five cases these negative feelings remained. As one mother said:

I didn't mind when they said he wasn't learning but when I walked round the school for the first time I nearly died of shock. I shall remember it to the day I die. All those mentally handicapped children together, putting their hands in his dinner. He hated it. He never wanted to go.

The ESN(S) school does seem to deal with a disparate group of children and young people in a basically similar way. This is reflected not only in the way most students regardless of ability go to ATCs, but also in other policies, like bussing. All but one of the young people interviewed were bussed to school, although ten felt they could get to school on their own if they were allowed; an index at least of their desire for normality and independence if not a complete reflection of their capability. While the headmistress spoke of continuous reassessment, two of the teachers agreed that when students came to the school it was assumed they would stay till they were 16. The headmistress said 'transfer is never easy', another teacher that 'It's not easy to upgrade a child.' The headmistress said that there was not a regular review of a child's placement in the school – just termly and annual reports and a review if called for. Two teachers referred to the unwillingness of the ESN(M) school to take any of their students; 'The headmaster is against children with Down's Syndrome – put it like that.'

There were frequent complaints from families about the effects of segregation. Thirteen thought employers were prejudiced against students from a special school. Twelve thought their child was discriminated against and stigmatised for the same reason — mostly by other children. One student described himself as going 'to a daft school'. While only one of the five workers interviewed wanted to see integration for special schools, 16 families said they would prefer it if their child with proper support and resources could go to an ordinary school — one of those who didn't, however, saying 'Ordinary schools have so many of their own problems anyway.'

The individual goals expressed by the staff are simply not attainable. It is not just that staff do not recognise or neglect the differences between the students but that the segregated setting, the constraints of preparation for adult training centres and the poor prospects of open employment narrowly limit their capacity to respond to them.

The staff adopted a very narrow definition of work and the possibilities for their students of fitting into employment even in a conventional sense. The characteristics they stressed as necessary for holding down a job included speech, ability to write a letter of application, money sense, time keeping. They made remarks like 'He couldn't hold a job down, he needs guidance all the time.' Yet there are jobs where these clearly need not apply. Certainly people without speech and who cannot read or write can get work even in the existing labour market, albeit with growing difficulty. Students' families were no less conservative in their view of work, assuming that their children would be excluded from the chance of employment because, for example, they couldn't read or write, had difficulties using public transport, couldn't count, had fits and couldn't concentrate unsupervised. There is no reason why any of these need be insuperable obstacles to working.

While as we have seen narrow market definitions of work seem to be accepted by both staff and families, broader, more individual orientated conceptions and forms of work are also possible. Such approaches which give priority to the wants and needs of workers rather than the market could readily draw on the varied abilities of young people now in ESN(S) schools, enhancing their development rather than conflicting with it. Simple work need not be synonymous with menial status and conditions or repetitive and unstimulating processes. This reflects only the market's division and valuation of labour. Co-operatives offer one model of self governing employment where such young people could work alongside others, with sufficient flexibility and mutual support to overcome their difficulties and maximise their skills and contribution in socially useful employment. Judging by their responses when asked what they could do that they thought would help them have a job, young people had a broader conception of work than teachers or families. Thus students referred, for example to their ability to wash-up, cook, mend a bike and draw.

It seems that recession and cuts in public expenditure are not only exacerbating ESN(S) school students' exclusion from the labour market, but also having a direct effect on their education. Some families stressed the need for more resources. There was widespread concern at the inadequacy of related services, from accommodation to social work. Teachers referred to the lack of adequate residential provision, one pointing to the need for money for community homes, another to the need for hostels for young people: 'There is so little provision.' One family spoke of the way in which lack of resources impeded the fulfilment of the school's individual-orientated goals: 'You're told the school will bring out the child's potential, but they say they haven't the staff and no money.' The teacher in the autistic unit felt little was done for mentally handicapped adults when they left school. The assistant education officer while referring us to the social services department for details of trends in expenditure on ATCs, remarked that 'There never seem to be enough places.'

Eighteen of the students surveyed were discussed at the November 1980 Leavers Conference. Eight have been offered full-time places at ATCs, including one who may be employed by the Pathway Scheme. One was offered two days at the ATC and one day on an OPEX course, and another, one day a week at ATC – the other days to be spent at home. One boy has been offered a place full time in a sheltered work-shop which a teacher said paid 'appalling wages', or a job at a shoe factory if his father can arrange it. Two students are leaving without being offered any placement; five others will stay on an extra year or more at school. One girl will be going to a new day care scheme for two days a week, just started in a hostel attached to an ATC. As the ESN(S) school headmistress said:

Until this term no one has ever left with nothing to go to. We try to justify the extra year educationally, but there are shortages of places in ATCs. If they say there's no place at Easter, that probably means there's no place for at least another year.

This lack of places seems to be indirectly due to the effects of a contracting labour market pushing more special school leavers towards ATCs, including those from ESN(M) schools.

The staff of the school and others concerned with the education of the mentally handicapped express a desire to see ESN(S) students achieving independence. But independence mainly follows from employment in a society where the work ethic is dominant. If mentally handicapped young people are to be like other young people then they must be brought more often and more closely into open employment. The families and the students shared these values of having a job and being independent. But the labour market largely and increasingly excludes such young people from work, except in its most marginal, menial, insecure and poorly paid sectors. At present the ESN(S) school actually seems to serve as a dumping ground for the rejects of mainstream schooling who in turn become the rejects of the labour market. Their experience highlights and exaggerates the fundamental question of whether broad-based, individual-orientated education will ever be possible for mentally handicapped and for other children and young people as long as employment and the labour market are not orientated to the needs of the individual worker, workers collectively and the community.

PART THREE:

PROCEDURES, PLACES AND CHANGE

35 STEVEN: LIFE IN A RESIDENTIAL SCHOOL FOR MALADJUSTED BOYS

Will Swann

The curriculum for a child whose 'special' education takes place in a residential setting involves far more than what is taught in formal lessons. The following description gives an impression of what life is like for a ten-year-old boy who for the past two years has attended a residential school for maladjusted children.

The last thing Steven can recall of his mother is her stockings going up in flames as she tried to commit suicide. At this time Steven was only six and his father had already left home. After the suicide attempt his mother was committed to a psychiatric hospital and she is now a long-stay patient. Along with his older brother and sister, Steven was admitted to a children's home in the suburban borough where he lived. This has been his home ever since.

It was around the same time in 1976 that Steven was first referred for special education from his infants school because of 'overactivity, inability to concentrate, tantrums, stealing and destroying of property and other children's work'. The family's problems had affected Steven much more than his brother and sister who were coping well at junior school. He was placed in an 'adjustment class' until he reached seven and when the case conference met to review his progress it was agreed he should be tried at a junior school, with support from the teachers in the local remedial centre. At that stage everyone knew that if he didn't cope the only alternative for a child in care was a residential school for maladjusted children.

It didn't work out, and the following year, 1978, he was referred again by the head of the junior school for 'overactivity, inability to concentrate, destroys classroom atmosphere by interference with and maltreatment of other children and their work, first noted at the infants school'. He was said to be 'illiterate, barely started to read, but having some knowledge of numbers'. During the summer of 1978 the referral procedures went ahead. The school medical officer described him as 'an impulsive overactive child of average intelligence', quoting, to the letter, from the educational psychologist's report two years earlier. The consultant psychiatrist at the child guidance clinic wrote of Steven: 'He is a child in poor contact with reality, lacking inner control, and I think that a disturbed inheritance underlies his instability. He needs as secure an environment as possible.' He was formally ascertained as maladjusted in the summer of 1978, aged eight, and placed at Ferney Hall, the borough's residential school for maladjusted boys. When his remedial teacher wrote her final report she said:

He seems most at ease when in the company of just one adult. Then he will talk quite freely. When other children arrive and join in he relates to them usually in unfriendly and aggressive ways. He has learned his sounds, he knows quite a few sight words and has made a start with reading. Steven is a likeable boy, I hope he will do well with you and acquire the stability he needs so much.

Ferney Hall is a former country house set in 11 acres of parkland with an ornamental lake, clipped lawns and fine gardens. Ducks, geese and coots wander round at will but a closer look reveals how the lack of money has meant that maintenance has been difficult and the fabric shows signs of deterioration. Apart from holidays and four weekends a term when Steven goes back to the children's home, his life is spent in this setting along with 44 other boys aged 7 to 16. Many of them, like Steven, have a troubled background, but many others are at Ferney Hall principally for disruption and delinquency.

When Steven first arrived, the school was not divided into any age departments, either administratively or geographically. In 1979 the school was split into two separate departments — junior and senior — and Steven is now in one of the three junior classes along with 13 other boys. The new organisational arrangements were set up mainly to control what the head describes as the 'Mafia element' in the older boys who were extorting and threatening the junior children to whom they had easy access. Steven's time is now divided between the junior department contained in converted outbuildings, his dormitory in a prefabricated building next door to the classrooms, and the main school building where the meals and assembly take place.

His day begins at 7.45 a.m. in Millwood, his 'house' where he shares a large room with two others. The room contains three beds, three metal lockers and three small bedside rugs, there are no partitions and nothing on the walls. He is woken fairly gently by the assistant matron and has half an hour to wake up and get dressed. Apart from his clothes for the day, his other clothes are kept in a separate room. The head visits Millwood in the morning and greets the children as they wake up. Breakfast is on a self-service basis and afterwards the boys play in the parts of the grounds to which they have access until 9.00 a.m.

School runs in the morning from 9.00 a.m. until 12.30 p.m. with assembly at 9.15 a.m. and break at 10.45 a.m. Steven spends his time in two classrooms, because although there are three full time teachers at any one time, one of them is off duty taking time off in lieu of a long duty that all teachers do in the evenings and at weekends. When he is in his own classroom, Steven shares it with four other boys. The room is sparsely and poorly furnished; there are some maths displays on the wall and a map of Europe, one corner has some broken-down second-hand settees where children can read, in the opposite corner there is a sink and art table with a few sheets of plain paper, poster paints and brushes. Two sets of bookshelves filled with rather battered reading and comic books, some empty cupboards, a cluster of desks and a blackboard complete the scene. The room could not be described as lovely and Steven's teachers feel the problem acutely: 'We can't offer as much as we'd like because the finances aren't there. It's a matter of living on a shoestring and doing as much as we can with very little money.'

Mornings are given over to English and maths. When Steven came to Ferney Hall aged eight his reading was not good enough to register a reading age. Two years later, he now has a reading age of eight. The department has a variety of reading schemes to draw on: Racing to Read, Flightpath to Reading and Reading 360 and the Trend reading books which are used throughout the school. His teacher, Linda Duncan, hears him read every day, as she does with all the boys and quite often Steven will ask to read to her. This is something of a special time for the boys and the others tend to leave teacher and pupil alone to read, but it is difficult for Steven to find any quiet place to read at other times. In the reading corner he is quite likely to be disturbed by other boys and there is little chance for him to read quietly in the rest of the day since he has no private place to go. When the junior teachers are on duty in the evenings they will often read the boys a bedtime story at 8.30 p.m. before the lights go out.

Steven also works through exercises in the Junior English Workbooks one or two mornings per week. Here he might have to add endings to words or complete sentences. He is developing joined up writing

with exercises in another workbook, and when he completes some of
the more difficult tasks Linda lets him complete exercises in another
book involving more simple skills. He writes regularly to the Children's
Home but he needs a lot of help with this as he is a considerable perfec-
tionist in such tasks, and his teachers can exploit such opportunities
for teaching spelling. In all Linda expects about 30–45 minutes of
concentrated work at English from Steven each day.

He is rather adept in mathematics and shows off his skills at any
opportunity. He will be the first with his hand up in assembly if there
is a problem to be solved about pocket money. The department uses
the Scottish Primary Mathematics scheme, and at Steven's stage the
children use workbooks covering a wide range of skills. Steven showed
considerable skill in identifying lines of symmetry in complex figures
one morning he was observed, and he stuck at his workbook for some
time; Linda is satisfied with 30 minutes work from him in a morning.

The class work individually, and Linda moves round supporting and
prompting them where necessary. Even so there is not enough time
even with only five boys to keep them all going. Steven will quite
frequently wander off the task either to stalk aimlessly round the room,
or do some work on a poster he is designing, pick up a book and glance
through the pages or annoy another boy. The atmosphere of the morning
fluctuates between periods of quiet and intensive work — especially
straight after assembly and break, and times when the boys are milling
round throwing the occasional insult or thump. It is this inconsistency
that most strikes the visitor; at one moment Steven will be tapping sticks
on desks or belting someone viciously for interfering with him; at the
next he will be quietly and warmly cuddled into Linda, reading.

At 12.30 p.m. the bell goes for lunch. Linda lets them go one by
one as they stand quietly behind their desks. Lunchtime runs until
2.00 p.m. and in the afternoon the junior department broadens the
curriculum to offer what they can from their limited resources. This
term, for the first time, the department will offer geography and
history: mapwork material is on order and they hope to start some
work on famous historical figures before the end of the year. They have
no resources for science work, so a project on sound with improvised
materials is planned.

The boys do cookery once a fortnight and all, including Steven,
enjoy this. He can follow a recipe independently and Anne Mason the
head of the junior department believes this is an important survival
skill. Art and craft covers a range of options, including tie and dye
printing, sewing, knitting, leather work, plaster of paris and claywork.

Much of this depends on off-cuts and oddments supplied by friends and staff members. One teacher unearthed some clay from the boiler room and there is now more on order. The staff have an arrangement with a local paper firm which supplements their very basic supplies of brushes, pallet paints and white paper with which children get quickly bored. Steven is quite skilled in craft and has made himself something of the class expert in cardboard box constructions but his efforts have to be treated carefully. If any faults are pointed out he will wreck them. He is often afraid that if he produces something better than the others someone will destroy it. He is very good at claywork and praise for his work has to come from the teachers. If he takes things home they tend to get broken so he often gives them to staff.

On one afternoon each week Steven does games and PE in the large, new, well-equipped gym. On pocket money day, the juniors are taken out to a local café across a field in the nearest village where they can spend their money on sweets and crisps. This system has been devised to minimise the chances of extortion and protection rackets run by the seniors: by the time the juniors return, most of their money, which comes from the school's funds, has been spent.

Afternoons are generally much less structured than mornings, and not all time is planned. In one 45 minute session observed before the weekly trip to the cafe, Linda had not got time to organise anything and the boys played, but somewhat aimlessly. Steven asked for a drill to drill some holes in a block of wood: 'so I got something to do'.

From the end of school at 4.00 p.m. until supper at 6.00 p.m. the boys are free to play out and supper finishes at 6.30 p.m. In the evening two of the teachers on a 'long-duty' are in charge of the boys and organise what activities they can. In addition to the common rooms where boys can watch TV, play snooker and games and read comics, groups often go out in the minibus to the local cinema, swimming pool or in the summer for a walk in the woods. Depending on the availability of staff and their perceptions of the mood of the boys, activities may be offered inside school, such as archery, rifle-shooting, or a teacher may take a group for some craft work. The boys are free to organise their own activities and from time to time do hold discos in the common room. In the winter the juniors usually go back to Millwood straight after supper and play in their common room, recently converted from a changing room, until bedtime at 8.30 p.m. They have just had a television installed. Bedtime is important: Steven along with the others gets a goodnight kiss and a story from the teacher in charge, and it is a chance for quiet private closeness.

Steven's experiences at Ferney Hall reach far beyond his formal education there: the head stresses the importance of those times of the day when a pupil is not under any demands from staff and he has the opportunity to be himself, express himself and form relationships with staff and other boys. This is a time when much can be learnt about Steven. He is free to leave the school grounds with a friend and with permission so long as he is back for meal times which are used as roll-calls. If he is out-of-bounds without permission he will be fined ten pence. Misdemeanours and incidents are entered in a day book by the duty teacher and at regular staff meetings the cumulative record is examined. Boys can be placed 'on restriction' if necessary, which means they are confined to parts of the school grounds for a week, are not allowed out on trips or to go home at weekends. On the other side of the account the junior teachers have organised a system of rewards for good work: stars and points are accumulated leading to prizes of money or sweets.

Steven sees the deputy head for ten minutes each day for a short therapy session. In these sessions, which began in the school a year ago, he may talk about problems he is having at home or at school, or he might just play some games and chat. About a year ago, when Steven was going through a very difficult time, these sessions did help him over the worst, although Anne Mason feels more could be done:

> I feel at fault here, but I don't get the opportunity to talk to Mr James very often. I only have one half day a week preparation time which is invariably taken up with something or other. So I don't find out what is happening at his pastoral times. There's no communication about what goes on there; I feel I ought to know more about what he's doing with them.

The other boys in the school have a major impact on Steven's experiences. A distinct subculture has grown up over the years with its own vocabulary and organisation. The school, and each class in the school, has a distinct pecking order. At the top of each group is a 'King'; Steven is currently one of two Kings in his group. The pecking order changes quite often as boys jockey for positions. Occasionally fights establish precedence but more often they will discuss who can beat up whom to work out the order. Violence is never very far from the surface: it is a strange experience to watch a group of boys engrossed in the 'Mr Men' on television and swearing at each other to shut up or stop playing about. There is intense competition between

Steven's group and the younger boys in the senior school who resent what they see as the juniors' privileges. This often breaks out in slanging matches or fights. Recently, Steven was being baited by Kevin, one of the seniors who had found out about Steven's past: 'Your mum's a loony, your mum's locked up, you're in a Home, you're fostered.' Steven gave as good as he got: 'Your mum's a thief,' although in fact it's Kevin who is the thief — insults tend to be directed at mothers. Steven is himself one of the worst offenders when it comes to insults, he and other juniors will often bait seniors beyond endurance and although they get a beating for it, it seems not to stop them.

And yet in the middle of all this, Anne Mason, head of the junior department, describes Steven as a very affectionate boy. When he is on view he tends to seek contact aggressively and will thump teachers to make them attend. On more private occasions, he will cuddle in and calm down, and it is individual attention that she feels is most important for him:

> At an ordinary school he'd be in a class of 30 plus, here he is in a small class where it is possible to provide individual work — far more individual attention — and as a result we would hope he is far less disruptive here than in a day school. It's attention that Steven needs. He might reject it but it's what he needs which he couldn't possibly get in a large class. We can overlook the upsets, whereas a teacher with 30 plus would probably wash her hands of him.

All this is true, and Steven's teachers carry an astonishing burden coping with the stresses and strains of working at Ferney Hall: that they manage to give real affection and attention to Steven and the other boys is a tribute to their devotion and determination. But how far the atmosphere of the school is conducive to Steven's growth and readjustment is not clear. There has been an improvement as Anne points out: 'He's a pathetic case really. I don't think he's ever known what it is to receive love and affection and cuddles. Two years ago you wouldn't have got near him. He isn't the same boy now.' Recently another boy broke a plastic gun of Steven's: 'A few months ago, Steven would have thrown desks and chairs, bookshelves, everything. But that morning he said: "I'll have to fix it when we have time." He's settled down a lot. I've known what it is to sit in the corner with him for an hour holding him down.'

But like everyone else at Ferney Hall, Steven is surviving. The school is surviving the lack of support from the LEA. This is caused partly by the special schools administration falling under the primary schools branch. For the past eight years the head has asked for a psychiatric social worker to be attached to the school and for a psychiatrist to conduct part-time sessions, but without success. Until 1978, educational psychologists only visited the school when new children were delivered. Then for two years one visited each term but she is due to have a baby and has not been replaced. Until last year there was no advisory support: 'I don't think we can expect someone who is in charge of all the primary schools in the LEA to give up any more time than they do. It is regrettable, but working for a small borough has its drawbacks in this respect.' To maintain a reasonable level of care in the face of cutbacks the head has had to cut the number of places from 60 to 45. The school used to have seven house parents under a matron and assistant matron, but to save funds all but the matron had to be replaced with qualified teachers who now spend half their time teaching, the other half in care and supervision duties.

Steven's teachers are surviving the lack of materials and equipment and their stressful life at Ferney Hall. One related her initial reactions:

I don't think I knew what being tired was before I came here. In the dinner hour I couldn't eat I was so tired. I'd go to bed for an hour. I'd go to bed at four. I used to be sick for hours because I was so tired. It still is a 12 hour day on Saturday and on Sunday. I do 12 hours on Sunday and then I have to get up at 7.45 a.m. But I'm so tired on Monday. I could be a much better teacher if I didn't have extraneous duties. After a weekend of duty, I can't prepare anything.

The staff also have to survive violence, both verbal and physical:

There is a limit. I object to waking them up in the morning and the immediate response is a mouthful of abuse and you get that constantly. It gets to the stage where you just do not accept that any more and you think: 'Nobody's going to talk to me like that.' If a child is in a temper and you have stopped him from doing something he wants to do, OK, but it's becoming so natural with them.

Teachers are sometimes at risk physically. On one occasion, one of the most unstable boys, Andy, flicked an elastic band at Steven. Steven swore back at him to which Andy started hurling Steven's nickname 'slashbed' at him. Eventually the dispute got so bad that Andy found a piece of broken glass and started chasing Steven. One teacher had to put himself between the two boys and brought Andy's wrath on himself. He had to avoid some thrusts with a piece of glass. Not surprisingly, staff turnover is high. Many teachers last one or two years only.

In the middle of all this, Steven, described by Anne Mason as 'an institutionalised child', is surviving too.

36 DEBBIE: A CURRICULUM FOR A PARTIALLY SIGHTED GIRL

Will Swann

Debbie was born with cataracts in both eyes. One of them was operated on but subsequently became infected and had to be removed, and her mother will not allow an operation on the other eye, in which Debbie has a slight degree of useful sight. Debbie is now 12 and enrolled at Featherstone School, a day special school for children with physical and visual handicaps and specific learning difficulties. However she also spends one and a half days a week at Dufton, a nearby high school.

Despite her severe visual impairment Debbie is remarkably mobile. Until recently she regularly rode her bicycle on roads round her home unperturbed by the number of times she fell off and unaware of the havoc she caused for other road users. Her mother eventually stopped her cycling, but she still skateboards and walks across narrow benches six feet up in PE lessons and her ease of movement gives little indication of her visual impairment.

Her school career began in a normal infants school, which she does not look back on with any great favour: 'I wasn't allowed to do any of the lessons they did ... I had to go with another teacher ... that kept me behind about two years.' Later she spent three years in the 'tutorial unit' of a middle school with which she was similarly displeased: 'I was one of the best at working but I was kept back by the others. I just had to do the same work they were doing.' (Debbie's tendency to blame her previous teachers is unjust according to Jane Nelson, her present teacher, who thinks Debbie makes sweeping statements.) She is much more satisfied with her present school: 'It's great ... it's the teachers. Jane's the main teacher ... she's like us really. Most teachers don't talk to you very much but she does. Everybody's at the same standard, so you don't stay behind, you just get on with your work.'

Debbie started at Dufton three months after it first opened. She had a trial week of French and English, two subjects that she and Jane thought were appropriate. French was not a success: the course was audio-visual, based on film strips using a class-centred approach and Debbie had missed the first term, but she continued with English. A number of difficulties had to be overcome: transport was irregular and unpunctual. Debbie attached herself constantly to a physically disabled girl who came with her from Featherstone, to such an extent that they had to be separated for lessons. She began to depend upon one or two girls who had volunteered to help until one visited the deputy head to say, rather embarrassed, that Debbie was holding her back. After this the teachers had to ensure that Debbie had sufficient assistance from a group of children. Debbie was put into a class judged to be most likely to accept handicapped children; the school was told of the arrival of children from Featherstone in assembly, and Debbie's class was given a more detailed briefing. Despite this, Debbie has not really become part of the group; she only comes into one out of five form periods per week, and her cautious approach to strangers has impeded friendships.

At Featherstone Debbie takes RE, history, art, PE, craft, French, drama, science, geography and maths. Dufton school provides a morning and an afternoon of English and an afternoon of drama, PE and music. Although she makes excellent use of her residual distance vision, her near vision is extremely poor. For close work she wears a telescopic low-vision aid which allows her to see print, but only with a span of two or three letters and only with reasonably large print size; average paperback print or the typeface of many textbooks, particularly mathematics, is too small. Debbie's impairment slows her down in many tasks and so Jane has to allow more time for Debbie to locate pages in books and sentences on pages. With the sight of only two or three letters at once Debbie has to scan everything systematically from top to bottom of the page. She can cope with most of the textbooks, but Jane has to write out the maths material for her — practicable when there are only eight children in the group. Blackboard work is not viable for Debbie, and this is a problem at Dufton where she is one of 25 to 30 children. Here Gill Graham, Debbie's English teacher, gives her copies of any work on the blackboard. Featherstone provided a reading lamp at first, but Debbie disliked using it and after some attempts at persuasion Jane abandoned it. Because writing is very difficult for her, Debbie is being taught to type which she much prefers to learning braille. At the moment she is slow — 15 words per minute — and has not yet developed enough confidence to avoid checking as she goes. She has a copy-holder placed at eye level that she was initially reluctant to use but now accepts as part of being a 'real secretary'. Another attempt to help overcome Debbie's impairment was a closed-circuit TV system under which books can be placed producing a greatly enlarged image on the screen. Debbie would have none of the first version, but a new improved model that can take a typewriter has proved more acceptable.

Debbie's reading age is 10 yrs 4 mths, and Jane considers this good for a partially sighted 12 year old. She enjoys reading and is currently working through the Oxford Progressive Graded Readers which have a good print size and she finds them interesting. She took a fancy to Dickens recently. Jane has now decided that Debbie has to learn braille. She feels that Debbie's eyesight will not improve and may deteriorate, the range of large print books is more limited than braille books, and the chances of ever getting an enlarging copier are remote. Debbie doesn't really want to learn braille and is simply going through the motions of learning at the moment. She only reads braille visually, but she should be able to use this knowledge to learn braille by touch more easily.

Most of Debbie's English takes place at Dufton in a mixed-ability class of 12–13 year olds. The curriculum structure has made flexible arrangements relatively easy: the day is divided into morning and afternoon sessions with two periods in each so changeovers between schools can always take place at convenient times. Her two half days are spent with two separate classes. For the first hour she works with one class, and then in the second hour repeats the same work with the other class; this system accommodates to Debbie's slowness but gives her only half the curriculum. For 25 per cent of the time the class works individually with spelling, reading, comprehension and composition work; the remainder is taken up in group activities: reading round the class, discussions, play-readings. Debbie joins in all this but to varying degrees: in play-readings she will follow the activity but does not read. Debbie's big problem is her spelling which is very idiosyncratic: she writes of Featherstone: 'First I fort it was horrible but now I think it is graet, but they are not stricked anuth.' She does get extra help with spelling from Gill Graham but at Featherstone she no longer does formal spelling work. Attendance at Dufton has so far increased Debbie's self-confidence rather than her attainments, but Jane Nelson has noticed an increasing concern with depth and quality in her work.

In mathematics Debbie is proficient at arithmetic, but does not always understand what she is doing. Nevertheless in her more recent work she has coped well with bar-charts, graphs and work on tessellations. Next year Debbie will do maths at Dufton, but Jane foresees some problems. She will have to enlarge the material in advance and she anticipates Debbie having difficulty fitting in to a cumulative curriculum much of which she has missed.

Social studies and science present difficulties for Debbie because of the need to use diagrams and other visual material. In geography, Jane has to ink over map outlines to improve clarity: she has not used raised diagrams because of Debbie's dislike of relying on touch. Much of the science curriculum — recently the class has studied freshwater plant life — relies on film strips which Debbie has difficulty seeing. History and RE are the subjects she likes best — arguably the least visual.

Debbie tends to see art and craft as a waste of time. She derives some pleasure from colour work, but baulks at drawing and gets little from modelling. Needlework proved similarly unmotivating: with so much close vision required this is hardly surprising. Eventually she switched to cookery and likes this rather better, but her limited experience showed up in not knowing the names and functions of most utensils.

She takes part in the full range of games and PE. At Dufton Debbie has begun to do tennis: 'I find it difficult, but I join in.' Where she is not reliant on fine vision — in running, some gymnastics and swimming, she can compete on equal terms with her normal peers. Even so, as she explained, in the noise of the swimming baths her hearing, on which she must rely for instructions from the teacher, is severely taxed.

At Featherstone, they use one morning a week with the older pupils for 'socialisation' which means 'preparation for work'. The week we spoke to Debbie she had been on the school's switchboard. Jane Nelson uses this time to observe Debbie's ability to work with others and to gain information on employment skills and self-confidence. Debbie enjoyed this greatly since it fitted in with her own ambition to become a receptionist/secretary — a realistic one according to Jane who foresees Debbie coping with a convential commerical FE course.

Debbie has firm opinions about her time at Dufton: 'It's the kids. You've got nobody to talk to and they take the mickey out of you and all this.' All of them? 'Not all of them take the mickey, but they don't like me.' Her feelings do not alter her continued wish to attend Dufton 'because if I don't work I won't get my exams'. Couldn't she do her exams at Featherstone? 'You could but if I go to Dufton I'm going to get more education . . . you get used to ordinary people around.'

Debbie's experience at Dufton has been encouraging enough to lead to her starting maths and science there next year. Unfortunately this will coincide with a change to a five period day to allow for shorter lessons and more flexible time allocation between subjects. This is going to make the arrangements more difficult for Featherstone who may have to ferry Debbie to and fro at awkward times. So far her success, according to Gill Graham, is due to her even temperament: 'She doesn't get easily frustrated and is not clamouring for attention.' She is in fact much less of a problem for Gill than a number of other children in her classes, and Gill would be happy to take her for as much time as she wants.

37 AFTER SCHOOL: FURTHER EDUCATION FOR HANDICAPPED ADOLESCENTS

June Statham and Richard Tomlinson

The following two curriculum guidelines for handicapped school leavers in FE colleges adopt contrasting approaches. The first, from a special residential college for young people with cerebral palsy, emphasises the 'personal growth' of its students and anticipates that by becoming more developed, whole people they will be better equipped to acquire the skills they need in life. It is strongly influenced by the 'personal growth' movement of the sixties and seventies which emanated from West Coast USA and gave rise to encounter groups as well as new forms of self-expression therapy like drama therapy and art therapy.

By contrast the second curriculum, describing a series of courses offered by an ordinary day FE college in London for ESN(M) and ESN(S) school leavers, focuses on a different American import; the task analysis, behavioural objectives approach which has its root in Skinnerian learning theory. Each area of skills is broken down into small steps, and this approach stresses the precision teaching of each of these steps in a developmental sequence.

1. A Learning Framework for Cerebral-palsied School Leavers

Beaumont College is a voluntary non-residential college for students with cerebral palsy. It has attempted to follow four basic guidelines in developing a curriculum for these often severely disabled adolescents, which are summarised by the college as follows:

First, the most significant function of a curriculum is that it answers the needs of the student population who partake of it. Be aware of the adolescent's need for a sense of identity and self determination; the need for independence and respect from their peer group and others, the need for satisfying relationships with the opposite sex

259

and the need to discover appropriate outlets for self expression.

Next, emphasise a holistic approach that maximises opportunities for personal and social growth. The importance of psychological, emotional and cultural factors should be recognised with as much readiness as intellectual and physical development.

Thirdly, remember that importance should be placed on adolescent developmental tasks. These typically include: achieving masculine and feminine role; achieving new and more mature relationships with age mates of both sexes; accepting one's physique and using one's body effectively; achieving emotional independence from parents and other adults; preparing for marriage and family life; desiring and achieving socially responsible behaviours and acquiring a set of values and an ethical system as a guide to behaviour.

Finally, avoid artificial subject boundaries. Be prepared to investigate and integrate new areas within the curriculum which include 'Personal Development', 'Communications', 'Interpersonal Relationships', 'Community Activities', 'Activities of Daily Living', 'Leisure' and 'Aesthetic Appreciation'. Emphasise pertinent processes such as perceiving, knowing, organising, creating, communicating, decision making, valuing and loving.

The philosophical and methodological basis informing educational provision for adolescents has been left unquestioned and unchanged far too long. What is needed is a scrutiny of the real needs of adolescents in the final years of schooling, links with continued education and community based activities and greater access to more appropriate provision.

The curriculum guidelines for Beaumont describe how students can be prepared to function as 'effectively and happily as possible within their community'. The college recognises that with increasing unemployment the severely handicapped are unlikely to obtain work, but it does not see its role simply as providing 'education for leisure'.

It should be recognised that for the severely handicapped, everyday tasks including personal care, mobility and travel often take the same amount of time that the non-handicapped person directs to work. Education for a worthwhile life without work should be provided in which, among other things, individuals can develop attitudes and abilities to 'work' in caring for themselves; in using the services and facilities available to them effectively; in development enjoyable leisure pursuits and in making their own contribution to the family and community in whatever ways become possible.

Rather than providing a curriculum which covers all that a disabled student might need to know, the staff at the college believe they are providing a framework which allows students to share feelings and experiences, and that this process will help them to cope with the adult world they are soon to enter. The college believes that 'The crucial point in the learning process is where the subjective or individual experience can become objective and shared.' Learning needs, they argue, should come from the student rather than be imposed by the teacher. The area of 'personal and social development' is seen as very important and centres around the drama workshop. The college makes great claims for what drama can achieve; the development of concentration, imagination, social skills and a 'realistic, satisfying perception of self'; the ability to think critically, act independently, apply original thought, listen and observe; the reinforcement of self-image through participation with others; the awareness of creative potential; the ability to project personality, to communicate and relate.

Most of the drama work takes place in The Studio; a small, well-equipped drama hall. Black curtains can be taken around the entire perimeter of the room or used to mask off specific areas, and the curtains can also be drawn back so that screens may be used for films or slides. The studio has versatile stage lighting, a portable music centre and video tape recorder, rostra and ramps, sag bags, chairs, movable partitions and a small permanent stage. Students attend at least one morning or afternoon session a week.

The Studio is seen as a 'safe and sensitive environment' in which students can focus on 'the reality of the limitations of handicap, and the recognition of their individual potential'. It encourages 'the transfer of situation between a student's specific stage of development and the next step into the expectations of the adult world'. The curriculum description goes on to state that:

The handicapped person's greatest need is to be recognised and accepted. The facilities within the studio provide a unique opportunity where aesthetically pleasing work, not previously experienced because of handicap, can be found.

Original thought and imagination can be developed and so many alternative channels to success are available, that strength in personality can be developed to the extent that handicap disappears. It is an art form in which all can be successful.

But it is not just inward looking. The work done in the studio is always aimed towards the students' future needs, and in the analysis within the lecture, where the students step outside the experience, the crucial relevance of concepts is related to the individual and his personal future in the real world.

A Studio Session

The following is an observer's account of what went on in one afternoon session in The Studio with a group of eighteen disabled adolescents.

The session began with an introduction by the lecturer who reminded the group what they had done last time. They then broke up for a relaxation session. Eighteen students (seven in wheelchairs) were asked to find a space in which they were comfortable. The wheelchair users were encouraged to get out of their chairs. Four did so and relaxed in the sag bags. Students were silent without prompting and were prepared to relax. The lights were dimmed. The lecturer talked about the need to work together, which was the main objective of this session. She then asked them to concentrate. 'Shut yourself off. Be in your own space. Don't mind the silence.' She inserted periodically some of the themes that they had decided they wanted to explore 'Think about things. Think about parts of you that work well, and things that don't. Think about feet first and relax them.' She encouraged them to think of ideas within the context of being at ease and comfortable with their bodies. A record was played quietly. If anything this was mildly intrusive and two or three students stirred. Previously someone had come into the studio but had in no way interrupted the atmosphere. The lecturer then initiated movement in the group, slowly bringing everyone back to life. The lights came full on again.

The theme for the session was then discussed. It was to be 'survival'. 'Why?' asked the lecturer. 'Because we might need it. Because it might help when we're out there on our own.' 'So what sort of thing do you want to do?' 'Want to use all the facilities. To use everything.' 'What ideas do you have?' Various suggestions were offered — something about handicap; aeroplanes; people making fun; learning to take situations as they come; being realistic about things you can't do.

'How are you going to set about it?' They decided to break into smaller groups to start off with and for each group to choose an idea. Two clearly defined groups appeared almost immediately.

There was one vague unsure grouping and three or four others meandered more or less aimlessly until encouraged to form their own group. Some started to get back into their wheelchairs. One boy went from group to group as a volunteer link. He was the one who stressed the need to eventually come together in one big group. He also encouraged people not to get 'bogged down in talk'. The lecturer reinforced this. 'Get up and do it. Try it out. Don't just sit and talk.' One group decided to leave and rehearse. Another started experimenting with the rostra, building a bridge. There was much discussion and experimentation as to how this could be used. Another group were discussing hobbies but only one seemed to express enthusiasm. She consulted with the lecturer about music, and a loud recording by the Tijuana Brass was put on. The bridge builders experimented with lighting effects. The general impression was of controlled constructive work. Only two or three were wandering or not concentrating. There was no disruptive behaviour at all. 'That's it, that's it. Got it,' said the bridge builders. It was noticeable that this group was full of movement, the other two in the studio, much more passive. The group who had left to rehearse returned.

The lecturer intervened. 'Right, let's stop it. How far have we got? Is everybody ready?' One group was reproached for lack of action. This was the fourth group made up of waverers and wanderers. 'You've got to do something. Don't tell me things. Don't wait for it to be done for you. You'll get left behind unless you *do* something about it.' She then generalised from this to say that too often had things been done for them in the past. If they applied themselves now, then this was going to help them in dealing with what was going on outside.

The group then broke for coffee with the understanding that they would all share their work after the break. I missed the first demonstration after break, and came in while the 'bridge building' group were getting prepared. Some of the group lay under the ramps. There had been an accident. One went for help to the station. 'My friends are trapped.' 'Rope snapped.' It was evidently a climbing accident. One person was badly hurt and they carefully lifted him onto a rostrum. He died with a minimum of fuss. That brought the scene to an end and the lecturer intervened in order to link what had happened to the wider theme in group activity.

'How does it relate to what happens outside?' The group were not clear. 'How can you transfer what you have been doing to any experience outside?' The group had not really understood the significance of this. They had seriously and intently been playing make-believe. This was not good enough for the lecturer: 'What we are dealing with has to be an actual thing.' Then focus was put back on the previous group who had simulated an aircraft crash. The lecturer encouraged them to take it further. One went to get help leaving his friend injured and the pilot dead. The audience was visibly moved by this. The lecturer pushed them further. 'How are you going to tell your friend about his injury? Is it permanent?' [It was.] The need to find a way of telling somebody about an injury (handicap) was discussed. This was real and the class recognised it.

Next we saw a group of beggars. A passerby agreed to help them if they came home with her. It was very brief, but encouraged a discussion. 'How would you feel if you had to beg for food?' 'Scary', said one. 'Is a handicapped person more likely to have to beg? Not just for food, but for favours?' Again this was real. Then returning to one of the main objectives, 'How can the work you've done be joined? Where is the link? What are the ideas that join everything together and involve everybody?'

Quite quickly with some prompting an idea was worked out whereby a crash was followed by telling an injured man about the nature of his injuries. This led to some of the consequences of the injury, one of which was begging, another, gaining access to a building.

The session then ran out of time, but a clear understanding was reached that they would start from this point next time. Various ideas came out about costumes and videoing it. 'Only if it's good', said one. 'But we can watch it and change it,' said another. One was convinced that they had messed it up. As they broke up one girl was apologetic for not being more actively involved. The lecturer agreed that she had waited around expecting 'to be told what to do'. They all wanted to continue the idea next time.

2. Ordinary FE College: Curriculum for ESN(M) and ESN(S) School Leavers

The general studies department of a large day further education college in South London has for several years been offering courses for ESN(M) and ESN(S) school leavers. There are six 'What Next?' courses of vocational preparation designed for school leavers with few, if any examination passes, as a transition into employment or appropriate alternatives. Three of the courses are aimed mainly at students from ESN schools; one is a two-year course for ESN(M) students; the second a similar course but lasting for one year, and the third a two-year course for students principally from ESN(S) schools. A few ESN students may also be considered for one of the other three What Next? courses; diagnostic, clerical or craft.

Students are recruited to the courses by direct referral from ESN(S) and ESN(M) schools, or by the careers service or adult training centres. The college describes the aims and content of these courses as follows:

The Course Aims

The course is designed to enable students to maximise their learning potential in basic skills by applying them to a range of commonly encountered contexts. Within these learning contexts, a programme of education will take place which is designed to lead by carefully measured steps to the achievement of the aims of the course, which are:

1. to assist further cognitive development;
2. to develop social competence;
3. to develop a variety of skills likely to be relevant in terms of vocation, occupation, or general development;
4. to provide opportunities for personal development;
5. to assess individual capabilities for employment or other future placement.

The Course Content

1. The curriculum will have as its core the teaching of basic skills of language, numeracy, decision making, motor and social skills.
2. The contexts within which these skills are to be taught will be as follows:
   2.1 the college and classroom;
   2.2 using the community;
   2.3 personal relationships;
   2.4 preparing for work and training centres;
   2.5 travel;
   2.6 leisure;
   2.7 self-help;
   2.8 manipulative skills in craft workshops.

The course structure is represented by a checklist (see Table 1).

Table 1: College Checklist

	Level 1	Level 2	Level 3
NUMERACY	Appreciates difference between weekdays and weekends Aware of classroom and daily routine Appreciates the passage of time e.g. coffee break Knows days of the week Recognises numbers 0–9	Can locate rooms by number recognition Knows the timetable Can choose appropriate coins to pay for a drink or snack and uses vending machines	Can keep appointments Calculates cost of lunch and pays appropriately
LANGUAGE	Can recognise own name Can copy name Can give name on request Follows simple verbal instruction e.g. Get your pencil, sit down Can seek help from appropriate person and act appropriately on information received Knows signs for men's and women's toilets	Can write name e.g. on luncheon voucher, library form, etc. Gives address Writes address Follows two part instruction Can locate member of staff, room etc., by asking for information Delivers a simple message Phones home Holds a simple conversation although may not always respond appropriately	Reads appropriate social sight vocabulary within the building Fills in library and enrolment forms Locates appropriate sections in the library and selects books Reads price list in the canteen Remembers and delivers messages within College and home Knows when someone is bored with conversation and changes subject or brings conversation to a close
MOTOR SKILLS	Can locate base classroom, canteen, toilets, library, entrance Can lock and unlock toilet door and flush toilet Washes hands after going to toilet	Locates and replaces equipment necessary for a given task Locates toilets on different levels, all rooms relevant to course and the staff workroom	Organises equipment appropriately on desk, workbench etc.

Table 1: Continued

	Can operate Sanitary Towel machine Can come downstairs appropriately Can carry a tray Can dress and undress	Can use vending machines in canteen Uses public phone	
DECISION MAKING	Responds appropriately to alarms e.g. fire Selects appropriate cutlery Chooses a drink, snack and full meal Solves simple problems for self e.g. broken pencil Selects appropriate dress for activities	Finds a seat in the canteen Chooses a well-balanced meal Can decide on appropriate member of staff in case of difficulty	Organises use of luncheon vouchers appropriately Accepts consequences of own actions
SOCIAL SKILLS	Knows names of peers, tutor, lecturers appropriate to course, classroom assistant Has appreciation of appropriate dressing and undressing behaviour e.g. in front of opposite sex Can behave appropriately in public places e.g. canteen, library, swimming pool	Has one or more friends within the group Has awareness of College rules e.g. no smoking in classrooms, punctuality, etc. Accepts blame for own mistakes Accepts criticism where appropriate Shows concern for the safety or welfare of others	Is a member of the Union and attends meetings Uses the Common Room Mixes appropriately with other students

Table 2: Student Record Sheet

LEVEL		COLLEGE AND CLASSROOM	USE OF THE COMMUNITY	RELATIONSHIPS	TRAVEL	LEISURE	WORK PREPARATION	SELF-HELP
3	Numeracy							
	Language							
	Motor Skills	X					X	X
	Decision Making							
	Social Skills							
2	Numeracy	X						
	Language	X	X	X	X		X	X
	Motor Skills	X						
	Decision Making				X			
	Social Skills							
1	Numeracy	X		X		X	X	X
	Language	X		X		X	X	X
	Motor Skills	X		X		X	X	X
	Decision Making	X		X		X	X	X
	Social Skills	X		X		X	X	X

Table 1 sets out the skills to be mastered in five areas of study at three different levels, which reflect the wide range of ability of students.

In the 'College and Classrooms' checklist, for example, a typical 'numeracy' skill at level one is 'appreciates the difference between weekdays and weekends'; at level 2 a comparable item might be 'locates rooms by number recognition'; at level 3, 'calculates the costs of lunch and pays appropriately'. Classroom activities are closely related to these checklists. As a group of skills is learnt, that section is ticked off at the appropriate level on the student's record sheet. The student whose checklist is shown in Table 2, for example, has mastered all of the skills in each learning context at level 1, has achieved some of them at level 2, and has begun work on motor skills in several areas of the curriculum at level 3. The checklists thus serve not only as a framework for the curriculum but also as an instrument of assessment. Some students will only achieve a very small part of the total skills taught in the course. A series of diagrams, one for each area of study, displays the interconnections between the main concepts in that area (see Figures 1-5 below).

Figure 1: The College and Classrooms

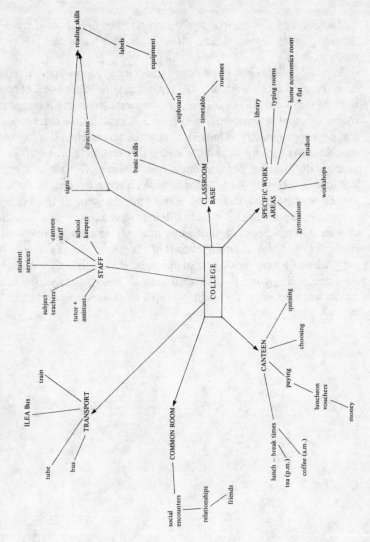

Figure 2: Using the Community

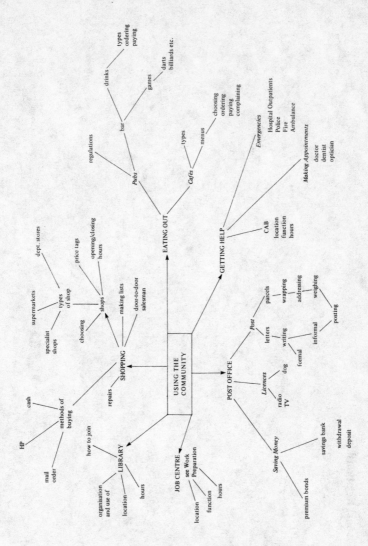

Figure 3: Personal Relationships

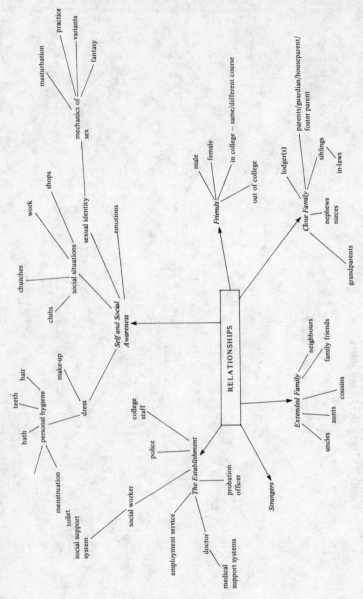

Figure 4: Self-help

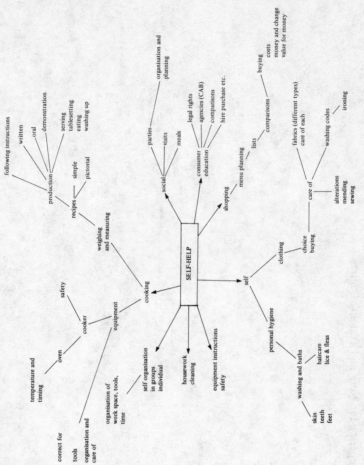

Figure 5: Preparing for Work and Training Centres

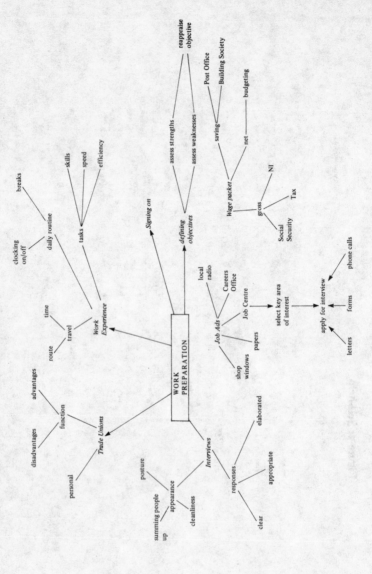

38 TOKENS AND TANTRUMS: A BEHAVIOUR MODIFICATION PROGRAMME

June Statham

Special schools often claim to offer a curriculum that differs in kind, as well as place, from that offered in ordinary schools. One example is the use of behaviour modification techniques, based on Skinnerian learning theory, to 'shape' the behaviour of pupils in a desired direction. The school attended by Emma Canny, who was described earlier in this book, adopted the following token-economy system and 'extinction' procedures in an attempt to control her night-time behaviour problems.

A year after coming to Beech Tree House, Emma was still causing problems at night. The residential therapist on duty on her first night back after the summer holidays estimated that Emma had no more than three hours' sleep, and described her behaviour in her notes:

Emma vomited, urinated and produced her usual range of screaming and banging. Every time I went to another child, she heard me and got out of bed. She took her duvet cover off the duvet. On occasions she was forcing mucus down her nose ('snotting'). This and attempts to vomit increased in frequency when I went in to see her. When I went in after she had vomited she looked at me defiantly, leant out of bed to reach her vomit, picked up a small piece and ate it. I responded crossly and smacked her hand. I at no time put her back into bed but always told her to go herself, firmly and crossly . . . She was not observed to produce any self-destructive behaviour. She was awake at 7.05 screaming and out of bed, so did not need to be raised. Nevertheless, she appeared to be tired during the day.

The staff decided that ignoring Emma's bad behaviour was not having sufficient impact, even when coupled with making her clear up the mess the following morning and lavishing praise when the room was clean, so they decided to introduce her to a more structured token-economy system.

Phase I: Establishing that Tokens have Value

During the first three weeks of the project staff attempted to 'hook' Emma on tokens, by giving them to her during the day when she did something well and allowing her to immediately exchange the tokens for smarties dispensed by a whirring, flashing sweet dispenser. The smarties were later replaced by pop music playable on a token-operated cassette machine. Staff collected blue tokens from the office before going on duty and returned them when going off duty. A clipboard headed 'Emma tokens' was available in a rack in the office, and staff recorded how many tokens they had given Emma each day, aiming for between ten and fifteen. At this stage the withdrawal of tokens was not used as a threat to control Emma's behaviour.

Phase II: Using the Now Valuable Tokens to Reward Clean Bedroom Behaviour

Emma soon learnt the value of the tokens and began asking for them in sign language whenever she was praised. As her messing showed no sign of abating, it was agreed at a team meeting to use the tokens to reward her for not dirtying her room at night. Each member of staff was given a duplicated sheet of instructions describing the procedure to be followed:

BEECH TREE HOUSE INDIVIDUAL TRAINING SCHEDULE
Action to Be Taken to Reduce Emma Canny's Messing Behaviour
1. Emma will be rewarded with five tokens if she has refrained from defecating, vomiting and urinating in her room throughout the night.
2. These tokens will be exchangeable only for music played on the token-operated cassette.
3. She will not be allowed to exchange her tokens until she has tidied her room, replaced her duvet cover and pillow case and so on.
4. Emma is to be taken to the toilet every night at 22.00 — whether or not she says she wants to go. She is to be taken to the toilet as soon as she wakes after 6.00, but then taken back to her room.

5. The token giving should be done as follows:
   (a) Enter room — preferably when Emma is quiet. Have the tokens with you as you go in. Say 'Hello' in a friendly manner.
   (b) Note whether she has messed her floor or bed, but give no apparent attention to this.
   (c) Sit on bed (if clean) and give Emma her five tokens. Then ask 'Have you been sick?'; 'Have you done a wee?'; 'Have you done a poo?' Ask these so that the question referring to the offending act (if any) comes last.
   (d) If the floor/bed is clean, praise Emma and let her keep the tokens. Remind her that she can spend them on music as soon as her room is tidy.
   (e) If the floor/bed is dirty, the tokens should be taken from Emma and she should be 'told off' very firmly.
   (f) Emma must clean up her own mess. This should not be allowed to become fun or a social activity between her and the member of staff.
   (g) Once the floor is clean, Emma should be showered in a socially non-committal manner.
   (h) Once Emma is dressed, she should tidy her room. No tangible rewards to be given.
   (i) Once her room is tidy, Emma should be treated as if nothing has happened. It is suggested that no discussion about her behaviour should be conducted in front of her.
6. The token-operated cassette should be used in the battery powered mode. Emma should listen to it in her room.
7. Please note whether tokens are given, what actions are taken and Emma's responses to them.

Extinction Procedure for Night-time Tantrums

It was also felt important to try to reduce Emma's night-time tantrums and periods out of bed. Unless these could be reduced, Emma was unlikely to be able to return home or even to live in another institution, unless heavily sedated. The staff felt that her future depended on eliminating some of the difficult behaviour which she had learnt over a long period.

The persistence of Emma's behaviour was viewed as evidence that she received some benefits from it. Being angrily reprimanded and placed firmly in bed many times each night might not seem like a pleasant experience, but it succeeded in gaining her adult attention and company. The staff decided to see if an extinction procedure could reduce the amount of time Emma spent out of bed and screaming.

They decided to ignore her night-time tantrums but installed a one-way intercom in her bedroom as a safety measure. Emma had not had a fit for well over a year, but the staff wanted to be sure that if they were not going in to her room at night they would hear if she did have one. Her room was also fitted with a bed-bug, an electronic gadget attached below the child's bed which bleeps every five seconds when the child gets out. An unbreakable observation panel was fitted into the door. The night staff were issued with record sheets marked in hourly and 5-minute intervals to record Emma's periods out of bed and to write comments about the night's activities. They were to take her to the toilet at 10 p.m., whether or not she said she wanted to go, and then not enter her room again until morning.

Extinction procedures are often used together with reinforcing other more desirable behaviours, but in Emma's case this was considered impracticable, as any rewarding technique would have been likely to distract her from the object of the exercise, which was going to sleep. The staff did consider using an automatic token display to reward Emma for staying in bed quietly. After a given period of time in bed a token would be released behind a perspex display, and these tokens would build up so that Emma could clearly see the consequences of her behaviour. The token-dispensing equipment would be wired up to the bed-bug, and if she got out of bed the pile of tokens would disappear into a hidden box below. However Emma might have become interested in the token display and wanted to get up to take a closer look, or have been disturbed by the intermittent clicks it made. It was for these reasons that the machine developed to dispense and withdraw tokens was not in fact used. A few minutes of adult company used as a rein-forcement for staying quietly in bed would similarly not do, since her constant demanding of adult attention at night was precisely what the programme aimed to eliminate.

Both aspects of the behaviour modification programme, the token-economy system to control Emma's messing behaviour and the extinction procedures to reduce her tantrums and periods out of bed, began to have an effect. The number of times Emma got out of bed went down to two or three times a night, and after about six weeks the frequency of her messing behaviour had dropped to not more than once per week. Her parents supported the programme and tried to use the same tech-niques at home, although circumstances made it more difficult for them. At Beech Tree House Emma's sound-limiting, waterproof and well-monitored room made it much easier to safely ignore her. Emma's room at home was similarly adapted, but her parents had neighbours to worry about if they ignored her screaming, and relatives around who thought they were being cruel by not going in to comfort her. For example during an early phase of the training, Emma's grandparents were visiting when she went home for a holiday, and they overruled her parents' instructions not to pay attention to her tantrums. She returned to Beech Tree House after the holidays with her night-time behaviour as bad as it had ever been, and the behaviour modification programme was back where it started.

Two years later Emma is still on a token-economy system. She rarely messes in her room now, and has lately begun to go to bed on her own, rather than having to be taken. The bed-bug device is no longer necessary. Her parents recently asked the school to extend the programme to try to stop Emma removing her sheet, duvet cover and pillow case at night. This has worked to some extent; she now leaves on the fitted sheet, but still takes off the pillow case and duvet cover. The staff think that the three extra tokens she was offered for not removing her duvet cover, pillow case and sheet were an insufficient incentive, since she is still receiving five tokens for not messing in her room. These she exchanges at a rate of one minute's worth of pop music per token on the token-operated cassette player. Three extra minutes of music are perhaps not enough of an added attraction.

The staff have not tried to phase out the token-economy system used with Emma, although there was a period recently when the cassette recorder broke and Emma could not exchange her tokens for music. She reacted by beginning to urinate in her room again — not badly, but enough to register her disapproval and indicate the extent to which the token system was controlling her behaviour. If Emma had been going on to an institution which couldn't or wouldn't use the behaviour modification programme, then the staff would have tried to get her off it before she moved, but at the moment her future is uncertain, and at Beech Tree House they feel that the benefits provided by the programme in terms of controlling some of Emma's more difficult behaviour far outweigh the efforts involved in administering it.

39 THE REFERRAL PROCESS: DANIEL AND HARRIET

Dennis Briggs and June Statham

The decision to transfer a child from ordinary school to special school, or occasionally vice versa, often involves the completion of four forms; a headteacher's report (SE1), medical report (SE2), educational psychologist's report (SE3) and a summary sheet of recommendations (SE4). With so many different professionals involved, it is not surprising that opinions sometimes conflict. In the first of these two case-studies, the school medical officer's recommendation that a recently disabled boy be transferred to a special school for the physically handicapped is questioned by the educational psychologist, who feels that Daniel would benefit educationally from remaining in his comprehensive school, with support and checks on his progress from the medical officer. In the second case-study, medical opinion and the educational psychologist's recommendations are again in conflict, but this time in the opposite direction. It is Harriet's opthalmic consultant who feels that, although partially sighted, she should be allowed to attend an ordinary school, and it is the educational psychologist who thinks she would be better remaining in her special school.

1. School for the Physically Handicapped or Ordinary Comprehensive School: Daniel's Story

In October 1979, the special services education department received a letter from the senior medical officer in their area enclosing a copy of his medical report (form SE2) on a twelve-year-old boy, Daniel Burgess. Daniel was attending Parks Middle School, and had been taken into hospital at the beginning of the year suffering from a hip joint defect diagnosed as *protrusio acetabulae*. He was likely to improve, but would be confined to a wheelchair until at least age sixteen. He was unable to walk, but was permitted to swim and use an exercise cycle.

280

The school medical officer had ticked the boxes on the SE2 form indicating that Daniel needed 'some' physical help in class 'occasionally', and under the heading 'other special needs' he had specified 'daily transport to school'. On all the other sections of the form — vision, hearing, speech and language, physical health, behaviour and emotional development, intellectial development, ability to care for himself, family history; the medical officer had entered 'normal'. He nevertheless felt that Daniel ought to transfer to a day special school for physically handicapped pupils, and had recommended this in the 'additional notes and comments' section at the end of the form.

Having received this SE2 form at the beginning of October, the special services education department contacted the educational psychologist responsible for Daniel's school area, and asked her to complete the SE procedure. Two weeks later she sent back the following memo:

25/10/79
From: Educational Psychologist
To: Special Services Education Dept.
Re: Daniel Burgess, attending Parks Middle School

Thank you for your memo of 11.10.79 accompanying a copy of Dr White's SE2 on Daniel. Since receiving it I have requested an SE1 from Parks Middle School and been to see the family at home twice.

It appears that there is no urgency about this suggested placement at present, as Daniel is coping (and being coped with) at his present school very well. His parents are naturally very concerned about the quality of the education offered at Greyfriars as they see Daniel as 'normal' and do not wish him to be placed somewhere where educational opportunities may be restricted. With this point of view I wholeheartedly agree, and on the basis of the assessment which I have undertaken to date feel unable to recommend transfer to Greyfriars as in any way appropriate — other than on the grounds of the case of use of a wheelchair there. In view of this I feel that any recommendation which I will make on SE3 will conflict with the current medical recommendation. Perhaps you would consider calling a Case Conference when you are in receipt of the SE papers? SE papers to be forwarded as soon as completed.

9/11/79
From: Educational Psychologist
To: Assistant Education Officer, Special Services Education Dept.

Please find enclosed completed Forms SE1-3: the procedure having been instigated by Dr White's recommendation for placement at Greyfriars School.

I do not agree with this recommendation and have therefore not completed Form SE4 (summary and action sheet). I presume this will be done after the case conference on Daniel which has been arranged for Wednesday November 21st.

Form SE1: Report by a Headteacher on a Child who may Require Special Education (summarised)

1	Background details.	Daniel Burgess, etc.
2	School attendance.	Good.
3	School's organisation.	Middle School (9–13 years). Four year groups. Daniel is at present in a 4th year mixed-ability class group of 20 children. Some of his time is spent in a middle group for maths/science/French.
4	Brief description of child's difficulties, when they were first noted.	Daniel was first absent from school early in 1979. A course of treatment, including traction, was given, and after diagnosis of a hip joint defect a wheelchair was provided for his use. Daniel first used the wheelchair in May 1979.
5	Do you suspect any physical condition which might cause or contribute to the difficulties?	No other contributory difficulties apparent.
6	Do you think that the child's difficulties could be caused, wholly or partly, by circumstances outside himself, e.g. irregular attendance, frequent changes of school or teacher, oversize classes etc.?	No. Difficulties purely of medical origin i.e. hip joint defect.
7	Has special attention already been provided in the school?	No special attention provided in *form* of education. A careful watch is kept on Daniel's movements at breaks and lunchtimes.

		His wheelchair enables full participation in all aspects of the curriculum except PE and games. Where equipment is to be used e.g. science, craft etc. provision is made for ease of use.
8	**Educational level**	
	Level of speech and understanding of speech.	Normal for age.
	Any significant aspects of child's play.	No.
	Reading level, fluency, comprehension.	Average.
	Spelling level.	Normal for age.
	Numeracy, level of mathematical thinking.	Average/above average for age. May 1979, NFER test 113.
	Practical and creative skills.	Average.
	Physical skills and co-ordination.	Not applicable.
	Specific skills and interests.	Shows some talent with craft and artwork.
	Progress in the last 12 months.	Normal progress in academic areas — reading, written language skills etc.
	Intelligence and other test scores.	Verbal reasoning 104 (test given Easter 1978). Higher IQ.
9	**Behaviour and disposition**	
	a. Relationships with other children	Normal — although activities restricted by wheelchair.
	b. Relationships with adults	Normal — quite relaxed, but respectful.
	c. Any special characteristics	None.
10	Interests.	Swimming.
11	Parental attitudes.	Parents were very upset on first knowing of hip joint defect. Mother and father have felt able to visit school at any time to discuss matters concerned with Daniel's adaptation to wheelchair life. They have been aware of the psychological effects of sudden restriction to a wheelchair.

	Parents have indicated that they will be pleased to accept arrangements for special education, if they are in Daniel's interest educationally.
12 Class teacher's observations.	—
13 Conclusions.	Parents have indicated that they have been pleased with the facilities made available at Parks School in accepting Daniel with his wheelchair. Daniel certainly seems settled in this environment and has made average academic progress. In understanding that Deanside Comprehensive School, by nature of its building, cannot accept Daniel for the next phase of his education, it seems reasonable that a form of special education is thus required. Certainly his parents are happy to accept this situation. From an educational point of view, it would also seem reasonable to expect Daniel to continue at his present rate of academic development if stretched to his full potential.

Form SE3: Report by Educational Psychologist on a Child who may Require Special Education

Reason for child being referred for examination.	Suffering from hip joint defect and is required to stay in a wheelchair. As a result of medical examination (SE2 dated 2.10.79) has been recommended to attend a School for Physically Handicapped Pupils.
Do you suspect any physical difficulties not so far detected?	None detected.
Description of child's behaviour in classroom, playground or home.	Until confined in wheelchair, normal.

Assessment of ability and personality.	Wechsler Intelligence Scale for Children (24.10.79 at CA 12½ years) Verbal IQ 118. Performance Scale IQ 139 (Prorated from 4 sub-tests). Full scale IQ 131. Performance and co-operation on test were entirely appropriate and concentration and perseveration were maintained throughout testing.
Implications of above observations.	Daniel is a 'normal' boy of well above average intelligence.
Assessment of educational performance	
a. language development.	Normal language development and above average level of verbal reasoning.
b. literacy.	Neale Analysis of Reading Ability Form A (at CA 12½ yrs.). Accuracy 'Age Score' – 12.2 yrs – appropriate for age and at 'ceiling' for this test.
c. mathematical knowledge and understanding.	WISC Arithmetic sub-test scale score = 11. Slightly above average for child of his age.
d. special interests or abilities.	Particularly likes maths, science and art; and hopes to do technical drawing.
e. subjects the child dislikes or finds difficult.	Finds French difficult.
Educational implications of the above.	Daniel's attainments are appropriate for a child of his age and he has clearly made normal progress during his school career. In view of this, and in the light of his 'potential' (see above), his main educational need is to continue to be exposed to a full normal school curriculum. He is NOT in need of special schooling for educational reasons.

Child's family background.	Normal so far as is known.
Child's views (if any) of his difficulties and the kind of help required.	Probably favours PH school placement as a way of avoiding the social difficulties which he has in adjusting to being wheel-chair bound. In fact knows nothing of PH schools and would miss or lose the friendship of local children if he attended a different school.
Parental attitudes a. level of support and interest.	High — extremely concerned that he should not be deprived of opportunities.
b. understanding of child's disability.	Seems good and reasonable. They are making realistic adjust-ments while remaining hopeful for the future.
c. ability and readiness to promote his growth and development.	Have done so far, no reason why they shouldn't in future.
Implications of the above for special education.	Daniel's proven educational ability combined with his parents' concern that he should not be deprived of normal educational opportunities con-traindicates special school placement. He should not be placed in a special school if it is at all possible for him to be catered for in a normal comprehensive school.
Type of placement required.	To remain in present school with no special arrangements other than a continuing review of progress.
Teaching arrangements required.	i) education appropriate to a child of high ability or special aptitudes (as provided by a normal school curriculum). ii) Continuing help from support-

	ive services to enable him to remain in ordinary school. (He needs monitoring by school medical officer and educational psychologist so long as he remains in a wheelchair in normal school.)

The case conference which the educational psychologist had recommended was held at the end of November, and at it she restated her opinion that Daniel should not be transferred to a special school. The main problem seemed to be that the comprehensive school where Daniel was due to transfer the following September was unwilling to take him, so the educational psychologist approached another school, and then wrote to the area education officer recommending that Daniel be sent there.

14/12/79
From: Educational Psychologist
To: Area Education Officer, Special Services Education Dept.
        Further to the Case Conference held on 21.11.79, I have been to see Mr Williams at Grange Comprehensive School to discuss the possibility of admitting Daniel.
        Mr Williams was most helpful and appeared prepared to do all possible to enable Daniel to attend the school. The site is not ideal but with relatively minor alterations a wheelchair bound pupil could have access to most teaching areas and the existence of service lifts suggests that the cost of installing an appropriate lift there could be less than at another school where such provision does not already exist.

Daniel's parents visited the school early in the New Year, and arrangements were made for him to start there in the following September.

2. School for the Partially Sighted or Ordinary Junior School: Harriet's Story

Harriet Withers has been seriously visually handicapped from birth. Her condition is described as 'bilateral nuclear cataracts, nystagmus, high myopia/photophobia, alternating squint'. When she was five she was admitted to a day special school for partially sighted children, which took boys and girls aged 5 to 16. Teaching was organised in six mixed-ability classes of no more than fifteen pupils, and three tutorial teachers provided extra instruction on both a group and an individual basis. A minibus took Harriet the six miles to and from school each day. Mrs Withers was very pleased to have Harriet accepted there, and the head considered it a 'very satisfactory placement'.

Five years later, when Harriet was ten, the child guidance department received a memo from the education office requesting them to 'set up the full SE procedure on Harriet Withers, whose parents have requested a transfer to an ordinary school'. The department requested and received SE forms from the head teacher at the special school, the senior medical officer and the educational psychologist. The head teacher was doubtful about Harriet's ability to cope in an ordinary school, especially as she had missed a lot of schooling due to respiratory infections and seemed to find many subjects difficult. He described in detail on the SE form Harriet's level of achievement and the kind of teaching she had received at the special school.

Extracts from Form SE1 (Headteacher's Report)

Educational level	
Level of speech and understanding of speech.	Her speech is clear and her vocabulary and comprehension commensurate with her general ability.
Any significant aspects of child's play.	Timid. Very clean. Never gets dirty.
Reading level, fluency, comprehension.	Schonell word test 8.0. Reads mechanically.
Spelling level.	Schonell 8 3/12.
Numeracy, level of mathematical thinking.	Knows number bonds to 10, slowly to 20. Above 20 poor. Able to tell time mechanically but severely limited in use and application at present.
Practical and creative skills.	Very slow in needlework. Simple work with assistance.
Physical skills and coordination.	Timid and apprehensive. Poor coordination. Tends to use poor vision as an excuse not to

	perform.
Specific skills and interests.	—
Progress in last 12 months.	She is making slow but steady improvement in reading, spelling, English, number, swimming etc.
Intelligence and other test scores.	WISC 75 (1974).
Behaviour and disposition	
a. Relationships with other children.	Generous with her possessions but does not make friends easily. Tends to buy friendship.
b. Relationships with adults.	Constantly seeking attention and approval and therefore enjoys a one to one relationship.
c. Any special characteristics of child.	Timid, occasionally spiteful. Possibly a little spoilt.
Interests.	Enjoys swimming at school. Likes painting.
Has special attention already been provided in the school?	She has been taught in small classes by very experienced teachers and received considerable individual and group instruction, with the most up to date aids available. She has been visited regularly by the peripatetic teacher for her area who has observed her working in class. She has followed specially prepared programmes of work including the new 'Look and Think' programme devised by the local university. She is a subject of the longitudinal research programme carried out by a research fellow at the university.
Parental attitudes.	Mrs and Mr Withers have been most co-operative and helpful in all school activities, attending open days and fund raising events regularly. They appear to have expected Harriet to try the

	entrance examination for Finmore School which seems to indicate that they do not appreciate the child's learning difficulties. Present attitudes may arise out of disappointment.
Class teacher's observations.	Harriet is a delicate, immature girl who although coming from a very sheltered, secure home is constantly seeking attention and approval. She has the approach, attitudes and ability of an eight year old. She has very limited reasoning ability when answering questions in English and maths. She can be a charming and generous girl, though sometimes petulant.

The senior medical officer submitted Form SE2 in which he described Harriet as 'signficantly visually handicapped (reduced acuity in both eyes which cannot be fully corrected by optical aids); squint under regular surveillance of opthalmic consultant; prognosis: unlikely to improve'. He recommended under the teaching/management heading of the form that Harriet should wear her spectacles constantly, sit 'mid class', work in better than average lighting conditions and engage in unrestricted physical activities. The areas of hearing, speech and language, motor functions, physical health, behaviour and emotional development, ability to care for herself and family history were all described on Form SE2 as normal, although under the heading 'intellectual development' the senior medical officer had written 'possibility that mother had Rubella during early pregnancy'. In his additional comments, he noted that 'Opthalmic consultant suggests transfer from special school to an ordinary day school is feasible in this case. Parents are anxious for such a trial. It is recommended that an experimental period at an ordinary school be arranged, subject to review both medically and educationally, within one year.'

In contrast to the senior medical officer's brief entries on Form SE2, the educational psychologist's comments on SE3 were very detailed.

Form SE3: Report by Educational Psychologist on a Child who may Require Special Education

Reason for child being referred for examination.	Harriet attends a school for partially sighted pupils, having been registered partially sighted. Recently her mother, family doctor and Mr Bowers (consultant opthalmic surgeon) have suggested that she would be better off attending a 'normal' school; a review was therefore instituted.
Do you suspect any physical difficulties not so far detected?	Visual conditions already known. No other defect suspected.
Description of child's behaviour in classroom, playground or home.	See also SE1. Harriet appears to adopt an easy, but superficial manner with adults, often appearing charming and verbally competent — this was certainly the impression gained of her in testing. With other children at school she is reported by her teachers to have difficulty making friends and sometimes to be spiteful. In contrast to this, Mrs Withers reports Harriet to be charming and friendly, and while agreeing that she is exposed to a predominantly adult group at home, claims that she has several friends locally with whom she plays. (There is no necessary contradiction in these reports as behaviour is often situation specific.)
Assessment of ability and personality.	In testing Harriet was most co-operative and appeared to understand all the demands made of her. When dealing with visual material she adopted a working distance of about six

inches and her performance on such items (e.g. Reading Test, Performance Items on WISC) was good enough at the lower levels to suggest that she had adequate vision to perform the items. Harriet's responding during testing was slow, long silences following questions, as if she was expecting further helpful questioning to aid her in answering.

On performance items, as the difficulty level increased so she became less persevering and attempted to involve the tester in solving the problem. Both responses are suggestive of a child who is dependent on, and expects, frequent help from adults in solving problems and who has little personal confidence and few adaptive strategies to call on when faced by such problems.

Wechsler Intelligence Scale for Children (6.12.78 at CA 10.3 yrs). Verbal Scale IQ 82. Performance Scale IQ 67. Full Scale IQ 72.

In view of Harriet's handicap some interpretation of the scores obtained is required. Although in testing Harriet appeared to have adequate close vision to perform the test items, it is to be anticipated that a child with a longstanding visual handicap would be at some disadvantage when their performance is compared with that of normal

	children on a test such as this.
Implications of above observations.	In spite of making allowance for the possibly depressing effects of handicap on her overall test performance, it still appears that she is currently functioning at the bottom end of the 'normal' range on such tasks. She will therefore appear in school as a 'slow learner' and extensive individualisation of her learning programme will continue to be required. Were she not already attending a special school where such individualisation of teaching is possible, I would seriously consider recommending such a placement on the basis of the test performances reported above, and the attainments reported below. However, it should be remembered that there are likely to be other children of her age in normal schools at present who perform at similar levels.
Assessment of educational performance a. language development.	See also SE1. Harriet's level of language development appears appropriate though in testing she did have difficulty elaborating some responses (WISC Vocab. Raw Score = 27, age equivalent of approx 9 years).
b. literacy.	See also SE1. Neale Analysis of Reading Ability Form C (6.12.78 at CA 10.3 years). Accuracy 'Age' 8.4 yrs. Comprehension 'Age' 8.7 yrs. Reading Rate 6.6 yrs. Schonell Graded Spelling Test. Form A Spelling 'Age' 8.4

	yrs.
c. mathematical.	See also SE1. WISC Arithmetic Sub-Test Scale Score 9. (Raw Score = 8; age 'equivalent' of approx 9½ yrs). Performance on this sub-test suggests Harriet is capable of simple mental arithmetic involving addition, subtraction and multiplication of numbers up to twenty.
d. special interests or abilities.	None noted but see SE1.
e. subjects the child dislikes or finds difficult.	None noted, any visually presented task poses difficulties and very slow working rate would give rise to difficulties in any normally paced teaching situation.
Educational implications of the above.	Given commonly held assumptions of the relationship between 'IQ' and attainments, Harriet appears to be performing at an appropriate level. However, her attainments are considerably less than those of an 'average' child of her age and her working rate is very slow indeed. On this basis I would anticipate that she would have great difficulty coping with and keeping up with the work of a class of 'average' children of her age. Because of her relatively poor attainments, Harriet will continue to need systematic basic subject teaching preferably on an individualised programme. While such provision can be made in both junior and comprehensive schools it is at present ideally provided by her present placement i.e. Greenbank School for the partially sighted.

Child's family background.	Both parents work. Harriet has older siblings, the next being a brother of 15–16 years – this makes her the youngest of the family by some years.
Child's views (if any) of her difficulties in the kind of help required.	Harriet is keen to attend normal school. I think she is not really aware of the difference between her own sight and that of a normally sighted person and, having always attended a special school, she is unaware of the environmental and social demands which might be made on her. Her mother reports that Harriet is increasingly aware of the 'special' nature of her present school and is beginning to resent this.
Parental attitudes.	Mrs Withers displays a very high level of concern and support for Harriet and maintains that she tries to treat her as normally as possible. She is undoubtedly able and ready to help Harriet in any way and appears to have taken a sensible approach to her visual disability. However, I feel that her understanding of Harriet's problems relates purely to the nature and extent of her visual problems; she regards her daughter as normal in other ways, which obscures her understanding of the real educational difficulties which Harriet has, and would have even if normally sighted.
Implications of the above for special education.	Mrs Wither's determination to regard Harriet as a normal child with a visual disability has led

	her to increasingly resent Harriet's placement in a special school, and since the opthalmologist (Mr Bowers) has suggested that Harriet could cope with attending normal school, Mrs Withers has sought to secure a transfer for her. Therefore while I feel sure Mrs Withers could continue to co-operate with the special school if Harriet is to remain there, she would not be happy with such a placement and, I suspect, would continue to attempt to have Harriet transferred. If such efforts on Mrs Wither's part continued I feel it might have an unsettling effect on the child.
Type of placement required.	To remain in present school with no special arrangements other than a continuing review of progress (i.e. Greenbank School for the partially sighted).

The educational psychologist sent the three SE forms to the special services education department, together with a covering letter:

8/1/79

I enclose herewith the completed SE Forms. I hope it is clear from the comments contained therein that the issue is not simply one of the degree of Harriet's visual disability, but rather of the total handicapping effect of the visual disability and other factors.

The idea of a 'trial' return to normal school appears to be supported by both medical opinion and Mrs Withers, who says that she would accept Harriet returning to Greenbank School if it was felt that such a trial had failed. The problem here seems to be setting the criteria whereby a trial might be judged as successful or otherwise, and the timing of such a trial — if Harriet were to transfer out now, she would go to junior school but would be due for secondary transfer in September. Because opinions differ on the most appropriate placement, I have not completed SE4 fully. Given the disagreement, you may feel that a case conference is necessary and, if so, I hope both Dr James (the family doctor) and Mr Bowers (consultant opthalmologist) can be invited. It appears that they are largely responsible for supporting Mrs Withers' feeling that Harriet is misplaced, and if she is to remain at Greenbank School, it could be helpful if they could agree with the decision and tell Mrs Withers that they do.

The case conference was held at the end of the month, and Harriet's mother attended. A week later the director of education wrote to Mr and Mrs Withers to confirm that he had agreed 'with some reservations' to Harriet transferring to Brandwell Junior School immediately after the forthcoming half-term. He added that 'Her transfer will be on a trial basis and will be reviewed in summer 1979 in the first instance.'

The responsibility for coordination of advice and help for Harriet fell to the peripatetic teacher of the visually handicapped. Three months after Harriet's transfer on trial to the fourth year of Brandwell Junior School this report was compiled:

24 May 1979

At her mother's insistence, Harriet is now placed on trial in normal school. This note is a review of her performance so far.

Sight.

As expected, Harriet's loss of distance acuity puts her at a considerable disadvantage. Visual work cannot always be adapted to favour her and it is not always possible to provide substitute work or individual explanation. Her near sight is adequate, although low-contrast, fine visual work such as maps slows her down. Her photophobia can be a problem on a bright day, and if she stays at Brandwell next year we may have to supply blinds for her home room. However, she is making brave attempts to take part in activities that are visually difficult for her (PE and sport, for example), she is mobile within the school, and she is not posing a safety problem.

Schoolwork.

First impressions are that she is bearing out our estimates of her ability. She learns slowly and finds it hard to retain new skills and knowledge. Mr Jones (the educational psychologist) will comment on this in more detail in due course.

Social integration.
My observation and discussions with Harriet's teacher and with her mother are encouraging. Harriet has made some friends, and her handicap is accepted and allowed for by other children. She relates satisfactorily if rather immaturely to her teachers. In this respect I think the transfer has been much to her advantage, for the present at least.

Other circumstances.
Mrs Withers is very apprehensive about the outcome of the trial; as before, she is desperate for Harriet to remain in normal school. Mr Jones and Harriet's class teacher have stressed again the need for staffing levels at the school to be maintained or raised. There is no doubt that Harriet does need individual help, and I hope that Brandwell's requests for staff can be sympathetically considered.

Harriet's trial period ends with this term, and we hope to be able to make a recommendation about her future shortly. It is worth noting that Harriet was born prematurely; if her birth had been at full term she would be due to transfer to secondary school in 1980. For this and for other reasons, it would be possible to justify keeping Harriet at Brandwell for an extra year.

Teacher of the visually handicapped.

The Director of Education passed on this recommendation to Harriet's parents two months later:

23 July 1979
As you are aware, Harriet's progress at Brandwell Junior School has recently been reviewed, and it is thought that, whilst she has made satisfactory progress during the period of her attendance there, a transfer to a comprehensive school would be premature at this stage. It is suggested, therefore, that she spend a further year at the junior school and I can make arrangements for this if you are in agreement. Perhaps you would let me know your views in the matter.

As an extra year at the junior school was precisely what Mrs Withers herself had requested six weeks previously, her reply was understandably exasperated.

3rd August 1979

    With reference to your letter of the 23rd July, I would like to say that I am pleased that my daughter's progress at Brandwell School has been recognised.

    I am in full agreement with her staying at that school for a further year, although I am surprised that you should ask for my views on this matter. As you will see from my letter of the 13th June, that is what I requested, and a copy of my letter to Mr Jones was sent to the various departments concerned.

Harriet's presence in the normal school was thus guaranteed for another year. However the reservations expressed by the educational psychologist, the head teacher of Greenbank School and the director of education meant that her future would again be subject to review when that year was over and a decision needed to be reached about Harriet's secondary schooling.

40 INTEGRATION IN PRACTICE: A SMALL RURAL PRIMARY SCHOOL

Patience Tuckwell

Peartree School is a small Church of England Primary School serving a fairly tightly knit rural community in Oxfordshire. All its children are from Peartree village or its adjoining hamlet and outlying farms and cottages. In a larger or more urban school, some of them might be recommended for education in a special school, but at Peartree they learn alongside the other children from that village, as Patience Tuckwell describes.

There are 70 children on the roll at Peartree School, three full-time teachers, including the headmistress, Miss J, who takes a class, and one part-time teacher. There is also a part-time secretary. Dinner attendants and a caretaker are local village people. This is the official complement of personnel but Peartree School can also draw on the help of some 20 voluntary helpers. These people are parents and grandparents of school children or simply village people with an interest in the school's work, who come in regularly to help in various ways, from hearing reading to giving cooking lessons, music tuition, games practice and so on. Several of these helpers are in fact qualified teachers who have children at the school.

The school, like most village schools, is the only educational establishment in the village and is perhaps the most important of the village's institutions. It is in the main street, close to the church and shop, two other pivots of community life. The life of the school overflows continually into that of the community, partly, no doubt, because of Miss J's strong belief in the importance of the role of the school in the village and also because inevitably, the resources of the school alone are poorer than the combined resources of school and environment. What might be seen as a disadvantage (the limited facilities of a small school) becomes a means of compelling the school to be outward rather than inward looking, warm towards, rather than isolated from, the people it serves. The school needs the community as the community does the school.

There are distinct disadvantages attached to a small, rural school. A drop in the birthrate is reflected in the school's roll and may result in a cut in staffing allowances so that while classes are certainly smaller than in large, urban schools, the constant worry is that they will have to be allowed to get larger as teachers are withdrawn. The fact that the staff is small must also limit the chances of getting excellent teachers and limit the opportunities of such as are recruited for the exchange of ideas and philosophies with colleagues.

Peartree teachers are encouraged to go on courses and mix, both formally and informally, with the staff of other schools. It has taken six years for Miss J to build up a good staff whose philosophies of education are compatible with her own very strong belief in the rural school's importance in the community. In spite of the precarious position of any small school in the face of falling numbers and financial restraint, Peartree has made a virtue of necessity. Miss J explains:

Vertical grouping ... mixed ages and abilities ... these are not new ideas for the village school, but have always been part of its life. We are small and perforce each group has a wide age range. Bill, aged 8½ and rather slow, works in the same room as Hugh, just 7 and rather bright. It is impossible to class teach anyway; each group of about 4 children has different needs. Our 'integration' does not have capital letters. The rural school is naturally integrated.

This state of affairs of course, has its potential drawbacks. There is concern, Miss J tells me, that brighter children do not get enough stimulation. 'It's not a question of competition', she says, 'but of finding kindred spirits, friends, if you are brighter than everyone else.' A bright eight year old will find himself working with eleven year olds and may have to draw his friends from older children, who leave long before he does. He may have to work alone as he gets close to leaving himself and to adopt a 'tutorial' relationship with his teacher. He may be lonely and suffer from a sense of isolation. The village school has a challenge to meet in the way it deals with its bright children no less than that of its slower ones.

A Peartree child may have the same teacher for three or four years or even longer. He may be in the same class as brothers, sisters, cousins, even young uncles and aunts. 'Peartree is a family school, a family affair.'

A child's parents probably attended the school. His parents, or one of them, may actually work in the school, even in the child's class, even with him. He can expect not only his parents, but also his relations, neighbours and the parents of his friends to note his progress and care about his achievements. Everyone knows him. Most people know his strengths. His academic weaknesses are important but so are his social and emotional difficulties and talents. The bright child, no less than any other, has his weaknesses and the education of children in Peartree is not solely concerned with academic achievement.

It could be said that Peartree School belongs to and is an asset of, the whole village and that few villagers are untouched by it. The school managers are not a remote body of people that nobody knows. Some of them are the parents of friends or the grandparents of friends. One of them is the Rector, who also comes into school, teaches and takes prayers, prepares children for confirmation, visits their homes and knows their parents. The school has no PTA organisation mainly because there seems to be no need for it. The school welcomes parents at any time and their occasional queries and demands are expected rather than dreaded by the staff. Difficulties are settled, as far as is possible, informally. Miss J also feels that a PTA in a village such as Peartree, where there are as many professional people as there are labourers and the school is naturally socially comprehensive, might result in a class barrier, the more articulate or prosperous parents having more to say than anyone else. Parents do meet on social occasions, to hear about and discuss teaching methods, to raise money and so on. There can be few Peartree people, parents of schoolchildren or not, that at one time or another during the year, have not 'been up to school', if only for the reason that the school provides diversions; it puts on shows, holds sports, has sales, organises special services in church in a community which is relatively poorly served by public transport and is some distance from the diversions of the urban setting.

The familiarity of the school with the lives of our children works both ways. Not only does the community know the school as it were, but also the school and its staff know the community, even though it is unusual for teachers to live in the village in which they work. You have to compensate for that. If there's a new baby, an illness in the family, a problem or a bit of good news, we know too and we generally know exactly the circumstances in which the problem or delight is being experienced. This makes it easier probably when there are things to be argued over with parents, problems, things we don't see eye to eye about. One has become involved in the lives of the children in a more intimate way than is possible in larger schools. Certainly, in larger schools, it is easier to escape involvement. This intimacy carries over when the children go on to their secondary schools. Our children come back to visit frequently and we encourage it. Peartree, we think, is still their village school, even though they have grown past its academic fare. A child who experiences difficulties with the 3Rs, say, and who, from a school point of view, might be considered to be dull, may, in his outside school life, have things of which he can be justifiably proud. Thus, the eight-year-old farmer's son, whose academic progress is painfully slow, is valued for his intimate knowledge of farms, his social adeptness, his leadership qualities. His academic progress is only one side of him with which we are concerned. His other facets are just as relevant in our concern for his education. (Miss J)

Miss J does not believe in shunting out the less able into special schools. 'The village school is not only for one class of person, not only for the bright or the average, the rich, the poor. Peartree School is for Peartree children.' It simply does what Miss J considers to be its duty; it educates the children presented to it. Thus, out of 70 children, there are six who, in different circumstances, might be eligible for special schools. But Miss J says:

We don't shunt them on. We educate them. Six is the most we have ever had in my time and we have not yet had to deal with a child who has severe mental or physical handicap. I should certainly want to accept such a child as I would any other from Peartree as long as I could be sure that I had enough help, perhaps an extra welfare assistant. The responsibility of the head is to keep a learning environment that is balanced for all children. As long as I could do that, I would accept any Peartree child. I think we cope well with our six but I would not like the school to become one that accepts 'Handicapped' children and 'Integrates' them. Not with capital letters. We are not an experiment, to be dropped when the researcher gets tired. The reason we integrate is because we are a community school and such children as we accept are part of that community. That's why we're here.

I asked Miss J. to describe the children:

Don (8.5) is the youngest of a large family, an over-protected little boy who couldn't swallow or use a knife and fork when he first came to school. He has very little number sense and doesn't play well. His development seems to depend entirely on his own confidence in himself as a person. He is gradually being enabled to think and reason because he has never been made to feel that he is a failure. Now that he is no longer one of the smallest in the school he is coming out of himself. I have him in my class, the smallest class and I teach him by himself and with one other child but he also joins in all the school activities. He has many of the same difficulties as Bill (8.6). Their backgrounds are entirely different. While Don is from an old working class village family, Bill is the second son of prosperous farmers. His problems have been his disappointed parents. His elder brother goes to an academically orientated private school. Bill suffers badly from asthma and eczema and he also has a sense of failure from the school he attended before the family came to Peartree. Bill's head is very slightly over-large and some of his coordination problems would seem to suggest possible minimal brain damage. Unlike Don, he is very popular, something of a leader, naughty and a good player. He is rather spoilt at home and at school occasionally kicks against authority. He is in my class too and for the 3Rs he works alone or with one or two others but for all other subjects he is extremely capable of joining in with the others.

Sarah (9) is the youngest of three in a family with a lot of problems. Her mother suffers from nervous troubles. Sarah is spoilt and has been babied. She lacks confidence and is slow and unresponsive. She hardly reads and shows one or two marked dyslectic symptoms. Work with Sarah has to be slow and patient and in small groups or by herself. If she had lived in a city she would be very likely to go to an ESN(M) school.

Sue (9), whose basic difficulties resemble Sarah's, is however, socially and physically able and very practical. She is very much the older sister and is full of good sound common sense. She learns slowly but thoroughly and progresses slowly as long as she can go at her own pace. Her brother, Simon (7), was very slow in learning to read and has many of the difficulties of his sister. Both children are popular at school.

All these children might be categorised as ESN(M) but I'm not sure how it would really benefit them. They receive their education at Peartree without ever thinking of themselves as special or handicapped.

It is a special education however. Certain goals are set for them and because of the smallness of our classes teaching is given individually and in small groups. Parents are encouraged to follow up teaching at home, hearing their children read or practising basic skills. Some of their family troubles have been ameliorated. For instance, Sarah's mother has been persuaded to work at school as a 'dinner lady' and Bill's mother has been encouraged to be firm with Bill and to praise his achievements. Praise is a great enabler and never hurt anyone.

The 6th child at Peartree who could be considered to be handicapped is James (10). He has troubles of an emotional rather than an academic nature. He is perhaps the most difficult of the six to educate in an ordinary school because he needs so much individual attention. He is light-fingered and the sort of child generally described as a 'nuisance'. His family is split and he now has half-sisters, a new 'father' and a new half brother to put his nose out of joint. It is not surprising that he feels rejected. Peartree doesn't reject him and can deal with his difficulties. His mother has been impressed at the academic progress he has made since he came to Peartree from a large urban school. James is very popular with other children.

Peartree is perhaps not much different from other small rural schools insofar as it has a head teacher whose principles and ideals are very clearly formulated. What is significant about it is that policies such as 'the integrated day', the 'open door' and 'community involvement' are not seen as revolutionary new ideas or as bandwagons on which it is safe to climb for a season, but are calmly and matter-of-factly practised because they make sense.

41 SCENES FROM WARD 7

Maureen Oswin

Source: Edited version of Maureen Oswin, *Children Living in Long-stay Hospitals*, Appendix 1: Scenes in Ward 7 (Spastics International Medical Publication Monograph No. 5, 1978).

In her book Children Living in Long-stay Hospitals, *Maureen Oswin describes the lives of some of the severely handicapped children living in Ward 7. The following extract includes a detailed description of only one of the children, Tom, but the sections describing a typical afternoon and evening in the ward convey a vivid impression of the kind of lives led by most of the children there.*

Background

Ward 7 accommodated 21 multiply handicapped children aged from three to 14 years. Eighteen of the children were receiving permanent long-term care, two were weekly boarders, and one was in for short-term care. Nine of the 18 long-term children had been admitted for permanent care before the age of five years.

Thirteen of the 21 children were non-ambulant, 19 were incontinent, four were known to be blind, 19 were speechless. 20 did not wash or dress themselves and seven did not feed themselves. All had the ability to grasp objects in their hands.

A Typical Evening

At 4pm

Two of the 21 children had been taken home for the night, and one was out with his foster-mother. Nursing Assistant Jones, and State Enrolled Nurse Smith were on duty for the remaining 18 children. There was a new little girl in the ward today: six-year-old Mary. She was ambulant, and had been admitted to the 'sick' ward a week ago for short-term care, and had just been transferred to Ward 7. She stood in the middle of the day-room, cuddling a soft toy hippo which she had brought from home, and looking timidly about her.

The day-room contained a battered settee, a large air-bed, and some wooden boxes with holes in and square boxes arranged as three steps. Ambulant children were walking about; the non-ambulant children were lying on the floor. A few children sat under the radiators and held the warm pipes with their hands, others rested their bare feet on the pipes. There was a sense of poverty in the room, and it was slightly cold.

A narrow corridor led from the day-room, on each side of which were linen cupboards, store-rooms, a bathroom, washroom and lavatories. The corridor led into the bedroom, which was so small that the beds were in rows across the centre of the room as well as all around the sides. The children's clothes were kept in two large cupboards just inside the bedroom. There was no room for individual lockers. The day-room had a newly-built extension to it, known as 'the sun-lounge'. At one end of this sun-lounge there was a colour television, a plastic settee, three plastic armchairs and a strip of carpet. At the other end there was a sideboard minus its doors, four tables, and ten kitchen-type chairs; this was where the children ate their meals.

At 4.15

Supper started. There was a shortage of clean bibs, so soiled ones were reused. These dirty bibs were lying in a damp heap in the broken-doored sideboard, and as the staff lifted them out a sour smell of stale food arose, and lumps of cold porridge, potato and sponge-pudding fell from them. They were shaken and then tied around the children's necks. There was also a shortage of bowls and spoons, which caused a major inconvenience during supper because the two staff had to keep leaving the children and running to the kitchen to rinse bowls and spoons. When they did this, some of the more able children went to the trolley and ate scraps from the scrap bowl, or grabbed food from the plates of the less able children. As it was so inconvenient to keep going to the kitchen to wash dishes in the middle of feeding the children, the staff eventually gave some of the children their puddings in unwashed bowls which had been used by other children.

Fourteen of the children could feed themselves, which was said to be due to the psychologists of the hospital directing the ward staff in the principles of behaviour modification. The ability to feed themselves appeared to be an isolated skill, for only two of the 14 children were also reliable about the lavatory, and only one of them could wash and dress himself.

The children were given their meals in two sittings, so that they could be individually supervised. Those who could manage without help were encouraged by praise, and the others were encouraged to lift their spoons to their mouths on their own after being helped to load them. Thus while actually sitting at the table with a plate of food in front of them and spoons in their hands, the children received attention. However, immediately a child finished eating he ceased to receive attention. Some of the non-ambulant children were then carried silently back into the day-room and placed, still sticky, onto bean-bags. Others remained sitting at the tables; their faces were covered with food and they sucked at their food-covered hands. A few of the children got off their chairs as they finished eating and went under the tables, where they used their hands to shovel up spilt food into their mouths. Some of the ambulant and crawling children went to the waste-bowl on the trolley and picked at the slimy mess of everybody else's leavings, and poked into the bowl containing the dirty cutlery to suck off the food which had been left on other children's spoons. Then they went to the slower eaters and tried to take food from them.

At 4.55

The staff cleared the tables, went into the kitchen and remained there to have a cup of tea. Nursing Assistant Hartley arrived at 5pm. She would be on duty until 8pm. She joined the other two staff in the kitchen.

The 18 children were left without supervision. Eight-year-old Monty (two years in hospital) and 14-year-old Douglas (11 years in hospital), both ambulant, began to tip over the chairs in the sun-lounge, and leant on the window-sills and opened and slammed the windows. They were high-spirited and healthy, and this was their usual behaviour after meals. Seven-year-old James (five years in hospital) was sitting in a baby-buggy at the end of the sun-lounge. His buggy got tipped over during the rompings of Monty and Douglas. He was unharmed but very startled. Monty began to loudly slam the low gate between the lounge and the day-room.

Nine-year-old Shirley remained sitting at the table where she had eaten her supper. She was a weekly boarder, and spent most of her time between Monday and Friday sitting at a table in the sun-lounge, in a state of silent, abject misery. She had a frail appearance, and wore a caliper on one leg. She had had a stressful time towards the end of supper today, because her plate had been snatched first by 13-year-old Elizabeth and then by Douglas (who had proceeded to eat her supper with his fingers). Shirley always ate very slowly, and she often had her food stolen by the more able children.

Three-year-old Tom, ambulant, but with very little sight, wandered about the two rooms. Sometimes he sat down on the floor. He had been admitted to the hospital only a few days before, and was in for long-term care. Mary, the new little girl, stood looking through the day-room doors into the corridor. Her toy hippo appeared to be lost. She held her hands limply at her sides.

At 5.30

The children's drugs were given out. This was the first staff involvement with the children since 4.55. The SEN stood in the corridor beside the drug trolley. The two Nursing Assistants stood by her with dessert spoons in their hands. The SEN put the appropriate drug for each child into one of the spoons held by the NAs, who had meanwhile filled the spoons with jam from a pot standing on the drug trolley. The NA then opened the day-room door, found the right child for the drug, and pushed the spoonful of jam and the capsule into his mouth. (This was the usual procedure for giving drugs in Ward 7: it was done hurriedly and without conversation with the child.) Because so much jam had been put into their mouths the children became very sticky: they continued to sit with sticky faces and with jam trickling down their chins onto the front of their clothes. Little streaks of dried jam, long there and hardened now, were stuck on the radiator in the day-room because the children on numerous previous drug-giving occasions had wiped their sticky mouths along the radiator by which they had been sitting when given their drugs. There were also streaks of fluff-covered jam down the sides of the wheelchairs.

SEN Smith went off duty at 5.35. NA Hartley and NA Jones would be in charge of the ward for the rest of the evening, and would have to get the 18 children ready for bed, and their clothing sorted out by 8pm. Neither had had any training in looking after handicapped children, or in residential care work. NA Jones was middle-aged and had started working in the hospital 18 months earlier. She said that on her first day she had been given the choice of spending a week looking around the hospital at the various wards, or starting work straight away as an NA on Ward 7. She had decided to begin as a nurse immediately, but had been very upset for a few days because of the children's grave handicaps. She had not attended any lectures or been given any guidance. She said that she 'just picked up what to do' from the other staff. She was kind to the children, and with different leadership would have made an excellent houseparent. NA Hartley was in her late twenties and had been working in the hospital for seven months. She said that she had applied to the hospital for domestic work but had been offered a job as a nursing assistant.

5.40 to 7.25

NA Hartley and NA Jones had to be in the bathroom, washroom and bedroom during this period, and a number of children were left unsupervised in the day-room. Non-ambulant children who were waiting their turn to be bathed or washed, or who had already had their turn, were lying on the floor by the radiator or sitting in wheelchairs or baby-buggies. The ambulant children wandered about the day-room and sun-lounge. Douglas and Monty continued to rampage about in the sun-lounge, shoving at the tipped-over chairs. Nine-year-old Dermod (four years in hospital), cerebral-palsied but able to crawl, remained in the corner where he always put himself after meals. He rested his bare feet on the warm pipes.

Shirley still sat alone at the bare table in the sun-lounge, where she had been sitting since finishing her supper at 4.55. She had shrunk into herself as Douglas's romps with the chairs continued unabated around her, and, completely still, she stared blankly at the untidy, comfortless scene in front of her.

Mary began to strip little pieces of wall-paper off the day-room wall. She dropped the paper on the floor. Six-year-old Jill, who had been admitted to the hospital the year before, bottom-shuffled along behind Mary, picked up the bits of wallpaper and ate them.

NA Jones was working in the small bathroom, undressing and washing one child at a time on a large table. NA Hartley was with a group of children in the wash-room/lavatory area. She was following the usual wash-room routine of sitting four or five children on the lavatories and then partially or fully undressing them as they sat there. After sitting on the lavatories for about 10 minutes, each child was taken across to the wash-basins to be washed. If he was non-ambulant, he was lifted onto a large table in front of the lavatories and washed as he lay there.

The children in the washroom were being washed with one shared flannel. There appeared to be a shortage of bathroom commodities; nappies were being used as towels, and there were only two hairbrushes for all the children. All underwear and nightclothes were communal, including the standard issue dressing-gown made of towelling.

Twelve-year-old Brian (in hospital for nine years) had dried mucus caked on his face because his nose had not been wiped for him for many hours. The mucus could not be moved, even after being soaked with the flannel. NA Hartley decided to leave it on in case his face was made sore by too much rubbing. Brian was a very big boy, and it was difficult to find pyjamas to fit him. The jacket eventually put on him was too tight and came high up his back.

Some of the children were returned to the day-room after being put into nightclothes. They were not wearing slippers, and their feet were cold.

Although the two NAs were almost overwhelmed by their chores, they were very kind to the children during the getting-to-bed routines. NA Jones called me into the bathroom to see a child smiling as she washed him, and she took me to see children whom she had put to bed. She went to each bed and peeped at the children. She said: 'It makes you wonder, doesn't it? I wish there was more time to spend with them and play with them as we could our own'.

At 7pm the washing and changing of children was all finished. Eight children were in bed; 10 were back in the day-room, dressed in their nightclothes. It had taken the two NAs 1 hour 20 minutes to attend to the 18 children. The NAs began to tidy up the bathroom and washroom, and pack up the dirty clothes. The 10 children in the day-room were in the following positions:

10-year-old June sat in a wheelchair, sucking her hands;
nine-year-old Dermod was in the corner where he was always to be found; he was stripping off his nightwear;
six-year-old Jill was shuffling around the room on her bottom;
13-year-old Elizabeth sat beside Brian on the air-bed, on which eight-year-old Monty lay asleep;
six-year-old Mary walked wearily up and down the room;
13-year-old Charles, blind, stood holding the radiator;
14-year-old Douglas was kneeling in the middle of the day-room floor;
three-year-old Tom stood holding the radiator.

At 7.25

The two NAs had just finished packing the laundry. They walked through the day-room into the sun-lounge, turned on the colour television and put Jill in front of it. Then they went into the kitchen, where they sat smoking and drinking coffee. While it seemed wrong that the children were left alone so much, these two women must have been very hot and tired because they had washed and changed 18 children since 5.40pm and had tidied up the bathroom and packed up all the dirty laundry.

At 7.30 the positions of the children were:

June was in her wheelchair, as before;

Dermod was still in his corner, now stripped, and he lay on his back playing with a wheelchair tray that had been on the floor near him. He held it onto his face and twiddled with the rods and screws;

Jill was crouched in front of the television in the sun-lounge;

Elizabeth, Brian and Monty were still on the air-bed;

Mary stood in the middle of the room, now sucking her hands;

Charles had sat down on the floor, his back against the radiator, and his hands and arms stretched out each side of the warm pipes. He looked very cold;

Douglas was still kneeling in the middle of the floor;

Tom still stood by the radiator.

At 8pm the staff were still in the kitchen and the 10 children were in the same positions as before.

One Afternoon, for Four Children

Again, the ward was under-staffed, and from 1pm until 4.30pm the staff were not involved with the children at all. During these hours the staff were in the bedroom, day-room or kitchen.

At 1pm, 12-year-old Percy (six years in hospital), partially sighted, cerebral-palsied and non-ambulant, was in a wheelchair. The chair did not have a foot-rest, and Percy's feet were dangling just above a narrow metal bar. At 1.15, 13-year-old Elizabeth crawled across to Percy and removed his socks. He continued to sit in the chair, bare-footed, until he was taken to the table for his supper at 4.30. By that time his bare feet had been hovering just above the metal bar of his broken wheelchair for 3 hours 15 minutes. His feet looked thin, cold and frail, and appeared to need some warm support, such as a cushion, to be placed under them.

At 1pm, eight-year-old Hector (four years in hospital, cerebral-palsied and non-ambulant) was lying on his back in a bean-bag in a very awkward position. He remained in that position until lifted for supper at 4.30.

At 1pm, 13-year-old Angela (nine years in hospital) was in her wheelchair in the sun-lounge, when she began crying. She cried unheeded until 4pm, and then became quiet. She was put to the table for supper at 4.30.

At 2pm, six-year-old Jill (one year in hospital) became very miserable at seeing two mothers and a father come to visit other children. She crouched at the door of the day-room, weeping and moaning, for 20 minutes. Then she resumed her usual behaviour of bottom-shuffling about the day-room, endeavouring to get staff attention. When the staff were in the bathroom or bedroom, Jill sat by the day-room door and tried to prise it open by curling the fingers of her 'good' hand under it, hoping to open it and get through to the staff. Whenever the staff came through the door they inevitably bumped into Jill as she crouched by the door. This appeared to irritate them, especially when she also tried to catch hold of their feet as they entered. She was not a popular child. Eventually the staff placed Jill on the air-bed, where she was anchored for some 15 minutes before managing to crawl off and once more resume her place at the day-room door.

The Loneliness of Three-year-old Tom

Tom had just been admitted to Ward 7. He knew the hospital through coming in for occasional day-care, but this was his first experience of residential care. He was ambulant, frail-looking, and described as 'almost blind'. The staff thought that he would remain permanently in the hospital because his family had complicated housing, financial and health problems.

Saturday Afternoon, a Few Days after Tom's Admission

From 1pm to 3pm there were 16 children and four staff in the ward. Ambulant children were wandering aimlessly about; non-ambulant children lay on the floor or sat in wheelchairs. Tom walked up and down, his head on one side. Sometimes he stood motionless in the middle of the room, or by the window. Sometimes he stood tapping his mouth with his hands. Several times he went and pulled at the curtains. Once he twirled himself up in a curtain, standing under it and folding it around him, and then whirling round and round on the spot until the curtain enfolded him like a cocoon. He unwound himself, then lay beneath the curtain and held it in one hand, and moved his body round and round in a small circle by pushing and tapping on the floor with one foot. A passing member of staff said 'I think he might be blind and deaf.' Tom received no attention from anyone during this two-hour period.

A Few Days Later: Mid-morning

There were again four staff on duty. Tom had been standing holding the radiator for some 10 minutes, then he moved away and walked across the room. He did not see nine-year-old Dermod lying on the floor, and almost trod on Dermod's face. Tom stumbled, bent down, felt at Dermod with both hands, stumbled again, and then pulled gently at Dermod's clothes. Dermod, partially sighted, pushed gently back at Tom. Tom swayed back and sat down hard on the floor. He remained sitting, felt all around him with one hand, bottom-shuffled around Dermod, felt his way to the wall, and then stood up. He then walked to the middle of the room and stood there tapping his mouth with one hand.

This episode, with staff guidance, might have been a valuable opportunity for the two little boys to learn more about each other. But Tom and Dermod had coped with the situation alone and come through it in muddled isolation. Not being taught to identify themselves and each other, these two poor-sighted children were developing into solitary beings without any meaningful experience of communicating with other people. Of course it is common for three-year-olds to be unsociable, but the organisation of Ward 7 encouraged the staff to develop habits of non-involvement with the children, and was likely to keep Tom at this solitary stage in his development. No attempts were being made to encourage social interaction between the children in Ward 7, not even in such primary ways as feeling each other's hands, and finding pleasure and recognition in touching each other and hearing their own and each other's names.

Later that morning Tom had his first bit of mothering. As the staff brought the lunch-trolley into the day-room, he fell over and began to cry. He cried for four minutes, then a nurse picked him up and cuddled him for one minute. He stopped crying. When the nurse put him down he immediately resumed his crying, whereupon another nurse picked him up. He stopped crying again. She held him for a moment, then went to put him down. He wound his legs around her thighs and knees, slipping to her calves and feet as she struggled to lower him to the ground and let go of him again. He would not easily be put down, he clung to her and his cries and protests increased in volume. 'I don't like to put him down', the young nurse said as she finally managed to extricate herself from his entwining legs and arms. She walked away. Tom remained in a heap in the middle of the floor, weeping. Such a situation caused by the organisation (i.e. lunch was about to start) not only teaches a young child about rejection; it also teaches a young nurse how to steel herself, *against her better judgement*, to ignore a child's appeals for mothering.

Throughout the afternoon Tom wandered about the room, wound himself up in the curtain, or just stood sucking his thumb. In mid-afternoon a member of the staff took him for a 20-minute walk in a baby-buggy around the hospital grounds. When he came back he was placed in the day-room and the staff went into the kitchen for their tea. Tom then went to the curtain and again began to wind himself up in it.

That Evening: 5.45

Tom was looking very distressed and tired. His day had been lonely and wearisome. I had been in the ward since 9am and had not seen him receive any direction to his activities, nor any rest or security. Like Mary, the other new child in the ward, he had spent the day walking about the day-room and sun-lounge. The staff had not settled him into a spot which he might have felt was his own, perhaps giving him a small chair and a table of his own with familiar toys on it, the company of nearby children, and cuddles from the staff, all of which might have helped to reassure him as a young handicapped child away from home for the first time.

He came to where I was sitting and seemed to want comforting, but he pulled away as I drew him to me. Suddenly he began to rush about and rattle wheelchairs, in a burst of anger. He hurled himself at seven-year-old James' buggy and shook it, then shook Percy's wooden chair, then went to 13-year-old Angela and punched her knees and legs, but his small fists did not seem to disturb Angela. He then rushed back to me and burrowed into my lap. His sleeves were wet where he had been sucking them, and he looked flushed and exhausted.

The three nurses who were on duty came across and looked at Tom. They said that he had only started to suck his sleeves since he had been living in the ward full-time for the last week or so, and they thought he probably copied the habit from other children. Several of the children in Ward 7 had a habit of drawing their jersey sleeves down over their hands and then sucking the material and their hands at the same time. This meant that they often had long damp sleeves hanging down over their hands. Tom had not picked up this habit when he had been coming to the ward for day-care only, but had started doing it about a week after becoming residential. It would seem that such habits are likely to develop when a child has prolonged periods of family deprivation and lack of attention, and when he spends many hours witnessing the long-established institutional habits of other deprived children.

At 7pm

Tom was put into his pyjamas and returned to the day-room to continue his wanderings. Just before 8pm he came again to me and sat in my lap. When I left at 8.15 he did not want me to put him down. He clung around my knees and feet. When I finally managed to get out and shut the ward door I could hear him hammering with his fists on the other side of it, and crying.

A Few Days Later: 5pm

There were 20 children in the ward, with three staff. The staff had just finished giving the children their supper, and were now in the kitchen having their coffee. I heard Tom crying in the sun-lounge and went to see what was happening. He was being hurt by six-year-old Jill, who was holding him down, pressing on his face and pinching him. He had no trousers, pants or nappy on, and he looked dishevelled and tired. I picked him up and took him to the day-room. He was so upset that he broke away, tore across the room in anger, punched Angela (who looked very surprised), and then ran crying into the sun-lounge again, where he flung himself against a radiator and sobbed.

Tom appeared to be in a grave state of homesickness and grief, and seemed to be getting more disturbed each day. It was noticeable that he had deteriorated emotionally during the two weeks since his admission. He was panicky, cried more, sucked his sleeves, got angry and hit out at other children. It was disquieting that the doctors had only that same day said 'that child *has* settled in well'.

The Same Evening: 7pm

The staff were in the bathroom, changing children. Tom stood in the middle of the day-room. He was bare-footed and dressed in hospital pyjamas which were too big for him. The floor was wet because the domestic worker had just washed it. When Tom moved forward his bare feet slipped on the wet floor; he sat down and began to cry. Then he got himself up again. The day-room door opened and one of the staff put six-year-old Mary into the room, and just at that point Tom slipped over again on the wet floor. He got up and ran crying to Mary, who was probably the nearest person he could see with his meagre sight. Mary stood bare-footed in her nightie, and Tom clasped her round the waist and tried to climb into her arms. Mary was startled and stepped quickly back; she swayed and nearly fell. The nurse took the weeping Tom away from Mary and put him to one side, then she went back to the bathroom.

[. . .]

Whose Responsibility?

Which professionals could be held responsible for the deprived conditions in Ward 7, and the appalling loneliness of the children there?

There were no therapists working in the hospital; social workers never visited the ward; the doctors gave no guidance at ward level, apparently because they were engrossed with committee work and with out-patients; the nurses appeared to be fighting a losing battle because of shortages of staff, and their goodwill and kindness was being dissipated by the poor conditions and lack of support.

Fourteen of the children could feed themselves because psychologists had instructed the ward staff in the principles of behaviour modification.

It cannot be denied that it is valuable for ward staff to understand the principles of behaviour modification, because they can then appreciate how a child learns and how he may systematically be taught acceptable skills. However, it seems that although much patience had gone into training the children in the physical skill of feeding themselves, the psychologists took no further part in improving the children's environment. It was disquieting to realise that the children's ability to feed themselves was a social skill made almost meaningless because it had no carry-over into the rest of their lives. It was merely a physical performance, and even a misleading one insofar as it was likely to convince people who did not recognise the children's deprivation that the hospital was providing good care — because the children had been taught to feed themselves.

In this same context, one might well ask what use it was to have taught a child to load his spoon with food and lift it to his mouth if he later crawled under the table and licked up other children's dribblings because there were too few staff to give him constant attention. The psychologists could be said to have created a false situation in teaching children a social skill without at the same time taking action about the deprivation which is inherent in under-staffed institutions, and which denies the children the mothering they need and eventually distorts their development. Perhaps the first priority for the psychologists should have been to effect changes in institutional care rather than to teach children how to manage their spoons.

How much responsibility did the hospital school-teachers take for the care of the children in Ward 7? The teachers said that they were well aware of the poor child-care in the ward, but felt unable to do anything about it in case they spoilt the good relationship which existed between the school staff and the hospital staff. Their lack of action prompts the questions of how much will professionals shut their eyes to in the interests of preserving 'good relationships', and when do professional responsibilities towards the children have to take priority over good relationships?

42 TOWARDS A SCHOOL POLICY FOR REMEDIAL PROVISION

Jane Collins, Ronny Flynn and Bob Moon

This case study describes the development of remedial provision in a new comprehensive school between 1974 and 1981, as perceived by Bob Moon, head of Bridgewater Hall School, and Jane Collins, head of the 'Progress department'. From the outset the 'Progress department' provided a supportive service by taking children from mixed-ability classes for relatively brief sessions rather than teaching them in separate classes. Clearly there were differences of opinion about this within the school which found expression in the formation of separate 'City and Guilds' classes for older pupils in the school. The study forms an interesting contrast to the study of Chalkway School.

Background

Bridgewater Hall School is the first of three comprehensive schools planned on Stantonbury Campus in the city of Milton Keynes, fifty miles to the north-west of London. Eventually three schools of up to 1,500 students will be joined together on a large campus which already includes shops, health, leisure, youth, resource and ecumenical centres, as well as theatre and extensive sporting facilities. By 1981 Bridgewater Hall was complete with a full complement of staff and students, and the second school, in the process of construction, was expanding to take the new students (age 12 plus) entering the city. The catchment area of the school covers some established communities, although new estates provide the bulk of the student population. People move to Milton Keynes from all over Britain primarily from urban conurbations. Inevitably the consequent disruption to schooling presents a challenge to a new school and remedial provision was anticipated to be a critical factor in responding to this.

Development

The school opened in 1974 with 26 teachers. One of these, a senior head of house, was designated as responsible for remedial work. The title of 'Progress department' was adopted in an attempt to provide a more positive and broader definition of 'remedial'. The number of implicit ideas underpinned the provision: a concern to involve all teachers in the overall provision of programmes for special needs; a wish to avoid the stereotyping of students into remedial classes or separate groups, and an acknowledgement within the overall philosophy of the campus and school of the 'worth' of the range of individual abilities. This latter factor was an important characteristic which, in the early years, gained for the institution a national reputation as a 'progressive' school. Locally, many people viewed with some apprehension the implementation of these new policies.

Students (not pupils) and teachers used first name terms, there was no school uniform and no corporal punishment. Mixed-ability teaching was the norm and considerable emphasis was placed on teachers working together in teams, often producing their own curriculum materials in the form of booklets, within a new 'open' timetable devised around large blocks of time. Many teachers had high hopes for the potential of new technological teaching aids. Community relations, particularly parental contact, were seen as critically important in establishing a new style of relationship within the comprehensive school. All of this had implications for the development of remedial education, although at that time the links were less than clearly articulated. As will be seen, this led to a measure of confusion and perhaps misunderstanding as policy was developed.

The growth of the school allowed the appointment of a further remedial specialist in 1976 and a third in 1977. In 1978 another remedial teacher was appointed. One of the team moved to the second school on the campus in 1979 and there is at present a team of three teachers. The styles and methods of teaching which have developed in the department reflect both the differing backgrounds and training of the teachers and their commitment to working as a team. All three teachers are graduates, but one came from primary education, another from working with mentally handicapped adults, and the third from teaching English in a secondary school. The department meets fortnightly to discuss individual students' problems and teaching plans.

Parallel with this development however, a further area emerged which aimed to complement the 'Progress department'. It occurred only after considerable staff debate. A number of teachers argued strongly that, for a small number of 14–16 year olds, the six or seven subject course offered in the fourth and fifth years was totally inappropriate. It was, they said, a built-in failure mechanism which provided an unsatisfactory experience for the 'non-exam' student at the end of a school career. Their proposal was to establish two small 'units' in each of these year groups that would enable close tutorial oversight and more individualised teaching.

There was, inevitably, opposition to this move. Some teachers argued that such separation was arbitrarily excluding many students with needs and including some whose needs were more appropriately met by other means. They suggested that such provision would deflect attention within the 'common core' curriculum away from the development of materials and expertise that stretched across the ability range. They were concerned that teachers with specialist skills and experience would be isolated from the mainstream school curriculum, and worried about the possible stigma attached to such 'units'.

Those teachers who were in favour of the special units viewed the situation differently. They saw themselves as able to positively improve the self-image of students who had often suffered a series of failures in their previous schools. Their arguments eventually won the day and in 1978 two groups of about 15 students each were established, one in each of the fourth and fifth years. At first there was disagreement over which students should attend; those who were deficient in basic skills, those who were 'maladjusted' and often disruptive, or those who had social difficulties which were expressed in non-attendance at school and isolation within their peer group. Most of the teachers who had reservations about the setting up of the special units could see some justification for providing a more 'nurturant' environment for the latter category of students, and over a three year period this became accepted as the rationale for placing students in the special units.

For historical reasons to do with the allocation of positions of responsibility, these units were not considered as part of the provision offered by the Progress department but instead functioned separately, with four specialist teachers working under a senior member of staff. Programmes of work were linked to the Foundation Level courses of the City and Guilds, to enable students to acquire practical qualifications. Students in these units were offered the same remedial provision by the Progress department as the fourth and fifth year groups, ranging from punctuation and spelling to essay writing and understanding literature, but there were sometimes problems in relating the two forms of provision, from a Progress perspective at least.

> We tried to pick out the students from the City and Guilds classes
> who were wanting specific teaching in areas like reading. We saw
> them on a one-to-one clinic basis, and there'd be a session where
> they'd come individually to do some reading and have some set
> work and take it away and come back. That was the most successful
> way of working – we couldn't work with them as a group because
> their self-image was not very positive and it was very hard to get
> them to be open about their problems.

Teachers in the Progress department saw this as partly due to their
different philosophy. One said:

> In Progress we are committed to mixed-ability teaching and see
> remedial teaching as an aid to subject teachers who want to teach
> mixed ability and need specialist help or extra teaching time. Whereas,
> the philosophy behind City and Guilds is that you start by taking
> the students away because they can't cope with the mainstream
> curriculum.

By 1981, seven teachers from amongst a staff of 75 had a main
teaching commitment in the area of remedial work; four in the City
and Guilds classes and three in the Progress department. Economic
cuts began to place pressure on this level of staffing and the head
of the Progress department prepared a document describing the school's
current remedial provision, which she distributed to all members of
staff to stimulate discussion about the place of remedial work in the
school. This document forms the basis of the following description of
work in the Progress department.

The Progress Department

1. Aims and Objectives

The aim of the Progress department is to enable students to take
maximum advantage of the education which the school offers them. In
specific terms this means both giving students intensive and highly
focused teaching in specific language skills (reading, handwriting,
spelling). In a more general sense it means giving support to those
students who may find the work in some subject areas difficult to
understand or who may need help in making their 'understandings'

explicit. Underlying these aims are the beliefs that:

a) 'remedial education' is not essentially different in its aims from 'mainstream education';
b) the work of the Progress department should extend to students of all ability and that all teachers should share the responsibility for the teaching of the less able;
c) students will benefit by coming to a mature awareness of their own weaknesses and strengths and should be able to take increasing responsibility over the years for their own learning;
d) honest and understanding staff/student relationships are fundamental to facilitating the process of developing self-awareness.

2. The Pattern of Provision

What this means in practice is a pattern of provision staffed by three teachers, which includes both withdrawing individuals or small groups from their lessons and also working alongside the class teacher in the classroom, either sharing the teaching of the lesson, working in small groups within the classroom, or providing additional individual attention. In each of the five years (foundation, third, fourth, fifth and sixth) there are different emphases and objectives. Students are referred by tutors in the foundation and third years, whilst in the fourth and fifth years students are encouraged to come on a voluntary basis. In the foundation year reading ability is given top priority: it is hoped that no student will leave the foundation year with a reading age of less than nine, and that the substantial numbers of students who come to the school aged 12 with reading ages of 9–11 should have the further reading experience that will enable them to become fluent readers. To this end, a very small number of students have daily help with reading during the foundation year. In the third year there is a continuing effort at consolidation of skills in handwriting and spelling. For the first two terms of the fourth year work is concentrated on the language skills that the student will need, both to achieve the level of literacy required by society at large and to meet the demands of examination courses in English. Beginning in the summer term of the fourth year and continuing through the fifth year there is a specific focus on the pieces of writing which students will submit for assessment purposes as part of their assessment in English.

3. Methods and Approaches

The department tries to provide a balance between building up reading skills and encouraging students to enjoy and appreciate books. The importance of word analysis skills is acknowledged in the large bank of resources for the teaching of phonics, but the department tries to make reading work interesting and varied. A 'typical' reading lesson might include a period of silent reading, some written work on phonics and a word game, listening to a story on tape, or work on a project. Writing and spelling lessons might involve tracing and copying writing, completing worksheets containing anagrams and quizzes, writing a group story, comparing dictionary definitions or writing spellings from memory. Although the department has recorded several BBC and ITV series on Video cassette, the simple playback tape recorder has proved to be the most valuable audio-visual aid. A small library of stories have been recorded on tape.

4. Assessment and Record Keeping

In keeping with the aim of developing student autonomy as learners, students are involved in some record keeping from the beginning. Both student and staff records are mainly used as a self-monitoring system. Although records are not normally open for inspection by students, staff are committed to being as honest as possible with students and every attempt is made to make the records objective.

The process of assessment begins in the foundation year when, during the first half-term, students are given a sentence-type group reading test. After the class teachers have had the opportunity to get to know their students, the teachers are asked to refer any individuals to the department, primarily for help with reading, writing or spelling. All students who come to the attention of the department in this way are interviewed individually by department staff. Students are asked about their own view of their problems and information about any previous help that they have received is noted. Students whose reading ability is very limited are given simple tests of letter/sound knowledge and phonic perception. On the basis of these interviews, groups are formed and initial teaching programmes are planned. The record sheet which is used at this interview is kept and updated by the teacher termly. When teaching begins, each foundation year student is given a record sheet of their own. Students make a record of the books they have read, the sounds they have studied, and the writing and spelling activities and project work that they have completed. There is space for both students' and teachers' comments. This record stays with the student for two years, being filed with the teacher's record sheet at the end of the third year. Records kept by staff in the fourth and fifth years indicate which students have received help. The department also works with heads of house to monitor the progress of students who are worrying them.

The Scope of the Department

If Progress department staff feel that they need further advice about the best way to help a particular student, they can call in the county's remedial advisory team. This sometimes gives a fresh perspective on a student's problems. If a student fails to make progress or has needs outside the range of available provision, in a very small number of cases he or she may be referred for special education. Several students have in the past been transferred to the behavioural unit in a nearby town. The Progress staff feel that they are not there to deal with children with behavioural problems unless there are associated learning difficulties, and that there were several misunderstandings over this in the early years of the school.

> There will always be teachers who find they can solve a problem by sending a student to the remedial department. It's just the easiest thing to do when you've got difficulties. And the more that student is away from them the less the teachers are really aware of the problem. We find that staff expectations of us are often still inaccurate, although much clearer than they were. The problem over students who are disruptive being referred to the department is less substantial now, because we've made it clear that we don't see that as our role and most staff accept this and try and see it as a school problem.
>
> (member of Progress department)

The problem has also been eased in the past year by one teacher in the school being given full-time responsibility for children who are disruptive. He has five students under his wing at the moment, and although he provides a 'home base' for these students he attempts to find out which lessons they can cope with and gradually to reintroduce them into ordinary lessons.

The Progress staff try to look at each student's individual situation when considering how best to meet their educational needs. They see this as sometimes a case of balancing the social benefit they would probably obtain from staying at Bridgewater Hall, with the academic benefit they might receive by attending full time or part time at another institution.

> I tend to try, although it's sometimes very difficult, to be absolutely logical and cold and clear cut about it and see whether the needs of the student can be matched by what we provide and if I really think that the child's needs greatly outweigh what we can possibly give them, then, rather than tucking them away — which would be easy — I try and define the problems and see where else they could be helped.
> (member of Progress department)

The school's philosophy however is to keep students within the comprehensive wherever possible. They have recently been involved in a very successful liaison and integration programme with a nearby school for deaf children. The scheme allows deaf students to spend, in some cases, up to eighty per cent of their time in classes at Bridgewater Hall School.

Student Attitudes

An important aspect of the work of Progress staff has been in educating student attitudes. All of the foundation year classes visit the departmental area in the first term of the foundation year. The aim is to remove both mystery and possible stigma from the Progress department and to encourage students to consider both their own strengths and weaknesses and the advantages of co-operation in learning.

> The students' expectations affect our image, so now in the Lower School we try to bring all the classes to the remedial department and talk about our ideas — how everyone has strengths and weaknesses. We find the students appreciate and understand this image. I don't think this is dishonest — if you look hard enough everyone has strengths. Giving them a sense of their own worth is partly what we're about. Then we go on to talk about specific problems people may have, for example, because your handwriting isn't good, it doesn't mean you're 'thick'. It's really important that the work happening here is seen in a positive light by the students.

Time spent by staff in this way has been very profitable and most students who come to the department seem to view their work in a positive way, as some of their comments indicate:

> When I'm in lessons, I don't seem to have a lot of time to write, and when I'm working I have to write fast and it doesn't come out very good. I need longer to do it.

> It's hard, I find it really hard. I think this is a lot easier so I like coming here.

> I know my writing isn't good so I'm just trying very hard to get it better. You have to write and it's best to do it properly.

> The main thing I want to do is learn to read and write; I really want to do that 'cos there's exams coming up.

And from a member of the Progress staff:

> We're better now at dealing with the image of remedial work. Most kids like to come now. We're trying to get around the bad image held by some students who don't come. We're trying to eliminate the mystery.

Relationship with Other Departments

The work of the Progress department is not seen in isolation from the rest of the teaching and learning that goes on at Bridgewater Hall School, and relationships with staff outside the department are very important. Staff in other areas need to know what sort of help the department can provide, while the Progress department needs to consider the situation of each faculty when planning its own programme. Many issues are raised and discussed between staff in Progress and other departments, for instance:

a) Should remedial teaching time be used for the teaching of skills or for the reinforcement of subject teaching?
b) Should students have 'extra' remedial help in place of some subject teaching, e.g. French or German?
c) Should the department provide alternative mainstream teaching materials for less able students?

d) Should the department set separate homework for students?
e) Should the Progress department deal with students with difficult behaviour?
f) Should counselling be offered by the department instead of remedial teaching for students whose learning problems seem to be caused by emotional factors?
g) What is the role of the department in formulating a school language policy?

The answers to these questions, where they have been found, have involved both formal and informal discussions between teachers. Particularly significant has been the recognition of the role of Progress staff outside their own department. Positive professional relationships between staff have allowed Progress teachers and some subject teachers to work together, with Progress staff providing the expertise on subjects such as appropriate reading levels for school-written teaching material and teaching strategies for less able students in mixed-ability groups. Such co-operation is possible because most teachers accept that less able students are the equal responsibility of everyone, not just remedial specialists, and that resources, teaching materials and expertise must not therefore be located only in the Progress department, but in other teaching areas as well.

The Progress staff want to extend their work in this area. At the moment they work fairly closely with the humanities and English departments, but provide less help with other subjects. Most teachers welcome the contribution of the Progress department, although not all of the problems of co-operation have yet been ironed out, as some of their comments indicate:

We haven't really got our own curriculum worked out for Progress kids who go away and miss half or two thirds of what we're doing, then they come back at awkward times and they can't always fit exactly into what you've been doing with the rest of the class.

There should be a lot more liaison between Progress and us. What should be done is to get together with them and work on the materials that we are generally producing for everyone, and see whether we need to fit into that piece of work something that those who go to the remedial department can come back and handle more easily, or whether we need to change all of it, or produce separate materials on the same topics for the students who have gone out. That's an area which needs developing.

Because kids are extracted from us, producing materials for them is not a problem we set ourselves to deal with much. If we were keeping the students within the group then we'd have to get ourselves worked out and find a way to spend more time with individual children.

Future Developments

Staff in the Progress department are themselves aware of several areas where current work is either incomplete or unsatisfactory.

a) The records kept by both staff and students in the department. In their present form these are almost wholly retrospective. It is hoped that in future, development evaluation and planning will be included in the record keeping process.
b) Testing. The department has in the past been responsible for testing in the school. Further consideration of how standardised testing might be used is likely to take place as part of a wider consideration of school policy on assessment and evaluation.
c) Individualisation of teaching. A continuing concern of the department has been the degree to which they are able to individualise teaching. This remains a problem with students for whom even small group work is unsatisfactory. Further involvement of sixth form students or parents may be a possibility.
d) An attempt has been made in the past to run a small scale experiment in counselling and although some of the ideas explored at the time have been taken up in tutorial work, there would appear to be a continuing need for individual and small group counselling.
e) The relationship of the department to English and humanities has been made explicit, but work with other faculties needs to be considered.

Conclusion

Looking back over the past seven years, the staff in the Progress department can identify a number of difficulties and contradictions in remedial provision at Bridgewater Hall. The categories of student problems that this remedial provision was aimed at were never clearly defined; at times they said it felt like 'every deviation from an undefined norm'! The confusion over criteria for allocating to City and Guilds groups, some early misunderstandings of the role of specialist remedial teachers, limited attention to what 'remedial work across the curriculum' might mean, and occasional bursts of interest by remedial specialists in the gifted student, were manifestations of the difficulty.

Being attached to all teaching teams rather than having a specific 'class' of students meant that there was a risk that Progress staff would be regarded as playing a marginal role in the school, although in practice this seems to have been avoided by virtue of the personalities of the Progress staff. Other factors impinged on the remedial provision offered by the school; changing ideas about the value of different screening and testing procedures; a growing disillusionment with the technological aids which in the late sixties and early seventies had seemed to offer so much; and a critical appraisal by staff of the curriculum materials produced by the school in the context of more individualised teaching methods. The initial production of these materials had often failed to meet students' needs across the full ability range and caused problems for the Progress staff:

> Rather than developing our ideas alongside other people in subject areas we came in after they had arranged their teaching organisations and after they had written the first series of booklets, and then had to work with them to make the necessary changes.

Against these problems must be placed some measure of success. The department's efforts to change the quality of the school 'climate' or 'atmosphere' have certainly helped to promote a more caring attitude towards the student with special needs. The faculty teachers are willing to design courses and programmes across the ability range, although the way in which their willingness can be harnessed has been the subject of considerable debate, as this account has illustrated. The main problem now facing the Progress department focuses on the consequences of economic recession and educational cuts. Ironically, the 'old' pattern of remedial classes taught by specialists for a large part of the week makes best sense when student-teacher ratios are being cut back. Help by 'extraction' from the mainstream curriculum or 'alongside' the teacher in the normal class implies that the remedial specialist becomes immediately a 'bonus' provision within the school's staffing allocation. Holding this bonus against all the other pressures of the institution can prove difficult and at certain levels of provision well nigh impossible. The long discussions that Progress staff have held with Faculty teachers means that the importance of their department's role in the school is mostly recognised. However further cuts in staffing will inevitably increase the pressure they are under, and may well radically alter the form of remedial provision at Bridgewater Hall School.

43 THE CURRICULUM AT COATES SCHOOL FOR ESN (S) CHILDREN

Ronny Flynn and Will Swann

Coates is a day special school for severely mentally handicapped (ESN(S)) and multi-handicapped children aged five to sixteen. The following account gives a picture of the wide range of capacities and interests of the pupils, and describes the form of care and education they receive.

It would be easy to drive past Coates School without noticing it. The modern single storey building is tucked away behind a pleasant street in a small town. Visitors have to go down a short drive to the back of the houses to find this school, where eleven teachers and ten welfare assistants care for and educate 75 severely mentally handicapped children. A few things distinguish it at once from an ordinary school. It is smaller, with less bustle and noise; the smell of disinfectant barely covers several rather less pleasant odours; there are lines of wheelchairs waiting in the hall for the children to arrive on the morning buses. These things apart, Coates looks like a small primary school. The staffroom and offices lead off one side of the small entrance hall, and the school hall containing PE equipment off the other. Beyond that are the school's housecraft and craft rooms and the dining hall with access to teaching areas. In the acre of grounds is a fairly new covered swimming pool, paid for by local charities.

It is not only the wide age range in the school that may surprise the outsider, but also the diversity of the children there. Luke is in the school's special care unit. He is seven, suffers from severe cerebral palsy and cannot sit up unaided. He takes some notice of people but doesn't play with toys on his own. He has trouble holding objects and understands very little of what is happening around him. Brian is different. He is just 16, and although he looks younger he is physically active and alert. He can be found playing snooker with his friends at lunch-time or holding a simple conversation. Richard has Down's Syndrome. He is seven, like Luke, but taks an intense interest in new people who come into the classroom. He asks their name, plays with their jewellery or badges, grins happily.

The staff try to respond to the children as individuals; that is what makes the education they provide 'special'. They believe that whereas in an ordinary school the children have to fit into the system, they make the system fit the children. They have no public standards of achievement to take the place of examinations and no agreed curriculum although the head has produced curriculum guidelines in terms of sequences of normal development in various areas. The staff do however talk about standards of behaviour: 'We expect higher standards than other special schools; our children behave better on outings than children from other schools.'

Some children at Coates School cannot feed or dress themselves and are not toilet trained, and this does not only apply to the younger children. The head feels that teachers must constantly remember that they have a teaching function as well as a caring and child-minding one:

> If we find ourselves acting in a non-teaching role we have to pull ourselves out of it. We are paid to be teachers and the children need to be taught. There are other schools where children just sit and do puzzles all day. You have to think of moving the children forward.

This teaching, he feels, is facilitated by the absence of discipline problems:

> In ordinary schools, before you can get down to teaching, you have to penetrate several layers of school routine, discipline and so on. The layers are much thinner here. There's no worry about conforming to conventions and expectations about discipline. You can get straight down to teaching.

The staff also feel that they have more contact with their children's families and know the children better than most teachers in ordinary schools. Parents are all seen at least once a year. Each child's progress is reviewed with his or her parents and the child's future discussed. Some parents are seen much more often, in some cases once a week, and the school's swimming pool has recently been opened to families in the early evening to encourage more contact. Much of the parent-teacher co-operation is seen by the staff as involved with lowering parents' expectations of their child to a 'realistic level'. Many parents, they say, want their children to read and do number work, to be 'nearly normal'. The teachers are generally less optimistic, and frequently find themselves 'letting parents down gently'.

To cope with the age and ability range of the children, the school is divided into four 'units'. The junior and senior units take children from 5 to 13 and from 11 to 16. These are the more able children who generally do not have behaviour problems nor are severely physically handicapped. The special care unit takes children of all ages who are profoundly and multiply handicapped, and the 'link unit' takes the children who are not physically handicapped but often have behaviour problems that compound their severe mental handicap.

The Junior Unit

Like the other units, this part of the school is a self contained group of rooms. The large main room is filled with toys, balls, rocking horses, and mats. Leading off this are four more rooms. One contains the unit's own toilets and washroom, another is a music and TV room which is also used for withdrawing small groups of children for structured lessons. The junior unit is divided into two classes and the other two rooms, which are fairly small by ordinary school standards, serve as a 'home base' for each class. 'Concertina' partitions between these rooms and the main area make for flexible use of space.

Chris French takes nine 5 to 9 year olds, and Joan Marsh teaches the older half of the group, nine children aged 8 to 13, in the classroom next door. Both class teachers are helped by a welfare assistant, making four full-time adults for 18 children.

Chris does have a timetable, but what actually happens depends a great deal on the mood of the children. No planned work is done before 10.00 a.m. because children arrive at different times on their buses. Chris uses the first 30 to 45 minutes as a time for quiet play. They mainly work alone: the lack of talk between children is very noticeable. Language groups are next, followed by orange juice and a half-hour playtime in the shared area or outside. The remaining hour and a quarter before lunch is different every day — it might be rotating 'activity groups', swimming or music and movement. Afternoons, which last for 90 minutes, are given over on three days to classroom work, on one day to swimming and on the fifth to PE in the hall. In the classroom sessions, Chris gives her welfare assistant a number of activities to do with groups of children and she concentrates on work with individual children on the targets she has selected.

In both groups the children vary enormously in ability and behaviour. One of Chris's group, Mary, is a seven year old who suffered early brain damage and has been brought up by her grandmother since her mother rejected her. Chris suspects that a lot of Mary's problems have to do with her social background. Mary is Chris's brightest child. When she first started school she was speaking in single words and didn't play at all. Since then she has advanced rapidly by comparison with other children, and now 'stands out a mile, she can sit at a table and concentrate on one activity'. Mary may eventually move on to an ESN(M) school.

Chris lists activities to work on over a three month period in four areas for each of her group: gross motor work, fine motor work, communication and 'social education'. The targets Chris had set Mary at the moment in these four areas are: walking on a narrow bench at various heights from the floor, with help at first; developing pencil control by colouring in shapes, cutting shapes with scissors and threading laces; using complete sentences with words properly joined, and learning to deal with the numbers 1, 2 and 3 using colour pegs, matching sets and number puzzles.

Kevin aged 8, was also brain damaged at birth and he is mildly hemiplegic. His ability to concentrate is much less than Mary's, and Chris believes he needs a lot of simple play where he is gradually learning to listen and attend, before she trys anything more complicated. He came from a more formal special school where 'he wasted his time'. He can count to 14 but cannot give two objects when asked. The targets she has set for Kevin in the same four areas are: throwing and catching a ball from several feet; connecting drawings like cup and saucer with a pencil line; learning to carry out two-part instructions like 'put the blue bead in the car and put the car in the box'; grading objects from largest to smallest.

The least able child in the group is Timothy. Chris describes him as 'low level' but she doesn't yet feel she knows his potential. She is concentrating on teaching him to post shapes into a box, to obey simple commands and to repeat single syllables.

Chris stresses the importance of teaching concentration. She uses free and structured play with the hope of laying the foundation for more formal work when the children move up the school. 'We've really got to give them as much experience as possible, which is why we have lots of PE, lots of outings, because that's the only chance they'll get to have a really concentrated time on those activities . . . The kids must enoy it.' Most won't learn unless they enjoy it. She also emphasises self-help skills. All her children need help to get dressed, and their three visits to the swimming pool each week provide plenty of practice. Chris uses all activities to provide language experience to supplement more structured teaching in the language groups.

In Joan Marsh's older group the ability range is equally wide. Colin is one of the most able children in the group. At the moment Joan is teaching him to use money. He can count in coins but he doesn't yet realise that a 2p coin is worth two 1p coins; to Colin they are just two coins. He can write his own name without help and can neatly copy writing from a book rather than just write underneath a line of writing. He is learning to swim and making good progress.

Alan at 13 is the oldest but in Joan's estimation is the least able. 'He needs motivating much more; the problem is to find something he'll cotton on to to get him going.' She says that he 'eats beautifully' and she devotes much more time to self-care skills with him. She is trying to get him to understand single words using photographs and he can point correctly to various objects. In the long term she wants him to understand what she says and act upon it. He rarely talks and when he does he tends to whisper — except when he goes swimming which he loathes. Then he'll shout at her.

All the children have their own writing books, most can read their own and some other names from the name plates on the back of chairs. Maths activities are drawn from schemes like Fletcher Maths, and Joan spends more time than Chris on reading and number activities. She also talks more about the need for a warm relationship with the group:

I love the children. They're so affectionate — not a bad thought in their heads. I need affection from children — I don't like older children so much as they have a mind of their own . . . If we could raise the children's IQs by 40 to 50 points the school would have enormous problems: they wouldn't be our children. They'd become more intelligent and more difficult; they'd want more autonomy and would challenge authority.

Most of Chris's and Joan's teaching is confined to their own groups but there is some joint organisation. Fifteen minutes every morning except Wednesday are devoted to language groups. Each of the four staff in the junior unit takes a small group augmented by one or two children from the special care and link units. One group is being taught the Makaton signing system; one group concentrates on making and listening to sounds; one group uses the Distar Language programme — a highly structured kit aimed at teaching children 'classroom language', and the fourth group focuses on making conversation using sentences. One other part of the timetable is co-ordinated between the two groups. For an hour on Thursday morning the four members of staff provide individual activities and groups of children might rotate between art and craft, music, bathing dolls and building colour patterns, spending around 15 minutes on each.

The Special Care Unit

The first impression of the special care unit at Coates is of entering a well-equipped nursery. The rooms are full of toys, colour and stimulating objects. There is very little noise and the atmosphere is peaceful. Some children are involved with adults, some are on their own. The unit occupies one large main room, two smaller rooms, a toilet, washing and changing area, and two medical rooms used for physiotherapy and speech therapy. One of the smaller rooms has been converted into a soft-play area. It is covered in foam, with panels of different textures, like cork, plastic and sandpaper. Mobiles and baby-bouncers hang from the ceiling. The other room is an 'activity room' with toys, music, noise boards, telephone dials and so on. In the large room are tricycles, walking frames, padded chairs and cradles, with mobiles hanging from the ceiling.

The unit is staffed by Pat Francis, a teacher who has worked in a hospital school for handicapped children, and Sandra Preston, who has also previously worked with severely mentally handicapped children, including those in special care. They are supported by three welfare assistants, part of whose job is to take responsibility for toileting, dressing and feeding these children. Between them they provide for 19 of the most severely handicapped children at Coates, divided into two groups aged 3 to 9 and 10 to 15. All the children are severely handicapped physically as well as mentally, and it is this unit that least resembles an ordinary school. The staff provide education, care and physiotherapy for their children; most of the children have yet to develop mentally beyond the level of a normal six month old baby. Several are subject to epileptic fits even though they are often heavily drugged to control these. Some are in wheelchairs, others can barely move at all and rely on the staff for all their needs.

There is a photograph of each child on the wall of the large teaching room and pasted beside it are details of that child's requirements for physical care and physiotherapy as well as an individual teaching plan. Pat Francis describes Luke, a seven year old child in the special care unit:

Luke is severely spastic and cannot sit independently. He observes people, laughs and gets very excited when something amuses him. He is very affectionate. We are not sure how much he understands. He is interested in people but not in toys unless people are involved. He can communicate through eye pointing to some extent, but is too undemanding to need to communicate. Reaching, grasping and letting go are very difficult skills for him. In terms of physical development, he needs special physiotherapy exercises like rolling over, sitting balance, supporting with arms when sitting, weight bearing on arms or legs, reaching and grasping. He needs general movement experience to increase awareness of his own body and learn how to respond physically to different things that happen to him, for instance in the swimming pool, in the soft-play environment, in different positions on different foam shapes, in carefully adapted 'rough and tumble' play. Luke likes to be rolled, pushed and pulled around the soft play environment and finds it fun having his feet high and his head low down. He also likes being pulled along the floor in a blanket and is particularly fond of swimming. The experience of moving the whole of his body freely and feeling the buoyancy of the water makes him very excited. I let him decide which way to go, upright, on his back or his tummy so he'll learn what is the effect of his movements. Luke needs to learn that objects and people have names. He needs to be motivated to want things and then to learn that he can do something (look, point, call, pull adult's sleeves) as a means to get what he wants. He is on a toileting programme which takes some time, and a feeding programme which takes much longer than if he were just fed.

Much of the time is taken up with physiotherapy. Some times this consists simply of frequently changing the position and posture of immobile children who would otherwise become uncomfortable and never get a change of scene. Other times children receive specially designed exercises to improve head control, walking skills or their ability to bear weight on their arms and legs. They are also given more general movement experience, often in the soft-play area or the swimming pool, to increase their awareness of their own body and the effect it can have on things around them. Parents help out in swimming sessions, and children who are really inert in the classroom can suddenly become active and interested in the water.

The unit's 'educational' curriculum is based on normal development in the first few months of life. For most children it consists of trying to interest them in the world about them, and helping them to see that they can affect it. For example, Pat is currently trying to interest Erica and Nigel in toys and games where things disappear and reappear, hoping to help them to develop a sense of expectation of events to be repeated. For some children, other problems hinder their experience. William is so heavily drugged to control his epilepsy that he is rarely alert; Angela who is 9, is preoccupied most of the time with her breathing and with putting her hand in and out of her mouth. Nevertheless all the children show signs of sociability. Even Angela likes company; 'She often comes and touches you; sometimes she gets upset and seems jealous when you ignore her and play with somebody else.' In everything they do, the teachers try to engage the children socially and to develop their social awareness.

Not all of the children in the special care unit are equally profoundly handicapped. One child is likely to move to the junior unit in the near future and Mark, who is seven, already joins the junior Distar Language group four mornings a week. A year ago he used a few phrases without any meaning, but he can now hold a very simple conversation. Teaching has helped, but Sandra Preston believes that the six months he spent this year in a children's Home with normal children was important too. By contrast, Barry has made no progress for years. He recognises his name, but he never makes sounds. He has a bad heart condition, which means he can only have very gentle exercises on his infrequent good days. He has fits and is also almost completely blind, so most work with him has to be done through touch. He does respond to close bodily contact. Sandra says of him 'One of the most disheartening things about working in special care is when you've got a really profoundly handicapped child like Barry. You know that he's never ever going to improve. He'll only get worse.'

Pat Francis finds that there is never enough time to give each child all the attention she would like:

You never get around to doing all the exercises you ought to be doing with all the children, and you always end up by leaving this child or that without attention for too long a period. Ideally I'd want to carry through a comprehensive teaching programme systematically and regularly so that I can check the progress and know whether the teaching is effective. But what is possible is very limited. And often it is more important to play with the child spontaneously in many different ways and respond to the child's slightest hint, at least as much as I want the child to respond to me.

The Senior Unit

Like the junior unit, the senior unit has two classes based in small rooms off a larger shared area. One other room is used for group sessions, watching TV and storing some shared resources like tapes and records. The 19 children aged 13 to 16 are divided roughly by age into two groups, the younger children are taught by Frances Blake and the older ones by Brenda Simpson. These are supported by two welfare assistants. The unit has a busy air about it, and the visitor is likely to find children engaged in tasks, with teachers and assistants moving around giving them any necessary support. There is much more talk than in the junior unit. The children not only do more but they also joke about things and ask questions more often. Frances and Brenda have very different styles: Frances is quieter and more relaxed, Brenda has a sharper, louder and more jokey approach with the children.

The curriculum in the two classes also differs. Brenda takes a more formal approach. She does not provide any play sessions except at break and children do not use Lego, sand or water. She combines structured individual work with a practical curriculum which she believes will prepare her children for leaving school and for further education. During the first session every morning the students do colouring, copying, tracing, drawing or counting work in their individual work books. Brenda tries to extend their concentration so they work for longer than a few minutes at each task: 'I think it's something you don't give up on very easily because it makes life hell otherwise . . . The long term aim is when you know you can walk away and a child will stay at it.' The unit is regrouped for language work for a half-hour session three mornings a week, as in the junior unit. Nearly all the children in Brenda's group are relatively proficient speakers. Only Sally is very limited in her use of language, and she is being taught the Makaton system with the junior group. Three other 30 minute morning sessions each week involve number, money work and calendar time. The rest of the timetable is divided between PE, games and swimming;

craft and practical activities like homecraft, gardening and doing jobs around the school.

Brenda is more concerned with social maturity and social acceptability than academic achievement:

> I'm not wishing to sound pessimistic, but I think these children reached their ceiling for any measurable academic achievement a long time ago ... so the thing you tend to notice more is how far they are showing signs of some sort of maturity, if at all. You don't plan a programme for maturity for these children. All you can do is expose them to the kinds of attitudes and behaviour you expect when you take them out and hope it will rub off, in their desire for approval from you.

Brenda will teach academic skills if a child shows some knowledge of an area:

> If they can read a few street signs, I'll plug reading street signs. If they have some semblance of time then I'll extend that a bit ... Very often it's just instinct and trial and error ... trying to create a stimulating environment and out of that stimulation to grab hold of something that has not shown itself before. Within that atmosphere you can get them to respond to things that you know can be good for them. But they don't realise it. You have to use the kids' enjoyment of activities to control their behaviour.

Frances takes the ten younger children aged 11 to 14. She sees her long-term aims as the development of self-confidence, a sociable personality and independence. In much of her teaching she tries to use real situations. When she started with her group they had done a lot of written arithmetic, and she took them back to practical work. At first this presented a problem: 'They like to please their teacher, and they couldn't understand why I didn't want sums. It had become a rote task.' Now she uses everyday tasks such as table setting. She is teaching volume and fractions with water in containers. When the children need to find a pencil or an apron in preparation for a craft lesson, Frances waits for the children to do it themselves so they get practice at following instructions.

In the more structured lessons, which are usually in the mornings, Frances takes groups of four to six children for reading, language and maths. Children who are not involved in these groups are given activities and take them to the shared area. She is using the Breakthrough to Literacy reading scheme, but she does not wait for any particular level of language development before starting with reading. Simon, aged 13, speaks very little indeed but he is beginning to read, and is enjoying it. The most capable child in the group just registers a reading age of six. In reading sessions, as in any activity, opportunities for language work are exploited. Frances talks about words and sentences with the reading group, discusses what a word means and counts words in sentences. In language sessions, she recently did two terms work based on teaching certain grammatical structures organised into degrees of complexity. Although this was successful and the children did learn some new language, she now concentrates more on language use in real situations such as using the telephone, knowing people's addresses and summarising the stories she often reads. A lot of language work is done in the mornings in group discussions about what happened at home or about things the children have seen. Unlike Brenda's class, Frances allows the children a free choice of activities at certain times, even sand and water play if they so wish.

Although the future of the children in these groups is much more on their teachers' minds, they do not prepare the children for particular jobs or placement in an adult training centre. They know very little about what will happen to the children. Neither teacher is very optimistic about the children's chances of employment. Brenda in particular believes that although some children might have the skills to do a job, they would fall down on time-keeping or would be unable to take criticism. She thinks that sheltered supervised employment like that provided by the Home Farm Trust is more realistic, but she does not believe it is particularly important to know about their future: 'It's probably a good thing that we don't know.' Frances takes a different view: 'I still think we have to work with an optimistic outlook ... sometimes it's better to aim a bit higher.' And whereas Brenda sees preparation for jobs as the responsibility of the FE unit, Frances thinks the school could aim towards employment: 'I think if I knew what would happen to each child I would change my teaching methods accordingly. But we really don't know what will happen.' There is in fact an acute shortage of even 'sheltered' facilities for these children. Many will not be able to obtain a place at an adult training centre: only three children from the school have gone to an ATC in the past four years.

The Link Unit

The link unit was created recently in an attempt to allow other teaching groups to run more smoothly. It contains the least able children from the senior group as well as children from both junior and senior groups who are found to be disruptive. The unit is rarely a full-time base and many of the 'link' children join the junior and senior units for activities such as language work, riding, swimming and singing.

The unit is well staffed. Two teachers (one the deputy head, Frank Moss) and three welfare assistants look after up to 16 children aged 9 to 17. One of their teaching rooms has been designed as a 'soft and quiet' room intended for slower and gentler activities; one is an audio-visual room where the staff have set up equipment for the children to operate themselves, such as tape recorders, a TV and games; and the third room is for more conventional individual teaching.

Janet, aged 16, is the most able of the group; she talks well and enjoys singing, cooking and needlework. Whenever she feels under stress, however, she starts to scream and to hit herself. She spends one morning a week in the senior unit, Wednesdays at the local training centre and on Fridays she goes riding with the seniors in the morning and sings with the school choir in the afternoon. By comparison Helen, aged 12, cannot move about without help, she can be placed in a sitting position but if she topples to one side she cannot get up by herself. When this happens it may lead to a petit mal seizure. She is just learning to co-ordinate her eye and hand movements, and can grasp objects with her whole fist. Her communication is limited to gurgling, screaming and laughing sounds to express her emotional state. She has to be fed and toileted by the staff.

Frank Moss has developed an elaborate and carefully organised curriculum for the unit designed to ensure that the children spend their time fully occupied in tasks matched to their level of ability. Pinned on the wall in the unit are clipboards, one for each child. On these are a set of 'job sheets' which describe a range of activities for that child, the resources needed, and the time to be spent on that activity.

On one typical day, Helen's activities involved some gross and fine motor work and some 'cognitive development' tasks. She was put on a small bicycle and helped to hold the handlebars with both hands and to push with her legs. This was designed to help her use both sides of her body and to strengthen her leg muscles. Another task designed to get her to control her immediate environment involved sitting her at a specially designed table and getting her to hit bells and plastic toys so they would move about.

Tommy is rather more capable than Helen, and his tasks include learning to use pencils and crayons, climbing steps and stepping across small gaps up to nine inches wide, or sorting objects by colour. In the soft and quiet room, he practices throwing sponges at people.

Job sheets change regularly as the staff review progress on various activities, each activity becoming a little bit more demanding than the last.

Co-ordinating the Curriculum

With such a diverse group of children trying to develop a curriculum for the whole school presented major problems, but Geoff Bennett, the head, felt it was important to try. He felt that some of his staff needed guidance and that work in the different units needed to be co-ordinated. The result has been the production of what are now known as the 'green sheets', drawn up by Geoff Bennett and Frank Moss. These sheets describe many different skills grouped into a number of headings such as: 'Achievements in Early Cognitive Development' and 'Achievements in Money Handling.' The former group of sheets begins with the following skills:

1. Following a slowly moving object through a 180° arc.
2. Noticing the disappearance of a slowly moving object.
3. Finding an object which is partially covered.

These achievements at the beginnings of development contrast with the most advanced skills in the 'Social Competence for Older Pupils' sheet which include carrying a message, eating in a café and borrowing a book from the library.

Four groups of sheets — language, number, reading and fine motor skills — are backed up by a central pool of resources. For example, if a teacher is working on the skill 'Language 1/3: Pointing to Familiar Parts of the Body,' he or she has available a box labelled 1/3, containing large jigsaws of boys and girls, face puzzles, mirrors and so on.

The intention of the system is that teachers choose from the many sheets which describe skills appropriate to their children and these sheets then become the curriculum. The teacher's job is to decide how to teach those skills and what material to use. The sheets have only recently been introduced, but the intention is to use them as a basis for the annual review held for each child and to use them at these meetings, which are attended by teachers, parents, the head and other professionals, to plan the next year's curriculum.

Although the implementation of these school guidelines is still at an early stage the only unit where they are very much in evidence is the link unit. Here Frank Moss uses the green sheets as the source of activities for the job-sheets. Elsewhere the sheets are not very apparent either in the way the teachers talk about their work, in the way they write their timetables, or in what they do with the children. A number of teachers look on the green sheets as just one other source of ideas for what to do. Chris French, when asked where she got her ideas from for her curriculum, said: 'You've got in your mind what a child starts with, say in language – they listen to their own voices, they start to repeat things you say, and you just kind of work through. There are checklists you can use but generally I make up my own. I use ideas from other checklists as well as the school ones.' Brenda Simpson uses developmental scales and the school guidelines as a 'jumping off point' but she was sceptical about their value:

I feel sometimes as if we work from an academic point of view simply to get our minds straight. It's totally unrealistic to pretend that you can just plough through this programme and move from Stage 1 to Stage 2 in a normal way because these children's reactions are so unpredictable. There's no way you can plan for the child's development, no theory to help you understand it. The only way to deal with it is by sheer spontaneity and instinct.

44 CROFTON INFANTS SCHOOL: A UNIT FOR ESN(S) CHILDREN

Ronny Flynn and Will Swann

Crofton is a large infant school with 557 children aged five to seven years in 18 classes with 20 teachers. It is a single storey building in a quiet part of Bromley, built in 1952. Since September 1971 it has housed a unit for up to ten mentally handicapped children aged three to eight years. In Autumn 1980, seven children were based in the unit and participated to varying degrees in the educational and social life of their school.

When local education authorities became responsible for the education of all mentally handicapped children in April 1971, the policy makers in Bromley looked at the available provision for mentally handicapped children. It consisted of one overflowing junior training centre, and hospital care. In developing the gap in services for children aged three to seven years they took the unusual step of placing young mentally handicapped children in units in ordinary infant schools. This was a unique arrangement and nearly ten years on, it remains a policy unadopted by any other authority.

In 1973, Anne Pierse, the head of the school, wrote about the early stages of the unit at Crofton:

Over the preceding six years, four special opportunity classes had been established within the borough for children between the ages of five and seven years whose needs could best be catered for in small classes of 10 children, within the ordinary primary schools. These classes comprised hyperkinetic, disturbed and backward children who in due course were passed on to other primary schools, special schools or to junior training centres. Whilst these classes did not encompass the severely mentally handicapped child, their success must have lent support to the idea and purpose of integrating the young mentally handicapped child with his peers in the infant

346

or primary school. In addition there was strong pressure from the vocal parents of the Bromley Society for Mentally Handicapped Children to admit their young children to ordinary primary schools.

So it was that in 1970 a class was formed for extremely retarded children at St Paul's Wood Primary School, which has most attractive buildings in a beautiful setting and a headmistress who could win the confidence of the children and their parents. The children's response to the environment created by their gifted young teacher and her assistant led the chief education officer to proceed with his aim to establish similar classes in other appropriate schools geographically suited to serve this very large London borough. A further class (for hyperkinetic children) was opened at St Paul's Wood, another at Alexandra Infants' School, Beckenham, during the summer term of 1971, for children of three to eight years, and in June 1971 I was approached with a view to opening a nursery class at Crofton Infants' School in the following September.

The unit began as a nursery class and the facilities were planned for children who might be at a developmental stage of 15 months upwards. It seemed essential, therefore, to incorporate within the room many of the features of the home environment, such as carpeting, large cushions to sit on, armchairs and curtains, together with a wide variety of equipment and materials for play. Structural alterations were planned to provide access to a garden area and to equip a domestic unit to meet all personal hygiene needs.

The unit is in the heart of the school; the door opens onto the dining area and it is close by the offices and staff room. The original reception classroom needed only minimal modification to convert it. Two toilets, a washing area and a cloakroom are attached to the unit. Outside, a paved, partly-covered play area surrounded by a fence overlooks the main school's play area and a number of the other classrooms. The unit looks like almost any other stimulating nursery or infant school: it is light and bright, with children's pictures on the walls, a carpeted area containing comfortable seats, and plenty of toys, books, games, puzzles, wheeled vehicles, sand and water. The school receives a special allowance for the unit, with which it can buy extra materials. As well as sharing the resources of the main school, the unit has the use of a minibus each Tuesday morning for outings and has its own tape recorder, piano, Language Master (a glorified tape recorder that simultaneously presents spoken and written words or pictures), and a colour television.

The children in the unit are a carefully selected group. They are all mobile and do not have major behaviour problems, although they are certainly not toilet-trained when they arrive, and they usually have very little language. They start at three, after thorough assessment and discussions between the school, health service, schools psychological service and parents. Multiply handicapped children do not attend the unit, but are instead placed either in a special care unit in another infant school or in a subnormality hospital school. The staff at Crofton look at both the individual and the group when admitting a new child: they are anxious to maintain a 'balance' in the unit, which means, for example, that they would not be keen to take only Down's Syndrome children.

Although the unit is staffed and equipped for ten children, there are only seven at the moment. Janice and Patrick are both eight years old and will be leaving the unit soon. Simon, Stephen and Lorna, all five, have like Janice and Patrick been attending one of the ordinary classes for some of the time. Luke and Martin aged six are not at present attending any classes in the main school and are the most limited in ability in the group. There is a chance that both the older children will move on to a school for 'moderately subnormal' children when they leave Crofton.

Responsible for these seven children are three full-time and one part-time members of staff. The one full-time teacher, Sheila Hart, is infant trained and has worked at Crofton for ten years, both in the main school and in the unit. Two welfare assistants also work in the unit full-time; Jane Scott, a trained nursery nurse who previously worked with 'special care' children in a nearby hospital school, and Pat Jones, who used to be a lunchtime supervisor in the main school and has done much voluntary work in the local playgroup for handicapped children and on holiday schemes for handicapped children. On one day a week Mary Croft, another trained teacher, supervises mathematics and reading activities, and two of the school's lunchtime supervisors are specifically allocated to the unit children.

The School Day

School for the unit children runs from 9.15a.m. until 3.00p.m. All seven spend their morning in the unit with occasional forays out for some of them for TV, assembly, and music and movement with the reception classes. Lunchtime runs from 12.00 noon to 1.30p.m. and then Simon, Janice and Patrick go off to one reception class until

2.30p.m., and Stephen and Lorna to another. At 2.30p.m. the children are all together again in the unit for milk and orange, tidying up and getting ready for the bus which collects them all at 3.00p.m.

One Monday when we visited the unit, events were a typical mix of academic and creative work, segregated and integrated activities. By 9.30a.m. all six children expected that day had arrived on various buses. Until 10.00a.m. each morning the children choose their own activities and the staff are ready to fit in with them. Today Patrick, Simon and Janice were watching TV with one of the reception classes from 9.30–9.45a.m. At 10.00a.m. the children are together for a mid-morning drink and break for 15 minutes, and then the time up to 11.30a.m. is the main teaching period of the day. On this occasion painting was interspersed with reading. One or two children at a time were painting with Sheila Hart, beginning with planned work on animals and then moving to whatever the children chose: usually cars and houses. At the same time Jane Scott was listening to individual children reading flash cards and reading them stories. Supporting this activity, the other welfare assistant helped children with their painting and washed the hands of and toileted those children in need. In the background, the large equipment − sand tray, large toy car and bicycles − provided activities for children who strayed from their work. This period was interrupted for Janice and Patrick who went off for a 15 minute assembly with the reception classes.

From 11.30a.m. to lunch at 12.00 noon some of the children sang with Sheila Hart at the piano, while others attended a party in the Wendy House organised by Pat Jones. Lunch is delivered to the unit for the two children who have their meal there; Simon, Janice, Patrick and Sally go to eat with the main school. For the rest of the lunch break, however, all the unit children are together, engaged in games, stories and play helped by the two lunchtime supervisors until 1.30p.m.

Straight after lunchtime this day the group watched TV for 15 minutes − a programme on heaviness and lightness which the staff used to talk about these ideas with the children. Then at 1.45p.m. all but Martin went off with the welfare assistants to two of the reception classes for three-quarters of an hour to an hour. Simon, Janice and Patrick in one class spent the time on maths and writing, while Stephen and Lorna watched 'Words and Pictures' on TV, had some milk and then played outside. Martin, the only child in the unit for that period, worked on a picture book with Sheila Hart, naming and pointing to objects and repeating their names. He also worked on his own at the

Language Master to which, according to Sheila, he is addicted.

At 2.30p.m. the school day begins to draw to a close as all six children return to the unit for a drink and tidy up. Buses begin to arrive at 2.45p.m. and by 3.15p.m. all the children have gone.

The Curriculum

The staff in the unit try to give the children a curriculum as varied as that given to a normal child. Reading, language, maths, stories, music, poetry, drama, science, PE, art and craft are all taught, albeit at a slower pace than for most children. Much of the work is based around a topic which lasts for several weeks. When we visited Crofton the curriculum was organised around the topic of 'small animals'. The walls were decorated with pictures of ducks, birds, worms and tadpoles as a basis for teaching single words; stories, music and poetry were selected around the topic; cutting out and painting involved swans and ducks; one to ten owls were counted and visits were organised to ponds in search of tadpoles, to a pet shop to stock up on water flies and weed for them to eat, and to a local farm.

Sheila aims to cover reading, writing, language and number each day with every child. Painting takes place twice a week and other activities like home corner, shop, sand, playing with large vehicles and caring for class pets are background activities.

Reading for the unit children begins with their own names, then progresses to matching words, using the unit's own flash cards. The children produce their own 'books', for instance on 'My Family', with the children drawing pictures and an adult writing in an appropriate sentence like 'This is my mum.' This becomes each child's own reading book. Children are also encouraged to read words from charts around the classroom. Reading is not restricted to the more articulate children. Sheila Hart told us:

> We wouldn't get anywhere if we waited for a certain language level before teaching children to read. Some children who can't speak very well are reading. Their understanding is OK, they can give the correct flash card if asked 'give me cup', but they can't reproduce the words.

Language teaching in the Crofton unit similarly involves much work with individual children, getting them to name objects by pointing to them and then later saying the word. For example, on one occasion Sheila was looking through a box of coloured photographs with Martin; she was encouraging him to imitate sentences describing the pictures, like: 'The baby is crying.' He repeats phrases like 'jump up in the air' but is not observed to say anything longer or more complex. When he was left alone he turned over the pictures saying 'What's that?' to each and replying to himself: 'Clap hands the boy', 'Boy kneeling', 'A boy is drinking orange.'

Number work begins with counting objects, recognising numbers, using songs and finger plays. The children also sort bricks and other objects, and learn to count and recognise numbers up to 5, then 10, then 20. Numbers may be chalked on paving slabs, and the children jump from number to number when instructed. Jane, one of the welfare assistants, records how she and the two lunchtime supervisors worked with the children during the lunch hour:

> Heather, Margaret and myself begin to organise the room for some number games and singing, making a line of 10 chairs. The children and adults sit on the chairs for 8 little speckled frogs, each 'frog' jumping off the chair in turn, counting down to one frog. I join in for '7 currant buns in a bakers shop'. Heather takes the part of the boy and Margaret is the shopkeeper. Counting down again to one currant bun.

All staff participate in learning activities with the children, and there seem to be no strict role divisions. Staff in the unit are involved in more caretaking functions than teachers of non-handicapped children, and this tends to fall more heavily on the welfare assistants than on the teacher, but even the toileting sessions are used for teaching purposes, with the children being taught parts of the body and learning songs and games.

Decisions about the curriculum of the unit rest firmly with the unit staff, and in particular with Sheila, the full-time teacher there. She says: 'The unit has more autonomy than other classes. Other classes work to the same basic schemes of work and curriculum (with individual teacher variations) but the unit has independence in deciding and planning work for individual children.' Much of the curriculum is similar to that of a normal infant class, but the unit staff see some major differences in the way they teach their children:

> We spend a very long time on their understanding and their spoken

language which you don't need to do in a reception class. That's the most important difference. Things they do learn to grasp, we just have to spend a lot longer on, like colour work; most of the children in the school know their colours or pick them up quickly if they don't — but we're a long time teaching them . . . Teachers who like to depend on results might get a bit frustrated (teaching these children) because the results take so long to come. You've got to be satisfied that you're doing the right thing yourself without getting the results, until eventually you do. But you can't be looking for quick results and feedback from the child. You've just got to keep going. Obviously not all the children are going to benefit to the full from it, but it's repetition for them and we find, all right, they didn't get it this year, but next year when it comes round, they'll get it that time, because they've been through it. We aim for everything; there are no time limits. We just hope the children will get some way there before they leave.

Monitoring the children's progress, like designing their curriculum, is more flexible in the unit than in the main school. There, standard maths and reading records are submitted yearly for each child, and each teacher provides the head with a monthly report of work that has been covered, but in the unit no standard school records are kept of the children's progress in basic skills. Sheila keeps her own records and observations continually throughout the year, but only formally updates each child's record every six months because 'Progress is so slow that it's not necessary to document changes more often, a mental note is enough.' The children arrive at the unit with a file of reports from the schools psychological service, local health clinic and the medical profession, and Sheila fills in the schools psychological service's annual report form for each child every year.

Integration

One of the most positive features of the special provision at Crofton school is the effort made to integrate children from the unit into normal reception classes wherever possible. The head feels that these classes, with their emphasis on play and basic skills, are the most suitable, as she says: 'They couldn't integrate mentally with the older children, and play wouldn't be going on in the older classes in the same way.' Not all unit children attend reception classes, only those whom the teachers feel would 'get something out of it'. They are expected to be toilet-trained, able to play and fit in with ordinary children, able to communicate well enough to be understood and capable of eating with 'adequate table manners'. Of the seven children attending the unit at present, only Luke and Martin do not fulfil these criteria. Janice, Simon and Patrick attend Sarah Ritchie's class; Stephen and Lorna, Denise Wall's class. These two teachers have both expressed a particular interest in the unit though they have not had any special training or preparation for this work. Sarah did work on summer playschemes for mentally handicapped children and feels she is familiar with handicap through her mother's work as a health visitor. Denise had less previous contact with handicapped children, though she now also has a physically handicapped child and two children with speech problems in her class. Neither teacher sees their lack of special training as a particular problem; there is a free exchange of information with the welfare assistants and with Sheila Hart.

Simon, now five, has been attending Sarah's reception class for a term. She feels he would have benefited from more free play when he first came to her class, and that he missed out because her children were past that stage. However he is, she says 'friends with everyone'. In her class he mixes socially with the normal children and his fellow unit children and flits between activities in much the same way as he does in the unit. On the day we watched him he began his afternoon in the reception class watching Patrick sewing a bean-bag with a parent who helps in the class. He then began his own sewing, aided periodically by the parent. Noticing Sarah taking the toy trolley outside he became rather more interested in that but was persuaded to finish his sewing. He called to Sarah that he had finished and she started him on some number work; he traced over a number four, although she had asked him to draw four cars. During this time he was exchanging comments with other children at his table: he needs regular support to keep him on a task. 'Ugh, look at his writing, it's big', said another child. Simon didn't reply. He turned to one of the other children with his writing: 'What does that say?', he asked. 'Nothing', came the reply. 'What does that say, Jamie?', 'I don't know.'

Stephen and Lorna have been attending the other reception class for nearly two terms, and have benefited from the flexibility of the system. Sheila comments:

It started off them just going into music and movement and PE two afternoons a week. They'd all been going in for singing anyway

— so that was three afternoons. Then, when they got used to the children, and the children knew their names, Pat started taking them over on Mondays and Tuesdays. Because it's a reception class they're usually playing in the afternoons and doing individual work with the teacher, so they can just join in any activity they like.

Integration also takes place outside the classroom, with five of the seven unit children spending lunchtime, playtime and assembly with the rest of the school. They fit in well, talking to the other children and being talked to by them.

Not all the unit children have been able to join in normal classroom lessons successfully. Sheila Hart mentioned two children who had not seemed to benefit from integration in a previous year: 'Barry and Graham both had terrible speech problems and the other children couldn't understand them. This was a great difficulty. We didn't really feel it was successful.' Pat Jones, who was the welfare assistant supporting them, commented:

> With Graham, I found that he was playing on his own, and he could have been playing on his own over here, because the children would only play with him if I sat down and was doing a jigsaw. But really they weren't playing with Graham, they were doing it with *me* and Graham happened to be there . . . We stopped it in the end. We didn't think the children were getting anything from it, and we didn't think the rest were getting anything from it. We did find that the children who weren't particularly happy there would want to come back on their own . . . The language is a very big problem; this is why we have to do so much work on it.

Even the children who cannot attend reception classes still have more contact with non-handicapped children than they would in a special school. Other children visit the unit, especially those from the reception classes attended by unit children, to watch television or to join in birthday parties. Teachers also come over, some just to visit the unit, others because they know the unit staff well. The unit probably has as much contact with other staff and children as many of the ordinary classes do.

For those children who can cope in the ordinary classes, the benefits are many. All the staff mentioned the advantages of their mixing with normal children, seeing normal behaviour and taking part in normal infant school life. The unit staff were unanimous; that the presence of normal children set high standards and provided them with the right model for their behaviour: 'They see us telling off the other children if they're doing something they shouldn't, so they learn that everybody gets corrected.'

Sarah, one of the reception teachers, felt that talking to the other children benefited the unit children's language development, and that mixing was good for the children socially, helping them to make friends and learn new games like 'Cowboys and Indians' which they might not have come across in the unit. The normal children were seen as providing a reference point for the behaviour of the unit children. Sharing resources was also seen as a beneficial outcome of integration, permitting the unit children access to a large school's facilities and enabling them to take part in outings, use equipment and cook like the other children.

It was clear that the unit children were not encountering teasing or labelling. They were not thought of as 'odd' or 'handicapped' by the other children they mixed with, who 'just think its another class called "the unit"'. This must help build children's self-esteem, and working alongside normal children who will help them should also decrease the unit children's dependence on adults.

It is not only the handicapped children who benefit from their presence in the ordinary classrooms. There are also advantages for the normal children. The head teacher said that: 'They get used to children who are different; they see handicapped children as part of school society and become more accepting of handicap.' Reception class teachers agreed:

They learn to be more tolerant, to make allowances. They may be more willing to help the handicapped when older . . . When I taught an older class and didn't have any unit children, my class were frightened of visiting the unit, they called it a 'bogey room'. The older children now who have worked with unit children are not afraid and will speak to them.

One common misconception remains however, even among pupils who know the unit children — which is that they live in the unit all the time. Children in the main school rarely see the unit children arrive or go home; they generally join the reception classes for afternoon activities and spend their last half hour before going home being washed and taken to the toilet back in their unit.

The adults involved with the integration of the unit children also benefit from the arrangement. The staff in reception classes receive extra help each afternoon from a welfare assistant and learn a lot about their own class from watching their interaction with the unit children. The head teacher feels that staff see how handicapped children could fit into ordinary classes, and has found that prospective teachers generally react positively when told about the unit. The unit staff themselves feel that it is good for other parents to see handicapped children in the school, and they make sure that all parents know of the existence of the unit by going along to the school's coffee mornings for new parents. Main school children's parents often help with reading, sewing, cooking and outings, and some have also offered to help in the unit. Parents of the unit children have more difficulty participating because they often live further away, but they are encouraged to come to an open evening every term and to occasions like Harvest Festival, with transport offered if necessary. The staff feel that parents benefit from seeing their child with normal children, becoming more able to put the handicap in perspective and see guidelines for their own child's development.

The Next Stage

What about drawbacks to the policy of integration? One of the reception teachers commented:

> Only that at Janice's age [8] it would help if they could integrate full-time with someone with them to supervise. They would then become more independent and be trusted more to go about on their own ... It wouldn't work with large numbers of children in each class. Two is a good number to cope with. In the unit, children are much more individuals. When they are in a class they are moulded together and have to work in a class or group. They should integrate only in small classes, too.

More worries were expressed about the future of the children after they left the unit at age eight, and were faced with placement in either an ESN(M) or ESN(S) school, a residential or a hospital school. Although when the classes were established it was hoped that integrated provision might become available at the junior level, a second ESN(S) school was built for children from seven upwards as well as the most profoundly handicapped and disruptive younger children. This school still has plenty of available space. Under the present system, the unit teacher fills out an SE (special education) form for each child due to leave, commenting on their performance in areas like play, reading, writing, spelling, numeracy, practical, creative and physical skills and speech, and a referral is made to a particular special school taking into account the views of parents, staff and outside professional services, with the educational psychologist's and doctor's reports generally carrying most weight. The head teacher feels that 'Teachers of unit children are not as objective in their assessment as outside professionals, as they know the child and have seen the changes.' The reception class teacher is not formally involved in this assessment process.

Several of the staff were unhappy about the kind of schooling the children would go on to receive, and would like to see similar units introduced for older children. 'Integration after 8 is very necessary. It's criminal to "put away" children at 8. They learn so much here, and it must be detrimental to be put away.'

45 WESTHALL SCHOOL FOR CHILDREN WITH LEARNING DIFFICULTIES

Tony Booth

Westhall is an unusual special school. It has a high staff-pupil ratio which permits its teachers to work with pre-school children in their homes and with children with learning difficulties in their neighbouring schools. The following case-study describes the establishment and organisation of the school and the progress of these two out-of-school projects.

Before the headmaster was appointed to Westhall in 1977 the local authority special education advisers and schools psychological service were keen that the school should not be used as a traditional ESN(M) school. One suggestion was that the school act as a resource centre for children with learning difficulties; taking children on a relatively short-term basis to improve their basic skills before returning them to mainstream education. As the headmaster recalled:

> There was a possibility of looking at this place as somewhere kids came in, had their top-up of skills and went out again. That was one potential way of looking at it and at least it was more flexible and less unsatisfactory than thinking you had kids in within a certain category and kept them until they were sixteen.

A second view of the school was that it would be an in-service centre for teachers, but the head was dissatisfied with this approach.

> Some teachers have come and spent a week here. But I prefer the notion of a 'service centre' rather than a 'workshop centre'. People can come here and learn about what we are doing but there's no way of ensuring that it makes any difference to their practice. You need to start a scheme and then check and monitor it if it's to keep going.

358

The head sought a method of working which involved more sub-
stantive contact between his school staff and children outside special
education. He also envisaged the school making a contribution to the
broad group of children with learning difficulties rather than a subset
of these characterised by the possession of a vague 'ESN(M)ness'.
These guiding thoughts were put together with a further principle in
shaping the formation of his school. He rejected the idea that an
ESN(M) school should offer a watered-down ordinary curriculum; a
typical mainstream curriculum only taken at a slower pace and with
reduced options. Instead he instigated the development of a specialised
curriculum in basic literacy and numeracy and encouraged new staff
to specialise in one particular curriculum area for a period of time,
such as 'language' or 'reading'.

> The first aim of the special school is to take an area of special
> needs, whether it's learning difficulties or visual handicap and
> concentrate on giving a good deal in that area, and only then to
> provide a comprehensive curriculum. I think it helps to have the
> kids on site so that you can generate and develop expertise. You
> use the staff and the kids you've got to generate a whole lot of
> practical useful skills and materials. But it's what you can do outside
> the school that really counts; so that you're actually using your
> resources to prevent children having the need to come to your
> school; you must at least attempt to alter the status quo in their
> homes, and schools.

Very early on it was realised that any additional contribution his school
was to make would require a favourable staffing ratio:

> We started off with an agreement on what class sizes should be. At
> the time most special schools had ten or twelve pupils to one
> teacher but we managed to get acceptance for eight to one. That
> was a very important decision. It gave us leeway to start thinking
> about alternative ways of using people. Looking back I suspect one
> of the main ideas was that this was just for us to have good group
> sizes here so that we could do a super job of getting them back to
> their schools quickly.

The curriculum, jointly developed by the staff, is highly formalised.
In each of the four areas of number, reading, language and fine motor
co-ordination the staff have produced graded materials along a

developmental sequence. Children at a low level in basic skills all
follow a broadly similar curriculum though they differ in their point of
entry for any particular area:

> We decided that if a kid wanted to learn to read it wasn't any use
> delving into the reasons for the failure. We took a behavioural
> objectives approach, though instead of writing a long list of state-
> ments about what should be learnt and in what order, we actually
> produced materials that could be used to provide each step in the
> learning chain. We also wanted to use them to systematically chart
> the progress of pupils.

The school has produced its own reading scheme which concentrates
on developing a sight vocabulary of 150 words before moving on to
phonics. Besides 30 reading books there are flash cards, tapes, and
numerous word games. The idea is to ensure that a child has mastered
each new stage in a number of contexts before moving on to a new
one. The worksheets, books and games are stored centrally and produced
in a form in which they can be easily replaced.

The most salient visual feature of the school is the individual educational plan and monitoring system for each child in each area of basic
skill which is pinned up on boards in each teaching area. There is a
strong emphasis on child-centred, individual education and the headmaster has eschewed the use of the blackboard. When I first toured the
school a group of teachers had written up some instructions about the
Christmas play on a blackboard and made exaggerated attempts to
conceal it from the headmaster's view as we entered the room.

The physical shape of the school is well suited to the headmaster's
conception of its function. It was built as four units around a central
hall. The children, ranging in age from four to sixteen, are grouped
into a nursery/reception unit, a unit for 6–9 year olds, a unit for
10–12 year olds and a unit for 13–16 year olds. Each of these units
has a number of linking rooms and is assigned a team of teachers, each
specialising in a different area of basic study which they develop within
their particular home classroom. The three units catering for the
younger age range organise their days in a similar way. The mornings
usually involve a varied use of the highly structured core curriculum in
basic skills. The afternoons are used for freer activities which take the
form of project work built around a half-termly or termly theme for
the middle two units. For the oldest group, work in basic skills is

more closely integrated into their curriculum as a whole. At the centre of their education are a series of interdisciplinary courses. They also spend half a day a week using the craft facilities of the nearby comprehensive school.

The differences in the educational plans for the younger and older children reflect a difference in the reasons for their referral to the school. The younger school-age children come because they are failing in basic literacy or numeracy. The referrals for the older children are often initiated because their teachers find them a nuisance or because the children dislike and cannot cope with the organisation of their comprehensive schools. As yet most of the older children are new to the school rather than graduates of the younger units. The complexion of the school will change when this is no longer the case. In the four years of its existence about 10 per cent of the children have been returned to mainstream education. If this trend persists many younger children will remain in the school until they are sixteen and there will not, in future, be space in the upper school for as many new recruits.

The staff of the school, then, are committed to team teach a jointly prepared highly structured core curriculum in basic studies. As each new member has been appointed it has been made clear at interview and when seeking references that a desire both to work in a team and to continually prepare and revise teaching materials and resources were essential requirements for the job. The preparation of a tangible and transportable curriculum in reading, number, basic concepts and language has been conducted with the intention that the materials — worksheets, booklets, tapes, cards, games — could be used outside the school. Resources have been allocated for the printing of materials which can be adapted for use by Westhall children or by others. One group of teachers keeps a book where they write down any need for adaptations or additions to materials. The team approach and favourable teacher-pupil ratio enable teachers to be freed for work on the curriculum and personal visits to other schools, as well as the two out-of-school projects which are the basis of Westhall's attempts to influence events beyond the boundaries of the school.

The first community project to be established was a home-visiting scheme for pre-school children based on the Portage project in the USA. The educational psychologist for the school had been impressed with the philosophy behind a scheme in operation in the Wessex region and had suggested the use of the school as the focus for a similar project in his area, though involving their own materials. The second contribution was a school-visiting scheme in five nearby primary schools working with children with learning difficulties and their teachers.

The Portage Project

The head teacher of the school and the educational psychologist were quick to envisage the benefits that a home-visiting scheme would bring to their work. For the psychologist it increased his 'referral options' and enabled him 'to get at a lot more children and help them in the most effective place — in the home'. By trying to alter home circumstances he felt he could 'make more fundamental changes for comparatively little cost'. The head teacher was keen on the preventive aspects of the scheme as well as the scope it permitted to concentrate solely on the development of the children:

In the Portage scheme we can concentrate on teaching rather than nose-wiping and group interaction. Mothers can put in more time to teach their child than could a teacher with a group of children. For example, you can have a language scheme which involves several individual sessions a day and that would be very difficult in school. We find that we can monitor a child's progress more carefully because we're able to stand back from it slightly.

We hope that by getting at such young children we can prevent them needing to come to places like our school. Only one child from the project has come here.

The scheme started with a small grant from special education funds and as well as Westhall staff it involved a few interested professionals who absorbed the work into their existing professional roles. After a year they applied for and obtained joint funding from Health, Education and Social Services. The project had a low-key start drawing on the interest and goodwill of other staff. They felt strongly that 'Nothing would have happened if we'd asked for it all before it had happened.'

The 'original' Portage project fits in closely with the philosophy behind the structured incremental curriculum at Westhall. It divides child development into a number of separate aspects and identifies a developmental sequence in each area. Children who are retarded in some way can have their profile of development pinpointed by matching their skills and behaviour against a checklist which divides development into 'infant stimulation', 'socialisation', 'language', 'self-help', 'cognitive' and 'motor' areas. A sample of items from the cognitive section is included below:

Cognitive development

Age	Item	Behaviour
3–4	41	Names big and little objects
	42	Points to 10 body parts on verbal command
	43	Tells if object is heavy or light
	44	Puts together two parts of shape to make whole

The aim of the home-teacher is to work with parents in order to identify and specify what is required to shift the child along the developmental sequence and to monitor progress. The responsibility for teaching the child rests primarily with the parent.

Children from a limited part of the city in the neighbourhood of the school are eligible for the scheme; they range in age from a few months up to five years and are specified in the project booklet in the following way:

The service is organised to cater for a wide range of problems, including the following:
— Children with severe or moderate delays in their physical or mental development. It is hoped that all the mentally handicapped children in these areas would be included, wherever possible.
— Children with physical handicaps.
— Children with language difficulties.
— Children with sensory difficulties.
— Children whose independence or self-help skills are delayed or problematic (i.e. dressing, toileting, feeding).
— Children with behavioural difficulties (children in this group will often have normal development but pose grave difficulties *to their parents* in the management of their behaviour — temper tantrums, bedtime difficulties, aggressive behaviour, non-compliance, etc).

Children attending a nursery school either part-time or full-time are 'not normally considered' for the scheme and children who have both parents working are specifically excluded because it is felt that they would not be able to find sufficient time to teach their child.

Referrals to the project come from a variety of sources including health visitors, social workers, GPs and sometimes parents themselves who hear of the scheme through the 'parents' grapevine'. They are sent initially to the educational psychologist, who is the 'project supervisor', and if the child is thought by the team to have an appropriate problem then a home-teacher is assigned to the family. Both the teachers in the nursery unit at Westhall act as home-teachers for the project, as well as a speech therapist, health visitor, a community nurse, and a social worker. At present there are 12 children involved though the group hope to raise the number to eighteen. Each home-teacher takes on responsibility for one, two or three children whom they visit once a week.

The home-teacher discusses the nature of the problem with the child's parents (almost always the mother) and when appropriate uses the Portage checklist to give an indication of what the child might be taught next. Together they draw up an activity chart which specifies, in behavioural terms, what the child will be expected to have learnt in the following week. It also details the materials used for teaching the task, the number of teaching sessions and the materials on which the child will be assessed. The home-teachers draw on materials, housed in a project room at the school, which include toys, puzzles and language schemes. The activities usually involve a relatively brief daily session between the mother and child and the visits themselves last about one and a half hours.

When the home-teacher returns the following week she assesses progress and then negotiates new objectives. There may be disagreement between the teacher and the parent arising from differences in the way they perceive the problem. The parent may, for example, be concerned with the child's day-time wetting or naughtiness whilst the teacher might regard the child's language development as the most appropriate focus for intervention. In such circumstances a negotiation process may occur whereby the parents' support and co-operation on the scheme is secured by an initial agreement to approach the problem from their point of view.

The home-teacher discusses the children in her care at a weekly support meeting attended by all six project teachers and by others with a wide range of skills. The ideas she brings to the next meeting with the parent and child are a product of wider experience and knowledge than her own. The project is also subject to a termly meeting of the management committee who are responsible for its overall direction.

Bridget, one of the teachers in the school's nursery unit, joined the Portage project six months after it started. She works with two children altogether. One child who is now off her lists is a five year old, Tony, with Down's Syndrome. Tony was referred by his health visitor when he was two and a half and before Bridget joined the project had a different home-teacher. His problems were identified as toilet training, language development and feeding. Both his parents are teachers and his mum is regarded as an 'ideal' participant in the scheme. She was able to write her own activity charts and establish her own weekly 'behavioural' goals. Bridget used materials from Bill Gilham's first hundred words programme as well as work on basic concepts. Tony made steady progress and when he was four and a half he came into the nursery group at the school. He had been attending a playgroup but he had been a 'loner' there. 'He just played on the big toys; they didn't try to involve him with the other children.' His mother had wanted him to go on to an ordinary school but after Tony had been on the Portage scheme she became very keen for him to attend Westhall. He started there although she was told when he came that it wouldn't be a permanent arrangement. Tony is more able than some others in his group but concern has been expressed about the effect that the presence of a child with Down's Syndrome might have on the parents of other children. The people in the area do not categorise the school and the uncertainty about Tony's stay in the school was part of an attempt to avoid it becoming labelled as a school for mentally handicapped children.

Other difficulties arose when Tony came to Westhall. The school language curriculum is different from the published materials on which Tony was working and Bridget regards it as less detailed and efficient. But he now comes under the jurisdiction of a different teacher and his language work has changed. Bridget also recognises that his mother isn't as involved in his education as she was, although she visits the school and is aware of what he is doing.

Not all the parents find it as easy to appreciate the details of the scheme as Tony's. William was referred to the project by the educational psychologist because of his destructive behaviour at home and his poor language. At first his foster mother found it impossible to stick to the instructions on the chart and would give him clues and change the instructions. But the visits have been a success. When Bridget first started going he would 'take the toys I had brought and fling them around' but 'now he's dying to look in my bag'. He is much calmer although he still gets upset after visits to his mother or when the social worker calls and will 'lapse into baby talk'. Bridget feels that he is no longer a candidate for a special school provided his family circumstances do not alter substantially. Of the other families who have been attached to the scheme there are only a couple of cases in which communication with parents has seriously impeded the children's progress.

Although Bridget has no children of her own, is younger than many of the mothers and has no specific training for this kind of work, she feels that 'working as a team provides the qualifications'. In working with Tony for example, she was in constant touch with a speech therapist and a physiotherapist. She has never been challenged by the parents about the relevance of her skills. She identified one area in particular where parents and the home-teacher need much help and reassurance: when a programme is started for a child with 'difficult behaviour' things may get worse initially as the child fights and then adjusts to a new regime.

The school's Portage project has been the subject of an independent evaluation though the staff felt that with the amount of monitoring they had done they knew in advance that it was successful. In the event, the evaluation confirmed their 'knowledge' and formed the basis on which funding for the project was agreed. Whether ultimately such a scheme should emanate from a special school or an ordinary nursery school is a question that the evaluation was not set up to address. The head does not feel that their intervention takes away the initiative of parents; a possible explanation of the disappointing results in other home-visiting schemes:

> The whole idea is to gradually reduce the amount of direction you give. After a while you may only need to discuss the general drift and leave the parents to specify the activities and the materials they need. We have mothers who have been on the project over a year who write their own activity charts.

Delivering a Service to Neighbouring Schools

Once the Portage scheme was underway, the Westhall staff began to develop their intervention scheme with primary school children with learning difficulties in ordinary schools. This scheme was also developed with limited funding; the school spread its own capitation allowance to cover the costs of extra materials. However they are now given additional money for the eighty children attached to the scheme. The philosophy behind the two schemes is broadly similar though with the school children the idea was that the learning sequence would be negotiated with the child's classroom teacher instead of her parents. The teachers felt that if children could follow an appropriate curriculum in their own schools then there would be no need for them to be referred and transferred to Westhall.

The school envisaged an ideal form of intervention which would involve the joint development of educational plans with classroom teachers, drawing on Westhall curriculum materials, with the progress of children being monitored by Westhall staff. The idea was for the Westhall teachers to gradually withdraw from direct contact with children and for the classroom teachers gradually to take on greater responsibility for setting weekly objectives for each child. The history of this particular scheme can be seen in part, as the progressive discovery of the factors which impede this simple relationship between a Westhall teacher and the teacher of another school. Unlike some parents, with only one or two children, teachers rarely have an opportunity to give one child their undivided attention; schools already have a curriculum and may find it difficult to fit in new methods and materials; staff regularly leave schools; the organisation of a school may be totally changed — one school in the project changed from vertical grouping to age-grouping when a new head arrived; staff may see children with learning problems as of only peripheral concern; some head teachers may attempt to control, personally, all outside contact with their school; where schools recognise or elevate the needs of children with learning problems they have a tendency to specialise — the appointment of a remedial teacher may reproduce and solidify the gap between the outside helper and the classroom teacher.

These then are some of the problems which the project has rediscovered; problems which may occur whenever an attempt is made to intervene in the life of a school. However it would be a mistake to think that they imply the lack of success of the project. They only serve to show, as one might expect, that the degree of success that Westhall teachers have had, varied from school to school.

Catherine is responsible for adjacent infant and junior schools which she visits each week. In the infant school, where the scheme has probably adhered most closely to Westhall's first principles, she has close contact with all the staff, and the children on the scheme come from a variety of classes. Children are jointly identified for inclusion in the project by Catherine and their classroom teacher. The school have set aside a resource area where Westhall materials are kept together with an adapted tape machine (Syncrofax) where children can work on pre-recorded materials. The welfare assistant in the school has taken on some of the responsibility for supervising the children's daily tasks but the class teachers are involved in formulating objectives. When she visits the school Catherine checks the progress of some of the children, talks to all the teachers involved as well as the welfare assistant, and monitors the revision of activity sheets. She feels her presence and support are essential for the scheme: 'If I didn't go in it would collapse in three weeks, it's not that the staff do not work hard on the scheme themselves but it is an interruption to their established routine and it would be the first thing to go.'

As in the Portage scheme, there is a system of monitoring the monitors. Catherine writes up her own set of short-term and long-term learning objectives for each child for whom she is responsible and the dates on which these are reached. She admits that strict conformity to a particular style of record keeping may be illusory at times, as she said: 'The long-term objectives are really records of completion of a section of work which I write in after they've been reached, but the school like them to be called long-term objectives.'

The project has made a big difference to the educational lives of a large number of children as well as to the quality of the working life of the Westhall teachers involved in it. However, Colin the teacher who has overall responsibility for the project is guarded in his assessment of its success. He feels that they have 'made some mistakes by homing in on children and not taking sufficient account of other factors'. He is keen to retain the central position of the class-teacher and to develop a scheme which will last:

> Success of the project depends on classroom teachers really needing help rather than us waltzing in as experts, telling them we've decided your kid needs help and this is how we'll set about it ... at the moment it revolves around our internally produced resources; there's a need to look at commercially produced materials that are commonly used in the schools and to create support materials for them; we'd have more chance that way of involving classroom teachers ... We mustn't lose sight of the original intention; monitoring the progress of the children is the most important role of the visiting teachers, they should have very little contact with the children themselves. We have to be careful that we don't sacrifice quality for quantity and abandon the central position of classroom teachers. I want to see the project having long-term validity rather than being dependent on the enthusiasm and energy of the particular staff doing the job. My time will have been wasted if the scheme collapses when I'm

gone.

There has been some discussion about ways in which the project might include secondary age children but as things are, Colin even has doubts about the work with the junior age children: 'There's far more value in working within the infant school to reduce the numbers of problems they pass on. In the junior school children with learning difficulties may not be central to their pattern of working.'

The difference in concerns of secondary schools in the area were emphasised by the school psychologist: 'The secondary schools are a different animal altogether. Their major concern is disruptiveness. You can count the referrals about learning problems on the fingers of one hand.'

The head did feel that they could play a similar role in secondary schools though it might be through the design and delivery of appropriate courses rather than plans for individual children. However both he and the psychologist stressed that any such plan would depend on an appropriate organisation within the school. As the psychologist put it:

Its not just a matter of providing the right materials or course, you would have to work in the context and organisation of a secondary school and that can be a hell of a problem. It would be no good where all the children with difficulties are placed in a D stream or sink group. You would need a resource base like the basic studies department at Drayton through which you could deliver your services.

Realising the Aims of the Schools

Westhall is, clearly, an unusual special school; it has developed its own structured and transportable curriculum; the staff are involved with as many children outside the school as there are on the school roll and the school receives funds for this work. But perhaps the most striking feature of the school is the level of staff involvement and commitment to the school aims. All of the staff who work on the community schemes enjoy the variety, stimulation and contact which they bring. Apart from the difference these schemes make to the children, parents and schools involved, they greatly improve the quality of life and sense of purpose of the staff within Westhall. As the headmaster remarked:

'The projects have given Westhall an identity and role in the community.'

It is difficult to assess whether the school has been successful in its aim to prevent children needing special education in special schools. At the same time as they were establishing their preventive schemes the school has filled and remains full; in the words of the school psychologist 'If it's there it will get filled — that's in the nature of things.' However there have been far fewer referrals from the five neighbourhood schools since the scheme started. The school has always had a very wide catchment area and what seems to have happened is that the reputation of the school now draws in more children from other wider areas.

Even Westhall with its favourable staffing ratio is limited in the number of directions in which it can expend its energy. The encouragement and involvement of parents in the education of their children is largely confined to the Portage scheme. The school-link project involves very little contact with the parents though, in theory, they could participate in the teaching programmes. The staff also recognise that they might do more to bridge the gap between ordinary and special school for their own children. But they have gone further in this direction than many other schools. The secondary age children have their craft lessons at the local comprehensive school on half a day a week, taught by Westhall staff. Five of these children attend the school itself for additional periods of time, some with a view to eventual full-time transfer. There are regular liaison visits by staff, in both directions. Although no Westhall junior age children were attending ordinary schools part-time, at the time of this study, a support system is already there in the shape of the school visiting scheme. About 10 per cent of the intake to Westhall have returned to ordinary schools.

One area where there is scope for change, at least in theory, is the extent of co-operation with the city remedial service. The developments at Westhall have taken place in close consultation with the schools psychological service but without co-ordination with the peripatetic remedial teachers. If the distinction between special help in ordinary and special schools is to be blurred then it would make sense to bring 'remedial' and 'special' services into a common system. There is however ample evidence, from other schools, to testify that this is often no easy task.

The head sees the character of his school as a stage in the development of the organisation of special services. He is not committed to special schools as the long-term future provision for children with persistent learning difficulties. He argues that 'Children are often better off staying in ordinary schools with access to the kinds of materials that Westhall can provide as well as access to their own school's resources in terms of music, games and subject specialists.' The school psychologist highlighted the dilemma involved in keeping the best of both worlds for children:

> Suppose you had units for children with learning problems in junior schools, how could you make those match up to Westhall where you've a group of people who know each other and work towards a common end for children with problems? In a unit the teacher might have to develop her own materials with indifferent or even bad relationships with the rest of the school. How could a unit teacher gain access to all the resources she would need? The system here delivers the goods and doesn't leave teachers stranded. In devising an integrated system we need to retain these advantages.

Westhall has been in a good position to innovate. It is a new school and the head teacher by guile, good friends and good fortune as well as deliberate policy, has acquired a staff who share his aims, and advantageous staffing levels and funding for the school. It would be far harder to reorganise a well established school along totally new lines unless there was a definite consensus of opinion among the staff and a willingness on the part of a local authority to take on additional staff or to reduce school numbers and permit staff to develop new roles. It is, too, a relatively easy matter to create an initial purpose in a school but it may be far harder to actually keep it on course. Most institutions suffer from hardening of the arteries after a fairly brief life. It remains to be seen whether Westhall can adhere to the purity of its initial aims and keep control over its future development.

46 DEVELOPMENTS AT PINGLE SCHOOL

Graham Fisher, Les Roberts and Irene Williams

Sources: Graham Fisher, 'Integration at the Pingle School', *Special Education/Forward Trends*, *4*, 1 (1977), pp. 8–11; Les Roberts and Irene Williams, 'Three Years on at Pingle School', *Special Education/Forward Trends*, 7, 2 (1980), pp. 24–6.

In Swadlincote, a small town in South Derbyshire, almost all the children with special needs within the area are educated in ordinary schools Springfield primary school contains units for ESN(M) children and severely mentally handicapped children including the most profoundly multiply handicapped. All their children, apart from the profoundly handicapped group who remain at Springfield until they are sixteen, transfer at eleven years of age to Pingle Comprehensive. Pingle school thus provides a unique example within the UK of a comprehensive school educating children of all ranges of ability and handicap. The mentally handicapped children have their own base attached to the main school whilst within the school are separate ESN(M) and remedial classes. Despite the retention of these distinctions it is striking how much the school has achieved in making mentally handicapped students part of the educational community. Details of the integration scheme at Pingle school were first described by the ex-head of the school's Slow Learner Department in an article in Special Education *in 1977, and the developments that have taken place over the subsequent three years are recorded in a second article by the present head and deputy of the department in the same journal in early 1980. The following account is taken from these two articles, and illustrates the perspective held by these heads of department about the developments in their school.*

Background

The integration system originated in 1970 when the Derbyshire education

372

authority was concerned with providing secondary education for South Derbyshire area ESN(M) pupils who were in a small, recently opened unit attached to a junior school in Swadlincote. There was no area special school and so the education authority decided as a matter of policy to transfer all children reaching the age of 11 from the junior school unit to the Pingle School which was then an 11 to 15 junior high school, one of three serving the urban district and surrounding rural areas.

It was decided to reorganise remedial provision at the Pingle School so that low ability children needing extra help in the basic subjects would be placed in mixed ability classes but would be formed into small groups for specialist remedial teaching in English and mathematics. It was further decided that, from the beginning, ESN(M) children would be in a 'special' class within the school, spending part of their time with specialist remedial staff and the remainder with specialist subject teachers, most in mixed ability groups.

Thus the structure for ESN(M) children was to be much like the 'remedial class' in other schools. They were to comprise a class in their year group like any other and as such would take part in all corporate and social activities. Academic work was to be a mixture of separate and integrated teaching.

In September 1971 the first class of ESN(M) children from the junior school unit was formed. Learning materials, compatible with those which the children had used before, had already been acquired and were added to resources already available in the school. Teachers, mainly with special training, were recruited from outside the school to teach them. No welfare assistants were provided at first, which caused practical difficulties and, in 1974, one was appointed.

New Unit for Mentally Handicapped Pupils

The next year the Pingle School was reorganised into a comprehensive school for children aged 11 to 18. By this time, encouraged by the successful integration of the ESN(M) children the reorganised school was planning to accept all South Derbyshire area ESN(S) children too (with the exception of 'special care' children). These pupils were at the time accommodated in a temporary all-age unit on the outskirts of the town and it was agreed that after the integration of the ESN(M), the ESN(S) children aged 11 and above would also come to the Pingle School, with one member of the unit staff who would be the teacher in charge of the new unit.

Possible methods of integration were discussed within the school and the Derbyshire education authority went ahead with the planning of a self-contained and specially equipped unit, to be sited adjacent to the existing remedial department and to be made an integral part of both department and school. Although it was to be self-contained, possible ways of integrating children on an individual basis were discussed. A planned programme of liaison was conducted with children and teachers already in the school and with parents, teachers and children who were to transfer. This included staff seminars, films and discussions with the comprehensive school pupils, meetings with parents and teachers and visits to the school by the ESN(S) children.

The unit, built for a maximum of 20, opened in February 1974. The Pingle ESN(S) unit does not have a special care section — non-ambulant children or those requiring constant medical care remain at the junior unit where the extra help is provided. The new junior unit was opened later in the same year at the junior school which was already accepting the ESN(M) children. The younger ESN(S) children left at the temporary all-age unit were then transferred there, and others added, so that this new unit now provides for children from pre-school age to 11 years.

Structure of the School in 1977

The ESN(M) and ESN(S) children are now part of a school which has reached the final stage of its development with the building up of the sixth form completed in 1975. The total of pupils on roll is 1,060 and the annual intake of approximately 190 pupils is divided into seven forms. These are organised into two broad bands of ability (those with IQs below about 95 and those above), each of three forms, and a special class for ESN(M) children; banding continues for the first three years.

About half the fourth and fifth year ESN(M) pupils then join mixed ability classes and follow the appropriate part of the option system which allows for examination and non-examination courses. There is also a special class for the other half, the older ESN(M) pupils aged 14 or above who still need special educational support.

The Slow Learner Department

The Slow Learner Department has responsibility within the school for the teaching, curriculum and welfare of children needing remedial help and the ESN(M) and ESN(S) children. It has four full time ESN(M)/

remedial teachers, two ESN(S) teachers, two who spend part of their teaching time with ESN(M)/remedial groups, two full time and one part time welfare assistants. With this organisation it is easy to place or replace a child in an environment in which he can thrive — either integrated or partly integrated or, very occasionally, in totally separate specialist care within the department. Many children in the department spend some of their time in different teaching groups such as remedial and ESN(M), or ESN(M) and ESN(S), if their abilities suggest it. The kinds of provision are regarded as a continuum rather than as separate entities, thus helping to ease the problem of borderline children. Because of this, labels descriptive of ability tend to become meaningless and disappear. Such a flexible structure allows for the often considerable performance differences with the same child. Alan, for instance, is a 13 year old boy who entered the ESN(S) unit at 11. After one year he was spending half his time in the ESN(S) unit and the remainder in the first year ESN(M) class. Now he spends most of his time in the ESN(M) class and attends some full mixed ability art and craft classes, although he still uses the ESN(S) unit as his 'base'.

The philosophy of the Slow Learner Department rests on criteria which, it is hoped, bring about the meaningful integration whereby handicapped children genuinely participate in some of the activities and life of the school and where contact with normal children is not artificially contrived. Fulfilling these criteria depends on the capabilities of the individual children, their social and emotional stages of development, the provision of suitable resources, the presence of teachers with appropriate special knowledge and skills, the involvement of parents, 'normal' staff and outside specialist agencies, and a structure which allows both for flexibility and for a firm 'home base' with a caring atmosphere.

Remedial Groups

As indicated above, there are no full time remedial classes in the school. Those children in the lower ability band who are backward or show specific retardation in the basic subjects are formed into small groups — one or two both in English and mathematics per year — taught by remedial teachers. These subjects are set throughout each year and the Slow Learner Department supplies teachers to a lower band set, thus enabling it to be split into two groups of approximately 10 and 15 children, according to need. The smaller group normally consists of those children with the most serious difficulties. These children spend the majority of their time in a normal lower band mixed ability class.

The small remedial groups are regarded as a normal part of the setting organisation.

ESN(M) Special Classes

About 12 ESN(M) children with IQs between 50 and 75 come yearly from the junior unit, for which they were chosen on a basis of area sweep testing in consultation with the educational psychologist. It is normal for all the ESN(M) children from South Derbyshire to proceed to the Pingle School at the age of 11 — there is no special selection of those of higher academic or social performance. To this group, a few more children may be added to make a special class of about 15 or 16 in each year. These extra children come from the school's normal catchment area and are those who would be the slowest learners in the more usual remedial class situation. If they would be unlikely to cope academically and socially in a lower band mixed ability class, even with the support of remedial groups in the basic subjects, the special class provides them with a more suitable learning environment.

Approximately half the weekly teaching time is spent on basic subjects (reading, number, language, cognitive skills and social studies) with various members of the department's specialist staff. This provision of a 'home base' to which the children can relate is considered important in the establishment of a caring environment. The children spend the remaining time about the school, taught by subject specialists. Art, crafts, games and swimming are taught in full mixed ability groups; for science and music, the children stay in the special class group.

Participation in Group Activities. Socially these children constitute a normal class in their year group and join in all group activities, such as dining and play, with the rest of the school. Movement from the special class into the lower band is not unusual — one or two children in their first upper year do so annually — and some lower borderline ESN(M) children spend some of their time with the ESN(S) group for particular basic skills.

Recently has come the formation of football and swimming teams which have played the remedial departments of other schools. In this way, the children have gained the satisfaction of representing the school and integration has been carried beyond its walls. We hope such contacts with other schools will increase.

The department is responsible for pastoral care with the support of the school's year heads. Many children in the fourth and fifth year are able to join a mixed ability class (with remedial support) as their social development tends to be similar to their peers. However some children, even at this stage, need the support of a special class, as mentioned earlier.

Teacher expectation is found to be an important influence, especially in social behaviour. The children also tend to adopt the norms and standards they see around them and generally their standards differ little from those of the other children in the school.

ESN(S) Special Unit

These children normally come from the junior ESN(S) unit around the age of 11 and their recorded IQs are below 50. Again, they are not selected on the basis of a hypothetical suitability for the unit which is provided at the Pingle School.

The mentally handicapped children spend more time than other children in the department as a homogeneous group using their own self-contained unit. It is recognised that such children – and the ESN(M) group to a lesser extent – have educational needs that require, in part, separate teaching, with the appropriate specialist staff, including welfare assistants, similarly to other identifiable groups within the school, such as the sixth form, GCE groups and non-examination courses.

Integration proceeds according to individual capabilities. Some children eat in the main dining room with other children. One attends normal mixed ability craft groups. Some play with and amongst 'normal' children during breaks and lunch time. Some attend lessons with ESN(M) groups and some do none of these things. All use the school's swimming pool, assisted by the sixth form, and other areas and resources of the school for activities like gym and movement.

Two-way Integration. Integration with the ESN(S) also works the other way. Older pupils across the ability range go into the unit to help voluntarily with working sessions and at break and lunch time, and on a rota for the school's community care scheme. Some subject specialist teachers come in to teach, and often take the children back to their own specialist rooms, while ESN(M) classes make use of the unit, including the kitchen and colour television. Such knowledge and contact should ensure that generations of 'normal' school children will accept mentally handicapped children as an integral part of the school and of their own society. There has never been any bullying, jeering or other overt forms of hostility directed to them from children in the main school. Socially, the teachers in the special unit are a part of the main school staff. Teachers unconnected with ESN(S) or ESN(M) children visit the unit to dine.

The ESN(S) children know their way around the main school on their own and are accepted by staff and children. Frequent visitors comment on their happy outlook, apparent lack of mental stress and 'mature' social behaviour, which their acceptance by the main school encourages.

Other Considerations

Some factors are central to the operation of the system. The role of head of department involves much liaison with parents, teachers and other children. New entrants to the department and their parents are seen before entry, at home or in the junior school and they visit the school and meet the appropriate staff. When possible, teachers from the Slow Learner Department work with the children in the junior setting to create relationships and ESN(S) children attend the unit part time for a term before entry. In addition junior school heads and teachers discuss potential remedial or special class children with the department's staff.

Liaison continues with parents as the child progresses through the school — and with other departments within Pingle School, as staff attitudes are crucial in establishing a caring atmosphere for the handicapped. It is frequently said that integration of handicapped children in ordinary schools is not more widespread because of the hostile attitude of many teachers. No such attitude has been found in this school and many of the staff are extremely supportive when they have the opportunity to see what is being done. Feedback from teachers involved has been found to be very helpful in promoting the welfare of the children. Art and crafts teachers, for instance, come to the department to discuss the work and behaviour of ESN(M) children they are teaching. What is necessary is attitude *formation* in schools rather than attitude change. Attitudes of parents and of 'normal' children in this school are similarly positive.

Equipment and Supportive Services

Adequate equipment and learning materials for all ability levels have been forthcoming since the outset of special education provision at the school and when necessary there are the wider resources of the main school to call upon. Much material has been bought to preserve a continuity between the junior units and the department.

Various support services cooperate and good informal working relationships have been set up with psychological, medical and social services, the speech therapist and education welfare officers. The speech therapist visits the school one half day weekly and the educational psychologist, who is 'on call', holds interviews and case conferences at the school.

Problems in establishing and developing the structure described in this article have been remarkably few and are mainly ones of organisation. Initially teachers found it difficult to spend adequate time on individual and small group work with lower ability ESN(M) children but the opening of the ESN(S) unit provided a continuum of provision and sufficient staff to enable further help to be given to these borderline children. Time, of course, remains a constant problem. Many hours have to be spent in compiling a school time-table flexible enough to meet individual children's needs and in staff liaison, case conferences and help for children with social problems.

The Future

Indications like the ESN(M) children's reading ages, which compare favourably with those in previous studies of ESN(M) children, and the level of their social adjustment suggest that the integration of the handicapped children is developing satisfactorily.

We are sufficiently encouraged to hope that the integration of handicapped children within the specially planned structure of the Pingle School will stimulate further ventures by other schools which are also prompted by the advantages of educating children with a very wide range of abilities within the normal school.

Three Years On: Provision in 1980

We now have a school of 1,073 children aged 11 to 18 which includes a remedial department responsible for the needs of mentally handicapped children in an ESN(S) unit, ESN(M) pupils in five special classes and a further 100 children who spend part of their time in remedial groups formed as part of the general 'setting' arrangements in the school for basic subjects like English and maths. We also have a number of ambulant, physically handicapped children and others who are emotionally disturbed, partially sighted, partially hearing, epileptic or speech impaired. The junior school half a mile away has two separate units for ESN(S) and (M) children, and across the school field is a newly built adult training centre and a residential hostel. This extended campus thus provides the education and training for almost all individuals with learning difficulties in the area.

The Present Structure

Children in the ESN(S) unit spend most of their time there but may join children in the main school for physical education, lunch and other corporate activities like those of the youth club. The unit is 'open house' with mainstream staff and pupils 'popping in' at breaks or lunch times or helping during lessons.

Children in the special classes spend a proportion of their time with their mainstream peers which varies from one fifth in the first year to half by the fifth year for activities like craft and games. The remaining time is spent in their own classes with specialist teachers and subject teachers for music and science.

Like all the others at Pingle, their class is known by its year number and the number of the room in which they register. Form 1/6, for instance, is a first year class which registers in Room 6; it also happens to be the first year special class. Using the same class numbering system, wearing the same uniform and observing the same rules as the children in the mainstream all help to make pupils in the department an integral part of the school.

Mainstream pupils in the lower ability levels who have difficulties in basic subjects are 'set' into small remedial groups for these subjects but pass most of their time in the ordinary classes following their class timetable.

New Developments at Pingle

How has integration at Pingle School developed since the description in the first half of this chapter? While the basic structure, summarised in the paragraphs above, has remained the same, its *uses* have constantly changed.

The first development is the increased involvement of mainstream staff in the integrated provision, particularly in the past two years.

Any member of staff experiencing difficulties with a pupil who is the responsibility of the remedial department can ask us to arrange a case conference at which he or she will have every opportunity to air views. As a result of such a case conference action is either immediate or deferred for further information.

The main school teachers take part in the decision making which may lead to temporary transfer of a pupil to the unit. If a psychologist's opinion is sought, here again, mainstream staff have the opportunity of discussing the child with him. As staff time is always at a premium, such meetings take the form of working lunches. Everyone welcomes this development and finds it extremely worthwhile. As well as such meetings, informed two-way traffic of information and advice continues daily between the department and the mainstream staff, who are given every opportunity to talk at length with visitors to the department.

The Multi-disciplinary Team

The second development is closely related to the first. This is the building of a multi-disciplinary team to help children with learning difficulties. It stretches beyond the local education and health authorities and into the neighbouring community. The senior educational psychologist, psychiatrist, medical officer, social workers, the local authority's senior adviser for special education and the remedial advisory staff are all part of the team. So, too, are the careers officer, staff of the nearby adult training centre and local employers who offer work experience to the pupils. Parents are also encouraged to become active members of the team. They are consulted whenever any changes in their child's educational programme are introduced, encouraged to visit school whenever they wish or are visited at home and are invited to attend occasional coffee mornings to meet other parents and see their children at work in the classroom.

All of the staff listed above attend the case conferences at the school, which are arranged as working lunches. These are split into two specific types. In one members of local firms — 14 at present — who will be supervising children at work experience can discuss the individuals with staff and careers officers. In the other the multi-disciplinary team meets, coordinated by the department, to discuss individual pupils and proposed developments. It is here that the senior educational psychologist, school medical officer and the psychiatrist can exchange further information with teachers on the treatment of pupils experiencing difficulties whom they meet to discuss regularly at one of their clinics.

In addition, the senior educational psychologist may visit the school to discuss educational and general problems with the teachers and parents, and a psychiatric social worker may be called in to help the family. The school medical officer and social workers may visit parents at home or in school, to advise, for instance, on medication at the suggestion of the department, and the representative of the LEA's remedial advisory team frequently calls in to advise on new developments or to offer practical help. Sometimes teachers have talks with the pupils' GPs (general practitioners) when they have to take children to the surgery. They can also meet the educational welfare officer who is concerned with individual children. In sensitive cases and where a family is under considerable stress social workers may be used instead of education welfare officers. The teachers also have strong links with the nearby adult training centre and two from the ESN(S) unit teach literary skills at the centre one morning a week and have assisted staff in initiating their own educational programmes.

The cooperation of this multi-disciplinary team is crucial to the success of the integrated provision at Pingle School. It is essential to have a supportive environment of this kind.

The third new development is that the ESN(S) unit has become a temporary haven for children from the mainstream who are under emotional or social pressure. Joan, for instance, was admitted to the unit in January this year from an assessment centre in Derby which she had been attending as a result of an interim Care Order. This had been the culmination of several court appearances for non attendance at a local secondary school. She attends at the unit daily, is beginning to spend some time in the special class provision and may later return to full time education in the mainstream. Another child, Sally, was transferred to Pingle School from an ESN(M) unit at the local primary school. She was suffering from severe hallucinations which culminated in her cutting herself with blades about the arms and legs, implying that imaginary males had inflicted the wounds. She was transferred to the special unit in November 1978 and with close cooperation between the teachers and the consultant psychiatrist she has increased in emotional security. She is now following a special class curriculum although she is reluctant as yet to return to the special class itself. The alternative to being transferred to the unit at the time of the hallucination crises would have been a hospital psychiatric ward.

Thus a short term transfer to the unit can give a child an emotional shield if pressure elsewhere becomes too great. For a few weeks, or sometimes longer as with Sally, the child can be given essential social training. Indeed we are now planning to use the material facilities of the unit much more for the rest of the department, in promoting personal hygiene, self help, for instance. This will, it is hoped, break down any barriers that may exist and will make the unit an even more integral part of the department. With such a development the work of departmental staff based in the unit will be extended beyond that unit and their commitment to other departmental areas, which already exists, will be widened. Placement of children within the department is under constant review and changes can be initiated, dependent on their individual progress. Four fourth year pupils, for instance, not so long ago in a special class, are now following a mainstream course. We also have a pupil who was originally in our ESN(S) unit, who transferred to a special class, followed our works experience programme and was recently offered open employment in a local firm.

In the last year there have been two major developments which have also extended considerably the scope of provision offered. These are the works experience and the 16 plus programme.

The Works Experience Scheme and the 16 Plus Programme

The works experience scheme began in September 1978. Each Monday, special class and selected ESN(S) pupils work one full day for a five weeks' period in local firms. Monday has been purposely chosen to ensure that pupils have to rely totally on themselves to get in after a weekend. Before their first day's work they are informed of the structure of the firm they will attend, the products or services it provides and the working arrangements. They are also introduced to personnel officers and the people they will be working with. While on work experience, the children are visited daily by a member of staff who can help overcome or ease any problems that arise.

Each pupil participates in three cycles. The first venue is chosen by the member of staff in charge, the second is the pupil's own choice and the third is decided after joint consultation. Written reports are provided by each employer.

Initially, this programme was devised for special class pupils and individual ESN(S) children who were likely to benefit from it. An ESN(S) pupil now on the programme, for instance, has had good reports from employers and it seems likely that he will be offered employment when he leaves in the summer. Already the programme has been extended to include the more difficult remedial pupils.

Although 90 per cent of school leavers with learning difficulties found employment before the introduction of the programme, thanks to a very efficient careers officer in our area, several of them began to drift from job to job very quickly, rapidly descending to dependence on the State. One of the big spin-offs from this programme is that during weekly visits to employers, a distant eye can be kept on past pupils who are in full employment. Out of this programme will, it is hoped, emerge a very useful after-care service.

Pupils take part in the 16 plus programme if they are likely to gain socially or emotionally. It has four elements. The first, survival skills, includes mobility, shopping, cooking and household management and encourages pupils to embark into the community at every opportunity.

The second, the extension of communicative skills, includes writing, conversation and eventual use of the telephone.

Practical skills comprises gardening, do-it-yourself (DIY) and environmental studies. We intend to send small, supervised groups of special class, selected ESN(S) and more able pupils out together to do a survey of a local village and to develop further courses along these lines.

The fourth element, careers, is possibly the most significant. It includes the work experience programme and also one to two days weekly at the nearby adult training centre (ATC), which is very cooperative and forward thinking. We hope that school leavers who join the ATC will, in time, be able to live in specially adapted council houses which the social services department is providing nearby. The teacher organiser of the 16 plus programme teaches one half day weekly in the education programme run by the ATC, assisted by one of the unit staff.

As the works experience programme develops we hope to include more and more suitable ESN(S) pupils for whom employment is not ruled out. There is also a growing range of residential courses which are recommended to parents where appropriate. Fortunately, two further education colleges are nearby too, and both run courses for the moderately handicapped.

Conclusion

At Pingle School we have developed as a cohesive remedial department despite the wide range of handicaps encountered by the pupils. We have the active support of the head, the main school staff, parents, the community and a multidisciplinary team; and we feel we have achieved our original aim of providing as full integration as is practicable within the normal school environment. We are now involved in developments outside the Department itself. We have initiated and gained acceptance for a core curriculum for non-examination school leavers and have recently set up a Community Care Planning Team which aims to coordinate all the facilities and services offered to the mentally handicapped in our locality.

47 PROVIDING FOR HANDICAPPED CHILDREN AT J T COBB

Keith Pocklington

J.T. Cobb Elementary School in Michigan, USA, opened in 1976. It takes non-handicapped children from the age of six to twelve and handicapped children from the age of two and a half to thirteen. It was purpose-built to foster the mainstreaming of physically handicapped and hearing impaired children. By June 1978, out of a total school roll of 650 pupils, 80 were physically handicapped and 37 hearing impaired.

Legislation in Michigan had anticipated the content of Public Law 94–142 by some years. This law made all handicapped children the responsibility of an education system obliged to provide for them, in ordinary schools and classrooms whenever possible. Act 198, implemented in 1972, had decreed that each school district should make educational provision for all handicapped individuals from birth to 25 years. However, it is easy to stipulate that all handicapped children are entitled to education within the regular school system but quite another matter to put this into practice. School administrative districts in the USA are small, sometimes containing as few as 3,000 pupils. Where there is a high incidence of handicap, for example mental retardation, or learning disability, then special class provision can be arranged within any particular school district. However, for less common handicaps, such as physical handicap, hearing and vision impairment, the smaller numbers mean that group provision is much less tenable within any one district. The school district which contains J T Cobb School has come up with an innovative solution to this particular difficulty; they combined with 12 other school districts to form a co-operative. Individual districts retain responsibility for the education of the high incidence categories of handicap but for the low incidence categories the co-operative exercises joint responsibility. By this means the group of school districts can ensure that appropriate provision is made for all types and severity of handicap.

The co-operative operates two basic forms of special provision for physically handicapped and hearing impaired pupils: special classes and a peripatetic teacher-consultant service. Before J T Cobb opened, the needs of such pupils were met in different ways. The physically handicapped were in a school which had become grossly overcrowded and which did not meet the conditions for unrestricted access to all areas of the building stipulated in the federal law. The hearing impaired received their schooling at three quite separate centres depending on their age. This necessitated their developing relationships with three different groups of hearing pupils before they were thirteen and presented difficulties for curriculum continuity.

The proposed new school embodied three broad aims: first, it was to be a barrier-free environment, with no part of the campus inaccessible to any pupil; secondly, whilst there were already local opportunities for severely handicapped pupils to attend regular classes after the age of twelve, J T Cobb was to integrate them from the start of official schooling; and thirdly it was to adopt a team-teaching approach.

The building provided lavish accommodation. One of its main features is the grouped open-plan teaching areas, with small rooms opening off them for quiet study, individual instruction and specialist support. The specialist teaching areas are in the centre of the school and such an arrangement provides almost ideal opportunities for educational integration both of children and of regular and special classroom teachers and specialist staff.

The school offers an extensive range of specialist research to provide the children with intensive support. The full-time staff consists of thirty-two 'regular' and special teachers, twenty other specialists including physiotherapists, occupational therapists, social workers, psychologists and an audiologist, and thirty-six teachers' aides. In addition the school has a half-time community co-ordinator, an ortho-paedic physician who holds clinics at the school several times each year, and visits from peripatetic teaching consultants.

Staff Preparation

Considerable efforts have been made to ensure that all staff are knowledgeable about the handicapping conditions in question, and that they hold attitudes conducive to the efficient practice of mainstreaming. All teaching staff were appointed before the school took in its first pupils. Potential employees had to fulfil a number of conditions, including some prior teaching experience, preferably some experience of team-teaching, and a desire to work with these particular handicapped pupils in a context of active mainstreaming. Special education staff, in addition, needed the appropriate qualification required by law.

However, some prior teaching experience coupled with the appropriate attitudes was not all that was required. It was recognised that regular teachers might need additional information about the particular handicaps. They all attended a 20-week inservice course, three hours per week, in advance of the school opening. This provided a general orientation toward handicap, with a specific grounding in physical and hearing handicap. Considerable use was made of expertise residing in the staff of the school, supplemented by other specialists. The school devised its own training programme for its teaching aides and training sessions were held weekly during school hours.

It is fully appreciated that knowledge about the educational consequences of handicapping conditions and about appropriate teaching or management techniques is constantly evolving. Accordingly, seven hours per term are put aside for some form of continuing 'professional development'. In addition, two 'floating' teachers, one for the regular teachers, one for the special education staff, are available on a day-a-week basis in order to free any member of staff from his or her teaching duties to engage in curriculum development, discussing a problem he or she might be experiencing, or visiting other educational establishments.

Admission of Handicapped Children

The school accepts handicapped children from two and a half years of age, and they may stay there until the age of 13. While the hearing impaired generally attend full-time from two and a half years, the preschool physically handicapped child is only likely to attend half-time initially. From six years upwards all handicapped pupils work the full school day.

The placement procedure typically commences with a hospital referral at around two years of age. Within 25 days a psychologist and nurse from the school visit the home to see the child for themselves. The former may carry out basic psychological assessment, while the nurse records the child's medical history. There follows a clinical evaluation at school involving either physio- and occupational therapists, or speech therapist and audiologist, depending upon which set of professionals is most relevant. Placement decisions are arrived at on the basis of the individual's need for educational assistance or specialist help being greater than could be met through the peripatetic service.

Handicapped pupils who attend the school are, therefore, all in need of intensive specialist treatment, be it educational, therapeutic, or a combination of the two. Many of the physically handicapped have severe physical impairment but the most severely multiply handicapped are placed elsewhere. Those pupils with impaired hearing have severe, even profound deafness. Only the hearing-impaired multiply handicapped child whose primary handicapping condition is other than deafness would be placed elsewhere.

If the staff agree that the child would benefit from attending the school, the next stage is for a formal EPPC (Education Planning and Placement Committee) meeting to be convened. This has two purposes; firstly to determine the primary disability, and secondly to identify the special education and/or related services necessary. School authorities maintain close contact with the home throughout the process, explaining parental rights as guaranteed under federal legislation, the EPPC and IEP (Individual Educational Programme) procedures. Parents are invited to attend all formal meetings. Once a child has commenced his or her schooling, then within a further 25 days a meeting of representatives of the various professional services involved is called to plan the detailed educational programme. School authorities are legally obliged to re-appraise this at least annually, and a full-time substitute teacher is made available each year so that school staff can be released to discuss programming matters. Parents have the right to request a new IEP at any time.

Meeting Special Needs

There is a definite orientation towards 'mainstreaming' whenever it is appropriate, but *not* just for the sake of being seen to uphold the integration principle. The hearing impaired are mostly provided for in self-contained classrooms with a maximum of four pupils per teacher. Integration for them tends to involve a whole group going into a regular class, accompanied by their teacher. Regular and special teachers either engage in team-teaching, or the special teacher functions as translator or individual supervisor of work. For the physically handicapped a rather different approach prevails. Some of them have few educational difficulties; their special needs may be primarily for physiotherapy and they may spend considerable time as members of a regular class with any special educational needs met by weekly (or occasionally twice weekly) visits from one of the two teacher-consultants employed by the co-operative. The teacher-consultants are each responsible for up to 25 pupils. They may work with the pupil in the regular classroom or, where there is already extensive integration, may withdraw the child for direct one-to-one teaching into one of the quiet rooms attached to each open-plan teaching area. The special needs of those physically handicapped pupils who are less extensively integrated are met by special education staff within the school and when they do join ordinary classes they are generally accompanied by a teaching aide. A videotape record is made twice yearly for all handicapped pupils. Typically they are put through a series of exercises by one therapist while other members of the team watch and note down their comments on the child's responses.

Handicapped pupils play as full a part in the life of the school as possible. They are included, as a matter of course, in the wide range of social and cultural activities that take place: school dinner, lunch and break-time activities, school plays and assemblies, thanksgiving activities, school outings, graduation ceremonies and so on. It undoubtedly helps that there are no physical obstacles to their getting around the school premises, but all members of staff, not just teachers, take every opportunity to develop an expectation for their active involvement in school life. Deliberate steps are taken to educate able-bodied and hearing pupils about handicap; they try out hearing aids, crutches and wheelchairs; and some ordinary pupils learn the rudiments of a manual system of communication. Handicapped pupils, for their part, are encouraged to talk openly about what it is to experience, for example, muscular dystrophy or to have seriously diminished hearing. While this may give the impression of a 'freakshow', in fact it is carried out quite naturally, and reflects the more open attitude toward handicap that the Americans adopt. Extensive use is also made of the 'buddy system' whereby ordinary pupils, chosen for their sensitive manner and sensible behaviour, are teamed with particular handicapped children whom it is felt might experience difficulty in developing relationships.

The school staff are well aware, then, of the benefits inherent in mainstreaming and the effort that is required to make it effective. The co-operative of school districts have also taken steps to avoid the pitfalls of integration; for example the teacher who fails to insist upon a sufficiently high standard of work, or neglects the specific preparation for post-school life which many handicapped pupils will need. One teacher-consultant has established weekly meetings for physically handicapped pupils which are held at the school. These are opportunities for the pupils to meet others suffering from similar physical conditions and to offer each other encouragement. There is also an attempt to compensate for areas of the children's experience which has been limited by their handicap and they may visit institutions in the local community such as the banks, library and post office.

What Happens After J T Cobb?

Bearing in mind the considerable upheaval hearing-impaired pupils have experienced at frequent intervals in their school careers in the past, placement at J T Cobb can offer them ten years or so of stability. For the physically handicapped the intention is, wherever possible, to transfer them back to their local elementary schools with the continued support of the peripatetic teacher-consultant. In the first three years of the school's life, three pupils had transferred back to their local elementary school. A further three had moved on to a junior high school close by, and three others, whose physical conditions had deteriorated, had moved to a more segregated type of provision. The school is undoubtedly successful, and very popular with parents. Ironically, one of the principal's greatest problems is to persuade parents that their child is no longer in need of the specialist facilities at J T Cobb, but may instead return to their local school.

48 AN INDIVIDUAL TIMETABLING SYSTEM

June Statham

The timetabling system of a large conventional comprehensive school is often regarded as a miraculous accomplishment. It is a task generally assigned to a wise and experienced member of staff who is capable of simultaneously bearing in mind all the considerations of classroom availability, setting, options, free-periods, part-time staff and team-teaching which may have to determine who is taught what, where and by whom. The idea of imposing on this hallowed ritual, the desire to provide some children with a special timetable all to themselves would cause some senior masters and mistresses to beat their breasts in despair. In the following pages we have attempted to write down the way in which Drayton Basic Studies department produces individual timetables for children with special needs. It cannot be read as a recipe but it does provide clues for others who may wish to achieve a similar aim.

The Basic Studies department at Drayton Comprehensive school in Banbury has attempted to put into practice what many of those involved in special education are currently preaching; the philosophy of meeting children's individual needs. When Jim Conway set up the department five years ago, he hoped it would offer a different kind of help to children with learning difficulties than that found in many remedial departments attached to secondary schools.

> We don't think simply of withdrawing kids from an existing time-table, but as starting afresh from their basic needs. We ought to be thinking whether they *need* to go into geography lessons, or whether we can offer them a better alternative; how much reading support do they actually *need*. If they're very slow, let's not be frightened to forget about pushing up their reading age six months and try to meet other, probably more important, needs instead.

The aim of meeting each child's needs has led the department to adopt a system of individual timetabling. Such a system has two distinct stages; first finding out each child's special needs, and secondly tyring to meet those needs within a comprehensive school with over a thousand pupils. The Basic Studies department has developed various strategies to help them at each stage.

As a start in identifying children's needs, Kim begins in February to visit all the feeder primary schools and to collect information from teachers, head teachers and educational psychologists on those children most likely to need help from the Basic Studies department when they arrive at the school in the following September. Wherever possible he also likes to talk to the children themselves. From this information he prepares timetabling notes for each child. In July the main school's timetable is completed and lists are available of pupils definitely selected to receive the support of Basic Studies, so Jim can then spend several weeks of his summer holiday drawing up a master timetable sheet with an individual breakdown for each pupil. The final stage is the production of a departmental timetable which includes all the individual timetables; about ninety of them in 1980/81.

These initial timetables are often substantially altered during the first year. Jim feels that 'You can only learn so much from pieces of paper. We do individual first-year timetables, but we don't always get them to accurately reflect needs because at the time they're constructed we don't really known the children.' After the children have had time to settle into their new school, pupils who have already been identified as having special needs in the area of literacy are tested using the department's own assessment system. Similar testing is carried out in the area of numeracy, and throughout the year informal assessments of progress are made. This assessment often leads to timetable changes. All other pupils in the first year are given a standardised reading comprehension test and a spelling test so that those who are likely to need less substantial reading and spelling help can be identified and timetabled into withdrawal reading and spelling groups.

Pupils in Basic Studies have a good deal of say over the content of their individual timetables. Jim feels that 'If you don't have the child's approval or fail to explain why certain timetabling decisions must be made, you are not going to get very far.' Regular monitoring of progress is obviously essential, as they spend different amounts of time in the department doing different subjects. The structured workcards used by the department for individual learning programmes in literacy and numeracy make such monitoring easier, as progress sheets can be drawn up for each child listing objectives to be met. The teacher signs the sheet when the objective is achieved, and can thus tell at a glance what stage each pupil has reached. A sheet headed 'timetable notes' is also completed for each Basic Studies pupil by his or her 'special' (pastoral) support tutor, in consultation with the pupil. The sheet has columns for comments from both teacher and child, and ends with a request to 'Please identify the special educational needs of the pupil and indicate how we might organise his/her timetable in order to meet these needs.' These 'timetable notes' help the tutor and pupil to focus on what is happening to the pupil in school, including mainstream lessons, and also help the head of department to create an appropriate individual timetable for the child in the following year.

Around Christmas in each child's third year, a full multidisciplinary re-assessment of their needs takes place in order to decide on their individual programme for the final two years. A booklet is sent out to all parents describing the various courses offered by the school to all fourth and fifth years, and intensive counselling and discussion takes place between Basic Studies teachers, pupils, their parents and other professionals to decide on the best courses for each child.

Having identified each child's special needs, the next stage involves the mechanics of trying to meet those needs within the organisational framework of the rest of the school. The difficulty of this task deters many people involved in special education who are otherwise committed to the notion of meeting special needs in an integrated setting. Jim accepts that some compromises will be inevitable, and he has drawn up a list of constraints which he needs to keep in mind when designing each child's individual timetable.

Some of these involve considerations which have to be built into the timetable in an order of priority. Top of the list is the timing of mainstream lessons which the child will be attending, as no special concessions are made to Basic Studies and their pupils' timetables have to be fitted around that of the main school. The department pursues a policy of integrating children into main school lessons wherever it is in the child's interests to do so. Several children from Basic Studies are allocated to each form in their year group. In the early years of the department the usual policy was to place two children in each main school form. It was felt that if there were many more than two pupils there would be a risk of their forming themselves into a separate group, possibly ostracised by the rest of the class, while having only one pupil in a form would have been too isolating. However, recently the extensive screening undertaken by the department in the first year means that more pupils are identified as having special needs, and so a larger group has been allocated to each of the eight or nine first year forms, with few problems so far. By the second year the numbers are down again, because few of these pupils have long-term learning difficulties. For many special needs pupils, though not all, a common core of lessons consisting of drama, music, PE, games, design, library (first year only) and art is shared with the main school up to the third year. Jim feels it is important that Basic Studies pupils take these lessons with their mainstream form. 'If they're doing music it has to be with their own form, not switching forms because that's not integration.' Those students who do follow this section of the curriculum find it takes up between a quarter and a third of their timetable, depending on which of these 'common core' lessons they attend — the decision is made individually for each pupil. In addition, pupils with a special aptitude or ability may attend mainstream lessons in subjects like mathematics, physical science or biology. 'We operate on the basis of a continuum of special needs, whereby a pupil will attend as many mainstream lessons as offer him educational value and help satisfy his needs.'

The second and third constraints on Jim's list are also linked to the fixed points of the timetable in the rest of the school. Some Basic Studies staff also teach in the main school, and although their teaching load is small (Jim takes science classes, another teacher a few maths lessons, others some woodwork, games or history), this commitment has to be timetabled in at an early stage. So do the fourth and fifth year options offered in the main school which Basic Studies pupils might join. Although a lot of the options listed in the booklet taken home by all third years will not be practicable for many pupils using the Basic Studies department, most of them nevertheless join in at least some of the main school options.

Having taken account of the limits imposed on timetabling by the organisation of the timetable in the main school, Jim then turns to the curriculum offered by the Basic Studies department to see what they can add to each child's individual timetable to best suit that child's needs. The Basic Studies curriculum aims to 'broaden and balance' that in the main school. The school is organised so that each day is divided into twenty-minute 'modules', ten in the morning and four in the afternoon, and the department offers literacy (reading and writing), maths, social studies, science, domestic science, woodwork, art, craft, swimming and gardening, plus a two-year Leavers Programme and handwriting for first and second years ('It sounds old-fashioned but it's something at which slow learners can achieve success, and it's a useful skill when writing formal letters like job applications.') Some of these subjects are also taken by Basic Studies pupils with their mainstream forms, but Jim feels that extra work can be useful in certain areas of the curriculum where pupils can achieve some success, or where they may need extra teaching to help them keep up with their mainstream forms.

Within the Basic Studies department too there are areas that have to be considered before others. The Leavers Programme for fourth and fifth years is one example, because it is necessary to timetable certain teachers to teach specialist parts of the course like DIY, Health Education and the Practicalities of Independence. Swimming is another, because the pool can only be used at certain times. Next come subjects which are taught in year-groups, since the individual timetabling system means that it is often difficult to get pupils together as a group. At present handwriting, science, social studies and tutor-time are organised in year groups, while English and maths are organised on a totally individual basis. The department is in the process of appointing a new member of staff to develop individual programmes in social studies.

The next criterion is to obtain a balance in each pupil's timetable, so that they get between ten and twelve modules of reading/writing and eight to ten modules of maths each week, spread out over the week.

Sometimes a kid may get English twice a day and complain bitterly, but there's no way of avoiding it. We wring our hands about it, but then we think that they're getting a far better deal than three hours of remedial English followed by withdrawal for more English during French lessons, which is what they'd be getting in a lot of places.

Subjects needing large blocks of time, like domestic science and woodwork, are timetabled next, followed by those like art and gardening which are relatively easy to timetable as they are taken in mixed year groups. Jim hopes that the result is an individual programme for each pupil using the Basic Studies department, fitted to his or her needs and abilities as far as possible. A typical timetable is given below for a pupil whose learning difficulties are towards the severe end of the 'moderate to severe' continuum. Shaded lessons are taken in the main school.

Creating an individual timetable for each pupil is a time consuming task but Jim Conway is convinced of its importance:

It would be far easier from an organisational point of view to take the bottom fifteen to twenty kids and put them in a remedial class.

Figure 1: Sample Timetable for a Pupil with Moderate to Severe Learning Difficulties

MODULE:	1	2	3	4	5	6	7	8	9	10	11	12	13	14	15	16	17	18	19
MONDAY	Craft		English		Art			Rural Studies		TV	Club				Music			Maths	
TUESDAY	W/W / Craft			Music	Maths		BREAK	RE	English			LUNCH			Social Studies		English		
WEDNESDAY	Social Studies			Music	W/W Craft			Maths		English					Domestic Science				
THURSDAY	Assembly Design							English		Drama					Maths		Swimming		
FRIDAY	Games		Art					Form period		W/W Craft						PE	Social Studies		

But you wouldn't meet their needs, and you would create a clearly defined group to be identified and ostracised by the rest of the school. We've tried to avoid that. We don't draw any distinctions between ESN and remedial kids, they all need some form of special help which we're trying to give on an individual basis.

Its success also depends on the support and co-operation of the head of Drayton School, on the department's ability to argue for a high staffing level, and on the willingness of teachers to put in time and effort to making the system work. The Basic Studies staff hold a curriculum development meeting after school every Wednesday where they discuss the curricula offered by the department and if necessary make changes to individual pupils' timetables.

The complexities of the timetabling system do baffle some of the pupils; many of them would have difficulty following an ordinary timetable. It is hardly surprising that there is a steady stream of pupils knocking on the staffroom door to enquire where they should be going next, but the staff are prepared to give this level of support. In Jim's words, 'Individual timetables can be an organisational nightmare. I wouldn't accept this form of organisation unless I was absolutely certain that it was the best way to cater for the educational needs of the pupils with learning difficulties within our school.'

49 FOUR HANDICAPPED TEENAGERS IN TRANSITION

John Morton

In the summer of 1979 John Morton, head of a day ESN(S) school, spent a fortnight living with four mentally handicapped adolescents from the Leavers Group at his school, observing how they coped, living in an ordinary house where the adults involved (himself and an assistant observer) adopted a strategy of 'minimum intervention'. By withdrawing much of the help and support the teenagers were used to receiving he hoped to find out how autonomous they could be, and how effectively they had been prepared for an independent life by their homes and school. Here he gives an account of a typical day during the project, preceded by a description of the four teenagers. All four had Down's Syndrome, but their personalities and abilities differed greatly.

The Characters

Tony lives at the end of a Georgian terrace near the city centre, on the edge of a common. His home is comfortable, lived in, and relaxing. His parents and siblings (he is the youngest of four children) seem to have accepted Tony's handicap naturally and his sisters, brother and their friends include Tony in many of their activities. The family are well established in the neighbourhood, and Tony has many friends and acquaintances. He is often to be seen with his characteristic gait and modern teenage casual clothes, shopping bag in hand, crossing the common alone to go to the shops. He can manage the minor roads involved in this expedition and uses a controlled crossing to go to the swimming baths nearly every day in the summer. In other directions his independence is curtailed by the volume of traffic in the city centre.

The first contact with Tony can be slightly daunting as he approaches with a vigorous, gangling and uncoordinated gait, head

398

thrust forward, bespectacled, and his pronounced mongolian features very evident. His tongue often lolls out if he is concentrating or is taken by surprise, although he is quite capable of keeping it in if he is conscious of it. Reservations are quickly dispelled, however, as he has a friendly manner coupled with a diffidence suggesting that he is anxious to weigh up social situations and do the right thing if possible. He has a considerable speech defect that is hard for strangers to understand, particularly if the context is not evident. He is uninhibited about his speech unless he is asked to repeat something, when he becomes self-conscious and silent.

Records of pop music are Tony's great interest. He owns about one hundred, which he has chosen himself; he looks after them with care and is always saving for more. He has his own record player in his room and spends a lot of time playing records. He does not watch television very much and is selective about what he sees, enjoying war films, space fiction, and films about pop stars. He joins in some social viewing with the family. He can read simple material, and is proficient enough to read comics and magazines in comic form. His mother spoke highly of Tony's ability and willingness to help with domestic tasks about the home. He was about to leave for an interview for a place on a two-year training scheme in agriculture and horticulture, but she had reservations about this and wondered whether he was old and mature enough to go, although he is beginning to show signs of being ready to leave home. Also he is tending to lack company more and more as his siblings are less often at home and he particularly enjoyed his recent stay in the school hostel. She considers that Tony has developed to near his potential, and does not see him as being able to solve problems or deal with unexpected emergencies. She also has reservations about group homes without residential staff for Tony, both now and in the future, but she agreed that he is ready to leave home now, in many respects, and would expect him to do so before long although she would 'miss him about the house'.

Carol, whose seventeenth birthday fell halfway through the project, gives an overall impression of roundness. Her head is round and her short hair follows its contours; her hair and curved fringe making a circular setting for her face. Her glasses are also round. Her short body is round too, certainly in circumference, but seemingly in the other dimensions also. She is invariably neat, clean and tidy, wearing patterned dresses, trousers and jerseys, or tee-shirts in plain primary colours.

Carol is not shy or inhibited about speaking to strangers. She is aware of her considerable speech defect but seems to have adapted to it by using telegrammatic speech, concentrating on the key words in her gruff, rough-edged voice. She is quite adept at saying things another way round, or using synonyms, if she is not understood. She has a strong, forthright personality and enjoys managing other people and telling them what to do.

Carol lives with her parents in a neat spacious bungalow on seven acres of market garden midway between two villages, and about a mile from each. Her eldest brother has left home, and the next one is out for much of the time, so Carol has little company other than her parents. They have accepted her handicap realistically and evolved a way of life that is safe and suitable for Carol, but which is not very adventurous. Carol helps about the home and is able and knowledgeable about household chores, but Mrs King felt she had not encouraged Carol to develop as much independence as she might have done.

Carol's mobility and independence is curtailed by the heavy traffic on the busy country lane without pavements, and this means that she can never go out alone. She enjoys watching television and has her own radio on which she likes to play pop music. Carol enjoys simple sports, has a natural eye for ball games and has a type of golf and a swing-ball in the garden. She also helps her mother in the house and with shopping, and her father in the market garden.

Carol's parents appeared to be taking her imminent transfer to the adult training centre in their stride, and were mainly concerned about dates and buses. They have not thought seriously about Carol leaving home, and appear to assume that she will live with them for the foreseeable future.

Colin is very small. He often wears black shoes (size 2!), grey trousers and a blazer and, with his black spectacles, gives the impression of a man in miniature, although his face is rosy, smiling and boyish. He is outgoing and friendly when approached, but seems to prefer to be left to himself. His speech defect is slight, and he is easy to understand. He can be quite loquacious, aping adult gossip and repeating the ends of sentences in a garrulous way. Sometimes he takes off in a flight of verbal fantasy, often based on television programmes and usually involving war. He lives with his parents in a small, neat, Edwardian terrace house a mile or so from the city centre. His two elder brothers have left home.

Colin does very little to help in the house. He will wash up efficiently, 'when he is in the right mood', Mrs North said, but she does not encourage him to help in the kitchen if he does not want to. She has never expected Colin to help with meal preparation and has always kept him out of the way. Mrs North rationalises this by saying that the kitchen is a dangerous place, but admits that she may have repressed and over-protected Colin. She mentioned another handicapped boy who is allowed to cook, and the family eat whatever is produced! Mrs North obviously has high standards and perhaps considers that Colin would not manage things properly. I suspect that she does not expect her menfolk to help with any of the household chores that are considered, traditionally, to be the woman's province. Colin does not use reading skills at home, but he does study wrapping papers, and recognises products by colour and pictures.

Television takes up a lot of his time; he likes most programmes and happily watches what his mother describes as 'intelligent' programmes — that is current affairs or documentaries — if his parents are watching, and she feels guilty that he watches so much. I pressed her to say what else he does and he apparently enjoys a day, or a holiday, by the seaside. He also goes shopping with his mother although it sounded as though neither enjoyed the trip very much. Mrs North spoke of early problems, and her and her husband's lack of knowledge of Down's Syndrome. They built a high fence round the garden, but Colin tried to run away continually between the ages of four to eleven. She thinks now that he was bored and craved company. After he was eleven, or so, she let him go and play with the other children, who sometimes took him to the park and 'were quite good with him'. There are no children or young people about in the immediate neighbourhood now, so Colin lacks company.

Mrs North thinks that he is ready for a group home or hostel, as it would give him company. But she would not like him to go too far away, and wouldn't be happy unless there were resident staff. Colin used to go out by himself to the corner shop but now it is closed, and his mother thinks that he probably knows the environment round the school better than round his home. I gathered that he rarely goes out, and then only when his mother takes him.

Arthur has a puckish, quizzical look as he peers sideways from under a straight fringe; his slanting eyes, and ears exposed by a short hair-cut, make him look slightly startled. He is short but broad shouldered and powerful looking, although his mottled mauve and pink colour is evidence of a serious heart condition. Any physical exertion, even walking or slight emotional stress, causes breathlessness, the heightening of colour, and the need for an immediate rest. This necessarily curtails many of Arthur's activities. He wears neat and conventional casual clothes, and wears glasses for watching television or for close work. He has a bad speech defect and is hard to understand unless the context can be grasped; there tends to be a pause almost a stutter, before he speaks, and then all the words pour out rapidly.

The family live in a large, well-appointed Georgian house, set in several acres on the edge of a village. Arthur's parents are particularly concerned about him at present. His heart always gives cause for concern, but there is worry too about his transfer to the adult training centre, and the question of his leaving home to take up a residential placement. As Arthur, too, is worried by the pending changes in his life, his parents invited me to call when he was away, so as not to upset him. As two older sisters have left home, there is little company for Arthur except his parents, who seem very involved with work and social life. He lives in a rich and spacious environment, but seems cut off by the isolated position on the edge of the village, and appears not to leave the grounds unaccompanied. Arthur attempts several domestic tasks at home, but some things are not expected of him. His mother, like Mrs North, seems to have a traditional view of which jobs are the province of the woman of the house. I gained the impression that Mr Richmond mollycoddles Arthur to some extent, and has various routines like tucking him up last thing at night, although his mother seems to take responsibility for his physical care, and has a brisk and positive approach to managing Arthur. He often gets his own breakfast, after which (if it is not a school day) he enjoys a walk round the grounds. He has his own record player in his room and enjoys playing his record collection. He likes television but is selective about what he watches. He enjoys looking at football books, painting and colouring, playing with Lego, educational toys and toy cars. Arthur is helpful in the garden and especially enjoys a bonfire, but physical activity is very much hampered by his heart condition. He is very fond of animals.

Mr and Mrs Richmond think that Arthur should begin to make a break with home, recognising his need for more companionship with others of his own age. Thus they have already visited a local authority hostel and are considering the possibility of a village community placement.

The Project

The council provided a small terraced house on an estate near to the school for the two weeks of the project and I furnished it with borrowed furniture and crockery to a basic youth hostel standard. On Sunday afternoon I collected Colin and Tony from their homes, and we arrived at No. 27 Johnson Road at 5 p.m. Malcolm, my assistant observer, arrived a few minutes later.

I had already decided where everyone should sleep. Carol showed considerable interest in the boys and indicated that she would like to share a room with Tony. Somewhat taken aback, I naively suggested that people of opposite sexes do not sleep together unless they are married. 'They do', said Carol, but accepted her appointed room. Although independence, decision making and autonomy were to be encouraged I considered that sexual experimentation was not appropriate to the project. Indeed, Tony's mother, possibly the most liberal minded of the four about such matters, had warned me about 'how fond the boys are of Carol'. Consequently I directed Carol to a single room, Colin to another, while Tony and Arthur shared.

Carol and Arthur arrived with their parents; Carol at 5.45 p.m. and Arthur at 6.30 p.m. Arthur was feeling unwell so lay on the sofa; the others dashed about exploring the house, organising their rooms and making tea.

The project was not, ostensibly, concerned with a study of language used by mentally handicapped people, but from the first there was a remarkable amount of talk. The quality of language is described and quoted later in this account, but all activities should be imagined as taking place against a background of almost incessant chatter, especially during the first week; there were a few more pauses during the second week.

Arthur and Colin spent each weekday at the adult training centre, leaving for their bus at 8.10 a.m. and returing at about 4.30 p.m. Carol and Tony left for school at 8.55 a.m. and returned at 4.00 p.m. On most evenings we spent an hour swimming in the warm pool at Tony and Carol's school.

As well as trying to find out how independent such handicapped people could be, I also want to give a convincing impression of what it was like to live with the teenagers, and to show them as people in their own right, with physical, emotional and social needs, skills and abilities. The description of one specific day could not be representative of the whole project, but details of all twelve days would be repetitive.

Therefore I have taken self-contained episodes, most of which occurred in more or less the same form on several occasions, and put them together chronologically as though they occurred on a single day. The writer and the assistant observer are referred to as JM and M respectively in the account that follows.

A Typical Day

The first sign of life is M letting himself into the house at 7.20 a.m. He wakes Colin, Arthur and myself and makes a cup of tea. I hurriedly dress and clear my bedclothes from the sitting room and give Arthur and Colin another call. They need to leave the house by 8.10 a.m. to catch their bus to the adult training centre so there is not time to allow them to go at their own speed. Tony wakes and gets up quickly; he appears lively and alert, even though he repeats several times 'I'm tired.' Tony says 'good morning, Malcolm, good morning Morton'. We return the compliment.

M: 'Tea's made.'

Tony pours himself a cup. Carol can be heard upstairs washing in the bathroom. She is talking almost continuously to herself. Not everything she says can be heard but she seems to be talking herself through the washing operation and in between fantasising about her birthday.

Carol: 'Wash face next. Oh pie! Where's soap gone? My birthday
            Thursday — I'll have a game and records, lots of records and
            birthday cake.'
Tony: Says 'hullo' to each of us several times and says 'poor Mr
            Morton' a few times.

When I ask 'why poor Mr Morton?' he says 'because you're old'. Pause for tea-drinking.

Tony (briskly): 'Right! Breakfast!'

Arthur comes down and says 'hullo' or 'good morning' to everyone.

Tony: 'Sit down and wait for toast.'

Tony lights grill. (We have borrowed a rather old calor gas stove with a waist-level grill set far back. I tried to teach the group how to light this with a match, but unsuccessfully. They were not able to manage the skills needed to get the match well alight, put down the box, turn on the gas tap, turn the burning match to a vertical position and move it right under the grill. They were well aware of the danger of burns from the match but not of the possible result of allowing unlit gas to escape for a long period, so an automatic gas lighter was acquired which required a squeezing action from the thumb and correct positioning near to the gas jets. This still posed problems although the four could all manage it by the end of the project.)

We wait nervously as we hear the lighter ticking, in the knowledge that an interval of more than a few seconds will produce a minor explosion. However, Tony's cry of 'I've done it; I'm genius!' sets our minds at rest.

Tony puts four slices of bread onto the grill rack and places the rack under the grill. He then puts cereal, sugar, butter, four plates, bowls, knives, spoons, marmalade and honey on the table, glancing at the toast from time to time. Wisps of smoke emerge from the cooker, clear evidence that some action is needed. M and I resist the temptation to intervene. Tony pulls out the rack, stares at the toast and turns some pieces over and some round. The end result is that the toast is mainly black or white with not much of it the required shade of brown. Tony seems reasonably satisfied and puts it on the table.

Colin comes down and everyone says 'good morning'. He wanders about with his hands in his pockets.

JM: 'Aren't you hungry? We've got to go in a minute.'
Colin: Sits down and says 'just toast, Green'.
Tony: 'You china'.

Carol appears, very neat and tidy and in a clean dress. 'Good mornings' all round.

Colin: 'Hello, Carol.'

Carol looks at the piece of toast she has been allocated by Tony.

Carol: 'I don't like it black. Clean it off.'

Seeing her opportunity she exchanges it with Arthur's piece.

Arthur: 'Don't want it black.'
Carol: 'Eat it up.'
Carol: 'Where's my tea?'
Tony: 'Pour it yourself.' She does.

Tony helps himself to cornflakes.

Carol: 'Don't take all of it.' (cornflakes)

Carol helps herself to cornflakes and picks up the milk jug. It is empty.

Carol: 'It's all gone now!'
Tony: 'Look in the fridge.'

Carol either does not hear or disregards the suggestion.

Carol: 'Who took it all?'
Arthur: 'Colin.'
Carol, vehemently: 'Tomorrow I want milk. Right?'

Colin guiltily pours some back into the jug. M points out that there is a full carton in the fridge. Carol cannot open the carton so she passes it to Tony.

Carol: 'Pie!'
Tony: 'Don't say that, Chinese woman.'
Colin: 'Sausage.'

Tony manages to open the carton.

JM: 'What shall we eat for supper?'
Tony: 'Turkey.'
Carol: 'Roast chicken.'
JM: 'Do you know how to cook it?'
Carol: 'Light the oven.' Pause.

There are no more ideas about how to cook chicken or turkey so I suggest that they choose something they have cooked before.

Tony: 'Beefburgers. We haven't had them for a long time.'
Colin: 'And peas.'

Carol: 'And 'tatoes'. (We have instant mashed potato in stock.)

Prompted by M and me it is established that a few other items are required. I realise that time is passing and urge Colin and Arthur to finish their toast.

JM: 'We've got to go for the bus in a minute.'
Tony: 'Come on, you two boys.'
8.10 a.m.   Colin says 'good-bye' to everyone. Arthur wanders out with-
              out speaking. We start walking together to Colin and
              Arthur's pick-up point, which is some three hundred yards
              away. Arthur quickly drops to twenty paces behind. Colin
              and I walk very slowly and Arthur follows, but the gap does
              not widen. There is only one road to cross, a fairly busy
              one at 8.13 a.m., and near a corner, which complicates the
              road crossing procedure. I arrive there with Colin, he looks
              both ways, talking to himself through the operation. Having
              watched one or two cars pass he waits for a cyclist approach-
              ing from a long way down the road. He could have crossed
              easily before the cyclist, but preferred to be cautious. Colin
              goes on ahead to the bus stop. Arthur is seemingly prepared
              to walk straight across the road, presumably reckoning that
              I will stop him if it is not clear. I suggest that he looks both
              ways, and decides for himself when to cross. He does, also
              being rather cautious. I leave Arthur to join Colin by the
              bus stop and retreat up the road, out of sight, to make cer-
              tain they get on the bus. They can be seen both uncon-
              cernedly sitting on the pavement at the head of the queue
              of a dozen or so people. After a few minutes the bus arrives
              and they board it.
8.25 a.m.   back at the house. Tony is washing up while Carol is up-
              stairs cleaning her teeth and tidying her bedroom. M and I
              have breakfast. Carol and Tony join us after a few minutes.
Carol: 'Make list.'

I point at the items we had decided to buy. Carol and Tony can read most of them when they help each other. Carol draws small pictures by each word and can then read the list without making any mistakes.

8.50 a.m.
Carol: 'Get a move on − going to school.'

Carol thinks to bring a bag for the shopping, and both have their swimming things which they will be needing at school.

The walk to school is about one mile. I escort them for less than half the distance and see them across the one busy road. I am confident that they can cross the road safely alone but prefer to supervise the operation as there is a large volume of traffic at 9 a.m. There is also the further complication of road works during almost the whole of the project. I wait for them to tell me when the road is clear and, like Colin and Arthur, they are very cautious and consequently have a long wait. The road has a traffic island providing a refuge half way across, but traffic approaching from either direction will prevent them setting off. They do not have this problem on the second half as traffic from the right is passing behind them and they do not take it into consideration. I remind them to wait for me after school, without crossing the road if I am late. We exchange good-byes and they depart.

3.45 p.m.   I meet Carol and Tony who appear through crowds of comprehensive school children making their way home. I hear one of them saying to his friend, as a tease and indicating Carol and Tony, 'There's your bruvvers.' Apart from this Carol and Tony attract a few stares but otherwise no attention. We cross the road to the supermarket, Carol produces the list and I ask how much money they will need. Tony counts the items and says 'ten'.

Carol: '£5' – whether an inspired guess or not, this is about right.

I tell them that I have to do some shopping of my own, and some twenty minutes later I go into the supermarket to see how they are managing. They are queuing at the check-out and do not see me. When they are near the end of the queue Carol notices that one of the coca-cola tins they have selected has a sticky top. She sends Tony back to change it, and is able to explain this to the assistant at the cash desk. They have succeeded in obtaining all the items on the list.

JM: 'Did anyone help you?'
Carol: 'Yes, a man did.'
Tony: 'And a lady.'

On the way home a teenage girl in one of the gardens in our road smiles at them. There is a general exchange of 'hullos' and 'what's your name?' but no more conversation. As we approach our house we see Colin,

Arthur and M coming from the opposite direction. There is great pleasure expressed by Colin and Carol and Tony at the reunion. Everyone
piles into the house, which feels very crowded with six people milling
about. There are a lot of jocular remarks:

Carol: 'Out of the way, the way, big bum.'
Tony: 'Same to you, Chinese woman.'
Arthur: 'Hey! Stop that!'

(Carol soon removes herself from the scene in the kitchen and goes
upstairs to change from her neat dress into her customary informal
evening wear of tee-shirt and trousers.)
    Colin looks at the shopping with interest and anticipation. He says
'27 foods', rather illogically.

JM: 'What are you going to do with them?'
Colin: 'Put them in the fridge.'

He puts everything away, making an appropriate division between
items for the fridge and larder.
    Carol comes downstairs, and having rinsed her own and Tony's
swimming things, hangs them in the airing cupboard.

4.35 p.m.   Relative and temporary quiet descends as everyone gathers
             in the sitting room. I am privately hoping that someone
             will decide to make a cup of tea.
5.00 p.m.   Arthur gets out the record player and sets it up. He chooses
             records and puts them on; the others make no comment
             about Arthur's choice, nor do they make suggestions them-
             selves. The record player is on the floor; Arthur kneels in
             front, knees almost touching the box, head bent over the
             record. Tony and Carol are in identical positions to left and
             right of him. Colin sits in a chair a short distance away,
             occasionally getting up to dance in a desultory way.
5.30 p.m.   The jangle of an ice-cream van's chimes cuts across the pop
             music. Tony leaps up.
Tony: 'Don't panic! Don't panic! Keep calm! I've got money.'

He rushes upstairs to get his purse. There is no sign of panic from
anyone except Tony. He rushes down, asks M and me if we would
like an ice-cream; we decline. He departs into the street, the others

following more sedately.

Relative quiet descends again as they lick. Arthurs dabs nose and chin with ice-cream; this caused some amusement the first time he did it, but this being the third time no interest is shown.

The sight of them all refreshing themselves with ice-cream is too much for me so I go to make a cup of tea. I return with a cup for myself and one for Malcolm.

Carol: 'Where's mine?'

JM: 'There's plenty in the pot; go and help yourself.'

In spite of my example of pouring cups only for Malcolm and myself, Tony says 'Who wants tea?' Arthur and Colin ask for milk. Tony goes to the kitchen with Arthur and they bring back two teas and two milks. As they finish drinking, Arthur surreptitiously tries to remove Carol's slipper and tickle her foot; this starts a general episode of tickling, attempts to remove one another's shoes and wrestling on the floor. Colin goes up to M, pats him on the head and strokes his beard.

Colin: 'He's like a hairy gorilla.'

A few minutes later he comes up behind me and moves my ears from behind.

Colin: 'Here's an elephant with big ears!'

The general romping subsides. There are a few minutes of quiet.

Carol: 'Let's go swimming today.'

Everyone agrees but no action is taken. Arthur sets about putting on another record.

JM, intervening: 'Do you want to swim this evening or listen to
                 records?'

They agree they want to swim. Carol goes and gets everyone's swimming things, and standing at the sitting room door she throws them across the room to their owners.

We all go by car to the Rees Thomas School swimming pool, which is not normally in use around 6 p.m. There is some rivalry over who should sit in the front of the car. Tony gets there first and Arthur tries to remove him by ordering him into the back. Tony doesn't move so Arthur gives up the struggle.

When we arrive at the pool, Arthur disappears to change in the boys' toilet area. Carol strips off quickly, unconcernedly exposing her well-developed female figure, and the rest of us go through to change in the pool area.

We play a simple team ball game in the water, involving throwing, catching and tackling. Arthur enjoys the game but is rather nervous, so stays near the edge and does not take a full part. Colin, also, partly because he is so short, finds it difficult to participate fully. Tony, apparently not concerned about the competitive nature of the game, sends the ball either way indiscriminately, thus incurring some good-natured annoyance from his team. Carol is enthusiastic and skilful at catching and throwing just outside her opponent's reach. Eventually, after thirty minutes or so, everyone tires of the game. Carol obtains a hoop and encourages people to swim through it. She gets annoyed and sulks when everyone else decides to practice individual swimming. Carol eventually bullies the rest of us into taking turns at going through the hoop. She is good at presenting a task that is commensurate with each person's swimming ability. After an hour or so in the water we return to the house.

We all establish ourselves in the sitting room, after having put our swimming things in the airing cupboard. Arthur and Colin leave theirs in soggy heaps while the rest of us make some attempt to hang them out.

JM: 'Who's going to cook?'

Tony, Arthur and Carol volunteer. Arthur opts for doing the beef-burgers, apparently the most prestigious job, Carol frozen peas and Smash, Tony the Instant Whip.

All go into the kitchen leaving Colin looking at a newspaper. The following is a verbatim transcription of a tape-recording made while the cooking was in progress. The scene opens with Arthur struggling with the beefburger pack and Carol trying to open the frozen peas; Tony is hovering in the background.

Carol: 'I'll do it for you Richie (Arthur's nickname); come here, let me have a go.' She tears at the pack. 'Here, look here, Richie!' She opens the pack and Arthur puts them on the grill pan.

Tony: 'What do I do now? I'm stuck.' He wants to know how to deal with this Instant Whip.

Carol: 'You nana!' Admonishing Arthur for not being able to open the beefburgers.

Carol: 'Oh no! Got to do peas now. Get scissors. Cut it'.

She wants scissors to open the pea packet.

Carol: 'Get scissors and cut it, Mr. Morton?'

Carol (more insistent): 'Scissors please — nick, nick, nick, nick'.

She mimes using scissors while making an appropriate noise.

Tony: 'I'll try and find scissors, Carol.'

He rummages through the drawer containing kitchen implements and produces a fish-slice.

Carol: 'Not *that* — choc-ice!'

Tony: 'You old chicken-face. Clumsy.'

Arthur: 'You're stupid, Morton.'

I was unaware of doing anything at all, stupid or otherwise. Tony produces a potato masher from the drawer.

Carol: 'Mash.'

Arthur: 'No, not scissors — masher — mash, mash, mash.'

He demonstrates how it should be used.

Carol: 'Goody — oh choc-ice!'

Arthur is meanwhile trying to open another packet of beefburgers.

Tony: 'I'll do that, Richie.'

Arthur: 'Oh' (an indecipherable word follows).

Carol: 'Richie, move up.'

Arthur, protesting as Carol moves in to take over the beefburgers' department: 'I'm this cook.'

Tony, trying to attract attention: 'Mr Morton'.

Carol: 'Ya, ya, ya' (tussling with beefburgers) 'I can't do it, Mr. Morton.'

Tony, resignedly in the background: 'Oh dear. Instant Whip.'

JM to Tony: 'Right! Wait a minute.'

Tony: 'Yes, dearie.'

Arthur,   still trying gain control of the beefburgers, 'Me!'

Carol giggles.

JM to Tony, referring to the Instant Whip: 'You can make that in a minute. You can make it a bit later. You can rest now.'

In the meanwhile Carol has opened the pea packet with her teeth.

Carol: 'Come'. Trying to persuade the lump of frozen peas out into the saucepan.

Carol: 'Hey! How many peas do you want?'

Carol: 'How many? More than that?'

JM: 'How many do you think?'

Tony: 'We want five.'

He probably means enough for five people.

JM: 'Oh, do them all.'

Carol: 'All of it? Right!'

JM: 'We can eat them up tomorrow.'

Pause − the only pause in this language sample, filled with the rattle of peas into the pan.

Carol: 'Parsnips' (used as an ejaculation)

Arthur: 'You're parsnips.'

Tony: 'Can't eat them up tomorrow.' (He is referring to my last remark.)

JM: 'What did you say, Tony?'

Tony: 'Birthday tea tomorrow'.

Carol: 'I'll have some tomorrow'.

JM: 'Birthday tea tomorrow?' (trying to disengage from the action of the moment and look ahead) 'Yes'.

Tony: 'Yes.'

Carol, shouting: 'BIRTHDAY!'
Tony sings a whole verse of 'Happy Birthday' to You', Carol giggles.
Arthur: 'Shut up, Tony, that's silly.'
Carol: 'Take this over puck.'

She means move the beefburgers out of the way.

Carol: 'Let me do the peas. Lay the table. Out of the way, bur-
          gers.'
Arthur: 'Mind the burgers.'
Carol: 'Excuse me. Oh gravy!'
Tony: 'Oh monster!'
Carol, to me, as I am standing between her and the sink: 'Can I have
          some water for peas?'
Carol: 'Cold or hot water?'
Tony: 'Cold.'
Arthur: 'Hot.'
Carol runs water, 'whoa!' — she has enough.
Carol: 'Bum'
Arthur: 'Knickers'
Tony: 'Twist'
Arthur: 'Hog'
Carol: 'Chicken'
Arthur: 'Hedgehog'
Tony: 'Knickers-a-twist'
Carol: 'Why?'
Tony: (an indecipherable sentence in which he is probably talking
          about slippers)
Carol: 'I'll get yours. Stay there, I'll get your slippers.'
Tony: 'I'm too tired to slippers on. I want to go to sleep.'
Carol: 'Oh choc-ice! Oh beefburgers!'

Carol serves up the food with considerable concentration and very
fairly. Arthur gets a sliced loaf from the cupboard takes three slices and
puts them by his plate. He puts four slices on his lap for later. I suggest
he should leave the bread in the pack until he needs it.

M and I take our food, which we brought in for ourselves, into the
sitting room. There is not room for six in the little dining alcove, and
it is also unrealistic to expect our group to cook for six.

First there is a lull, and then quiet conversation.

Colin (having evidently enjoyed his meal): 'Good God, I needed that!'

They wander through into the sitting room and sit down in post-prandial peace and relaxation. No one has shown any interest in cleaning or washing up.

JM: 'Who's going to do the washing up?'
Arthur: 'I did the cooking.'
Carol (to me): 'Tell Tony and Colin to do it.' Vehemently, to the others, 'I take the orders here!'
Tony offers to do it; all volunteer to help him but he says he is happy to do it alone.

He carries all the dirty crockery to the sink, washes each item thoroughly with concentration, and places it slowly and methodically on the rack. When all the washing-up is finished he takes a tea towel and with some concentration and measured, careful movement, dries everything and puts it all away in the correct places. He then wipes the table and work surfaces, letting the crumbs fall to the floor. The job is solemnly, slowly and excellently done, although the sweeping of the floor and wiping the sink are disregarded.

Tony joins the rest in the sitting room. No one seems inclined to do anything.

Tony: 'Why don't we play records? Don't want to do nothing.'

No one moves. Five minutes later Carol gets the record player and Arthur helps her to set it up. They discuss which records to play and Carol puts them on. Carol and Arthur assume the characteristic pose, kneeling by the record player. Colin is stretched out on the sofa, apparently tired. Tony alternates between dancing and listening in an armchair.

Carol: 'What about a cup of coffee?'

No action.

9.45 p.m. Colin is almost asleep.
JM: 'You know you can go to bed if you want to, Colin.'

He stumbles upstairs, saying goodnight.

JM (aware that it is late and that Arthur, in particular, has problems in getting up and off to the bus by 8.10): 'Two more records and then it's bedtime.'

They play only one record.

Tony: 'I must tidy up this mess.'

He carefully collects his own records. Carol picks up hers and puts away the record player.

They sit around, apparently unable to take the decision by themselves to go to bed. I change the sofa into a bed, and say 'I'm tired.' They take the hint and go up.

I make a coffee for myself. Tony wanders down and seeing the coffee makes himself a cup.

Carol (calling from upstairs): 'Where's Tony?'
Tony: 'I'm downstairs drinking coffee.'
Carol (loudly): 'Coffee everybody, downstairs.'

She tries to wake Colin up, unsuccessfully.

Carol and Arthur come down, Arthur wearing an anorak over his vest and pants. They make their own coffee.

9.50 p.m.   Arthur goes up to bed. Tony and Carol wash the cups.
Carol: 'Stay here Saturday too.'
Tony: 'Oh yes, I forgot.'

They seem pleased.

Tony (to JM): 'Switch the light off when you've finished.'

They go up.

50 BLUEPRINT FOR INCREASING INTEGRATION IN AN INFANT SCHOOL

Sylvia Pollock

When Sylvia Pollock was taking an advanced diploma in special education she was asked as part of her continuous assessment to produce an essay describing the way the primary school in which she taught might be changed to permit a greater integration of children with special needs. If integration schemes are to be realistic then they have to be devised by the people who will implement them. In the following account, she assesses the work done in her school with 'maladjusted' and 'non-communicating' children and the improvements that might be made in incorporating them into the general life of her school.

I work in a local education authority infant school for 180 boys and girls aged 5-7. Besides the six regular classrooms the school also has two units, one for eight maladjusted children aged 5-8, the other for non-communicating children aged 4-8. It is in an urban area with a fairly mixed social intake. The units draw from a very wide area; some of the children travelling sixty miles a day.

The school, built 26 years ago, is a long, single storey building on three levels, linked by gentle slopes. There are ample hard and grass playing areas. A junior school on the same campus is the normal progression for most of the children, but not for those from the units. A few go on to their local junior school, some to an ESN day school or junior maladjusted unit and some to residential special school.

There are eight internal classrooms and a temporary room close to the school, currently used as a school library and parents' room. The two units are at the far end of the building, with a partition across the corridor separating them from the rest of the school. They occupy two adjacent classrooms and a small shared indoor area, with toilets and a bathroom. The accommodation opens onto a small, attractive playground, entirely separate from the other infants; they are not even

417

within sight. The junior girls are within loud hailing distance, and are frequently loudly hailed. They usually respond very satisfyingly.

There are two ways that the aim to achieve 'a greater integration of children with special needs' could be interpreted in my school. It could be seen as accepting children with a wider range of special needs, not only those ascertained as maladjusted or non-communicating, or it may be seen as a more extensive acceptance and inclusion of these two categories of handicapped children within the present structure. I intend to consider both these interpretations and some of the ways in which the first might possibly affect the second.

Accepting children with a wider range of special needs could be accomplished as part of a new approach to the concept of special education, and would involve policy change at area or county administrative level. It could mean taking children with physical handicaps or those designated as ESN(M) as well as the non-communicating and maladjusted children. I think there would still be some children who could not be adequately taught in a class covering a range of special educational needs; for example, children with severe hearing or visual impairments who need specific technological aids and highly specialised teaching, content and methods. There might be others with very special needs, either medical or psychological, which could only be met in a special school. There will probably always be some children who need residential placement. Wherever possible there should be a range of suitable provision, and the decision as to which is most suitable should be arrived at after consultation between the involved professionals, the parents, and when appropriate the child.

It would be essential to take into account the dynamics of the existing group when placing a new child. Although this is always theoretically desirable it is rarely practicable at present because of the rigidity of the system. If the system were changed it would become even more important, but should also become more practicable.

I can see many potential advantages of increasing the range of children with handicaps catered for in units in ordinary schools. A handicapped child might well attend the same school as siblings and neighbours, for a start. Parents are likely to feel more positive about such provision and will therefore give more support, especially as the school is likely to be nearer and so is easier for them to visit both formally and informally. The shorter journey would be a far-reaching improvement as it would cut fatigue, lessen a danger-time for problem behaviour, could lengthen the time in school, and would be less costly. A unit catering for 'special needs' could avoid the stigma of a child being labelled 'subnormal' or 'maladjusted', and should be more easily able to take account of temporary special needs in a mainstream child. A possible advantage from admitting children with a range of disabilities might be a more positive and understanding attitude from colleagues, parents and children within the main school, due to increased opportunities for two-way integration.

What of the second approach to increasing integration? How could existing groups participate to a greater extent in the present structure? The obstacles to be overcome involve the attitudes and even prejudices of some teachers and parents, as well as extensive, detailed and skilful organisation, and as such may be particularly difficult to change.

Locational integration can be achieved by an administrative 'stroke of the pen'. But if there is to be social and functional integration it is important that there should be prior consultation with the head and teaching staff and that there should be continued monitoring of all staff appointments. Without this there may be an unenthusiastic head and teachers who are unsympathetic, intolerant or even directly opposed to the whole idea of educating children with special needs alongside 'normal' children. This is a formidable obstacle. It may even be insurmountable and ultimately involve staff changes, or failing this, a change of location. You cannot change entrenched attitudes overnight by legislation or any sort of coercion. Discussion of the underlying principles has to be initiated and regularly encouraged, both formally and informally amongst teachers, parents and other professionals.

How, when and where the children with special educational needs can join with and be part of the main school, will depend on the success of the discussions, the quality of the detailed plans, and the skill and timing of their presentation. Another factor of vital importance is the staffing ratio in the main school and the units. This is controlled at area or county level, but it is essential that the officers responsible for staffing are aware of this aspect. A generous staffing ratio permits more extensive and flexible possibilities of integration.

Focusing on my own school again, I can envisage several ways in which a programme for integration could be initiated. A modest beginning would be to hold the school assembly at a time when all the unit children are able to participate, instead of the traditional nine o'clock. A second step could be to arrange for the unit children to sit amongst the others at lunchtime. This might involve organising an adult or perhaps another child to help or oversee the feeding; but the benefits could be wide ranging, both in offering good models to the handicapped child and encouraging understanding and social interchange.

Playtimes are often seen as a good opportunity for social integration, but since they are unstructured and often undersupervised, these times can be quite difficult and threatening. For some maladjusted, partially-hearing or sighted, for some physically or mentally handicapped children, the school playground might come at the end, not at the beginning of an integration programme. There are others who might enjoy and benefit from this experience. Since there are two teachers and two welfare assistants in the units, it would be easy for one to supervise children in the small unit playground with some children from the mainstream, whilst another went, as an extra adult, with those children who might benefit from playing in the main playground.

Another strategy would be to invite children from other classes to 'play' in the unit. This is nearly always popular with the mainstream children because of the wide range of activities that can be offered, as well as the extra attention and space. But it can present difficulties. Some teachers, aware of the popularity, are anxious that all children should 'have a turn'. This makes it impossible for the unit children to form any lasting relationships. Some see it as an opportunity to get rid of their more difficult children for a while. Again, this is not ideal for the unit children. Therefore, this form of integration can only be thoroughly successful after understanding of the problems has been reached by at least some of the mainstream teachers.

Unit children might also join mainstream classes for certain activities. This would need very careful planning on an individual basis and the child or children might at first need to be accompanied by the welfare assistant. They could join in for PE, music, story, play or even in a more formal learning situation. The possibility of being accompanied by an auxiliary helper might prove an incentive to some hard-pressed and unaided infant teachers.

Increased integration could be encouraged in various other ways. Mainstream teachers might ultimately think it useful and helpful to teach in the unit for specific periods or subjects. The unit teachers could occasionally take other classes with all or some of the unit children. Extra curricular activities, such as recorder, country dancing, games and clubs, could be arranged to include the unit children, preferably in the lunch break. All these suggestions would need to be carefully planned and constantly reviewed.

Attention would also need to be paid to organisational details. In an ordinary infant school, most aspects of the organisation are undertaken by the head or deputy head, but a special class teacher would need a certain degree of autonomy. Auxiliary staff are normally appointed by the head, but in the case of a unit for children with special needs, such appointments would need to be a joint decision between the head and unit teacher. Basic items of stock like paper, pencils and paints, would still be best ordered and stored centrally within the school, since it is uneconomic and time consuming to order separately, but there would need to be provision for the unit to order any items not normally ordered by the school. As far as equipment goes, it would be difficult but quite essential to insist that although there are only a few children in the group, the room needs to be at least as well equipped as any other classroom. Because of the age and ability range, the learning disabilities, and the fact that some children may be in the same class for three years, the unit actually needs to be better equipped.

Adequate cover for teachers who are absent would be another essential organisational aspect of increased integration. Because of the needs of the children, the absence of their teacher can be extremely difficult for them to accept and similarly difficult to cover the absence with another teacher. The Warnock Report recommends that a school with a unit is allotted an extra specialist teacher to its staffing complement for such contingencies. In a time of financial cut-backs this is unrealistic, but it should be possible to have one or two supply teachers who can build up a good relationship with the children and who could be called on in an emergency. A well-established integration policy would also help at such times.

Timetabling should be quite straightforward in an infant school since there are no specialist, part-time, or remedial teachers. Time-tabling entails allocating resources such as hall-times for PE and music, television, cookery, playground. Once the principle of integration has been accepted, the timetable can be a useful tool in extending the possibilities, since if the unit children are joining with other classes there would be more sessions available to share out.

The nature of the curriculum would also need to be carefully considered. In most infants schools the curriculum, traditionally planned by the head teacher, is based on aims to develop social awareness, confidence, independence and initiative, good attitudes to learning and a grounding in the basic educational skills. Although there would be a wide range in the attitudes, abilities, developmental levels and early experiences of normal infants, certain assumptions are made. In a class catering for a wide range of special educational needs, no such assumptions could be made. The broad underlying aims might be similar, but the curriculum would have to be planned around thorough assessment, and teaching methods would have to take account of very different objectives for each child. The need for continuous evaluation and modification is essential. The unit teacher would have to be free to plan the specific objectives and to provide the appropriate learning experiences for each child.

Finance and decision making would be two other areas needing consideration. The cost of providing special education is high and to provide comparable services and facilities in a number of special classes attached to ordinary schools will be even more costly. The only possible saving might be on transport contracts and the use of the specially qualified teachers in an advisory capacity in the main schools. Internal finance should be monitored by the LEA to ensure that the money allocated for the unit is benefiting those children for whom it is intended.

Decision making in a more integrated system could raise problems both within individual institutions and in the broader context of national policy. In the individual school there should be a balance between autonomy and *laissez-faire*. For instance, the unit teachers should be free to make curricular decisions and to plan home/school links. However, it is important that the head and preferably all teaching and non-teaching staff regard the unit children as just as much part of the school as any other pupil.

51 SOME ASPECTS OF SPECIAL EDUCATION IN OXFORDSHIRE: INNOVATION AND CHANGE

Tony Booth and Christopher Pym

There are two quite distinct ways in which the word 'policy' is used in education. In one sense it can be a summary of what is actually going on in a particular area, a post hoc *rationalisation or passive conception of policy. In its second sense it may define attempts to supply coherence and direction to what is going on. In this sense 'policy' carries connotations of central control over an area of practice, but in the permissive and hence diverse education system in the UK it can be difficult to discern any active educational policy developed beyond the confines of a single classroom. Education in the UK is often characterised by an absence of active policy making. Sometimes one school may appear to have a unified sense of direction but it is extremely rare for a local authority to attempt to impose a structure on the historical, economic and personal forces which can determine what happens between teachers and pupils. The beginnings of just such an attempt are discernible for children with special needs in Oxfordshire. The following case-study, which concentrates on secondary education, documents some aspects of these ideas of policy, their background and some of the problems that arise in attempting to implement them. It utilises information obtained directly from some of the people involved and from already published sources. Its purpose is to provide some indications for policy development in other areas and inevitably it is a very partial and incomplete picture.*

Background

Policy making in education never starts with a clean slate. Even in a new school a head teacher is constrained by the expectations of the local education authority, staff, children and parents as well as current

423

restrictions in expenditure. It is unlikely that anyone can document the myriad decisions that create future planning for a local authority. However a number of features stand out in the development of practice and in the administrative structure of Oxfordshire which contribute some measure of coherence to special educational policy. Oxfordshire never entered the movement in the sixties and seventies which equated the value of the contribution local authorities were making to the education of handicapped children with the establishment of new special schools and off-site provision, though this appears to have had little to do with a conscious adoption of an integrationist policy. In fact, in the absence of a large number of special schools of its own, the county sent out and paid for an unusually high number of children to residential schools for handicapped children outside its own boundaries. When they did begin to increase their response to the needs of handicapped children, in the new climate of opinion which was emerging in the seventies, they had a greater opportunity to innovate than existed in many other places. They could redirect a large proportion of the money previously expended on expensive out-of-county placements. There was already a tradition, too, for the use of ancillary helpers to support the education of individual handicapped children particularly at the primary level — a practice developed partly in response to the rural nature of the county and the large distances this necessitated for travel to more centralised facilities. In Alvescot Village School for example, in what might have been a one-teacher school, the headmistress has the assistance in her classroom of a full-time ancillary helper, an additional teacher in the morning, and a part-time welfare assistant. Handicapped children from the surrounding area come to the school and at present on the school roll are three children with cerebral palsy, one mentally handicapped, one with speech problems, one with spina bifida and another child with cystic fibrosis.

One of the most evident developments for children with special needs in Oxfordshire has been the establishment of resource bases or special needs departments in secondary schools in a number of parts of the county. The first of these to be established, at Coopers School in Bicester, was part of an initiative called 'the vulnerable child scheme' which was established to combat the problems produced within a rapidly increasing and mobile army population in the area. Additional support teachers were put into the area and special needs departments opened at the two comprehensive schools in Bicester. A peripatetic project coordinator was appointed to run the scheme, which aimed to identify the needs of all school children in the area who were at risk or vulnerable in any way and to help them, their parents and their teachers, within their schools. It involved members of support agencies such as the family and child guidance service and social services, as well as all those teachers in the area working in special and remedial education. The scheme provided backing and advice to those working in the units at the two comprehensive schools. In 1976 Jean Garnett,[1] the co-ordinator of education services at Coopers School, described how the unit there was set up and developed:

How the Unit Began

The unit opened in September, 1969, with 15 children aged 11 to 12 and one teacher. Its three classrooms were in premises situated within the grounds of this 11 to 18 comprehensive school of some 1,800 pupils, which serves a part urban, part rural community. It was attached to the main school for major administration, registration, assemblies, dinners and certain creative and practical subjects, but the unit children were to be taught separately from the main stream. To all intents and purposes it was a separate entity with its own way of life but obtaining 'pay and rations' from the parent school.

Three problems began to emerge during the first two years as the unit took on a third year group, a helper and a second teacher.

1. The children were seriously rejected by their peers in the main school and were often teased and bullied, being told to keep themselves to their own 'school'. It was not a happy situation for them.

2. The unit staff began to feel that, although they were welcomed as specialist teachers by their colleagues, they were neither an integral part of the school nor a special school in its own right, losing out on the advantages of both, particularly as regards practical facilities like well equipped craft rooms and spacious outdoor play areas.

3. Subjects like physical education and games became difficult to run with such a wide age range in one group. Although the physical needs of 14 year olds were recognised to be different from those of 11 year olds, the unit numbers were too small for them to be timetabled separately.

Move to Closer Integration

Developments during that second year took us to the decision that we should aim for greater integration, probably the most influential being the changing attitudes of the main school staff. A number of them had begun to question the segregated state of the unit, first the head of games, then the head of English, both of whom wondered why the children should not join their mixed ability classes. There had by now been some interchange between the remedial department and the unit and two or three unit children had joined a remedial class for some English work. We noted that they not only held their own with the others but also proved themselves more able to concentrate on the work in hand. It was therefore decided that the unit pupils should attend some ordinary classes but, where possible, their special teacher should accompany them and work with them, and with any others needing extra help, alongside the class teacher.

It became evident to the ordinary and special teachers alike that the majority of the ESN youngsters were able to cope as well in the ordinary classes as many of the other slower learners and sometimes rather better. It was not so much the slow learners who caused teacher anxiety as those with learning difficulties *and* serious behaviour problems.

Meanwhile the building of the new Lower School to take 11 to 13 year olds, was under way and we were soon involved in discussions on possible provision for ESN pupils in this age range there.

Oxfordshire education authority gave its blessing to the placement of the first and second year pupils in their own progress unit attached to the new Lower School across the town in time for the new school's opening in September 1971. A similar process of integration took place there. We therefore had two 'special' bases in Bicester School, each providing for about 30 pupils and staffed by two teachers and a helper.

Around this time we found ourselves wondering what was really meant by the term 'ESN' in the context of this school. Were all the children with special educational needs actually getting suitable help and was it time we looked more closely at the criteria laid down for this help (the main one so far being based on an IQ score of 75 or less)? And where did 'ESN' stop and 'remedial' start? Our local authority was prepared to allow us flexibility and to offer help to a slightly wider group of pupils in difficulty.

Becoming an Integral Part of the School

In the summer of 1972 the headmaster agreed that the Upper School unit should become an integral part of the school, moving into rooms originally built for remedial use in the middle of the school and taking some responsibility for about a dozen senior pupils still needing special help with reading and number and often with social adjustment too. It seemed that the barriers between the two notions of 'special' and 'remedial' were lowering and the concept of a continuum of difficulty and need (now generally accepted in most educational circles, was gaining credence.

Now we were in a position to plan for each individual according to his needs. Each unit became a kind of workshop centre-cum-home base.

By 1973 the children in both progress units were spending on average 50 per cent of their lesson time working in the main stream with small-group maths and language lessons in the unit where much of the work backed up that which they were doing elsewhere. Opportunities for a range of practical activities were provided, including a cooking area and a place where destructive/constructive work could be done. A special leavers' course was introduced in the unit in the Upper School because these pupils needed specialised training for competence in adult living. The local technical college offered day courses for them in building crafts, beauty care and horticulture and a work experience scheme was begun with local employers.

The identity 'ESN' was disappearing and the idea that these youngsters were different in what Wilson (1973) termed 'kind' from their peers was losing ground. The idea of 'degrees' of difficulty was taking on. We were happy to notice that the teasing and bullying had decreased considerably.

The children were still perfectly aware of their differences and disabilities and it is probable that they suffered more than their counterparts in the more protected special schools, where they do not have to cope with the buffetings of 'normal' society. But they still had special people in the units to help them come to terms with their differences and to build their emotional defences, in order that they should in the end be able to manage in that society. They have to manage when they leave school and perhaps we do many of them a disservice by removing them from it rather than helping them to cope in it. Perhaps we also do a disservice to 'ordinary' children by denying them the social experience of accepting their responsibilities towards people who need their understanding and support.

After 1974, the year of local government reorganisation, a number of changes took place which were to give further impetus to policy development. A new chief education officer arrived who was to take an active interest in special education. and later a new principal psychologist was appointed who was to share the day-to-day administration of policy with the senior adviser for special education. In a recent interview Jean Garnett reflected on the changes that had taken place.

> The guiding light behind the Bicester Scheme was the assistant education officer for special services. She was trying to develop a provision for ESN(M) children, which made it possible in a large rural authority for them still to go to school near home. The authority had an ESN school at Woodeaton, but children had to board partly because it was such a long way to go. The principal psychologist's view was that all these children were pretty dull, and we probably would not teach them to read and write — it was very much the notion that psychologists had in the old days that certain children really just needed looking after and needed to be given a happy life. He was certainly in favour of segregating these children. What we were doing in the first place was almost accidental. As things seemed sensible to do, so we did them, and it was not really the result of a carefully thought-out policy on my part, or I think on anybody's part. We were very fortunate in that people did not hold us back. Our own caution held us back more than anything else.

One of the main changes in the organisation of special services in 1980 noted by Jean Garnett was in the status of one of the county's officers. The principal psychologist, Neville Jones, appeared to be the driving force behind an extension of the plans to provide for special needs children in ordinary schools. Neville Jones, himself, described the developments within the authority in the following way:

> Local Government reorganisation in 1974 created the new County of Oxfordshire incorporating Oxford City, the old County of Oxfordshire, and part of North Berkshire. An identification with the new authority by staff working in it developed slowly but was

facilitated by the retirement in 1978 of the chief education officer, who previously had been chief officer to the Oxford City Authority. Different kinds of service, different personnel and styles of working, compounded to create a sense of loss among those who had personal allegiances to a management system superceded by something larger and seemingly more impersonal. The planning of services and resources during the immediate post reorganisation period was very much on an ad hoc basis and resulted in the opening of both new special schools and new units attached to ordinary schools. The reorganised county inherited three special schools from Berkshire catering for mild and severe mental retardation on the same campus. Two purpose built schools were opened for severely mentally retarded children; Bardwell in 1976 and Bishops Wood in 1977. Around the same time three purpose-built units for mildly mentally retarded children were attached to comprehensive schools; Chilton Edge (1976), Lord Williams (1976) and Drayton (1977).

Whilst these new units did enable some children who had been sent out of county to be educated within their locality, it was to some extent additional to existing provision of ESN(M) schools. These units were established, then, partly in response to previously unmet needs and involved some children in spending less time in ordinary classrooms than they would have done if the units had not existed.

The unit at Drayton School, called the Basic Studies department, combined responsibility for groups of children hitherto categorised as ESN(M) and remedial under a single head of department and organisation. The individual timetabling system which is a cornerstone of this organisation is described in another case-study for this book. Drayton is a new school and the Basic Studies department has its own separate resource block where some of the children do spend most of their school day. If one were consciously planning a school where the participation of children with special needs was at its maximum level then one might wish to avoid their physical separation from the rest of the school. Children are timetabled for ordinary lessons to the extent that they will benefit from them and in an educational sense are treated on a continuum of ability. In practice, however, the children who need a relatively small amount of support in literacy skills are withdrawn within the main body of the school and so a distinction between remedial and ESN(M) pupils does re-emerge to some extent.

In 1975 planning permission had been sought from the Department of Education and Science to open four further two-class units in primary and secondary schools and it was intended that the manner in which these units met the needs of a wide range of handicapped children would be monitored. A special resources department was opened at Carterton Comprehensive School in 1978 and a further special department at Gillott's Comprehensive School, Henley, in 1980. Elizabeth Jones, the counsellor at Banbury Comprehensive, spent a year evaluating the Carterton scheme. The concept of the department had been transformed from the idea of a separate unit into one which provided support for children to work within mainstream classes. Elizabeth Jones found that she was not looking at a small group of children with handicaps, but at issues like the financing of schools, pupil-teacher ratios, curriculum planning for the ordinary child, mixed-ability teaching, effects of streaming, setting, banding and group teaching, in-service training and teachers' attitudes towards any child who proves difficult to teach. Special education, she thought, was a mirror being held up to reflect educational processes for all children. Elizabeth Jones and Sandra Berrick described the Carterton scheme in an article for *Special Education* in 1980,[2] and we have included an excerpt here which describes the children and the forms of support they received:

The Special Resources Department (SRD) has built up its intake gradually. To have swamped a school with severely handicapped children at the outset, before the SRD staff had been given an opportunity to work together and test their own strengths and weaknesses, would have been tantamount to failure. To date, the range of disability presented by the 11 to 15 year old children in the SRD includes the following: the mildly mentally retarded, severely and mildly epileptic children, a leukaemic child functioning at ESN(S) level, a child with cystic fibrosis, a child disabled by polio, a child with Hirschprung's disease and others with cerebral palsy, arthritis, minimal cerebral dysfunction, partial hearing or severe learning disability. The majority of the children are aged 11 to 13 as this is the age range planned for in advance.

We recognise that some of the multiply handicapped children also have problems of emotional adjustment. Their management programme takes into account that, at certain stages of schooling, their educational needs due to maladjustment may be over-riding as compared with their other disabilities. There is continuing emphasis on meeting the child's 'total person' needs, rather than on planning for some specific disability in isolation which is commonly known to affect other areas of a child's development. Identifying a child as having 'special needs' as compared to being 'ESN' or 'maladjusted', for example, has helped in providing a flexible approach.

The Roles of the Special Resource Department (SRD)

To provide flexibly and with expertise for each child according to ability and disability, the staff have assumed various roles.

These relate to the following functions.

(a) A child may be withdrawn from ordinary classes for specialised help in the SRD. There will be no focus on remedial reading as such but rather on perceptual-motor skills and similar basic skills, for which the department will have responsibility to draw up and implement a detailed and appropriate programme. The withdrawal may be for specialised instruction, or to reinforce learning in a particular subject, such as a newly acquired numeracy skill. It may be for emotional support and encouragement for the child who, for example, finds it very difficult to return to school after illness or prolonged treatment. The withdrawal may also be an alternative to a particular subject such as swimming in a heated indoor pool, rather than games, for a child with spina bifida.

(b) A member of the SRD staff may accompany a child into a subject class for a variety of reasons: help in science practical lessons if a child cannot move about freely or keep up with the teaching or where the alternative would be to withdraw her completely from that subject. Not all main school staff feel entirely comfortable having another member of staff in their classroom, and this is respected, but this is a school where team teaching is an accepted practice and therefore the difficulties may be lessened. As most of the children in the SRD come from years 1 and 2, it does mean that an SRD member of staff may be monitoring several children in the same room or, as in Humanities, monitoring several children in several adjoining classrooms during the same lesson.

(c) The SRD may, in consultation with the subject teacher, provide appropriate work which the subject teacher monitors in his own class. For example, materials for Humanities lessons are not always appropriate in our experience of mixed ability teaching, the level is often pitched at the 'average' child in the group and may fail to meet the needs of certain children. Increasingly, the SRD staff are providing materials for a wider group of children within a teaching group than has been recognised up till now as having special educational needs.

(d) The SRD may act as consultants on a particular child within a teaching group. On occasions, the SRD staff have gone to observe a child within his teaching group and to offer advice and suggestions as to how to bring out that child's potential within his classroom. Another development worthy of note is that the head of the SRD has been asked by several teachers to give demonstration lessons on how to teach particular class groups — not classes necessarily recognised as having special educational needs but ones which are causing concern to staff. Another member of staff is on a working party attempting to draw up an appropriate programme for 'disenchanted' non-examination fourth and fifth year pupils.

(e) The SRD staff may ensure, through the form tutor, that the child has the appropriate equipment/timetable to enable him to join in with his peer group. For example, the child in a wheelchair can be made mobile because he has a timetable that allows him to move around the school on ground floor level.

(f) The SRD can offer specialist teaching and diagnostic skills, such as the setting up of an educational programme for a child who has a specific learning disability of a dyslexic nature.

(g) The SRD staff confer jointly with parents and form/subject teachers and they initiate separate parent conferences when needed.

(h) The SRD staff initiate the full time integration of children into the form/subject room and serve as supportive resource teachers until the child has made the complete transition.

(i) The SRD staff are responsible for the final evaluation report of each referral and also for a written evaluation of the child's progress in both the classroom and the SRD.

One major obstacle to developing a coherent plan for children with special needs in Carterton School is the persistence of a distinct remedial department. At the same time as the special resource department staff are attempting to break down a clear distinction between ordinary and handicapped children, the division between handicapped and remedial children is actually built into the organisation of the school.

One feature of the account of Carterton School is the reference to an American tradition of subskills teaching. The philosophy behind this special resources department and the attempts to formalise a policy plan for special education in Oxfordshire draw support from a further American influence; the 'resources approach' to children with special needs.

The Resources Approach

The 'resources approach' is an idealised conception of the delivery and management of services for children with special needs which was developed in the USA in the early seventies. It was part of the 'new philosophy' of special education arising in the wake of the mainstreaming movement. The 'old philosophy' placed the responsibility for meeting the needs of handicapped children on the special educators and specialist professionals to whom a particular child might be referred. The sphere of influence of these people was outside of ordinary schools and classrooms and as a natural result children with special needs often ended up receiving their education outside normal classrooms and schooling. The 'resources approach' aims to reverse this process. The idea is that the ordinary classroom teacher becomes the manager of special provision and can draw on specialist resources, both materials and people, as the need arises. The delivery of such services actually takes place in the ordinary classroom wherever possible, for example, in the form of an ancillary helper or a language and reading scheme. Where children have to move to a special place for some of the time they actually remain as full members of their ordinary class base. This is clearly a question of emphasis. Some special needs departments might see themselves as a child's base introducing a child from there into as many aspects of the 'normal' curriculum as is feasible. The resources approach sees special support teachers as sometimes taking children out from ordinary classes.

Most aspects of these ideas are entirely familiar and in one sense 'traditional'. They are implicit in the notion of remedial provision run on a system of withdrawal groups from mainstream classes rather than separate remedial classes. Such ideas are however extended to a much wider group of handicapped children who are to be provided with a varied continuum of support services. The less familiar aspects of the approach concern its management by classroom teachers and it is here that it can have far-reaching consequences for the work of teachers and professional support services.

Applied to the whole range of provision from special school to ordinary classroom, the emerging special education policy in Oxfordshire involves the provision of supports at each point on the continuum so that a flow can take place towards an integrated system. Mike Burnham, the senior adviser for special education, identified some of the developments that have been taking place at the special school end of this continuum:

At present three special schools are actively engaged in discussions which will result in special classes being set up in local primary schools, staffed and equipped by members of the special school staffs.

The idea is to create a series of bridges along which pupils can travel into the mainstream. Special school children will work alongside mainstream children in ordinary classes, we hope for increasing amounts of their time.

The authority have instituted an inservice course on 'handicap awareness' and intend 'within a two year period' that 'one teacher from every primary school in the county will have attended'. The course is backed by a specially prepared booklet which provides basic information on handicap and its educational implications for classroom teachers.

Ideas about how the 'resources approach' would be applied in Oxfordshire were set out in a discussion paper, 'Special Educational Needs in Oxfordshire in the 1980's', prepared by Neville and Elizabeth Jones. An idea which eventually emerged was for the county to be divided up into a number of sectors each containing a secondary school and its feeder primaries, which between them would share certain special resources in the form of support teachers, psychologists and educational social workers. Other resources would be shared between sectors — such as a teachers' centre and any support provision for infrequently occurring handicaps which needed to be concentrated together in one ordinary school to serve a wider area.

The initial report provoked a flurry of other reports in response, which brought to the surface the genuine and deep fears of those working in special education, particularly the special schools. Anxieties were voiced about the future role of advisers and specialist support services like the schools psychological service.

The chief education officer was closely involved in discussions about innovations in special education in the county. He responded to a suggestion for a thorough implementation and evaluation of the proposals within one area of the county by establishing a management team, under his chairmanship. This team consisted of local heads, advisory staff and psychologists.

Banbury was the area selected for special treatment. Several reasons were given for choosing this particular part of the county; it contained a mixture of social classes and urban and rural areas; it had older communities as well as new London and Liverpool overspill estates;

and the child population from five to sixteen had been screened and a record kept of all those children who had special needs relating to 'physical disorders, learning problems, maladjustment, giftedness, multicultural and home difficulties'.

The 'Banbury Scheme' was depicted by Maureen O'Connor in the *Guardian* on 20 January 1981:

In the north of the county all the schools in the Banbury area have been grouped into four partnerships — each consisting of a comprehensive secondary school and its feeder primary schools. These have been asked to work together to plan an integrated education for all the children in their area. This, says John Sayer, head of Banbury School, implies a far more fundamental change in approach to the education of the whole ability range than did the much-debated switch to comprehensive secondary schools.

[The great advantage of the scheme], as Stephen Friar, head of one of the rural primary schools involved sees it, is that it will enable children to get just as much or just as little special help as they need at any particular time. His school already has a specially staffed group originally set up to deal with ten disturbed children on a full-time basis. He has found that the most difficult children can spend some time with the rest of the school, while the smaller group can be used by children who need withdrawal on a short-term basis. This separate unit, he says, has turned into a resource for the whole school.

The whole scheme is the subject of an application for DES funding for support staff and an evaluation team. However, within the whole Banbury area, one sector consisting of Banbury School and its primary schools has been selected as a more concentrated spearhead for new developments. As an attempt to 'normalise special services' an educational psychologist and educational social worker as well as the existing schools counsellor and special needs teachers are all to be on the staff of the comprehensive school, under its head. However, they will also coordinate work for children with special needs within their primary schools. In addition hospital-based speech therapists and physiotherapists will be available to work in the sector and a considerable amount of ancillary help will be provided for physically and sensorily handicapped children. A system of school-based inservice education for all teachers within the schools is seen as a necessary support for the scheme. It has been suggested that the process of 'staff normalisation' might eventually be extended to include the peripatetic remedial service and to create a single administrative structure for all children rather than two relatively independent branches for 'normal' and 'handicapped' children. The scheme is seen as a devolution to local schools of central control over children with special needs.

One of the key features of this scheme is the commitment which the head of Banbury School has made to pursuing a policy of integration. His school has inherited most of the children from a nearby ESN(M) school which was closed down. A few more were attached to the unit at nearby Drayton Comprehensive, but in Banbury School they were fully absorbed into mixed-ability classes where they follow a full curriculum which includes French. He felt that the main school had always contained a larger number of children who had 'slipped through the net of ascertainment'. The school instituted a withdrawal system of helping all children who experienced difficulties.

Whilst many of the most recent developments have yet to be implemented it is interesting how the change in emphasis in Oxfordshire is beginning to take effect. Productive meetings are taking place between special and ordinary school staff and there is the start of a recognition of their mutual contributions; one of the primary schools in Banbury School catchment area which contained a separate language unit now places most of these children in ordinary classes in the afternoons. Of course most changes engender their own set of problems and John Sayer has highlighted some of the issues for Banbury schools:

The problem of embracing Warnock will be changing teachers' attitudes so that they no longer regard handicapped children either as a problem to be passed on to the specialists as soon as possible or alternatively, a cross to be borne within their own four classroom walls with no specialist help at all ... We're bound to change our roles. If you bring a wider spectrum of special needs pupils into the same school setting it is logical that you need a new relationship with people who have the skills to help children and to help teachers to help children. People like school social workers and educational psychologists will become advisers with a special concern for pupils who will be more closely related to ordinary schools than ever before. Somehow or other we have to find a new professional relationship at the same time as we're finding a new relationship with pupils with special needs.

Some Problems of Implementation

Despite the fact that there have been considerable attempts to promote a policy for children with special needs in Oxfordshire, there is as yet no single unified policy direction for such children, neither can Oxfordshire or any county be held up as an example of uniformly good practice. In Oxfordshire, for example, parents of some mentally handicapped children have been campaigning for the provision of further education for their children between the ages of sixteen and nineteen. This had been curtailed because of the closure of a hospital special school which had kept some students after statutory school leaving age. The parents are basing their fight on the possible legal obligation of authorities to make such provision and their efforts may set an important precedent for other areas.

Changes, in a permissive system, inevitably occur in a piecemeal fashion. Two years ago there was considerable pressure to establish separate disruptive units and further provision for maladjusted children. There was an agreement in Oxfordshire to set up three such units but after the 'outcry' died down the money was diverted into other projects. A new school for maladjusted children has been opened in Oxfordshire at a time when some teachers are suggesting that they could cope with such children in their schools, if they had been given the resources instead. Innovations too can only take place where they will be readily accepted. Councillor Westall, himself a former head teacher and in 1980, the Chairman of the county's Warnock Working Party, puts it like this:

> It must be remembered it very often rests on personalities. You can lead a horse to the water but you cannot make it drink. There will be a number of persons to be influenced, to be persuaded to adopt a different approach. It cannot be dictated from on high. These are head teachers. I'm thinking now of three schools which, as a unit, will persist in carrying out a traditional way of looking at themselves inwardly inside their own framework. There has been a desire to get them to work together, but it has been unsuccessful, and I am quite sure that none of them would be able to venture into this new form because of the traditional way in which they have been tackling life, remembering that they're all on the borders of retirement. And I wouldn't blame them for not moving.

The 'resources approach' is an ideal towards which the 'Banbury project' is aimed, and because it is an ideal there may ultimately be insuperable obstacles to its full implementation. Such a conclusion emerges from the results of special educational reform in the USA as well as from a consideration of the large changes it requires in the role and training of teachers and professionals in the UK. One of the reasons for a division of labour between ordinary and special education may be the limited time in which teachers are expected to fulfil an unlimited job description. Whether their role as managers of special services can actually be accomplished within their daily schedule depends on whether the degree of support they receive actually frees them to accomplish this task. The tendency to reward specialisation also acts to subvert the wish for class teachers to adopt a general responsibility for all their children. This can create a dilemma about the timing and nature of the additional resources provided to a school, as well as a need to prevent schools creating the area of 'special needs children' as a post of responsibility. There are considerable human problems to overcome if support teachers are not to regard some pupils as 'their children'.

There are more obvious ways, however, in which changes in professional roles may be uncomfortable, personally threatening and actually resisted. If head teachers of ordinary schools are to take greater responsibility for children with special needs, officers of the local authority who are used to being paid to make decisions may be unwilling to delegate their authority.

During a period of change there may actually be two systems of decision making in operation which can come into conflict. Some of the educational psychologists in Oxfordshire reacted strongly to the suggested appointment of a psychologist to the staff of Banbury School. They may have been worried about a possible loss of autonomy if such posts were to become more common and they also expressed concern about what they saw as the favourable workload involved in working with only a sector of schools.

Mike Burnham spoke of the reaction within ESN(M) schools to the burgeoning ordinary school units:

> We're doing this very slowly, but it's going to take a long time for the ESN(M) staff not to see this as a threat, that they're going to be done out of a job. We've also got to change attitudes about staff crossing boundaries. I see special schools staff in the future not necessarily working in the four walls of their own establishment, particularly in the world of the physically handicapped where those

teachers can give support to ordinary teachers in schools. Many of the teachers at present engaged in the work aren't yet prepared to do this. They feel very threatened by it, because it's a change. It raises the whole question of what is special about the curriculum and management of a special school. In some parts of the county you have a tradition of special schools and therefore the attitude is that if a child is in any way abnormal, he must go to a special school.

Nowhere are barriers more difficult to break down than between remedial and special education. We have seen how in Carterton a remedial and special department actually coexist within the same school, and this was also a feature of the early stages of Coopers School described by Jean Garnett. 'Remedial education' and 'special education' have formed separate arenas for the development of teaching careers and the final dissolution of the distinction may wait on the emergence of a generation of people who do not think in terms of such categories. Neville Jones has documented some of the administrative barriers to the joint formation of policy with the peripatetic remedial service:

The peripatetic remedial service to primary schools in Oxfordshire is not part of the county's service for children with special needs but is run by the Primary Advisory Services. One result of this is professional isolation of peripatetic remedial teachers from other special needs teachers in the county and also from primary heads who are engaged in a dialogue through meetings with colleagues and working parties linking with other support services. It is hoped that in time the Warnock recommendation that children with special needs will all come under a more generic category of Children with Special Needs will be implemented. That the 'normalisation' principle will apply in this area so that remedial teachers are school-based, and accountable to local heads, but with a work brief to a group of primaries.

He has also highlighted another important area which may not yet have been raised often enough to become a cause of contention; the pay differential between ordinary and special teachers and the staffing ratios in an integrated school:

Staffing ratios and finance are other areas of difficulty. Many special teachers have special 'S' allowances for working with special children. On an intervention model special children will be registered as normal members of a class but withdrawn to a resources base for those parts of the curriculum where their disability prevents them from partaking in main school. But do we pay ordinary class teachers a special allowance for having the same children in their lessons? Warnock advocated the abandonment of the 'S' allowance and for teachers to be placed on career structures comparable with other teaching staff.

A local authority may also have to consider the financing and staffing of ordinary schools in exactly the same way for special needs as is done for any other subject. What kind of criteria there should be for this has yet to be determined and there are no national guidelines or precedents.

Resistance to change does not only come from the teaching profession. In one particular instance parents mobilised support against the closure of an ESN(S) school and took their protest to Mrs Warnock, an Oxfordshire educational celebrity. She intervened on their behalf to such effect that the school was saved from closure, for the time being at least.

Despite this intervention, which was viewed as ill-advised by some of the main protagonists of the 'new approach' in Oxfordshire, Mrs Warnock has expressed considerable approval for the county's move towards integration. She felt that developments might be held back by 'the extreme conservatism in outlook among elected members [who had] a real difficulty in grasping the way we are trying to break down the huge dichotomy between ordinary children and handicapped children.'

The protagonists of policy in Oxfordshire were deeply disappointed by the failure of post-Warnock legislation to supply money for innovation. However they feel certain that they can make progress by redeploying existing funds, a sentiment echoed by Mrs Warnock:

> I don't believe that a plan like the Oxfordshire plan does really cost money. I think it's a matter of redeploying resources as much as anything else. Radical changes of any kind always look as if they're going to be expensive, but I don't believe it's true they always are.

It is clear however that policy change may have acquired a momentum which will only be satisfied by more change. Mike Burnham summarised the position in Oxfordshire at the present time:

> In our efforts to acquire new resources and to improve and rationalise existing ones we have had to look more closely at the needs of our pupils than we have done previously. The result in Oxfordshire has been a countywide debate on a scale hitherto unheard of, involving teachers in ordinary as well as special schools, interested professional bodies, advisers and administrators from every persuasion.

Elizabeth Jones has sounded a cautionary note about keeping change at a pace which only raises expectations to the extent that they can be met:

> The authority has put on a training course which was attended by seventy teachers from primary schools and twenty from secondary schools. But once you create an awareness in teachers about handicap you have to make a response to it. Unless we can actually meet the new needs of teachers such courses may only lead to increased frustration. We do not want to leave people doing the same things but with less satisfaction.

Mrs Warnock had expressed concern about the possibilities of a clash between the various services:

> The whole tone of the [resources model] report was extremely optimistic about co-operation with the other services, and this is one of the most difficult things to get right because at the assessment stage, when a child goes into school, and then again, perhaps, a year later, it is absolutely essential to get not only the social services and the psychologist, but the medical profession to come in on this.

This concern is perhaps most pertinent at the preschool stage and for the mentally handicapped, who of all the handicapped are still beset by demarcation disputes between health, education and social services. In 1980 the Oxfordshire community health council which represents the interests of the public in the National Health Service, deplored the failure of Oxfordshire county council to prepare joint proposals for the mentally handicapped:

> Frequently, parents do not know to whom to turn for help, or why, or how; responsibility is divided between health, social services and

education. Anxieties expressed at each public meeting we have held (including one in Banbury) have confirmed this problem. Parents comment on the boundary lines drawn by the various departments; lines which appear to do nothing but put obstacles in the way of those already so burdened they have no energy left to find a way through the maze.

It may not be possible ultimately, to persuade each service to jointly develop comprehensive plans for a community service for the handicapped though clearly it is important to make an attempt. The size of such a task might be ascertained by multiplying the difficulties of developing policy within any one of these services by three and then adding a factor which represents the pitfalls inherent in multidisciplinary co-operation. Whether any such macro-policy could be developed in the absence of directive legislation is open to doubt.

Notes

1. J. Garnett, 'Special Children in a Comprehensive', *Special Education, 3,* 1 (1976).
2. Elizabeth M. Jones and S. Berrick, 'Adopting a Resourceful Approach', *Special Education, 7,* 1 (1980).

APPENDIX: SPECIAL NEEDS IN EDUCATION: THE OPEN UNIVERSITY'S FIRST FULL COURSE ON THE EDUCATION OF HANDICAPPED CHILDREN

This course will be available from 1982 in both the undergraduate and associated student programmes — people wishing to take it on its own will be able to do so.

'Special Needs in Education' is a general introduction to the field drawing on many disciplines and approaches: psychology, sociology, economics, history and politics. No prior knowledge of the field is expected. The course will be of interest not only to teachers in special and normal education but also to any other groups who have an interest and involvement in the education of handicapped children and young people.

Course Themes

1. Understanding Special Education. We aim to describe what special education is like, and what it is like to be a participant in special education.
2. Meeting Special Needs in Education. Here we will be looking at how far children's special needs are met by existing provision, and how education might better meet the needs of handicapped children and their families.
3. Relating Special Education to the Education System as a whole. We will be examining how normal schools meet children's needs, how special education depends upon normal education, and how changes in one system affect the other.
4. Integrating Children with Special Needs into Ordinary Schools. The course examines the conditions for successful integration, the reasons for existing segregation and the arguments for integration.

443

Course Outline

The course comprises correspondence texts published by Open University Educational Enterprises, TV programmes, radio programmes, *The Nature of Special Education* and a second reader entitled *The Practice of Special Education* edited by Will Swann.

'Special Needs in Education' examines the whole range of special needs, arising from minor learning difficulties or profound and multiple handicap. It also looks at the full range of educational institutions that provide for these children, from remedial departments, through special units and schools to residential schools and hospitals. We shall be looking at all the participants in the process: children, families, teachers and other professionals. We will be trying to help students understand what the present system is like, why it is the way it is, and what the alternatives are.

Units 1 and 2 Special Biographies – Tony Booth

These units introduce students to special education. They describe children with a wide range of problems in the context of their families, neighbourhoods and schools. They show how handicap is the product of both individual characteristics and the social environment: children may be handicapped by physical impairments, social backgrounds and schools. The units also introduce the arguments for and against integration and shows the recent growth trends in special education.

Unit 3 Family Views – David Thomas, Will Swann

What is it like to be a parent of a handicapped child? What difficulties and pressures do families face? How does handicap affect their lives? Unit 3 looks at these questions through the eyes of families and of research workers. It examines early intervention by professionals and how they can both help and constrain family responses to handicap. The unit also studies the role of the family as an educator and how far partnership with parents in the education of handicapped children is a reality.

Unit 4 Education for Independence – Richard Tomlinson

This unit discusses the extent to which children are able and prepared for economic, social and intellectual independence when they leave special education. It asks whether independence is a legitimate or desirable educational aim for all children. The opportunities offered by schools, colleges or further education and universities are examined as is the contribution of careers officers. The way in which young handicapped people experience the problems and possibilities of independent living is discussed in detail.

Units 5 and 6 Special Places? Special Curricula? – Will Swann, Dennis Briggs

These two units introduce students to the institutions and content of special education. The first part begins to chart the many complex factors that contribute to the quality of life in special institutions and shows the diversity of provision for various kinds of children within and between LEAs. The processes by which children are referred and placed in special education are described and analysed, followed by a look at the features that comprise a special curriculum. Finally, the units look at studies of the effectiveness of special education. To what extent do special institutions meet children's needs? What alternative systems might better meet these needs?

Unit 7 The Professionals – Patricia Potts

Who is involved in special education and what do they do? This unit looks at professional involvement with handicapped and troubling children. It charts the historical emergence of a variety of professions, it examines their claims to expertise and raises the issue of over-professionalisation: when does practice go beyond knowledge? The difficulties of liaison between groups are considered and we ask: do professionals act only in the interests of handicapped children or also in their own interests?

Unit 8 The Powers That Be – Andrew Sutton

In this unit we look at how special education is organised, financed and administered, at how power is distributed within the system and the differences between formal structures and procedures and actual events. How separate is special education from the rest of the education system? Who controls policy-making in special education? How does change come about?

Unit 9 Origins – Patricia Potts

Special education has an involved and largely hidden past. This unit traces how the present system developed and the factors which produced change. It examines the legislation and moral debate on which acts were based, and charts the change in discussion from moral and social arguments to considerations of efficiency. It looks at the recent re-emergence of debate about the rights of the handicapped, and draws a distinction between change and progress.

Unit 10 National Perspectives – Tony Booth

Through a study of special education in the USA, Scandinavia and Italy, this unit explores the reasons for the diversity of arrangements and the rationale for recent changes. It concentrates particularly on the impact of legislation and how laws have been implemented in practice, to illuminate the likely effect of legislative changes in this country.

Unit 11 Biology and Handicap – Patricia Potts

This unit looks at the implications of biological knowledge for special education. It examines the legitimate application of biological principles in devising curricula and at their over-extension to encompass many groups of children. It describes arguments concerning the social origins of some biological impairments, via factors such as lead pollution, and it examines the general influence of medical ideas in special education. The meaning and functions of terms like 'hyperactivity' are explored.

Unit 12 Psychology and Special Education – Will Swann

Psychology has had a considerable influence on special education. This unit describes how that influence has grown, concentrating on the areas of psychometrics, behaviourism and psychoanalysis and the way these theories have infiltrated into the curriculum and organisation of schools. The unit looks at the possible benefits of more recent theories of child development and the links between psychological research and practice.

Unit 13 Handicap is Social – Tony Booth

This unit argues that all handicaps depend on cultural conditions which are independent of the difficulties of a particular individual. The meaning and value placed on a handicap may become part of the handicap itself. The unit discusses the beliefs and prejudices which give rise to stereotyped images of handicap and the processes by which these are incorporated into the identities of handicapped people.

Unit 14 Eradicating Handicap – Tony Booth

How can we prevent handicap and educational difficulties? This unit analyses medical, educational, social and political approaches to prevention. It presents a critical account of medical intervention as a model for other interventions, and it discusses the extent to which a handicap can be prevented by changing its social image.

Unit 15 Research in Special Education – Keith Pocklington

This unit describes the resources of manpower, money and institutions which are devoted to research into special education. How much of this research is relevant to education? Examples of research reports are examined to illuminate the connections between research and practice? What kinds of questions can be answered by research? Can research tell us how to implement integration?

Unit 16 An Alternative System. A Special Imagination – Tony Booth, Patricia Potts, Will Swann

The last unit in the course describes a possible alternative system where handicapped children are provided for in the mainstream. It brings together ideas from the course to show the impact this would have on normal schools and what services would be needed to support them. It includes studies of institutions in the process of changing towards integration and looks at participants' views on how they wish special education to develop.

INDEX